Public Management and Governance

Second edition

D1513175

The role of government in managing society has once again become a hot topic worldwide. A more diverse society, the internet and new expectations of citizens are challenging traditional ways of managing governments.

The second edition of *Public Management and Governance* examines key issues in efficient management and good quality service in the public sector. With contributions from leading authors in the field, it goes beyond the first edition, looking at the ways in which the process of governing needs to be altered fundamentally to remain legitimate and to make the most of society's many resources.

Key themes include:

- challenges and pressures facing modern governments worldwide;
- the changing role of the public sector in a 'mixed economy' of provision;
- governance issues such as ethics, equalities, and citizen engagement.

This new edition has an increased international scope and includes new chapters on partnership working, agency and decentralised management, process management, and HRM. Comprehensive and detailed, it is an ideal companion for undergraduate and postgraduate students of public management, public administration, government and public policy.

Tony Bovaird is Professor of Public Management and Policy at the University of Birmingham. He has published widely in strategic management, public policy evaluation and performance management in the public sector.

Elke Löffler is Chief Executive of Governance International. She has published widely in public governance and quality management in the public sector.

Public Management and Governance

Second edition

Edited by Tony Bovaird and Elke Löffler

Routledge
Taylor & Francis Group

LONDON AND NEW YORK

First published 2003
Second edition published 2009
by Routledge
2 Park Square, Milton Park, Abingdon, Oxon OX14 4RN

Simultaneously published in the USA and Canada
by Routledge
711 Third Ave, New York, NY 10017

Routledge is an imprint of the Taylor & Francis Group, an informa business

Typeset in Perpetua and Bell Gothic by
Florence Production Ltd, Stoodleigh, Devon
Printed and bound in Great Britain by
MPG Books Ltd, Bodmin

British Library Cataloguing in Publication Data
A catalogue record for this book is available from the British Library

Library of Congress Cataloging in Publication Data
  Public management and governance / edited by Tony Bovaird and Elke
  Löffler. – 2nd ed.
      p. cm.
    Includes bibliographical references and index.
  1. Public administration. 2. Government productivity. 3. Legitimacy
  of governments. 4. Public administration–Citizen participation.
  I. Bovaird, A. G. II. Löffler, Elke.
  JF1351.P824 2009
  351 – dc22   2008029203

ISBN10: 0–415–43042–9 (hbk)
ISBN10: 0–415–43043–7 (pbk)
ISBN10: 0–203–88409–4 (ebk)

ISBN13: 978–0–415–43042–5 (hbk)
ISBN13: 978–0–415–43043–2 (pbk)
ISBN13: 978–0–203–88409–6 (ebk)

Contents

v

CONTENTS

Figures

Tables

Case examples

CASE EXAMPLES

Contributors

Rachel Ashworth is a Reader in Public Services Management in Cardiff Business School. Her research interests include performance improvement and public services, organizational accountability across the public sector, public sector professions and the application of institutional theory to public service reform. She has published widely in a number of refereed journals including: *Journal of Public Administration Research and Theory*, *Public Administration*, *Journal of Management Studies, Policy and Politics, Government and Policy* and *Public Management Review*.

Christine Bellamy is Professor Emerita at Nottingham Trent University, where she previously taught public administration/public policy and ran the graduate school in Business, Law and Social Sciences. She has written and researched on e-government, e-democracy and information policy for the last fifteen years. She recently completed a major study funded by the ESRC on national policy and local practices in relation to information-sharing in multi-agency working, and has also worked as a consultant for the UK government in this field. She is a past chair and honorary fellow of the UK's Joint University Council (the National Association for Public Administration, Social Policy and Social Work Education), has served on the Research Evaluation Committee of the ESRC and is a member of the UK's Academy of Social Sciences.

Jürgen Blum is at the John F. Kennedy School of Government, Harvard University. He previously worked at the Public Sector Management and Performance Division in the OECD as administrator for the Good Governance for Development (GfD) in Arab Countries Initiative. He holds a Diploma in International Studies of Economics, Politics and Languages from Passau University, Germany.

Annette Boaz has recently taken up a new post as lecturer in translational research at King's College London. Prior to this she was a senior research fellow in the UK Centre for Evidence and Policy, also based at King's College. At the Centre she was involved in a programme of training, development and methodological work relating to evidence based policy and practice. Annette has previously worked at the Universities of Oxford and Warwick, carrying out research in a wide variety of policy areas, completing evaluations for the UK Cabinet Office and Home Office. Annette has also worked in the Policy Research

Programme at the UK Department of Health. Annette is a member of the editorial board of the journal *Evidence and Policy*.

Geert Bouckaert is Professor of Public Management and Director of the Public Management Institute at the Faculty of Social Sciences at the Katholieke Universiteit Leuven, Belgium. He is president of the European Group of Public Administration (EGPA) and the co-ordinator of the Policy Research Centre for Governmental Organizations in Flanders. His main research interests are in performance management, public sector productivity measurement, quality management and financial management techniques in the public sector. He was a member of the jury of the European Public Sector Award in 2007.

Tony Bovaird is Professor of Public Management and Policy at INLOGOV and Centre for Public Service Partnerships, University of Birmingham. He worked at the Department of the Environment, Birmingham University, Aston University and the University of the West of England, before rejoining INLOGOV in 2006. He has directed the national research team undertaking the meta-evaluation of the Local Government Modernisation Agenda in the UK from 2002–7 on behalf of the Department of Communities and Local Government. He led an evaluation for the Cabinet Office of the civil service reform programme. He has also undertaken research in recent years for OECD, the European Commission and many other public agencies in the UK and internationally. He was a member of the jury of the European Public Sector Award in 2007.

Mike Broussine was, until 2007, Joint Programme Director of the University of the West of England's MSc Leadership and Organization of Public Services, a programme designed to promote leadership development and learning across the public, private and voluntary sectors. His main research interests include: emotions and the politics of organizations; public services leadership; gender and diversity; and creative organizational research methods. Mike has written extensively about aspects of public services leadership, and has published critical reflections on the processes of organizational facilitation and consultancy. He is now a freelance organizational consultant and researcher and offers consultancy, action research, action learning and leadership development in client organizations. Mike is also a visiting research fellow at Bristol Business School.

James L. Chan became Professor Emeritus of Accounting at the University of Illinois at Chicago at the end of 2007, and now holds visiting appointments at the University of Cagliari, Italy, and at the Research Institute of Fiscal Science, SunYat-sen University, Central University of Finance and Economics, and Zhongnan University of Economics and Law, China. He was honoured with the Enduring Lifetime Contribution Award by the American Accounting Association's Government and Nonprofit Section in early 2008.

John Clarke is Professor of Social Policy at the Open University, UK. From a background in cultural studies he has developed a range of research interests around the ways in which welfare states are being transformed. These include: comparative studies, with a particular interest in the USA; the role of managerialism in reforming welfare states; and the significance of audit and evaluative practices in the management of public services. He is currently part of an international collaboration exploring how citizenships are constructed and contested in the encounters between juridical and everyday representations and practices.

Howard Davis is Acting Director of The Local Government Centre, Warwick Business School, University of Warwick, UK. He has undertaken a wide range of local government projects in both Britain and the countries of Central and Eastern Europe. Current research interests include local government modernization and improvement, inspection, local government contracting, transport governance, and joined-up services for people in later life.

Andrew Erridge is Professor of Public Policy and Management in the School of Policy Studies at the University of Ulster, UK. His main research interest is in public procurement, especially its use to deliver socio-economic benefits. In recent years he has contributed to the Gershon Review of Civil Government Procurement, advised the National Audit Office on their study on Modernising Procurement and carried out research for the NAO's Guide to the Audit of Procurement. In 2000 he completed a three-year ESRC-funded research project on UK Central Government Procurement, and he recently completed a project analysing the impact of using social clauses in major projects and service contracts in Northern Ireland. He has published four books, many book chapters and journal articles, and is a member of the editorial committees of the *Journal of Purchasing and Supply Management* and the *Journal of Public Procurement*.

Utz Helmuth is a Research Associate at the Public Management Centre of Excellence (PMCE), University of St Gallen, Switzerland. His research focus is on process management and on performance motivation in the public sector. He has participated in research projects and published on these topics. He is the vice-chairman of eCH's section on business process management – a standards committee for the Swiss government.

Sylvia Horton is Leader of the MPA Degree at the University of Portsmouth. She has published widely on British and Comparative Public Management. Her current research interests are in evaluating public sector leadership training and development. She is a member of the steering committee of the European Group of Public Administration and co-convenor of its study group on personnel policies. She is also a fellow of the UK Public Administration Committee and of the Chartered Institute of Personnel and Development and a visiting professor at the University of Leuven, Belgium, where she contributes to the Public Management Programme for top civil servants.

Peter M. Jackson is Dean of the Faculty of Social Science and Professor of Economics and Strategy in the University of Leicester School of Management, UK, and has had a continuing interest in public finance and public sector management for over thirty years. Since starting out his career as an economist with HM Treasury, he has made major contributions to debates on public expenditure management and control and on approaches to measuring the performance of public sector organizations. His most recent work focuses on public-private partnerships. In 2001 he was appointed as specialist adviser to the Finance Committee of the Scottish Parliament, assisting in its inquiry into the Private Finance Initiative.

Elke Löffler is the Chief Executive of Governance International, an international consulting company in the UK. Previously she was a staff member of the Public Management Service (PUMA) of OECD where she worked on performance and intergovernmental management. Elke studied economics and political science and got her Ph.D. at the Civil Service College in Speyer, Germany. For six years she has been scientific rapporteur at the European Quality Management Conference for Public Administration.

Nick Manning works in the World Bank as Manager (Public Sector) for the Latin American and Caribbean region. Previously he was the head of the Public Sector Management and Performance Division in the OECD and lead public sector specialist (South Asia) in the World Bank. He has been senior technical adviser to UNDP in Lebanon and adviser (Organization Structure and Design) to the Commonwealth Secretariat in London. He began his public sector career in local government in the UK.

Steve Martin is Professor of Public Policy and Management at Cardiff University. His research is focused on public sector reform and public service improvement. He has written widely on public policy and local government management, and has served as an adviser to the European Commission, Council of Europe and a range of UK government departments and agencies.

Janet Newman is Professor of Social Policy and Director of the Public Research Programme within the Centre for Citizenship, Identities and Governance at the Open University. Publications include: *The Managerial State* (with John Clarke: Sage, 1997); *Modernising Governance: New Labour, Policy and Society* (Sage, 2001); *Remaking Governance: Peoples, Politics and the Public Sphere* (Policy Press, 2005); *Power, Participation and Political Renewal* (with M. Barnes and H. Sullivan: Policy Press, 2007); *Creating Citizen Consumers: Changing Relationships and Identifications* (with John Clarke *et al.*: Sage, 2007); and *Publics, Politics and Power: Remaking the Public in Public Services* (with John Clarke: Sage, 2008).

Sandra Nutley is Professor of Public Management at the University of Edinburgh, where she is also director of the Research Unit for Research Utilisation (www.ruru.ac.uk). She has published widely in the area of research utilization and evidence-based policy and practice, including her recent book on *Using Evidence: How Research can Inform Public Services* (with I. Walter and H. Davies: Policy Press, 2007). Sandra is also involved in several other groups concerned with understanding and improving the linkages between research and policy. Prior to joining academia she worked in local government and since then she has been seconded to work with several public sector organizations, including the Scottish Government.

Christopher Pollitt is BOF/ZAP Research Professor of Public Management at the Public Management Institute, Katholieke Universiteit Leuven, Belgium. Previously he was Professor of Government and Dean of Social Sciences at Brunel University, London (1990–8) and Professor of Public Management at Erasmus Universiteit Rotterdam (1999–2006). Christopher is author of more than fifty scientific articles and author or editor of more than a dozen scholarly books. Several of the books have been translated into a range of other languages. From 1980 to 1989 he was editor of *Public Administration* and since 2005 he has been editor of the *International Review of Administrative Sciences*.

Kuno Schedler is Professor of Public Management at the University of St Gallen, Switzerland. He is director of the Institute for Public Services and Tourism and of the Sino-Swiss Management Training Programme, both in St Gallen. He has published widely on public management reforms, public governance and the reform of financial management in public institutions. His current research interest is focused on strategy processes in public administration.

John Tizard has been Director of the Centre for Public Service Partnerships at the University of Birmingham since January 2008. He was previously group director of government and business engagement for the Capita Group plc and, up to 1997, director of strategy and policy at Scope. John has had over eighteen years' experience as a county councillor and nine years as joint leader of an English county council. He has board level experience in a police authority, the NHS, business and the third sector. He writes and speaks regularly on public service partnerships and contributes to government and other working groups on this and related subjects.

Wouter Van Dooren is Assistant Professor at the Department of Political Sciences of the University of Antwerp, Belgium and senior researcher at the Public Management Institute of the Katholieke Universiteit Leuven, Belgium. His research interests are public sector performance, measurement and the use of performance information.

Xuyun Xiao is Associate Professor of Public Finance in the School of Economics at Peking University, China, and has held visiting appointments in Japanese and Korean universities. She teaches government budgeting, and is the author of a textbook on public choice and a dozen articles and book chapters on a wide range of topics in public economics.

Acknowledgements

The editors and publisher would like to thank the following for permission to use copyright material:

OECD for Figure 4.3 from Anne Ketelaar, Nick Manning and Edouard Turkisch (2007), 'Performance based arrangements for senior civil servants – OECD and other country experiences (OECD working papers on public governance)'. doi: 10.1787/160726630750. Paris: OECD. Reprinted by permission.

Abbreviations

ALS	Action learning set
BPMN	Business process modelling notation
BPR	Business process re-engineering
CAA	Comprehensive area assessment
CAF	Common assessment framework
CCT	Compulsory competitive tendering
CFO	Chief financial officer
CPA	Comprehensive performance assessment
CPI	Corruption perceptions index
CSCI	Commission for Social Care Inspection
CSE	Customer Service Excellence
DfID	Department for International Development
DPA	Data Protection Act
DSO	Direct service organization
DTI	Department of Trade and Industry
DTV	Digital television
EBPP	Evidence-based policy and practice
EFQM	European Foundation for Quality Management
EPOC	Effective Practice and Organisation of Care
EPP	Expert Patients Programme
ESD	Electronic service delivery
FOI	Freedom of Information
GDP	Gross domestic product
HEFCE	Higher Education Funding Council for England
HRM	Human resource management
ICAC	Independent Commission Against Corruption
ICT	Information and communications technologies
IiP	Investors in People
KM	Knowledge management
LAA	Local Area Agreement
LINks	Local Involvement Networks

LSP	Local strategic partnership
MBO	Management by objectives
NAO	National Audit Office
NCSC	National Care Standards Commission
NDPB	Non-departmental public bodies
NPFM	New public financial management
NPM	New public management
OFSTED	Office for Standards in Education
OT	Opportunities and Threats
OMB	Office of Management and Budget
PB	Participatory budgeting
PFI	Private Finance Initiative
PFM	Public financial management
PIU	Performance Improvement Unit
PPBS	Planning, programming, budgeting system
PPP	Public-private partnership
PRP	Performance-related pay
QA	Quality assurance
RCT	Randomized control trials
RIA	Regulatory Impact Analysis
RVEM	Remote electronic voting
SCS	Senior Civil Service
SWOT	Strengths, weaknesses, opportunities and threats
3G	Third-generation
TEN	Trans-European network
TPM	Traditional personnel management
TQM	Total quality management
VFM	Value for money
ZBB	Zero base budgeting
ZBO	Zelfstanding bestuurs organisaties

A guide for the reader

AIM OF THE BOOK

This book has been written with the aim of giving readers a clear picture of the current state of play and the most important emerging issues in public management and governance. We intend that it will help students of public issues to be better informed and managers who work in the public domain (whether in public, voluntary or private sectors) to be more effective.

The book is also written to help readers to understand what it means to become better citizens and, as such, to help to change the current practice of public management and governance. In this way, we hope that the ideas in the book will help readers to make a greater contribution to their neighbourhoods, their local authorities, their regions and the countries in which they live – and perhaps even to the quality of life of citizens elsewhere in the world.

STRUCTURE OF THE BOOK

The book comprises three main parts:

1   An *introductory* part, setting out the role of the public sector, public management and public governance, and how these have evolved in recent years in different contexts.
2   A second part on *public management for public sector organizations*, exploring the main managerial functions that contribute to the running of public services.
3   A section on *governance* as an emerging theme in the public domain.

LEARNING OBJECTIVES, CHAPTER BY CHAPTER

The learning objectives in each chapter are as follows:

1   ■ To be aware of the different meanings of 'public';
       ■ to understand the main differences between public management and public governance;
       ■ to understand the motives for studying public management and public governance.

2
- To identify recent changes in the context of public policy;
- to identify the major paradigm shifts in public policy making in recent decades;
- to identify the changing role of politics in public policy.

3
- To understand the role and scope of government;
- to be aware of the trends in social spending and to understand the forces that shape them;
- to be aware of the changing composition of public spending;
- to understand the implications of these trends for public sector management.

4
- To be aware of the changing expectations towards governments;
- to understand differences in public sector reform trajectories of OECD governments;
- to be aware of the unintended consequences of public management reform;
- to be aware of the new reform agendas.

5
- To understand what 'strategy', and 'strategic management' mean in a public sector context;
- to be able to prepare a corporate strategy and business plan for their service or organization;
- to understand the difference between strategic management and strategic planning;
- to understand the political dimension to strategy making;
- to understand how strategic management and innovation mutually reinforce each other.

6
- To understand the role of marketing in a public sector context;
- to be able to prepare a marketing strategy and marketing plan for their service or organizational unit;
- to understand how marketing is different in a politically driven organization working on issues with wide-ranging public implications, as opposed to marketing in private firms;
- to understand the limitations of marketing in a public sector context.

7
- To understand the meaning of contracting;
- to understand why contracting for services has been increasing over the past twenty-five years;
- to be able to identify the pros and cons of contracting out of specific services;
- to understand the links between contracting, competition and collaboration;
- to understand how contracting could be used to pursue the wider socioeconomic goals of government.

8
- To be aware of changes in governmental financial management systems and to understand their underlying conceptual models;
- to understand the context and content of each of the models discussed;
- to understand how each of the models is supported by its underlying disciplines.

9
- To identify the functions of people management in the public sector;
- to compare and contrast traditional personnel management and HRM;
- to examine some of the HRM issues facing public organizations today.

10
- To be aware of the changing understanding of the significance of ICTs;
- to understand their implications for public service delivery and democratic practice;
- to understand the need for active policies to minimize the 'digital divide';
- to understand the critical importance of protecting personal data and managing identity.

11
- To be aware of the evolution of performance measurement and management in the public sector;
- to understand the key concepts in performance measurement;
- to understand the key concepts in performance management;
- to understand the main lessons learned in performance management;
- to be able to identify the main traps in performance management.

12
- To be aware of the differences of quality management in the public and private sectors;
- to understand the key issues associated with quality assessment in the public sector;
- to be aware of the major quality assessment instruments used in the public sector;
- to understand the key obstacles to, and success factors in, quality improvement in the public sector;
- to understand how the concept of quality can be extended to quality of life and governance processes.

13
- To understand what a process is;
- to be able to distinguish different processes from each other;
- to understand how processes are measured and optimized;
- to understand the challenges that process management entails for the public sector.

14
- To be aware of the conditions leading to the recent 'audit explosion' in the public sector;
- to understand the new practices of audit;
- to understand the changing roles of scrutiny agencies;
- to understand the challenges to scrutiny of public sector organizations.

15
- To understand the key concepts of public governance;
- to be able to identify the most important stakeholders in public governance;
- to understand network management as a specific mode of public governance;
- to understand how the role of government is changing from the role of service provider towards the role of co-producer.

16
- To understand the different types of partnerships that are found in the public domain;
- to understand their benefits and limitations;
- to understand how to probe under the surface of partnerships to see the level of 'jointness' that they exhibit.

17
- To understand why the arguments for 'arm's-length' public bodies have recently proved so attractive in so many countries;
- to assess the evidence underpinning this fashion;
- to become able to identify some of the key contextual factors that help or hinder successful decentralization;
- to become equipped with a set of useful key questions with which to interrogate proposals for the decentralization of managerial authority to arm's-length bodies.

18
- To be aware of the current emphasis on leadership in public governance;
- to be aware of the history of the study of leadership;
- to understand the differences between leadership and management;
- to understand the interrelationships between leadership, power and politics;
- to be aware of the gender dimension in leadership;
- to understand the key issues in community leadership;
- to recognize the complex interrelationship between organizational leadership and political leadership;
- to understand what leaders need to learn if they are to become effective.

19
- To be aware of the arguments in favour of engagement with service users and citizens;
- to be aware of the main forms of public engagement;
- to be aware of practical approaches to public engagement;
- to understand the obstacles to effective engagement and ways of overcoming these.

20
- To understand the politics of equality, and the different notions of justice that it draws on;
- to understand how far equality and diversity policies may be viewed as simply a matter of 'good business practice';
- to be able to identify the difficulties inherent in translating policy into practice;
- to understand how to rethink equality and diversity in the context of new forms of governance.

21
- To understand the reasons for the current emphasis on ethics and standards of conduct in the public sector;
- to be able to identify the spectrum of unethical behaviour in the public sector, from corruption to minor infringements of ethical codes;
- to be aware of the rationale behind the recent move to strengthened codes of conduct in the United Kingdom and elsewhere;

- to understand the pros and cons of control-oriented and prevention-oriented mechanisms to ensure ethical behaviour;
- to understand the role of transparency as a mechanism for fighting unethical behaviour.

22

- To understand what counts as evidence for what purposes;
- to understand how evidence may be used to improve public services;
- to be aware of the obstacles to improved use of evidence in policy making;
- to understand how evidence-based learning can be encouraged.

From public management to governance

Part I forms an introduction to the key themes of the book and locates the public sector in its political, social and economic context.

Chapter 1 examines what is 'public' about the public sector and about public services. It distinguishes public management from the wider issues of public governance.

Chapter 2 explores recent changes in the context of public policy, identifies the major paradigm shifts in public policy making in recent decades and examines the changing role of politics in public governance.

Chapter 3 examines the size and scope of the public sector. It compares trends in the size and composition of public expenditure across OECD countries and looks at some of the forces that shape these trends. It then considers the implications of these trends for public sector management.

Chapter 4 examines the objectives and results of the generation of public sector reforms since the 1980s, the different reform trajectories across OECD countries and some of the unintended consequences of public sector reform.

Chapter 1

Understanding public management and governance

Tony Bovaird, University of Birmingham, UK and
Elke Löffler, Governance International, UK

WHY STUDY PUBLIC MANAGEMENT AND GOVERNANCE?

Welcome to *Public Management and Governance*. We aim to provide you with up-to-date state-of-the-art knowledge on what the public sector is doing, why it is doing it and how it might do it better. We hope also to challenge you to think out for yourself how your society should be governed – one of the questions that has fascinated people for thousands of years – and how your governors should be managed – a question that is much more recent. Along the way we hope to entertain you, too. Above all, we will be introducing you to the ideas of some of the leading analysts of the public sector around the world, so that you can weigh up their arguments and develop your own.

Actually, issues of public management and public governance are often very interesting (see Box 1.1). And we also want to warn readers of this book that it can no longer be taken for granted that the activities of public management and governance are 'worthy' – sometimes they are conducted by 'sharks' rather than by 'suits' (see Box 1.2). Indeed, even when public services are managed by 'suits', the people wearing those suits may seek (and partially achieve) the lifestyle of 'fat cats' rather than 'public servants'.

Consequently, nowadays public managers have to earn our respect and gratitude, rather than simply assume it. And the players in the public policy arena have to earn the trust of those for whom they claim to be working, rather than claiming legitimacy simply on the grounds that they were elected or that they are part of a prestigious profession.

LEARNING OBJECTIVES

The key learning objectives in this chapter are:

- ◼ to be aware of the different meanings of 'public';
- ◼ to understand the main differences between public management and public governance;
- ◼ to understand the motives for studying public management and public governance.

BOX 1.1 PUBLIC MANAGEMENT AND GOVERNANCE ARE INTERESTING . . .

Changing the course of history: the Paisley/Adams agreement in Northern Ireland

[I] observed at close quarters the process that led to the historic commitment by both Ian Paisley and Gerry Adams to share power together from 8 May . . .

. . . Peter Hain [the Secretary of State for Northern Ireland] decided to take the risk to win, by being prepared for it to collapse. That is why he legislated for a date for a government to be formed or for Stormont to shut down for who knows how long.

He also introduced policies – such as water charges . . . – which he thought correct but which proved hugely unpopular. These were the number one issue in the election three weeks ago.

In answer to protests about water or his ban on academic selection for post-primary admissions, or stopping salaries and allowances for the politicians, or banning discrimination on grounds of sexual orientation, his answer was: If you don't like these policies, get into government yourselves.

Significantly, both Paisley and Adams referred to stopping water charges in their historic statements.

Source: Norris (2007: 6)

BOX 1.2 . . . BUT NOT NECESSARILY 'WORTHY'

Dramatic cases of sick leave?

Is Joan Cogul really dead? Judges have been asking this question since Mr. Cogul, a former director of Catalonia's tourism board, was reported to have died of a heart attack in Thailand last month. He was shortly to return to Barcelona to stand trial on charges of fraud and embezzlement of millions of pesetas of public funds during the 1990s, facing a minimum of 12 years in jail, if found guilty.

When the investigating magistrate requested the repatriation of Mr. Cogul's body, the Spanish embassy reported that it had been cremated. Moreover, hospital records allegedly showed he had shot himself in the head.

The Barcelona judge has reason to be suspicious – Mr. Cogul is the second suspect to 'die' during his investigations over 3 years. Moreover, there are precedents for fugitives from Spanish courts faking their deaths. Five years ago obituaries appeared in *El Pais,* mourning the passing of Francisco Paesa in a Thai monastery.

Mr. Paesa, alias *El Zorro*, had fled Spain after being charged with laundering more than €100m in bribes and illegal commissions for the former head of the paramilitary civil guard.

Spanish police flew to Thailand, where their inquiries established that his death certificate was a fake; the Thai official who had signed it did not exist. Other signatures on the document were forgeries. His body had not been cremated in the Thai monastery mentioned in the obituaries.

Since then, *El Zorro* has been sighted in France and Switzerland, although he has always eluded arrest.

Source: Adapted from *Financial Times*, 10 and 11 January 2004, p. 22

WHAT DO WE MEAN BY 'PUBLIC'?

The essential task of the public domain can now be interpreted as enabling authoritative public choice about collective activity and purpose. In short, it is about clarifying, constituting and achieving a public purpose. It has the ultimate responsibility for constituting a society as a political community which has the capacity to make public choices. Producing a 'public' which is able to enter into dialogue and decide about the needs of the community . . . is the uniquely demanding challenge facing the public domain.

Source: Ranson and Stewart (1994, pp. 59–60)

Before we go further, we should explore what we mean by 'public'. We start from a clear statement from Ranson and Stewart (1994, pp. 59–60) as to what constitutes the public domain. (They wrote in the context of local government, but their analysis applies quite generally.)

This short passage explains how the public domain is the arena in which public choice is exercized in order to achieve a collective purpose. This is the arena which this book explores.

Ranson and Stewart also introduce another meaning of the word 'public' – the group (or groups) of people who inhabit the public domain. They clearly identify the political concept of 'a public which is able to enter into dialogue and decide about the needs of the community', which we might contrast with the marketing concept of different 'publics', each of whom expects to be treated differently by public services and public managers.

Another common usage of 'public' is to distinguish between the 'public sector' and the 'private sector', which essentially revolves around differences of ownership (collective ownership, in the name of all citizens, versus individual ownership) and motive (social purpose versus profit). This meaning is particularly relevant when public managers try to claim that the public sector is different from the private sector, and that therefore private sector management methods would not work in their agency (see Allison (1994) on the concept that public and private management are alike in all unimportant respects!).

However, there are other, wider meanings to 'public'. For example, 'public services' are sometimes delivered by private utilities or contractors, rather than public agencies. Here, the concept of 'public' generally means that the providers have to observe and satisfy some form of 'public service obligation'. Again, 'public issues' are those which cannot simply be left to the decision-making of private individuals – they typically necessitate mobilising the resources of public and voluntary sector organisations or regulating the behaviour of private firms or individuals or groups in civil society.

We shall examine each of these dimensions of 'public' in this book. Consequently, we shall take the word 'public' to be part of the problematic, i.e. the set of concepts to be explored in this text, rather than defining it unambiguously here at the outset.

PUBLIC MANAGEMENT AND GOVERNANCE: SOME KEY ISSUES

So, what is public management? And what is public governance? While most people will immediately assume they have a general grasp of what public management entails, fewer will have a feel for what is meant by public governance. Moreover, we want to argue that both concepts actually cover quite a complex set of ideas.

We shall take *public management* to be an approach that uses managerial techniques (often originating in the private sector) to increase the value for money achieved by public services. It therefore covers the set of activities undertaken by managers in two very different contexts:

- in public sector organisations; and
- in public service organisations, whether in public, voluntary or private sectors.

This raises a number of issues that we will consider later:

- What distinguishes 'public management' from 'public administration'?
- What is 'public' about public services?
- Are 'public services' always in the 'public sector'?
- Is public management only about public services?

We take *public governance* to mean 'how an organisation works with its partners, stakeholders and networks to influence the outcomes of public policies'. (You can see other approaches to defining 'governance' in Chapter 15.) The concept of *public governance* raises a different set of questions, such as:

- Who has the right to make and influence decisions in the public realm?
- What principles should be followed in making decisions in the public realm?
- How can we ensure that collective activities in the public realm result in improved welfare for those stakeholders to whom we accord the highest priority?

This chapter addresses these issues and sets the stage for the rest of the book.

Is 'public management' different from public administration?

In the middle of the twentieth century, the study of the work of civil servants and other public officials (including their interface with politicians who passed legislation and set public policy) was usually labelled 'public administration'. As such, there is no doubt that 'public administration' conjured up an image of bureaucracy, life-long secure employment, 'muddling through' and lack of enterprise – dark suits, grey faces and dull day jobs.

From the 1980s onwards, however, a new phrase began to be heard, and even achieved dominance in some circles – 'public management'. This was interpreted to mean different things by different authors but it almost always was characterized by a different set of symbols from those associated with public administration – it was thought to be about budget management not just budget holding (see Chapter 8), a contract culture (including contracts with private sector providers of services (see Chapter 7) and employment contracts for staff, which were for fixed periods and might well not be renewed, see Chapter 9), entrepreneurship and risk taking, and accountability for performance (see Chapter 11).

These differences can be (and often were) exaggerated. However, it appears that the expectations of many stakeholders in the public domain did alter – they began to expect behaviour more in keeping with the image of the public manager and less that of the public administrator.

What is 'public' about public services?

In everyday discussion, we often refer to 'public services' as though they were 'what the public sector does'. However, a moment's reflection shows that this tidy approach nowadays doesn't make much sense any longer, at least in most countries (see Chapter 4).

After all, we have for a long time become used to seeing private firms mending holes in our roads and repairing the council's housing stock. More recently it has become commonplace in many areas to see private firms collecting our bins and running our leisure centres. Moreover, whatever country we live in, there are very few services that are never run by the private sector – in the UK it is possible to find some places that have private provision of hospitals, schools, child protection, home helps for the elderly and disabled, housing benefit payments, and a local council's Director of Finance. (Indeed, in the UK we even had, for a while, provision of the post of Director-General of the BBC by a private company.)

Furthermore, there are some things that are done by the public sector that might cause raised eyebrows if described as 'public services' – such as running a telephone company (as the city of Hull did until comparatively recently), or a city centre restaurant (as Coventry did up to the 1980s).

So what *is* public about public services? There is no single answer to this prize question – but neither is there a lack of contenders to win the prize. The answer you come up with is very likely to relate to the discipline in which you were trained and to your ideological position.

For welfare economists, the answer is quite subtle but nevertheless quite precise – public services are those which merit public intervention because of market failure (see Chapter 3). In other words, any good or service that would result in suboptimal social welfare if it were provided in a free market should be regulated in some way by the public sector, and in this way qualifies as a 'public service'.

This definition of 'public services' is attractively rigorous, but unfortunately very wide-ranging. Almost all services, under this definition, exhibit some degree of 'publicness', since the provision of most goods and services in the real world is subject to market failure for one or more of the common reasons – chronic disequilibrium, imperfect competition, asymmetric information in supply or in consumption, externalities, discrimination based on criteria other than cost or technical ability to satisfy user requirements, uncertainty, non-rivalry in consumption, non-excludability in supply, or user ignorance of his/her own best interest. Consequently, this yields a definition of 'public services' that is only occasionally useful – for example, it suggests that all theatres and cinemas are worthy of public intervention (since they are at least partly non-rival in consumption), whereas anyone who has sat through a performance of most Broadway or West End musicals knows that there are real limits to the justifiable level of public subsidy to many theatrical events.

DIFFERENCES BETWEEN THE CONCEPT OF A CITIZEN AND THE CLIENT/CUSTOMER/USER OF PUBLIC SERVICES

A citizen can be defined as a concentration of rights and duties in the person of an individual, within a constitutional state, under the rule of law, and within the hierarchy of laws and regulations.

A client is a concentration of needs and satisfactions of needs in an individual, within a market situation of supply and demand of goods and services, and within a hierarchy of needs, subject to the willingness to pay. A citizen is part of a social contract, whereas the client is part of the market contract.

Source: Pollitt and Bouckaert (1995, p. 6)

An alternative approach to defining the scope of 'public services' comes from politics. It suggests that 'public services' are those which are so important for the re-election of politicians or, more realistically, of political parties that they are given a public subsidy. Under this perspective, where a service is so important in political decision-making that politicians are prepared to spend some of their budget on it, then its 'publicness' must be respected. However, the attractive simplicity of this stance has again been bought at the expense of mind-numbing expansion of the definition of what is potentially a 'public service'. There are very few goods or services that are never important electorally. However invisible is the widget in the sprocket in the camshaft in the car that is bought by international customers who have no interest in the producer or its location, when it is proposed that a local widget factory should be closed and the widgets should be produced elsewhere (especially if it is 'abroad'), so that local politicians are goaded into proposing public subsidies to keep the production going in its present location, then that widget becomes a 'public good' under this definition.

A third approach, which similarly sounds like commonsense, focuses on all those goods where providers are placed under a 'public service obligation' when they are given the right to supply the service. This approach defines as a public service all those services in which Parliament has decreed a need for regulation. However, this approach probably results in a definition of 'public service' that is too narrow. For example, there is a legal public service obligation imposed on the providers of all electricity, gas and water utilities, and broadcasters but not on the provision of leisure centres – yet the latter services may form a major part of the quality of life of certain groups, particularly young people and families with young children, and as such may be widely supported by politicians as important services to be provided in the public sector or through public subsidy.

What is public governance?

Trying to define public governance seems to open Pandora's box. Although there is a general acknowledgement that public governance is different from public management, the academic literature on governance (which each year increases exponentially) offers a myriad of definitions. Indeed, even the authors of different chapters in this volume offer different ideas of what is 'public governance'.

The definition of governance is not, in itself, of critical importance, particularly because many practitioners are widely familiar with governance in practice, although they may find it difficult to recognise it in the forms discussed by academics (see Chapter 15). Nevertheless, we have given a definition above, because we believe it is useful in order to focus discussion.

Whereas in new public management a lot of attention was paid to the measurement of results (both individual and organisational) in terms of outputs, public governance pays a lot of attention to how different organisations interact in order to achieve a higher level of desired results – the outcomes achieved by citizens and stakeholders. Moreover, in public governance, the ways in which decisions are reached – the processes by which different stakeholders interact – are also seen to have a major importance in themselves, whatever the outputs or outcomes achieved. In other words, the current public governance debate places a new emphasis on the old truths that 'what matters is not what we do, but how people feel about what we do' and that 'processes matter' or, put differently, 'the ends do not justify the means'. These two contrasting emphases make 'good public governance' exceptionally difficult – but they may well represent non-negotiable demands by the public in modern society.

The difference between a managerial and a governance approach is illustrated in Case Example 1.1.

CASE EXAMPLE 1.1 **DIFFERENCES BETWEEN MANAGERIAL AND GOVERNANCE APPROACHES**

Whereas public-management-oriented change agents tend to focus their efforts on improving street cleaning and refuse collection services, a local governance approach emphasises the role of citizens in respecting the communal desire that no-one should throw litter on the streets in the first place, and that materials should be recycled, not simply thrown away. This involves education (not only in the schools, since 'litter-bugs' come in all sizes and ages), advertising campaigns, encouragement of people to show their disgust when dirty behaviour occurs, and the provision of proper waste facilities (including those for dog waste) which will help to prevent litter and dog-fouling problems occurring in the first place.

The Chartered Institute of Management Accountants in the UK uses the following definition of corporate governance:

> Corporate governance is the system by which companies are directed and controlled.

Source: Cadbury (1992, para 2.5)

Whereas the governance discussion in the public sector is relatively recent (see Chapter 4), there has been a debate in the private sector for some time on one aspect of governance – *corporate governance,* which refers to issues of control and decision-making powers within organisations (not just private companies). The 'corporate governance' debate has been triggered by

9

the increase of the importance of transnational companies – today numbering more than 78,000 (UNCTAD, 2007) – which have highlighted problems of unclear lines of accountability.

International organisations like the OECD have issued guidelines as to how to improve corporate governance. Even though a lot of reforms have recently been implemented in many OECD countries, the fallout around the collapse of Enron in the US in 2001 shows that corporate governance is not only a matter of drafting a stricter legal framework but also of respecting societal values.

Another longstanding governance debate comes from the field of international relations where the issue of *global governance* has become very topical. In a nutshell, global governance is about how to cope with problems that transcend the borders of nation states (such as air pollution, the sex tourism industry or the exploitation of child workers), given the lack of a world government. Pessimists suggest that globalisation means that governments everywhere have become powerless, that managing globalisation is an oxymoron, since globalisation is shaped by markets in a 'race to the bottom', not by governments. Some have suggested that this powerlessness is reinforced by the coming of the Internet age – that there is no governance against the 'electronic herd' (Friedmann, 2000).

However, this pessimistic discourse on global governance was countered by a very different set of arguments by the UN Secretary General in his Millennium Report – he argued that globalisation needs to be 'managed'. This was close to the language used by the Communiqué of the 2000 Ministerial Meeting of the OECD, headlined: 'Shaping Globalization'. Yet others have proposed to 'govern' globalization and 'make it work for the poor' (IMF's Deputy Director, Masood Ahmed) or simply to achieve 'globalization for all' (UNDP Administrator Mark Malloch Brown). The task of the times was 'to get globalizing processes within our control and focus them upon human needs' (Anthony Giddens, LSE). The events following 9/11 2001 in New York City have cast a further, more troubled, light on the idea that global activities (such as terrorism) can be 'fought' through collective international action.

Whereas governance is a positivistic concept, analysing 'what is', *good governance* is obviously a normative concept, analysing 'what ought to be'. Even though particular international organisations like the United Nations and the OECD have excelled in providing rather abstract definitions of the characteristics of 'good governance', we believe that this concept is highly context-dependent. This means that instead of using a simple operational blueprint or definition, the meaning of 'good governance' must be negotiated and agreed upon by the various stakeholders in a geographical area or in a policy network.

'Good governance' raises issues such as:

- stakeholder engagement
- transparency
- the equalities agenda (gender, ethnic groups, age, religion, etc.)
- ethical and honest behaviour
- accountability
- sustainability.

Importantly, the implementation of all the governance principles agreed upon between stakeholders has to be evaluated – ideally, by those same stakeholders.

However, there is as yet no theoretical reason to suppose that all the principles which we would wish to espouse under the label 'good governance' are actually achievable simultaneously. This 'good governance impossibility theorem' (mirroring the 'general equilibrium impossibility theory', which shows that it is impossible for markets to deliver all the welfare characteristics which economists have traditionally held dear) is troubling – if valid, it means that politicians will need to trade off some principles of good governance against others to which they give a lower priority. This is not a debate that has yet surfaced explicitly in many countries – and it is one that we must suspect politicians will be keen to avoid.

What is the role of public management within public governance?

The concepts of public management and public governance are not mutually incompatible. Nevertheless, not all practices of public management are part of public governance, and not all aspects of public governance are part of public management.

For example, some practices of public management revolve around the best way to provide networks of computer workstations within the offices of a public agency (e.g. a personnel department). There are few public governance dimensions to this decision, which is a decision common to most organisations in all sectors. On the other side, there are issues of co-production of public service between family members and volunteers who come together to look after the welfare of an elderly person who wants to live an independent life in the community, but with enough support to ensure that no personal disasters occur. This is an issue in public governance but need not (and usually will not) involve intervention from any public manager.

Consequently, we suggest in this book that the realms of public management and public governance are separate but interconnected. One is not a precursor to the other, nor superior to the other – they do and should co-exist, and should work together, through appropriate mechanisms, in order to raise the quality of life of people in the polity.

Of course, not all aspects of public management and public governance can co-exist. When taken to extremes, or interpreted from very contrasting standpoints, contradictions between public management and public governance can indeed be detected. For example, Rod Rhodes (1997: 55), writing from a governance perspective, characterises NPM, or the 'New Public Management' (one branch of public management), as having four weaknesses: its intra-organisational focus; its obsession with objectives; its focus on results; and the contradiction between competition and steering at its heart. While each of these elements of NPM, if treated in a suitably wide framework, can be reconciled with a governance perspective, an extreme NPM proponent who insists that her/his view of the world is the only way to understand reform of the public sector is bound to antagonise a proponent of the governance perspective (*and vice versa*).

SO WHY SHOULD YOU STUDY PUBLIC MANAGEMENT AND GOVERNANCE?

Finally, we want to make a claim for this book that we hope will encourage you to read it with more enthusiasm – and to read more of it – than you otherwise might. We want to claim that the study of public management and governance will not only make you a more informed student, and a more effective manager (whatever sector you work in), but that it will also make you a better citizen. You should be able to make a greater contribution to the neighbourhood, the local authority, the region and the country in which you live. You may even be able to make a contribution to the quality of life of many citizens elsewhere in the world. And if you decide you do NOT want to know more about public management and governance – just remember that you will be making it more difficult for all those people who will therefore have to work harder to substitute for the contribution you might have made.

But our greatest hope is that, however you use this book, it will help you to find out more about and care more about what it means to be an active citizen, influencing the decisions made in the public domain.

STRUCTURE OF THE BOOK

The book has three main parts:

- an *introductory* part, setting out the role of the public sector, public management and public governance, and how these have evolved in recent years in different contexts;
- a second part on *public management for public sector organisations*, exploring the main managerial functions that contribute to the running of public services;
- a section on *governance* as an emerging theme in the public domain.

QUESTIONS FOR REVIEW AND DISCUSSION

1 How would you define public services? Show how this question would be answered by authors from different schools of thought and try to come up with your own definition.

2 In some UK cities, vandalism has become a serious problem. Think of a public management and a public governance solution to this problem. Why are they different?

READER EXERCISES

1 How do you think the image of the public sector has changed in the last five years? Have you personally experienced any improvements in public service delivery? If yes, what are these improvements and why did they happen? If no, why do you think this was the case?

2 Does ownership matter – i.e. does the efficiency or effectiveness of a service depend on whether it is in the public or private sector? Why? How would you collect evidence to support your view – and how would you collect evidence to try to refute it?

CLASS EXERCISES

1   In groups, identify the main differences between 'public management' and 'private management', and between 'public governance' and 'corporate governance'. Thinking about the news over the past month, identify instances where these concepts might help in deciding who has been responsible for things that have been going wrong in your area or your country. (Now try answering the question in terms of things that have been going right in your area or your country. If you find this difficult, what light does this throw on how the media shape debates on public management and public governance?)

2   In groups, identify some public services in your area that are provided by private sector firms. Each group should identify ways in which these services are less 'public' than those that are provided by the public sector. Then compare your answers in a plenary session.

FURTHER READING

Tony Bovaird (2005), 'Public governance: balancing stakeholder power in a network society', *International Review of Administrative Sciences*, 71 (2): 217–28.

Stuart Ranson and John Stewart (1994), *Management for the public domain: enabling the learning society*. Basingstoke: Macmillan.

REFERENCES

Graham Allison (1994), 'Public and private management: are they fundamentally alike in all unimportant respects?', in F.S. Lane (ed.), *Current issues in public administration* (5th edn). New York: St Martin's Press, pp. 14–29.

Adrian Cadbury (1992), *Report of the Committee on the Financial Aspects of Corporate Governance*. London: Gee & Company.

Thomas Friedmann (2000), *The Lexus and the olive tree: understanding globalisation*. London: HarperCollins.

Dan Norris (2007), 'Hain, not Reid'. Letter in *New Statesman*, 2 April, p. 6.

Christopher Pollitt and Geert Bouckaert (eds) (1995), *Quality improvement in European public services: concepts, cases and commentary*. London: Sage.

Stuart Ranson and John Stewart (1994), *Management for the public domain: enabling the learning society*. Basingstoke: Macmillan.

Rod Rhodes (1997), *Understanding governance: policy networks, governance, reflexivity and accountability*. Buckingham: Open University Press.

UNCTAD (2007), *World investment report*. New York: United Nations.

Chapter 2

The changing context of public policy

Tony Bovaird, Birmingham University, UK and *Elke Löffler*, Governance International, UK

INTRODUCTION

Public expenditure in most parts of the world increased rapidly after 1945, as the 'welfare state' in its various forms became widespread. However, by the early 1980s, budget deficits provided a major motive for public sector reforms in many parts of the world – reforms that covered both the content of public policy and the way in which public policy was made. Since then, many governments, at least in the OECD countries, have achieved more favourable budget positions (see Chapter 3), although another economic slowdown appears to be in train at the time of writing (mid-2008).

Meanwhile, other challenges have emerged since the 1980s to drive reforms in public policy. These new pressures on governments consist of a mixture of external factors (such as the ageing society, the information society and the tabloid society) and internal factors (including the consequences, both planned and unplanned, arising from the 'first generation' of public sector reforms, as outlined in Chapter 4). These new pressures have emphasised the quality of life implications of public policies and the governance aspects of public sector organisations. They have typically pushed the public sector in a different direction to the managerial reforms of the 1980s and early 1990s. In particular, they have re-emphasised the role of politicians in the public policy arena.

LEARNING OBJECTIVES

The key learning objectives in this chapter are:
- to identify recent changes in the context of public policy;
- to identify the major paradigm shifts in public policy-making in recent decades;
- to identify the changing role of politics in public policy.

RECENT CHANGES IN THE CONTEXT OF PUBLIC POLICY

Most policies have spending implications. If money becomes scarce, policy-makers have less space to manoeuvre. However, financial crises also have an upside – they put pressure on public organisations to become more efficient. In particular, the fiscal crises in most OECD countries in the 1980s (lasting in some until the 1990s) were a key trigger for public sector reforms (see Chapter 4). As these crises receded in many OECD countries by the mid-1990s, the financial imperative for public sector reforms became weaker, although clearly it remained important that public services should be managed in an economic and efficient way.

From the early 1990s, other pressures on governments became more important, consisting of a mixture of external factors and internal factors. Many of the external factors have operated for several decades (see Box 2.1), but some became significantly more important in recent years. A particularly powerful group of external factors pushing for reform since the early 1990s has been associated with quality of life issues. The first of these to make a major impact was the global environmental crisis, particularly since the Rio Summit in 1992. Since then, interest has grown in many countries around the world in the quality of health (not just health care), the quality of life of children, particularly the prevalence of child poverty (not just the quality of public services for children), and the quality of life of the elderly (not just the quality of their social care).

BOX 2.1 EXTERNAL FACTORS DRIVING PUBLIC POLICY REFORMS

Political

■ New political and social movements in many countries – and internationally – which contest the neo-liberal world view, especially in relation to world trade, the global environment and attitudes to civil liberties.

■ Changing expectations, fuelled by globalisation (particularly through tourism and the mass media) about the quality of services that governments should be able to deliver, given what is currently available in other countries.

■ Changing expectations about the extent to which public services should be 'personalised' to the needs of individual citizens.

■ Increased insistence by key stakeholders (and particularly the media) that new levels of public accountability are necessary, with associated transparency of decision making and openness of information systems.

■ Changing expectations that there will be widespread and intensive engagement with all relevant stakeholders during the policy-making and policy implementation processes.

■ Loss of popular legitimacy of some long-established public leadership elites, such as political party leaders, local politicians, etc.

Economic/financial

- Decreasing proportions of the population within the 'economically active' category as conventionally defined, with knock-on effects to household income levels and government tax revenues.
- Economic boom for ten years from the mid-1990s in most OECD countries and many other parts of the world, generally producing rising tax revenues for governments.
- Increasing (or continuing) resistance by citizens to paying higher rates of tax to fund public services.
- Weakening roles of trade unions as labour markets become more flexible.

Social

- Traditional institutions such as the family and social class have changed their forms and their meanings in significant ways, so that old assumptions about family behaviour and class attitudes can no longer be taken for granted in policy-making.
- Traditional sources of social authority and control – police, clergy, teachers, etc. are no longer as respected or influential as formerly.
- Changing expectations about the core values in society – just as the 1980s saw traditional values such as public duty and individual responsibility being replaced by values of individual self-realisation and rights, so in the 1990s there was a slow return to the understanding that caring and compassion are vital characteristics of a 'good society' and that 'social capital' is vital to a successful public sector.
- The ageing society, which means that much higher proportions of the population are in high need of health and social care.
- Changing perceptions about the minimum quality of life for certain vulnerable groups that is acceptable in a well-ordered society – especially in relation to child poverty, minimum wages for the low paid, and the quality of life of elderly people (especially those living alone).
- A revolt against conceptions of 'difference', whether of gender, of race, of physical or mental (dis)abilities, as 'given' rather than socially constructed, with consequences that new political settlements are sought in which disadvantaged groups have increased expectations.
- Changing perceptions about which behaviours towards vulnerable people are socially acceptable in a well-ordered society – particularly in relation to child poverty, child abuse, domestic violence and levels of anti-social behaviour.
- The growing realisation that public services not only alter the material conditions experienced by users and other citizens but also affect the emotional lives of users, citizens and staff, affecting their ability to form fulfilling social relationships within a more cohesive society.
- The growing desire by many citizens to realign the balance between paid work, domestic work and leisure time, particularly to tackle some of the gendered inequalities embedded within the current (im)balance of these activities.

continued

17

- The new level of scrutiny that the 'tabloid society' provides of the decisions made by politicians and by public officials (and also of their private lives), often concentrating more on the 'people story' side of these decisions rather than the logic of the arguments.

Technological

- Technological changes, particularly in ICT, which have meant that public policies can now take advantage of major innovations in ways of delivering services and also that the policy-making process itself can be much more interactive than before.
- The information society, in which a much higher proportion of the population can make use of new ICT technologies.
- Increased concern about the efficacy of 'hi-tech' solutions – e.g. renewed interest in 'alternative health care' and in 'alternative technologies'.

Environmental

- Increasing concerns with global warming.
- Willingness to take some serious steps to reduce the level of usage of non-renewable energy sources and to recycle waste materials.
- Increasing pressure for governments to demonstrate the environmental impact of all new legislation, policies and major projects.

Legal/legislative

- Increasing influence of supra-national bodies – e.g. UN, World Bank, IMF, WTO, EU, etc. – in driving legislative or policy change at national level.
- Increasing legal challenge in the courts to decisions made by government, by citizens, businesses and by other levels of government.

Many of these external factors have tended to push most governments in rather similar directions – e.g. the concern with child poverty has driven many governments towards 'workfare' programmes, the ageing society means that the pensions policies of most OECD countries are now under threat, the information society means that e-government is a major theme everywhere, and the tabloid society has driven governments in most countries to take public relations (now generally known as 'spin') much more seriously than (even) before.

However, the internal factors that are driving changes in public policy tend to be more context-specific. For example, in many countries governments are contracting out a high proportion of public services and also looking to the private sector for advice and consultancy on many policy-relevant issues. This is sometimes because of the superior access to capital finance enjoyed by the private sector, and sometimes because of the perception that the private sector has greater expertise in certain functions. This has had a number of important policy implications: for example, a new generation of public sector employees no longer expects to enjoy a 'job for life', which increases the flexibility of policy-making (but probably also leads to higher salaries and, where greater mobility occurs, may lead to a loss of 'institutional memory'). Moreover, in those countries where governments have gone far down the road of contracting out public services to the private sector (see Chapter 7), there have emerged new and serious concerns about fraud and corruption in privately run public services (see Chapter 21).

Again, the concerns about fragmented and disjointed public policies and governmental structures (often the consequence of 'agencification' or internal markets) have encouraged governments to find more mechanisms for coordination and integration, but in different ways in different countries. While it is widely agreed that today's 'wicked' problems can no longer be solved by a single policy or by a single actor, governmental responses have differed significantly, from the emphasis on 'joined up government' in the UK and 'whole of government' approaches in Australia, to the 'seamless services' agenda in the USA and the initiatives on 'one stop shops' for citizens and investors in Spain and Germany.

CHANGING PARADIGMS OF PUBLIC POLICY

In the 1980s, the drivers of change, particularly the financial pressures, pushed most Western countries towards a focus on making the public sector 'lean and more competitive while, at the same time, trying to make public administration more responsive to citizens' needs by offering value for money, choice flexibility, and transparency' (OECD, 1993, 9). This movement was later referred to by the academic community as 'new public management' or NPM (Hood, 1991) (see Box 2.2).

Whereas some scholars considered this reform movement as a global paradigm change (e.g. Osborne and Gaebler, 1992: 325 and 328) others were more sceptical of the transferability

---

BOX 2.2 ELEMENTS OF NPM

- emphasis on performance management;
- more flexible and devolved financial management;
- more devolved personnel management with increasing use of performance-related pay and personalised contracts;
- more responsiveness to users and other customers in public services;
- greater decentralisation of authority and responsibility from central to lower levels of government;
- greater recourse to the use of market-type mechanisms, such as internal markets, user charges, vouchers, franchising and contracting out;
- privatisation of market-oriented public enterprises.

Source: OECD (1993, 13)

of Westminster-type managerialism to Western Europe and other countries (e.g. Flynn and Strehl, 1996). Certainly, the credence given to the NPM paradigm by public sector practitioners in a major country such as Germany has remained rather low throughout the past two decades.

In the NPM, managers were given a much greater role in policy-making than before, essentially at the expense of politicians and service professionals. While this clearly helped to redress the traditional balance in the many countries where management had been rather undervalued in the public sector, it quickly led many commentators to question whether this rebalancing had gone too far. In particular, it led to a vision of the public sector that often seemed peculiarly empty of political values and political debate.

As Chapter 4 shows, different countries responded to the challenges in different ways, depending on a whole variety of factors. However, one factor that ran through most of these responses was a concern with the governance dimension of public policy and the governance of public sector organisations (see Chapter 15). This governance-oriented response tended to emphasise:

- the importance of 'wicked problems' that cut across neat service lines, so that 'quality of life' improvements are more important than 'quality of service' improvements;
- the need for these 'wicked problems' to be tackled cooperatively, because they cannot be solved by only one agency – thus the need for multi-stakeholder networking;
- the need for agreed 'rules of the game' that stakeholders will stick to in their interactions with one another, so that they can trust each other in building new joint approaches to the problems they are tackling – extending 'corporate governance' principles into the sphere of 'public governance';
- the critical importance of certain principles that should be embedded in all interactions which stakeholders have with each other, including transparency, integrity, honesty, fairness and respect for diversity.

Of course, the set of responses described above have developed gradually rather than overnight. Indeed, many of today's wicked problems are the emerging and unresolved problems from yesterday. Also, in many cases, fiscal pressures have persisted and have been mixed with the new demands on governments. Which pressures are dominant and which are less relevant depend essentially on the setting (see Chapter 4). As public policy contexts become more differentiated in the future, the variety of governance reforms are likely to be greater than in the NPM era.

These challenges put public agencies under pressure to adapt. Whereas some agencies respond to the new environment quickly or even proactively, others change more slowly or not at all. As a result, old and new structures and management approaches are often found side by side (Hood, 1991). This messy situation is multiplied by the many different kinds of reform going on – some of which are described in Parts 2 and 3 in this book. Figure 2.1 shows the main directions of reform as a movement from law-driven ('*Rechtsstaat*') to service-driven to citizen-driven agencies, but with each of these co-existing with each other to some degree in any given agency.

20

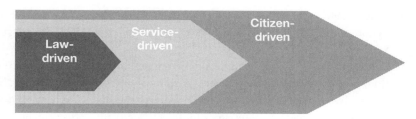

Goal:	legal conformity	competitiveness	community quality of life
Perspective:	state	public/private service providers	civil society
Control mechanism:	hierarchy	market	networks
Logic	legal		political

Figure 2.1 *Types of public agencies*
Source: Translated and adapted from Gerhard Banner (2002)

Of course, it is not enough to diagnose what is happening in the public policy system. It is necessary also to decide what to do next. Pollitt and Bouckaert (2004: 186–8) suggest that there are four strategic options (the '4Ms') for public sector reforms:

- Maintenance of existing relationships between the political system, the system of public administration and law, and the market economy – usually involving tightening up traditional controls (e.g. restricting expenditure, squeezing staff numbers, running efficiency campaigns, rooting out corruption, etc.).
- Modernisation of the system, by bringing in faster, more flexible methods in all aspects of the administrative system (e.g. budgeting, accounting, staff management, service delivery, etc.), with some knock-on effects on the political system – this option has one variant that emphasises the need for deregulation and 'empowerment' of lower levels of managers, while another variant emphasises the need for citizen participation and stakeholder engagement.
- Marketisation of the system, by introducing as many market-type mechanisms as possible (e.g. through competition), while still keeping the general shape of the existing system of administration and law.
- Minimisation of the administrative system, by transferring to the market sector as many tasks as possible, through privatisation and contracting out.

This latter option has been referred to by some academics as the 'hollowing out of the state', and they typically add other mechanisms such as the loss of national government powers to international organisations such as the WTO or the European Union. For much of the 1980s

21

and early 1990s, this option haunted the public policy arena as a spectre threatening the extinction of the public sector as we know it. As Dunleavy (1994: 58) suggested:

> Current NPM thinking identifies government's optimal role, its core distinctive function, as being an 'intelligent customer' on behalf of citizens, purchasing privately supplied services so as to maximize the public welfare. But consuming without producing is new territory for liberal democratic governments, and we have no developed guidelines that could prevent loss of core competencies and the creation of 'hollow state' structures.

However, such fears have now somewhat abated. The debate is now rather which (plural) roles the state should play, which (plural) reform modes it should adopt and in which context. As Pollitt and Bouckaert (2004: 188) suggest: 'Different regimes at different times appear to have leaned towards one or other of these strategies. The "4Ms" do not have to be taken in a particular order, but neither can they all be convincingly pursued simultaneously.' They go on to suggest that many reform programmes tend to opt for two of the strategies, in shifting combinations.

Moreover, a major theoretical critique of the 'hollowing out of the state' and 'network governance' perspectives comes from Mark Bevir and Rod Rhodes (e.g. Bevir and Rhodes, 2003). In their work, they undertake a 'decentred' analysis of governance, i.e. one that does not accept the 'truth' of any single narrative about what governance is and how it evolves over time. They attempt to 'unpack the institutions of governance through a study of the various contingent meanings that inform the actions of the relevant individuals' (Bevir, 2003: 209). They point out that the network governance narrative is only one of several that provides insight into the current state of governance in countries around the world.

Taking these various lines of argument into account, we would argue that the dilemma outlined in the 'hollowing out of the state' debate misinterprets the issue at stake. The most important question is not whether the state will remain more powerful than other players but which set of formal (legal) and informal rules, structures and processes will be needed so that the state, the private and third sectors, citizens and other important stakeholders can each believe that they exercise power over decisions by the other stakeholders, in ways that protect their interests and allow the creation of win-win situations for all parties concerned. And if this is not possible, what changes are necessary to these political rules, structures and processes in order to ensure acceptable minimum outcomes (both in terms of quality of life and in terms of quality of governance processes), from the viewpoint of key stakeholders, which we would interpret as meaning, in particular, the most vulnerable groups in society.

THE POLITICS OF PUBLIC POLICY

The role of politics in the public sector, which might seem in theory to be central, has for long been under pressure from two other major sources – the professional groupings who tend to believe that they are uniquely well informed about which policies are most likely to work and the managerial cadres who tend to believe that they are uniquely expert in getting the various professional groupings to work together effectively. More recently, a third set of actors has tried to push its way onto this already crowded stage – the groups of citizens and other stakeholders who have been told that they alone know best what they want, at least in terms of services that directly affect their quality of life. So is there still room for politicians to play a role upon this stage?

First, it is important to recognise that politicians play a number of roles – leadership of their polity (at a variety of levels), policy-making for society, strategy-making for the organisation, partnership building with other organisations and with other stakeholders (including other countries or other communities), watchdog over the decisions made within their polity, lobbyist in relation to decisions made in other polities, and last, but not least, representation of their constituents. Not all of these roles are equally supported by the bureaucratic structures of the public sector – in particular, constituency roles tend to be rather poorly supported by officials, being largely regarded as 'political' and therefore for political parties to support.

How does this role differ in different contexts? Not only do the fundamental roles of politicians alter, as we move from the global to the local stage, but so do the relative priorities between the roles and the dominant stakeholders with whom politicians have to interact. Furthermore, the political role varies depending on the balance in the polity between representational and participative democracy.

Starting at the global level, *global politics* is mainly about security, trade and environment, and is played out by heads of state and ministers. However, many of these decisions have major implications at national, regional, local and neighbourhood levels – e.g. the 'peace dividend' can be a bonus for national social programmes (more funds are available from government budgets) but very bad for local employment strategies in areas where army and naval bases are closed down. Again, global environmental strategy involves clashing national interests ('carbon guzzlers' versus the rest?), while global environmental improvement often entails 'think global, act local' approaches. So national and local politicians cannot ignore the global level in their policy-making, even though their role may often be essentially one of lobbying for their own interests.

National politics is often the most ideologically driven, as it is the main forum for the debate about ideas that determine election results and subsequent government legislation programmes. Here, there are frequently clashes between ideological viewpoints, between national power groupings (which have variously been viewed through the lens of classes, 'fractions of capital', dominant coalitions of stakeholders, communities of interest, etc.) and between the 'political' sensitivities of party politicians and the 'technical' recipes favoured by the 'technocracy'. Policy-making at this level has a strong emphasis on injecting 'political flavours' into professionally designed strategies.

Regional politics is driven by different considerations in many countries. In Spain, there is a clear desire to allow expression within the *autonomias* to feelings of national identity as well as differing local priorities. This is clearly the case also with Scotland, Wales and Northern Ireland in the UK. In other cases, regional government has been deliberately formulated as a counterweight to central government (e.g. in the US since 1776 and, nearly 200 years later, in the post-1945 German constitution, largely fashioned in the US mould). In some cases,

23

there is a mixture of motives – the slow movement towards some form of regional government in England may be seen as a partial recognition by central government of strong regional identities in some parts of the country, coupled with a desire to devolve some responsibility for unpopular transport and planning decisions away from Whitehall. At this regional level, politicians are in a half-way house between national and local politics. Where the region is strong (e.g. US states, some powerful Spanish *autonomias* such as the Basque Country and Catalonia, some German *Länder* such as Bavaria and Baden-Württemberg), then regional politicians can have a national and even international significance. Where regions are weak (e.g. Spanish *autonomias* such as Murcia and Rioja, the regions in France and the regions recently created in Central and Eastern European countries), regional policies mainly play merely a 'gap-filling' role between policies set at the centre and in localities.

Local politics still usually has some ideological flavour but this is often idiosyncratic (local political parties often deviate quite far in their views from their national parties) and often it is less important than stances on local issues. Part of the role of the strategic politician in a local area is to lead the local community towards new goals, partly it is to help the local area compete against other areas (particularly in the same region) and partly it is to represent the community where policies (at all levels of government) are believed to have failed. Clearly, many local politicians are non-strategic, worried only about 'patch politics' and working on behalf of their constituents to improve the outcomes they experience from public services and from their dealings with other organisations. This means that many officials experience local politics as an irritant in the policy implementation process rather than a contribution to the policy-making process, which may explain why many have such a negative view of it.

Neighbourhood politics is usually far from the ideological level and is dominated by local issues – it therefore often pits individual politicians against their own party colleagues and leaders. Indeed, neighbourhood politics often involves the balancing of interests within and between neighbourhoods, producing coalitions on issues and across interest groups that have little parallel at any higher level of politics – NIMBYism (the 'not in my back yard' syndrome) is the most obvious example of this. Consequently, highly rational strategies, cooked up by well-informed professionals and backed by top politicians in the local council and nationally, may still fail because they 'don't go down well on the street'.

Clearly, there is still a major role for political input into policy-making, even in this era of highly professionalised 'new public management' and partnership-based 'network governance'. However, the autonomy of political decisions should not be exaggerated. There are many different pressure points by means of which other stakeholders can drive politicians down roads that they do not personally like very much. For example, policy networks often contain strong voices from all the main stakeholders – politicians, by becoming involved in them, give credence to, and even magnify, these voices. Consequently, political platforms are usually designed to take on board the interests of a wide coalition of stakeholders. At worst, this can mean that politicians seek to 'please everyone, all the time'. In these circumstances, strategic policy-making becomes next to impossible. Only if politicians are prepared to weather adverse comment when they follow strategic policies in which they believe can they claim to exercise political leadership and help their organisations and partnerships to manage strategically.

24

SUMMARY

After the 1980s, fiscal pressures became less important as drivers of public policy change. However, since then, a large of number of major changes in the political, economic, social, technological, environmental and (international) legislative fields have impacted on public policy-making, the implications of many of which are not yet fully evident.

The paradigms of public policy-making have changed significantly during the past three decades – the 'old public administration' was partly replaced by the 'new public management', which in turn has been partly supplanted by the 'public governance' perspective. However, current public policy-making in most countries still has strong elements of all three approaches – and it is not clear how far or how fast these will converge to produce a more 'unitary' approach in the future. In any case, further perspectives will no doubt emerge that will partly borrow from, and partly replace, these perspectives.

Politics is integral to policy-making, but the role of politicians, which has never been as clear as the conventional model of democratic decision-making ('the primacy of politics') has tried to suggest, is today even more complex, given the roles that are played in public decision making by professional groups, managers, engaged citizens and other stakeholders.

QUESTIONS FOR REVIEW AND DISCUSSION

1   Which of the main groups of factors driving changes in public policy (listed in Box 2.1) have been of most importance in the last five years? Is this likely to continue in the next five years?
2   What are the main paradigms of public policy-making and what are the main differences between them?

READER EXERCISES

1   Get a copy of a serious newspaper, such as *The Guardian*, *Le Monde* or *Frankfurter Allgemeine Zeitung*. Try to find examples where factors listed in Box 1.1 are cited as influencing current government policy decisions.
2   In the same newspaper, identify ten politicians whose activities are being described in detail. Identify the roles that they are playing. How many of these roles would you describe as 'policy-making' roles? And at what geographical level is this policy being decided?

CLASS EXERCISE

Divide into groups. Each group should identify the four major policy areas (at national or international level) where it believes current government policy needs to change. For each of these, the group should suggest how such changes might be initiated in the current political climate.

25

The groups should then come together and compare notes. Where there are commonalities between the lists, suggesting that there is some consensus between the groups on the need for change, discuss why these policies have not yet been altered.

FURTHER READING

Peter John (1998), *Analysing public policy*. London: Cassell.

Christopher Pollitt and Geert Bouckaert (2004), *Public management reform: a comparative analysis*. Oxford: Oxford University Press.

REFERENCES

Gerhard Banner (2002), 'Zehn Jahre kommunale Verwaltungsmodernisierung – was wurde erreicht und was kommt danach?', in Erik Meurer and Günther Stephan (eds), *Rechnungswesen und Controlling*, 4 (June): 7/313–42, Freiburg (Haufe Verlag).

Mark Bevir (2003), 'A decentred theory of governance', in Henrik Paul Bang (ed.), *Governance as social and political communication*. Manchester: Manchester University Press, pp. 200–21.

Mark Bevir and Rod Rhodes (2003), 'Decentring British governance: from bureaucracy to networks', in Henrik Paul Bang (ed.), *Governance as social and political communication*. Manchester: Manchester University Press, pp. 61–78.

Patrick Dunleavy (1994), 'The globalization of public services production: can government be "best in world"?', *Public Policy and Administration*, 9 (2), 36–64.

Norman Flynn and Franz Strehl (1996), *Public sector management in Europe*. London: Prentice Hall/Harvester Wheatsheaf.

Christopher Hood (1991), 'A public management for all seasons', *Public Administration*, 69 (1): 3–19.

OECD (1993), *Public management developments*, Survey 1993. Paris: OECD.

David Osborne and Ted Gaebler (1992), *Reinventing government. How the entrepreneurial spirit is transforming the public sector*. Reading, MA: Addison-Wesley.

Christopher Pollitt and Geert Bouckaert (2004), *Public management reform: a comparative analysis* (2nd edn). Oxford: Oxford University Press.

Chapter 3

The size and scope of the public sector

Peter M. Jackson, University of Leicester, UK

INTRODUCTION

What is the appropriate scope and size of the public sector? The simple answer is, it all depends. It depends upon the vision of the state to which you subscribe and it depends upon your weighing up the costs and benefits of two highly imperfect social institutions: the market and the public sector.

The public sector is a ubiquitous social institution that has grown in size and complexity over the past fifty years. Nevertheless, this has not been a linear development. Whereas the development of the welfare state in the late 1960s and 1970s resulted in an unprecedented growth of the public sector in most OECD countries, the 1980s and 1990s were marked by concerns and attempts to reduce the size of the public sector, or, at least, to make it more efficient (see Chapter 4). In some cases this has meant privatization, in others devolving responsibilities to lower levels of government or simply the introduction of market-type instruments in the public sector (see Chapter 7).

Today, public expenditure in all developed countries accounts for between one-third and one-half of a country's gross domestic product (GDP). Given the fact that many OECD countries continue to suffer from budget deficits and high levels of debt, public expenditure management will remain high on the political agenda. Overall economic efficiency depends upon how well these public sector resources are managed, not only because of the opportunity cost of wasted resources but because of the impact of taxation and public borrowing on private sector decisions.

LEARNING OBJECTIVES

This chapter will look at the following key issues:
- the role and scope of government;
- the trends in social spending and some of the forces that shape them;
- the changing composition of public spending;
- the implications that these trends have for public sector management.

THE ROLE AND SCOPE OF GOVERNMENT

Variations in public expenditure across time and space reflect differences in the vision of the role and scope of government. What then are the appropriate role, scope and size of government?

There is no simple or straightforward, technically grounded answer to this question. Instead, there are conflicting perceptions of the proper scope of government. Nor is the question new. It has been the focus of an emotionally charged debate conducted by political philosophers and economists over several centuries. Central to the debate are the basic normative questions of 'what should governments do; how big should the share of public spending be in the national economy; and should governments engage in direct production activities?'

Recently, this debate has become more intense as those who advocate a minimalist state have sought to downsize, privatize, re-engineer or re-invent government. At the other end of the spectrum those who argue in favour of an active interventionist state emphasize the benefits of public policies and public spending programmes and the enlargement of the positive personal freedoms which accompany them. The position that any individual occupies on this spectrum reflects as much his or her preferences for what constitutes a 'good society' as any technical, philosophical or socio-economic arguments.

While this debate has been conducted for many years it has not been resolved. This is clearly demonstrated by the recent exchange between Buchanan and Musgrave (see Box 3.1) who each subscribe to significantly different answers to the fundamental question: what is the appropriate role of the state?

BOX 3.1 MUSGRAVE'S AND BUCHANAN'S VIEWS OF THE ROLE OF THE STATE

Musgrave is representative of a group of scholars who regards the public sector as having its own legitimacy and the public and private sectors as complements (rather than competitors) working together to achieve maximum social welfare.

While Musgrave sees the state as 'an association of individuals engaged in a co-operative venture, formed to resolve problems of social co-existence and to do so in a democratic and fair fashion' (Buchanan and Musgrave, 1999, p. 31), Buchanan's view of the world is that majority politics results in the formation of coalitions between special interest groups that produce policies that best serve their own interests. For Buchanan the issue is to constrain these tendencies by the use of fiscal constitutions and rules. 'My concern and my primary motivation here in a normative sense is preventing the exploitation of man by man, or woman by woman, through the political process. That is what is driving my whole approach.'

Source: Buchanan and Musgrave (1999, p. 52)

THE ROLE OF THE STATE IS . . .

. . . allocative
   – Correcting market failure through regulation, taxation, subsidies and providing public goods.

. . . distributional
   – Achieving a just and fair society by regulation, the adjustment of rights, giving access to markets in the face of discrimination, progressive taxation and subsidies.

. . . stablisation
   – Controlling economic growth, unemployment and inflation by demand and money management.

Source: Musgrave (1959)

Many years ago, Musgrave (1959) set out three distinct roles for an active state. This taxonomy provided a useful structure and fashioned the subsequent debate. For Musgrave a modern state transcends the primitive and minimal role of the 'night watchman' and embraces an allocative role, a distributional role and a stabilization role.

Within the allocative role, the provision of public goods is seen as a means of overcoming various market failures that can arise from ill-defined property rights, externalities, incomplete information, high transactions costs or non-increasing returns to scale. These sources of market failure had long been acknowledged by, among others, Adam Smith and John Stuart Mill. Markets are said to 'fail' when they either do not exist, because transactions costs are so high, or when they produce an inefficient outcome. Correcting market failure gives rise to what Musgrave (1998) has referred to recently as the 'service state', i.e. an essential role that is to 'repair certain leaks in the efficient functioning of the market as a provider of goods' (p. 35).

The second role of government is concerned with distributional issues and forms the basis of the 'welfare state'. Given any initial distribution of rights, including property rights, the unfettered market system will grind out a distribution of welfares that may or may not be considered to be socially just and fair. The objective of the distributional role of the state is to adjust the market-determined distribution of welfare by bringing it closer to what 'society' regards to be just and fair. This is achieved through regulation, the adjustment of rights, giving access to markets in the face of discrimination, progressive taxation and subsidies.

The third role of government is represented by the stabilization role. Unconstrained market forces can result in a general equilibrium for an economy that is accompanied by unacceptably high levels of unemployment. Classical economists in the early twentieth century argued that, if left alone, market forces would adjust and unemployment would be eventually eliminated. However, Keynes pointed out that an economy can become stuck in a state of high unemployment for many years because the speed of economic adjustment is very slow – 'in the long run we are all dead'. In order to speed up the adjustment process Keynes advocated corrective action through changes in public spending and/or taxation, in order to manage 'effective demand', depending upon where the economy is on the business cycle. From the 1950s up to the 1980s the Keynesian consensus was dominant. Demand in the economy was 'managed' to achieve the twin objectives of low unemployment and price stability, while acknowledging that there was a trade-off between these objectives.

From the early 1980s, monetary economists (harking back to the classical school) regained the upper hand with their insistence that controlling the money supply was the only practical tool of stabilization policy. By the 1990s, both schools were represented in the governments of major OECD countries.

While writers such as Musgrave and Arrow had earlier emphasized market failures, we now also acknowledge 'government failure' and policy failure. Recently, Musgrave (1998) wrote about the 'flawed state'. Both markets and public bureaucracies are flawed institutions. Public sector failures arise for reasons that are similar to market failure – high transactions costs and incomplete and imperfect information – but in addition there are the inefficiencies that arise from inadequate incentive structures, severe principal/agent problems and inadequate demand revelation mechanisms as in the case of voting mechanisms. These failures result in both allocative and managerial inefficiencies within the public sector, reflected in inappropriate policies being implemented through wasteful bureaucracies.

THE CHANGING BOUNDARIES OF THE STATE

There is a great diversity in the size and scope of government across the various nation states of the world. This in part reflects differences in preferences for the 'good society' but it also arises from variations in per capita real incomes and hence the capacity of countries to finance their public policies; differences in social factors such as population size and composition; and also differences in political institutions, for example, majoritarian compared with proportional electoral systems and presidential versus parliamentary systems.

The absolute and relative sizes of the public sectors around the world have shown dramatic changes over the past 130 years. IMF data show that in 1870 the average relative size of the public sector around the world, as measured by the ratio of government spending to GDP, was 10.7 per cent. This increased to 19.6 per cent in 1920; 28 per cent in 1960; 41.9 per cent in 1980 and 45 per cent in 1996 (Tanzi and Schuknecht, 2000).

Up to 1950 there had been a lengthy period of laissez-faire during which public expenditures and the boundaries of the state changed modestly, only periodically being disrupted by major world wars. During the 1950s and the 1960s there were many Keynesian economists who advocated increases in public spending. Galbraith (1958) dramatically referred to public squalor amidst private affluence. Bator (1960: xiv) argued that society was 'dangerously short-changing (itself) on defence, foreign aid, education, urban renewal and medical services'. Increases in public spending on infrastructure and human capital (education and health) promote economic growth but have to be paid for through increases in taxation. However, the growth in real per capita incomes is able to fund the increase in taxation.

Growth in public spending, however, is not inevitable. Some theories of public expenditure growth (see Brown and Jackson, 1990) such as *Wagner's law*, which relates public expenditure changes to real income growth, or *Baumol's cost disease model*, which relates it to changes in the terms of trade between the public and private sectors, are highly deterministic. These theories provide the means of carrying out an interpretation of historical trends but they ignore public choices. The demand for public spending comes from income growth, population growth, changes in the composition of the population, urbanization and the increasing complexity of society. The decision to spend is the outcome of public choices, which are shaped by changing perceptions about the role and legitimacy of government and hence where the boundaries of the state are drawn.

In examining trends in public expenditures and making international comparisons, we shall use two principal data sources – the IMF (as presented in Tanzi and Schuknecht (2000)) and the OECD. Their definitions and coverage differ somewhat from each other but both datasets give essentially the same qualitative picture of trends in public expenditure.

The rapid expansion in the absolute and relative size of the public sectors of the world took place during the period from 1960 to 1980, as shown in Table 3.1. This was a period during which there were no world wars and when demographic trends were not placing significant pressures on public budgets. It was, however, a time when attitudes changed positively towards an interventionist role for government reflecting the advent of the welfare state and also Keynesian demand management policies. Public spending increased owing to the introduction of new (especially welfare) policies along with expansion in the scope and coverage of existing programmes.

As one commentator has remarked, this was the 'golden age of public sector intervention'. It was also a period during which many had simplistic and romanticized views of how government worked and what government could achieve. These views played up market failure and were blind to the possibility of public sector failure – the costs of government intervention in terms of the distorting effects of taxation and public borrowing; the inefficiencies of public bureaucracies; the self-interest politics of pressure groups and the possibility of corruption on a significant scale. This idealized view of government assumed that politicians and bureaucrats acted to promote maximum social welfare while ignoring the realities and consequences of 'rent-seeking' behaviour (i.e. the search for personal gain) (Tullock, 1967). Furthermore, it was implicitly assumed that policymakers possessed considerable knowledge; for example, that they knew with certainty which policy levers produced what effect.

Public choice theorists and libertarians mounted a series of challenges to the post-war consensus that public sector intervention was at all times beneficial. They pointed out the potential efficiency losses resulting from the distorting effects of high marginal rates of tax; the effect on interest rates of large public sector deficits (which also crowded out private investment); and the frequency of policy failures. Whether or not there was any convincing empirical evidence to support the anti-government rhetoric of the 1970s (and there was little) is of no significance; the point is that these arguments won the day and ushered in the Thatcher and Reagan administrations and policies aimed at 'rolling back the frontiers of the state'. The 1980s and 1990s witnessed a series of initiatives that would change the balance between the public and private sectors: privatization; contracting out; reductions in public sector debt; balanced budget rules; fiscal constitutions; private finance initiatives and public-private partnerships, and so on.

Were the frontiers of the state rolled back? Table 3.1 suggests not. The relative size of the public sector was in most cases greater in 2004 than it was in 1980. Even in countries such as the UK where the relative size of the public sector is smaller, this has more to do with the growth in GDP than the reduction in the absolute size of public spending. Nevertheless the rate of expansion of the boundaries of the public sector slowed down after 1980. The exception is Japan.

THE COMPOSITION OF PUBLIC EXPENDITURE

Real government spending on goods and services has been very modest in its growth. The main element of public expenditure growth over the past forty years has been transfer expenditures on income maintenance and subsidies, due to expansion in the welfare state. This increase in social spending has not been due primarily to demographic factors, such as the ageing of the population, as so many commentators have erroneously assumed. Of course, there has been some pressure from demographic factors but these have been modest when compared with the real factors, which have been increases in the scope of social programmes to embrace more individuals along with increases in the rates of benefits paid.

Furthermore, social spending programmes cover more and more situations and therefore bring more people into the benefit net. The full impact of an ageing population has yet to be experienced.

Table 3.1 *General government outlays, by country (% of GDP)*

	1965	1970	1975	1980	1985	1990	1995	2004
Australia	24.6	25.2	31.3	32.3	37.8	33.0	35.4	30.8
Austria	36.6	38.0	44.4	47.2	50.1	48.5	52.4	47.5
Belgium	35.0	39.7	47.6	53.4	57.3	50.8	50.3	46.2
Canada	27.8	33.8	38.9	39.1	45.4	46.0	45.3	37.2
Denmark	31.8	40.1	47.1	55.0	58.0	53.6	56.6	50.8
Finland	30.3	29.7	37.0	37.1	42.3	44.4	54.3	43.6
France	37.6	37.6	42.3	45.4	51.9	49.6	53.6	50.7
Germany	35.3	37.2	47.1	46.5	45.6	43.8	46.3	43.6
Greece	22.0	23.3	27.1	29.6	42.3	47.8	46.6	43.4
Ireland	36.0	37.7	40.7	47.6	50.5	39.5	37.6	28.2
Italy	32.8	32.7	41.0	41.8	50.6	53.1	52.3	46.9
Japan	19.0	19.0	26.8	32.0	31.6	31.3	35.6	38.8
Korea	14.5	14.8	16.9	19.2	17.6	18.3	19.3	22.7
Netherlands	34.7	37.0	45.7	50.9	51.9	49.4	47.7	42.7
Norway	29.1	34.9	39.8	43.9	41.5	49.7	47.6	41.4
Portugal	18.1	18.0	25.2	28.1	42.9	44.2	41.2	43.7
Spain	19.5	21.7	24.1	31.3	39.4	41.4	44.0	39.2
Sweden	33.5	41.7	47.3	56.9	59.9	55.8	62.1	55.6
United Kingdom	33.5	36.7	44.4	43.0	44.0	41.9	44.4	39.7
United States	25.6	29.6	32.3	31.3	33.8	33.6	32.9	31.3
Euro area	33.1	33.9	40.9	43.0	47.2	46.3	49.1	46.8
OECD	26.9	29.2	34.4	35.5	38.1	38.0	39.4	38.4

Source: Adapted from OECD National Accounts. © OECD

According to IMF data (Tanzi and Schuknecht, 2000), on average, total real public spending around the world increased from 12.6 per cent of GDP in 1960 to 17.3 per cent in 1995. While this is a modest increase, it is nevertheless overstated because it is not adjusted for the 'relative price effect', i.e. the fact that public sector costs tend to go up faster than private sector costs.

In Table 3.2, which shows public sector consumption expenditure (the amount of goods and services for end-users produced by means of public sector funding), there was only a modest increase and much of that was due to the reasons given above, i.e. that the growth in GDP slowed down. The significant increases in public spending for all countries have come from the absolute and relative growth in subsidies and transfers (see Tables 3.3 and 3.4). Part of the expansion in governments' welfare role has been due, as mentioned above, to extending the coverage and benefit rates of these programmes. Another reason is the high levels of unemployment experienced, especially in European economies, during the 1980s and 1990s.

Table 3.2 *General government outlays, by economic category: consumption (% of GDP)*

	1965	1970	1975	1980	1985	1990	1995	2004
Australia	13.5	14.4	18.9	18.6	20.0	18.5	18.6	18.7
Austria	14.6	16.1	18.2	18.4	19.5	18.8	20.4	19.6
Belgium	16.7	17.6	21.4	23.0	23.0	20.3	21.5	21.5
Canada	15.6	20.5	21.8	21.3	21.9	22.4	21.4	19.0
Denmark	16.7	20.4	25.1	27.2	25.8	25.6	25.8	25.6
Finland	14.2	15.1	17.8	18.7	20.6	21.6	22.8	21.7
France	16.9	17.4	19.5	21.5	23.7	22.3	23.9	23.6
Germany	15.0	15.5	20.1	19.9	19.7	18.0	19.8	19.2
Greece	8.2	8.8	10.6	11.4	14.2	15.1	15.3	15.3
Ireland	13.3	14.3	18.2	19.4	18.1	15.1	14.9	12.1
Italy	16.2	14.9	16.1	16.8	18.6	20.2	17.9	18.2
Japan	8.2	7.4	10.0	9.8	9.6	9.0	9.8	10.6
Korea	9.5	9.7	11.3	11.9	10.4	10.5	9.7	10.0
Netherlands	23.6	24.9	28.2	29.1	26.4	24.3	24.0	23.5
Norway	14.6	16.4	18.7	18.7	18.1	20.8	20.9	19.6
Portugal	11.5	13.3	14.4	14.0	15.0	16.4	18.6	21.4
Spain	9.1	10.2	11.3	14.3	15.9	16.9	18.1	17.3
Sweden	17.9	22.5	25.2	29.6	28.2	27.7	26.3	26.8
United Kingdom	17.2	18.0	22.4	21.6	20.9	19.9	19.8	18.9
United States	16.4	18.5	18.1	16.8	17.1	16.6	15.3	14.7
Euro area	15.4	15.8	18.5	19.5	20.3	19.7	20.4	20.4
OECD	14.6	15.7	17.3	17.0	17.3	16.8	16.6	16.0

Source: Adapted from OECD National Accounts. © OECD

Capital expenditure is another element of public expenditure that has great economic significance, not only in terms of direct employment creation in the private sector but more generally in terms of the impact of public sector infrastructure on economic growth. Table 3.5 shows the net capital outlays of the public sector (i.e. net of depreciation). The data show wide variations. Because public sector capital programmes are easier to control than public consumption spending, they tend to be the first to be hit when public expenditure needs to be cut back. This is seen in the volatility of the ratio in Table 3.5.

As part of their welfare state role, governments provide 'positive freedom goods', i.e. goods that expand individuals' freedoms to access markets, which will then expand their opportunities. Examples of freedom goods are education, health services, pensions and unemployment benefits. Table 3.5 shows the variation in these different freedom goods across a number of countries. As expected there is a wide range, which reflects prevailing local

Table 3.3 *General government outlays, by economic category: income transfers (% of GDP)*

	1965	1970	1975	1980	1985	1990	1995	2004
Australia	4.2	3.9	5.9	6.8	7.4	6.9	8.5	8.7
Austria	12.9	14.1	14.9	16.2	17.9	17.7	19.5	18.6
Belgium	11.9	11.0	14.5	16.1	17.2	15.1	15.5	14.9
Canada	5.2	6.5	8.6	8.3	10.5	11.2	12.6	11.2
Denmark	6.8	10.5	13.5	16.2	16.1	17.8	20.4	17.8
Finland	7.6	5.9	8.7	9.5	11.8	12.6	16.1	13.4
France	11.5	12.0	14.1	15.5	17.7	16.9	18.5	19.2
Germany	13.0	13.0	17.2	16.6	16.0	15.2	18.1	18.7
Greece	6.8	7.6	7.1	8.9	14.4	14.4	15.1	16.8
Ireland	10.0	10.0	10.0	10.7	12.9	11.9	12.6	10.4
Italy	11.9	11.8	14.4	14.2	17.1	18.1	16.7	17.8
Japan	4.7	4.6	7.7	10.1	10.9	11.4	13.4	16.2
Korea	0.9	0.6	0.7	1.3	1.5	2.0	2.1	3.8
Netherlands	10.0	10.8	14.3	16.4	15.5	15.5	15.3	12.5
Norway	6.6	9.0	10.0	11.3	11.8	16.0	15.8	14.4
Portugal	2.3	2.1	5.2	7.0	7.8	8.5	11.8	12.8
Spain	4.5	5.9	7.4	10.9	12.7	12.7	13.9	13.1
Sweden	7.7	10.1	13.8	17.1	17.7	19.3	21.3	18.8
United Kingdom	6.9	8.0	10.2	11.6	13.7	11.9	15.4	13.9
United States	5.0	7.1	10.2	9.8	9.8	10.0	11.8	11.1
Euro area	10.9	11.2	14.0	14.7	15.8	15.5	17.0	17.2
OECD	6.5	7.5	10.2	10.7	11.4	11.5	13.2	13.4

Source: Adapted from OECD National Accounts. © OECD

circumstances (e.g. population size and composition, per capita incomes) and local political preferences and institutions.

Data from the IMF reveal a steady increase in public sector education's share of GDP from (on average) 3.5 per cent of GDP in 1960 to 5.8 per cent in 1980 and 6.2 per cent in 1995.

This has been due to expanding the coverage of education programmes (e.g. raising the school leaving age), but the main driver was demographic pressures arising from the post-1945 baby boom. An expansion in publicly funded university education, along with a general increase in entitlements at the tertiary level, has also contributed to the rise. While population increases have slowed down and will moderate the pressures on public education budgets, nevertheless there are new forces that will take their place (e.g. greater access to tertiary education and lifelong learning). Some of this demand may be met by greater private sector involvement.

Table 3.4 *General government outlays, by economic category: subsidies (% of GDP)*

	1965	1970	1975	1980	1985	1990	1995	2004
Australia	0.7	0.9	1.1	1.5	1.7	1.3	1.3	1.5
Austria	2.3	1.8	3.0	3.1	3.2	3.1	2.9	2.6
Belgium	2.3	2.3	2.6	2.8	2.4	1.7	1.5	1.7
Canada	0.9	0.9	2.5	2.7	2.5	1.5	1.1	1.3
Denmark	1.8	2.6	2.7	3.1	2.9	2.2	2.5	2.4
Finland	3.2	2.8	3.8	3.3	3.1	2.9	2.8	1.8
France	2.5	2.2	2.2	2.1	2.6	1.8	1.5	1.7
German	1.2	1.7	1.9	2.0	2.0	2.0	2.1	2.0
Greece	1.4	1.0	3.2	3.0	3.7	1.2	0.4	0.3
Ireland	2.7	3.4	2.5	2.6	2.3	1.1	1.0	0.8
Italy	1.7	1.9	2.8	2.9	2.6	2.0	1.5	1.3
Japan	0.7	1.1	1.5	1.5	1.	1.1	0.8	0.7
Korea	0.3	0.3	1.4	0.9	0.6	0.6	0.7	0.4
Netherlands	0.9	1.0	1.2	1.7	2.0	1.7	1.1	1.7
Norway	3.4	3.8	4.6	5.2	4.5	6.0	3.7	2.7
Portugal	1.0	1.3	1.7	6.0	4.2	1.8	1.4	1.3
Spain	0.5	0.5	0.7	1.1	1.3	1.1	1.1	1.2
Sweden	1.1	1.3	2.5	3.3	3.9	3.6	3.8	2.0
United Kingdom	1.6	1.7	3.6	2.5	2.0	0.9	0.7	0.6
United States	0.2	0.5	0.5	0.5	0.5	0.4	0.3	0.3
Euro area	1.6	1.7	2.0	2.1	2.2	1.8	1.7	1.6
OECD	0.8	1.0	1.4	1.4	1.4	1.1	0.9	0.8

Source: Adapted from OECD National Accounts. © OECD

Public spending on health services has also shown a substantial rise. Again, according to IMF data, public expenditure on healthcare increased from 2.4 per cent of GDP in 1960 to 5.8 per cent in 1980 and 6.5 per cent in 1995. Access to free healthcare at the point of consumption is regarded as a basic positive freedom right. Entitlements to healthcare have been expanded in many countries since 1950. At the same time, technological changes in the form of new equipment, new surgical procedures and new drugs have expanded the scope and quality of treatment and greatly increased healthcare budgets. An ageing population also places pressures on health spending. There is a life cycle in the use of health services. When individuals are very young or very old they make the greatest use. Furthermore, it costs on average three times as much to care for someone over the age of 80 compared with someone

Table 3.5 *General government outlays, by economic category: net capital outlays*[1]
(% of GDP)

	1965	1970	1975	1980	1985	1990	1995	2004
Australia	3.8	3.6	3.1	2.3	3.8	2.4	2.8	1.6
Austria	6.0	4.8	7.0	7.0	6.1	4.9	5.3	5.2
Belgium	1.3	5.3	4.9	4.9	3.5	1.8	2.5	3.3
Canada	3.1	2.3	2.2	1.4	2.1	1.4	0.6	0.4
Denmark	5.4	5.4	4.7	4.6	3.6	0.7	1.5	1.8
Finland	4.3	4.9	6.1	4.7	5.0	5.8	8.6	6.9
France	6.7	5.0	5.3	4.9	5.1	5.7	6.0	5.8
Germany	5.4	6.0	6.4	6.1	4.9	6.1	2.6	0.6
Greece	5.1	5.1	5.1	4.3	5.5	8.3	4.6	4.8
Ireland	5.0	5.0	5.0	8.5	7.2	3.6	3.7	3.5
Italy	2.0	2.5	4.4	2.9	4.5	3.5	4.7	3.8
Japan	5.0	5.2	6.3	7.5	5.6	6.0	7.9	7.8
Korea	3.8	3.8	2.9	4.6	4.4	4.8	6.4	8.8
Netherlands	2.5	−2.7	−1.0	−0.1	1.8	1.9	1.4	1.6
Norway	3.2	4.1	4.9	5.6	4.2	4.9	4.4	4.3
Portugal	2.7	0.8	3.4	−1.2	9.3	10.9	4.3	4.2
Spain	5.0	4.7	4.6	4.6	7.6	6.9	5.7	4.8
Sweden	4.9	5.9	3.6	2.7	1.6	0.2	3.6	3.7
United Kingdom	4.1	5.1	4.4	2.6	2.4	5.9	4.9	4.0
United States	2.0	1.3	1.1	1.0	1.4	1.4	0.7	1.1
Euro area	4.3	3.9	4.6	4.1	4.3	4.4	4.2	3.1
OECD	3.5	3.2	3.4	3.3	3.3	3.8	3.8	3.5

Note: 1 Net fixed investment plus net capital transfers.

Source: Adapted from OECD National Accounts. © OECD

who is 60 years old. Increases in life expectancy are due in part to improvements in healthcare but this then impacts on budgets.

The biggest time bomb that is ticking away in every country is the ageing of populations and the impact that this will have on pensions. Public expenditures on pensions have increased on average from 1.2 per cent of GDP in 1920 to 4.5 per cent in 1960, 8.4 per cent in 1980 and 9.8 per cent in 1995. Not only has the coverage of entitlements increased but so too have benefit rates. In many countries pensions are indexed to inflation and in Germany they are indexed to net wage growth (i.e. net of taxes). It is estimated that by 2020 the share of the population who are above the age of 60 will, in most countries, have increased to 25 per cent, thereby increasing the dependency ratio. The Ageing Working Group of the Economic Policy Committee of the European Commission has estimated that pensions expenditure will rise in the UK from 6.6 per cent of GDP in 2004 to 8.6 per cent in 2050 (EC, 2006) – this is a relatively slow rise compared with that expected in countries such as Portugal (11.1 per cent to 20.8 per cent) or Ireland (4.7 per cent to 11.1 per cent), and in line with the increase in countries such as France and Germany.

How countries will cope with this is currently an active topic of public policy debate. The retirement age could be increased. The age of 65 was introduced when life expectancy was lower. For example, in the UK the retirement age of women will be increased from 60 to 65 sometime between 2010 and 2020. In Italy the male retirement age of 60 was raised to 65 in 2001. Another means of dealing with the problem is to reduce the retirement benefits paid. In some countries (Japan, Germany, France and Italy) these are very generous. This does, however, break the implicit intergenerational social contract – a consequence of which would be that current generations would need sufficient warning in order to adjust their life cycle savings decisions. The role of private pensions is currently uncertain, given the loss in their portfolio values following the puncturing of the bubble of 'irrational exuberance' in the world's equity markets in 2002. Public sector pension schemes are in many cases uncovered, which means that, in order to cope with the future demographic time bomb, tax rates will need to increase or radical changes to pension schemes will need to be introduced.

THE PUBLIC/PRIVATE DIVIDE

In recent years, the boundaries between the public and the private sectors have become increasingly blurred as a result of policy innovations. Two important initiatives have been public-private partnerships (PPPs) and the involvement of the voluntary sector in the delivery of public services. The formation of PPPs is a worldwide phenomenon that makes greater use of private financing for public sector capital infrastructure provision. In the United Kingdom, the dominant PPP is the Private Finance Initiative (PFI) that was introduced in 1992, under which the private sector accepts responsibility (within the specification of a contractual relationship) for the design, build (i.e. construction) and operation (including maintenance) of public sector capital projects such as schools, hospitals and housing. The rationale for PFIs is that they are regarded as enhancing efficiency, delivering improvements in value for money and improving the public sector's management of risks. These risks are familiar and include the risk of cost and time over-runs on large capital projects; higher than expected maintenance costs; and unanticipated changes in the demand for the service. In

37

essence a PFI shifts the risk (or part of it) from the public to the private sector, but obviously at a cost that is reflected in the PFI contract 'price'.

As the United Kingdom Treasury points out, 'the Private Finance Initiative is a small but important part of Government's strategy for delivering high quality services'. By 2006 the United Kingdom Treasury was able to claim that, 'there are currently around 200 projects with a capital value of £26 billion in the procurement pipeline to 2010' (HM Treasury, 2006, p. 8). Looking over the period since PFI was introduced there have been completed 185 new or refurbished health facilities; 230 new or refurbished schools and forty-three transport projects. PFI represents about 10 per cent of total public sector investment. Involvement of the private sector and the use of private finance are means for the public sector to meet the investment challenge of filling the infrastructure gap while keeping within public sector borrowing limits and securing improvements in value for money.

Great claims are made for PPPs and PFIs. Obvious questions to ask are, have these innovations improved value for money, and have they improved the management of public sector risks? These are complex questions, and it is probably too early to provide definitive answers. Nevertheless, current research does call into question the positive claims and rhetoric that support PFI. Shaoul (2005) provides an excellent starting point, questioning the underlying assumptions and the methodologies used to evaluate PFI. She also throws into sharp relief the issues surrounding the political economy of PPP/PFI. She concludes,

> the analysis of the VFM methodology showed it relied upon a new methodology, expressly introduced for the purpose that was premised upon concepts such as value for money and risk transfer that despite their initiative plausibility have little objective empirical content . . . Value for money rested upon discounted cash flow techniques that were not value free. Political choices were exercised in the selection of the technique, the discount rate, and the appraisal process.
>
> (Shaoul, 2005, pp. 463–4)

CONCLUSIONS

The public sectors in the developed economies are now significantly different compared with their size and composition in the mid-twentieth century. Over the next thirty to forty years further radical changes will take place. The future shape of the public sector will be influenced by the demographic time bomb of an ageing population and the complementary role played by the private sector. This places greater pressures on those who have to manage public services with the objective of providing value for money. It offers opportunities to seek private sector solutions in a mixed economy model of PPPs, which will challenge public sector managers to work across new boundaries and interfaces between the public and private sectors.

SUMMARY

The boundaries between the public and the private sectors obviously vary depending upon the vision of the 'good society' that is dominant at any particular time. Irrespective of where these boundaries are drawn, and whatever the size of the respective sectors, the relationships between public and private sectors will need to be established and managed effectively.

Relationship management is central to public governance (Jackson and Stainsby, 2000). Deciding where the boundaries of the state should be drawn, and then managing the resultant cross-sector relationships, result in a new role for government, as a 'broker', of relationships in order to add value (Jackson, 2001).

Does the public sector have the capacity to design and deliver efficient and effective public services at a tax price that the electorate finds acceptable? This is the domain of public management, and it is within this arena that much of government failure is found. Central to the achievement of value for money is knowledge and evidence gathering (see Chapter 22). In many significant areas of public policy, including deciding the limits of the public sector itself, the knowledge of public managers and politicians is still severely incomplete.

QUESTIONS FOR REVIEW AND DISCUSSION

1   What are the main causes of 'market failure' in your country at the present time? Which state interventions are most likely to correct them in a cost-effective way?
2   What are the main causes of 'government failure' in your country at the present time? Which market-based solutions are most likely to correct these government failures in a cost-effective way?
3   In what ways are politicians and public sector bureaucrats likely to behave that undermine the achievement of social or public welfare? How might this behaviour be controlled to minimize the damage it causes?
4   Is it possible for public expenditure to comprise more than 100 per cent of GDP? Demonstrate how this might occur and discuss how it might effect the macro economy.
5   If private sector firms provide public services, funded by public money, what effect does this have on the public sector borrowing requirement and the level of efficiency in the macro economy?

READER EXERCISES

1   Choose a public service in your country in which you have a special interest. Find statistics on the level of expenditure on this public service, the level of employment and the level of usage over the past ten years.
    ■   Are the trends in spending change and employment change different? If so, why do you think this is? What evidence can you find on this?
    ■   Are the trends in line with the change in the numbers of clients? What has most influenced the cost of the service – the eligibility criteria for the service or the standards of service offered to eligible clients?
2   Pick out two different philosophies of the role of the public sector and highlight their contrasting views on the appropriate size of the public sector. What are the

underlying assumptions about economic, social and political behaviour in these two philosophies that have led them to such different conclusions? How would you test which of these philosophies is most likely to be able to explain the decisions made recently by politicians in your country on the size of the public sector?

CLASS EXERCISE

Divide into three groups. Each group should develop a case about what is the main economic role of the state – the achievement of allocative efficiency, distributive justice or macroeconomic stabilization? It should also consider which of these goals should be now given priority in your country, if there is any need to trade them off against each other. The groups should present their arguments to each other in a plenary session.

FURTHER READING

James M. Buchanan and Richard A. Musgrave (1999), *Public finance and public choice: two contrasting visions of the state*. Cambridge, MA: MIT Press.

HM Treasury (2006), *PFI: strengthening long-term partnerships*. London: Stationery Office.

Peter M. Jackson (2001), 'Public sector added value: can bureaucracy deliver?', *Public Administration*, 9 (1): 5–28.

Vito Tanzi and Ludger Schuknecht (2000), *Public spending in the 20th century*. Cambridge: Cambridge University Press.

REFERENCES

Francis M. Bator (1960), *The question of government spending: public needs and private wants*. New York: Harper.

Charles V. Brown and Peter M. Jackson (1990), *Public sector economics* (4th edn). Oxford: Blackwell.

James M. Buchanan and Richard A. Musgrave (1999), *Public finance and public choice: two contrasting visions of the state*. Cambridge, MA: MIT Press.

John Kenneth Galbraith (1958), *The affluent society*. Boston, MA: Houghton Mifflin.

HM Treasury (2006), *PFI: strengthening long-term partnerships*. London: Stationery Office.

Peter M. Jackson (2001), 'Public sector added value: can bureaucracy deliver?', *Public Administration*, 79 (1): 5–28.

Peter M. Jackson and L. Stainsby (2000), 'Managing public sector networked organisations', *Public Money and Management*, 20 (1): 11–16.

Richard A. Musgrave (1959), *The theory of public finance*. New York: McGraw-Hill.

Richard A. Musgrave (1998), 'The role of the state in fiscal theory', in Peter Birch Sorensen (ed.), *Public finance in a changing world*. London: Macmillan, pp. 35–50.

Jean Shaoul (2005), 'A critical financial analysis of the private finance initiative', *Critical Perspectives on Accounting*, 16: 441–71.

Vito Tanzi and Ludger Schuknecht (2000), *Public spending in the 20th century*. Cambridge: Cambridge University Press.

Gordon Tullock (1967), 'The welfare costs of tariffs, monopolies and theft', *Western Economic Journal*, (June): 224–32.

Chapter 4

Public management reforms across OECD countries

Jürgen Blum, Harvard University and *Nick Manning*, World Bank

INTRODUCTION

The conditions under which OECD governments operate are changing fundamentally, as expectations change (see Chapter 2). While ten years ago only a few countries were seriously involved in public sector reform, a government's stance towards the nature of public service is becoming a major policy issue across all OECD countries – and there is no reason to expect that the pressures for change will ease off in the next ten years.

This chapter sets out different public management reform paths that OECD countries have chosen in response to expectations that increasingly emphasise government responsiveness and performance.

In view of unintended consequences of past reforms and emerging challenges that OECD countries will face in the twenty-first century, the chapter predicts a new and possibly more modest future agenda for public management reform. It suggests that there is no generic flaw in existing public administrative arrangements that can be tackled by a universal set of reforms. Indeed, public sectors almost everywhere are adapting and evolving, but in different ways. Public governance and management are in a state of flux, and governments need a new capacity to understand and guide the adaptation process.

LEARNING OBJECTIVES

This chapter will look at the following key issues:
- changing expectations towards government;
- differences in public sector reform trajectories of OECD governments;
- unintended consequences of public management reform;
- new reform agendas.

CHANGING VIEWS OF GOVERNMENT

The last 100 years have seen an unprecedented growth in the tasks of the public sector (see Chapter 2) and in the complexity of the expectations placed on civil servants. Four key stages can be distinguished in the evolution of expectations towards the public service (see Figure 4.1)

These stages have been cumulative rather than successive, the complexity increasing as one piles on top of the other. They constitute a change from a public service that was primarily expected to serve as an apolitical bulwark of institutional continuity in the nineteenth century towards a public service increasingly oriented to demonstrate performance and responsiveness to political leadership and citizens' expectations.

In the nineteenth century, the role of public service institutions as a quasi-constitutional constraint on political institutions was emphasised, ensuring their adherence to constitutional and legal requirements. A wave of meritocratic reforms aimed at creating an apolitical public service, run on its own mechanical principles – primarily but not exclusively in anglophone countries. For example in the US, the federal Pendleton Civil Service Reform Act in 1883 put an end to the previous spoils system. It placed most federal employees on a system of merit-based appointments and established the United States Civil Service Commission. Previously, in the UK, the Northcote-Trevelyan report of 1854 had similarly recommended open recruitment and put an end to most forms of patronage. In continental Europe, the most relevant example was perhaps the 1875 decision in France that the *Conseil d'Etat* (an administrative body) had the right to judge the legality of a policy decision taken at a political level. The idealisation of the public service as an apolitical bureaucratic world continued until

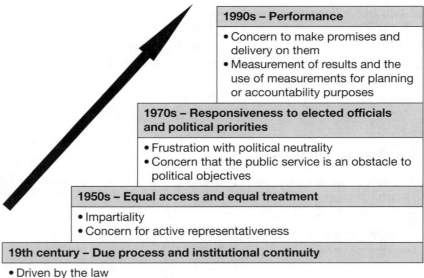

Figure 4.1 *Accumulating expectations towards the public service*

the middle of the twentieth century: Sayre suggests that the late 1930s was, at least in the US, the 'high noon of orthodoxy' in which 'administration was perceived as a self-contained world, with its own separate values, rules, and methods' (Sayre: 1958, 102). According to Max Weber (1956: 124), bureaucracy as an ideal type meant 'formally the most rational form of power'.

It was not until the 1950s and 1960s that a more active notion of *equal access and equal treatment* entered mainstream debate. Before, in what are today OECD countries, citizens' access to public services was distinctly unequal in practice, although impartiality was *de jure* guaranteed (see Chapter 20). As social values changed, it became increasingly believed that impartiality was impossible without representativeness. Equality of access and treatment found some expression within the European discourse on public administration in Council of Europe Resolutions and subsequently in case law set by the European Court of Justice.

Since the 1970s, as many countries faced significant fiscal pressures to reduce costs, there has been an increasingly explicit emphasis on balancing due process with *responsiveness to elected officials and political priorities.* Inevitably, public servants delivering public services to citizens have always played a quasi-political role in deciding who gets what from the public sector. Even at Sayre's 'high noon', the ideal type of the apolitical 'Weberian civil service' was rarely found in practice. However, in the late 1970s, the concern became more urgent that public service should improve its responsiveness to political priorities. For example in the UK, Prime Minister Thatcher explicitly identified 'an unresponsive civil service' as an obstacle to implementing her policy changes in the 1980s. Modern media have doubtless played an important role in raising expectations about responsiveness of government, e.g. through frequent opinion polls, call-in radio and blogs.

Over the past two decades, *performance* has taken on a special urgency for OECD governments. As many have noted (Matheson *et al.*, 2006; Schick, 2005), the notion of performance is seen as fundamental to the modern state: governments must increasingly earn their legitimacy by fulfilling their service delivery promises. Performance approaches have been strongly inspired by management ideas from the private sector, concerned with the measurement of results and subsequent use of those measurements for planning or accountability. As the pressures for fiscal consolidation have grown, the performance movement has emphasised the need to set targets and create incentives that focus on efficiency. Consequently, as Pollitt and Bouckaert (2004) point out, there has been a deluge of managerial and political rhetoric about the significance of performance, and something of an industry has grown out of its measurement (see Figure 4.2).

CHANGING STRUCTURES

How have OECD countries responded to this growth of responsibilities and complex expectations? Often, over the past thirty years the 'New Public Management Story' has grabbed the headlines. In reality, this perspective somewhat simplifies and distorts, suggesting a general movement of OECD countries from the 'old' ideal-type of the traditional Weberian bureaucracy towards 'new' efficiency-oriented public management approaches. In this vision, while some pioneering Westminster and Scandinavian countries have heroically shown the way ahead, other countries are seen as somewhat lagging.

Relatively simple measures	Business process measures	Compliance with delegated authority	All regulatory and legislative responsibilities complied with	
		Leadership style	Strength of internal governance and leadership, and maintenance of good working relationships	
		Facilitating learning and change management	Effectiveness of arrangements for staff learning, fostering innovation and change management	
		Human resource management	Good recruitment and retention decisions, and productive working environment	
		Stewardship	Operating resources, capital assets and IT infrastructure are well managed	
		Promoting/ preserving values	Effectiveness of mechanisms to promulgate public service values	
	Single results measures	Input usage	What goes into the system? Which resources are used?	
		Outputs produced	Which products and services are delivered? What is the quality of these products and services?	
		Policy goals achieved	Intermediate outcomes (direct consequences of the ouput)	
			Final outcomes (significantly attributable to the output)	These measures are valid for performance only, to the extent that there is a clear causal relationship between the individual or agency outputs and the measure
	Ratio measures	Efficiency	Costs/output	
		Productivity	Output/input	
		Effectiveness	Output/ outcome (intermediate or final)	
Complex measures		Cost- effectiveness	Input/outcome (intermediate or final)	

Figure 4.2 *Types of performance measures used in OECD countries*

Source: Developed from OECD (2007), Sterck *et al.* (2006) and material from the Canadian Treasury Board Management Accountability Framework, www.tbs-sct.gc.ca/maf-crg/ (accessed 16 May 2008)

In fact, OECD countries have taken strikingly different paths towards improving responsiveness and performance (Manning and Parison, 2003; Pollitt and Bouckaert, 2004). Diverse administrative traditions and the malleability of administrative systems play a key role in determining these differences.

The malleability of administrative systems strongly depends on the *nature of the executive* and the *structure of the state*. Single-party majority governments are particularly well positioned to drive through complex reform programmes that would create tensions within coalition governments. Coordinating public management reforms across government is easier if a powerful central agency can drive reform. Federal countries (e.g. Germany, Belgium, USA and Canada), where authority is divided vertically between levels of government, tend to be less able to drive through comprehensive and uniform reforms than unitary systems (e.g. New Zealand, UK, the Netherlands, France). However, the lack of uniformity in federal systems can also be an important asset as sub-national government entities can provide a natural testing ground for a variety of reform approaches.

Administrative cultures are a second major factor determining different reform paths. A helpful distinction is usually made between two types of administrative culture: the '*Rechtsstaat*' ('rule of law' or legal state) model versus the Westminister 'public interest' or 'civic culture' tradition.

Given the dominant role of the law in the Rechtsstaat tradition, it tends to bring forth a culture of 'correctness and legal control' (Pollitt and Bouckaert, 2004, p. 53), possibly making it less malleable to performance-oriented reforms than 'public interest' systems. In Continental Europe, legislative authority still provides the key legitimising mechanism in public administration, together with an independent administrative court system and the ethos of a professional civil service. As a result, managerialist ideas will generally have to show that they are compatible with the existing legal framework. There is even some debate as to whether they are needed at all – for example in Germany, the separation of policy and implementation (often achieved under NPM through the establishment of arm's-length agencies) is to some degree enshrined in the federal-state-local government structure.

By contrast, the Westminster 'public interest' tradition attaches much higher value to pragmatic and flexible decision-making for the public benefit. Governments in this tradition are regarded as a somewhat necessary evil that must be held to account at all times. The law is in the background, and enforcing the law is an implicit rather than explicit principle in the work of public servants. Public servants are regarded as employees more or less like any other, except that their employer happens to be the state. This tradition appears to be peculiarly compatible with more radical reform efforts. For example, a strong political lead in the United Kingdom was able to produce extensive changes in the pattern of public sector employment and reporting arrangements, with remarkably few legislative obstacles. That same malleability also facilitated the abolition of an entire tier of government in London and other major metropolitan areas in England – and a subsequent introduction of a variation on that tier of government – in a manner that would have been inconceivable in other European settings.

Many other factors can also play important roles in determining reform paths. For example, acute fiscal crises can trigger changes that would be very hard to accomplish under normal circumstances; the power of public sector unions to resist change varies enormously among OECD countries; so does the relationship between politicians and top public servants,

45

determining the ability of politicians to push through reforms. Despite these striking differences, some common trends can be identified in the way that governments have responded to changing expectations – and in particular to the growing concern about responsiveness and performance during the past decades.

Structuring for responsiveness . . .

OECD governments have developed many new institutions that foster openness and receptiveness to citizen concerns. An open government is understood as one where businesses, civil society organisations and citizens have gained in their relative powers: to know what has been decided (*transparency*), to obtain their legitimate service entitlement (*accessibility*), and to be heard (*consultation and participation*) (OECD: 2005a).

Freedom of Information (FOI) legislation has been an important means of establishing rights of access to information and has today been adopted by over 90 per cent of OECD member countries (see Box 4.1). It has combined with other transparency measures, such as the publication of service standards and performance results, helping the public to understand and assess what government is doing and how it is doing it. While the regulations imposed on businesses and citizens have become more complex in many fields, administrative simplification efforts (e.g. creation of one-stop-shops) have helped people to comply with these regulations and to access government services more easily. Consultation and participation in the development of regulation (e.g. through regulatory impact assessments) and the creation of ombudsman offices have provided citizens with a right at least to be listened to, even if the nature of redress available varies significantly. They have also helped both to improve the quality of public policy and to strengthen governments' legitimacy.

In parallel with these moves towards openness, there have been a variety of restructuring efforts to make government more agile in responding to expressed needs of citizens and service users.

BOX 4.1 VARIOUS APPROACHES TO OPENNESS IN OECD COUNTRIES

While building open government is now an objective shared by all OECD countries, their reasons for wanting open government, and their policy choices for achieving it vary considerably. Some countries, such as Korea and Mexico, have focused on making government more open to public scrutiny in the interest of fighting corruption and improving accountability. Others, such as Denmark, have concentrated on making government more user-friendly in order to improve service delivery, while Canada and Finland have been more interested in increasing government interaction and partnership with external stakeholders, such as civil society organisations . . . to foster better quality, and more inclusive, policy-making.

Source: OECD (2005b: 2)

Many countries, including France, Italy, Japan, Korea, Spain, Turkey and the UK, have *decentralised* some responsibilities to lower levels of administration, partly based on the conviction that this would make service providers more responsive to users. More subtly, the increasing application of vouchers (e.g. for public housing or education), individual budgets (e.g. for people with learning disabilities in the UK) and user charges (e.g. for car users in congested cities) provides powerful mechanisms in some countries for revealing the preferences of the public for different services.

In some countries, giving government responsibilities to bodies at arm's length from government (e.g. the UK executive agencies, and development of 'ZBO' organisations in the Netherlands) has significantly altered the traditional picture of direct hierarchical control by a minister. These agencies can have varying degrees of management autonomy, combined with contract-like accountability for results – interestingly, making them more responsive to politically defined targets.

In sum, the diversity of organisational forms – although it has always existed – has increased in recent years and now provides a choice of structures that can, in principle, be tailored more appropriately to the particular political and customer needs of a service.

. . . and for performance

Over the past two decades, measures of performance have been increasingly introduced into management and budgeting arrangements within OECD countries. Performance is a 'feel good' word that it is very hard to be against, generating a welter of rhetoric but also leading to some very clear structural changes. OECD countries have introduced procedures for defining performance in quantitative terms (sometimes within 'standards'), measuring it, turning it into targets, and linking it to incentives or sanctions provided by a superior agency or person to a subordinate one, generally coupled with some increased degree of managerial autonomy for the subordinate. Figure 4.3 indicates how performance targets are used both at the individual level and at different organisational levels.

While the scope, types and uses of performance measurement vary enormously across OECD countries, most countries have sought to change their budgeting, management and accountability approaches in ways that shift emphasis from controlling the mix of inputs and processes *ex ante* towards *ex post* monitoring and evaluation of outputs and outcomes. Relaxation of input controls gives managers more flexibility to improve performance, while in return they are held accountable for results. This has led to the development of stronger processes of *external control* on outputs, emphasising that results are (at least) as important as the means that delivered them. In parallel, *internal management control* for probity and compliance has also been strengthened as many financial and non-financial resource allocation decisions are now made at the discretion of local managers.

With regard to budgeting, many countries include performance information in their budgets, but few use it in their budgetary decision-making process and even fewer use it for the allocation of resources (with Korea being the major example). Performance budgeting rhetoric often suggests that the allocation of resources should be directly linked to the degree to which output targets are met – establishing automatic mechanisms for rewarding successful agencies. Although performance measures increasingly inform political judgements,

47

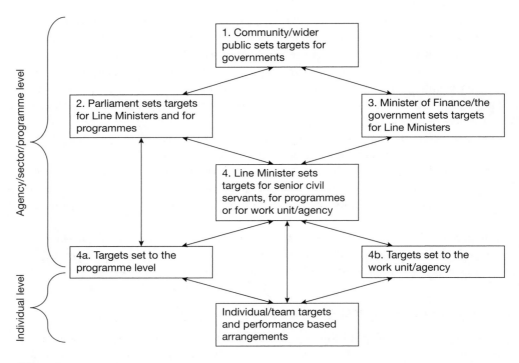

Figure 4.3 *Possible linkages between performance targets*

Source: Ketelaar *et al.* (2007)

the problems in attempting to use measures to allocate resources automatically are generally overwhelming. Obstacles include the obvious point that many government objectives are not measurable in terms of outputs (foreign policy, defence, etc.); moreover, there are problems if the results run against political priorities; and if performance measures directly affect real resources, managers have strong incentives for 'gaming' (OECD, 2007b).

Governments have to choose their performance measures and performance management approach carefully to achieve their desired performance result. Collecting performance data is expensive, and developing and implementing meaningful indicators takes time. More importantly, performance management systems are not an end in themselves – they can motivate public servants to be more attentive to public purposes and results – but this can nearly always be done better by using performance information for dialogue, rather than for control. Moves towards relating the employment contracts of individual staff to their performance have not, so far, been markedly successful (see Box 4.2).

PROGRESS – BUT WITH UNINTENDED CONSEQUENCES

It would be more than cynical not to recognise the productivity and quality improvements that the public sectors of OECD countries have seen over the last two decades. Arguably, these improvements are due in large measure to the quantum leap in human capacity within

BOX 4.2 INDIVIDUALISING EMPLOYMENT CONDITIONS OF PUBLIC SECTOR STAFF

Many OECD countries have placed new emphasis on individualised staff treatment, including recruitment, employment contracts, accountability and pay, in order to optimise each employee's performance.

The OECD countries that went furthest in individualising employment conditions broke completely away from the traditional public sector norm of guaranteed lifelong careers, introducing fixed-term employment under general labour law (e.g. Sweden). Other countries have maintained the lifelong employment guarantee but use time-limited appointment to more senior positions to increase individuals' responsibility for performance (e.g. Belgium). In such systems, public servants are guaranteed public service tenure, but can lose a senior position, depending on their performance. Moreover, most OECD countries have introduced individual performance appraisal systems which are usually linked to promotion and advancement. A majority of OECD countries have implemented performance-related pay policies, but there are wide variations to the application: in many cases, they are limited to managerial staff or specific departments.

the public sector: the coming of managerial age of the baby boomers, the continued recruitment of articulate and motivated graduates and the professionalisation of many previously somewhat bureaucratic backwaters. At the same time, major productivity gains in all services (not just public sector) have arisen from the extended use of ICT, both by staff and by service users. But there can also be no doubt that managerial reforms have played a significant role in these improvements.

However, reforms may have been more costly than anticipated – and they may also have had unintended consequences. This section explores selected examples of unintended consequences and the overall cost-benefit balance.

Reform overload

Could there be too many reforms? The results of a recent review of US government reforms concludes that

> the deluge of recent reform may have done little to actually improve performance. On the contrary, it may have created confusion within government about what Congress and the president really want, distraction from needed debates about organizational missions and resources, and the illusion that more reform will somehow lead to better government.
>
> (Light, 2006, p. 17)

This suggests the need to take into account such costs as the displacement/distraction of time and energy from core tasks, the loss of staff morale and motivation, negative productivity consequences for other related work areas and the costs of remedying problems in reform design. If each reform causes a productivity dip, and reforms follow in rapid succession, before recovery from the productivity dip caused by the previous reform, they could cause serious, detrimental productivity losses.

Moreover, it is possible that the risk of reform overload is increasing in a number of OECD countries because of shortening institutional memories. The spread of term contracts for senior officials and higher rates of staff turnover increase the likelihood that lessons from previous reforms are rapidly forgotten. One UK study of the Department of Trade and Industry (DTI) concluded that the 'constant re-organisation of departmental boundaries and structures . . . weakened the confidence of DTI staff and reduced policy quality' (Hood *et al.*, 2002, p. 11).

Governing in a fishbowl

While government's openness to public scrutiny seems a fundamental tenet of democratic governance, secrecy may be crucial for responsible decision-making (see Box 4.3). If policy deliberations are exposed to the public, this can undermine the quality of advice that public servants provide to policymakers. For example, applying FOI rules to senior public servants' emails can deter them from providing 'free, frank and fearless' advice to ministers via e-mail. They may react by replacing e-mail traffic with telephone conversations. In the extreme case, measures aimed at increasing public scrutiny may in fact lead to the opposite: they can provoke an incomplete audit trail so that key information is no longer preserved as a public record, amenable to parliamentary scrutiny.

BOX 4.3 THE NEED FOR SECRECY FOR POLITICAL DECISION-MAKING IN THE EUROPEAN COUNCIL OF MINISTERS

The example of the European Council of Ministers illustrates the potential harm of 'excessive transparency' in supreme decision-making bodies. Stasavage (2006) points out that closed doors in Brussels have allowed for some apparent hypocrisy, with significant contradictions between ministers' publicly stated and privately defended positions. While such divergences could impair trust in government if they become publicly known, the Council itself has been surprisingly frank about its vitality for reaching compromise:

> If agreement is to be reached, they [the members] will frequently be called upon to move from their positions, perhaps to the extent of abandoning their national instructions on a particular point or points. This process is vital to the adoption of community legislation.

Source: (Statement of Defence of the Council of the European Union in Case T 194/94, Brussels, 13 July 1994, quoted in Stasavage (2006)

That 'excessive transparency' in international negotiations can endanger compromise is no great surprise (Stasavage, 2006). Under uncertainty about the best reachable negotiation result, transparency can prompt representatives to 'posture' for recognition by their constituency by adopting overly hard negotiation positions – and thereby risk a breakdown in negotiations. Even worse, if the constituency favours a particular policy option, without understanding its likely outcomes, politicians will be tempted to adopt a 'pandering' strategy – playing to the public view for populist reasons, despite their better knowledge and against their private conviction about what could be the 'right' policy in the public interest.

Gaming

Holding organisations and individuals accountable for reaching performance targets can motivate them – but it can also encourage 'gaming' (see Box 4.4). If agents know the control mechanism used, they will be tempted and often able to find ways of short-circuiting it, in order to make their performance appear favourable, regardless of the impact on the public or policy outcomes.

Bevan and Hood (2005) have undertaken one of the few existing systematic studies on the extent of gaming problems, tracking gaming behaviour in the UK health sector, ranging from 'hitting the target but missing the point' all the way through to outright cheating. Gaming problems were endemic to the Soviet production target regime and it seems rather ironic that a phenomenon that is historically associated with discredited central planning also appears to afflict modern performance management systems.

While evidence of gaming may have made some sceptics call for totally abandoning target systems, Bevan and Hood (2005) point out that gaming can be significantly reduced by making it harder for agents to predict the control mechanism. This could be achieved by randomising performance measures, by reducing their specificity or by increasing uncertainty about when

---

BOX 4.4 CONCERNS ABOUT 'GAMING' IN THE UK

The UK House of Commons Public Administration Select Committee came close to recommending a significant policy reversal on performance measurement in 2003. The Committee considered,

> whether, in the light of the evidence of professional demoralisation, perverse consequences, unfair pressure and alleged cheating, the culture of measurement should be swept away. Should there be a cull of targets and tables to allow the front line to work unhindered by central direction?

In the end the Committee argues against this wiping the slate clean of these problematic measures – concluding that '[t]he increases in accountability and transparency brought about by the last twenty years of performance measurement have been valuable'.

Source: UK Public Administration Select Committee (2003: para 98, p. 29)

51

and how the measurement will take place. Better monitoring of gaming problems could also help to detect risk areas. Finally, if combined with reinforced face-to-face scrutiny, performance measures could become much less vulnerable.

Overall cost-benefit balance

There is insufficient evidence for an overall cost-benefit evaluation of public sector reform efforts (OECD, 2007b; Pollitt and Bouckaert, 2004). It is certainly paradoxical that the principle of rigorous cost-benefit analysis, while being at the core of the performance movement, has been applied to many public policies – but only rarely to public management reforms themselves. The actual cost-benefit balance of reform will vary from case to case and it seems unlikely that, on average, costs have outweighed benefits. However, the above examples of unintended consequences illustrate that reforms may have been more costly than anticipated – and do suggest the need for caution in future reforms.

CLOUDS ON THE PUBLIC MANAGEMENT HORIZON

The future of public management reforms must be seen within the context of the emerging policy challenges OECD countries face in the twenty-first century. Pressures for expenditure restraint are growing with the recognition that it would be undesirable to push borrowing and taxation further. At the same time, there are increasing demand-side pressures on the horizon. A particular concern is population ageing, which will boost expenditures for health, long-term care and pensions, and, in parallel, will reduce tax income and shrink the expertise available within government. Migration has emerged as another major challenge to policymakers and civil servants. On top of this, declining trust in OECD governments could reduce their capacity to take action.

Expenditure constraints

There has been growing recognition in many governments that borrowing and taxation should not be pushed further. Moreover, there is arguably less political confidence nowadays in the wisdom of spending, even if the money could be found. The track record of scaling up public expenditures has not been great. For example, in its 2004 review, the Netherlands Social and Cultural Planning Office cast doubts on the ability of the public sector to increase outputs at the same rate as inputs, at least in the short term – e.g. the benefits of introducing new technologies can be overwhelmed in the short-term by their disruptive impact on production processes. Moreover, when resources are scaled up rapidly, there is a risk that a significant part of these additional resources may be used to improve working conditions and incomes, or simply wasted, rather than being translated into increased outputs (Social and Cultural Planning Office, 2004, p. 25).

In parallel, OECD projections suggest that, without changes in work and retirement patterns, the ratio of older, economically inactive persons to active workers will increase from 1:3 in the OECD area in 2000 to just over 2:3 in 2050 (and to almost 1:1 in Europe).

The inevitable consequence is a decline in revenues and an increase in demand-side pressures. Age-related spending will increase substantially, starting from 21 per cent of GDP in 2000 to 27 per cent of GDP by 2050 (OECD: 2003).

Weakening capacity of government

Within this fiscal vice, senior public servants may find themselves with less capacity in their own departments and ministries than before. The retirement tsunami, the other side of the hiring frenzy of the 1960s and 1970s, is already impacting the public sector – e.g. the average age of the public service increases by one year every three years in Australia, every two and a half years in France and even every fifteen months in Ireland (OECD, 2006).

In addition, difficulties in attracting and retaining skilled staff groups, in particular senior managers, tax specialists, auditors and economists, ICT specialists and other technical staff, as well as new graduates, persist in many OECD countries. The attraction of the relative security is reduced by a negative image of the public sector, often associated, in the minds of many potential employees, with slow advancement largely unrelated to merit. In many parts of the world, e.g. in Central and Eastern European countries, low salary levels for civil servants mean that high-flyers prefer jobs in the private sector and international organisations. In practice, many civil servants need to take on additional work, which may even conflict with their public duties.

Declining trust in government?

The steady erosion of voter turnouts in elections and falling memberships in political parties suggest that something significant is taking place in the popular view of government. Two-thirds of the respondents to the 2004 Eurobarometer survey of public opinion in the twenty-five EU member states said that they tend not to trust national governments.

However, while there are few grounds for complacency, such assertions need to be regarded with care. First, they are by no means new: the persistent drumbeat of concern about a 'decline of trust' has been heard for over thirty years (Crozier *et al.*, 1975). Second, such assertions are not robustly supported by the limited evidence available. The authoritative World Values Survey data do not reveal a clear decline of trust over time. Third, it is far from clear what the relationship might be between management reform and public trust – some reforms, such as codes of conduct, may be taken by citizens as signals of potential wrongdoing, rather than of more careful scrutiny.

Moreover, it is important to ask to what degree citizens should trust government. History suggests that a certain distrust is surely healthy, and, in the 'age of spin', it is not surprising that citizens remain sceptical of how trustworthy their governments are (although this varies from country to country – traditionally, US citizens have been more distrustful of government than, say, German citizens).

Accordingly, rather than a fact, the 'decline in trust' might be a handy argument that has been used to legitimise public sector reform. The ambiguities in measuring trust seem to have facilitated 'hyping' of alleged declines in trust at key moments in the political cycle.

53

A MORE MODEST FUTURE FOR PUBLIC MANAGEMENT REFORM, MAYBE

The gathering fiscal and capacity clouds suggest that OECD governments will inevitably find themselves under increasing pressure of doing more with less. In view of these pressures and of a rapidly changing societal context, responsiveness and performance are doubtless here to stay as key concerns for the future public management reform agenda. The old ideal of bureaucracy as a 'self-contained world' clearly is an anachronism in times of a blurring distinction between public and private service provision, of careers increasingly moving between the two sectors and of networks replacing traditional hierarchies.

However, not all answers to the challenges on the horizon are to be found within public management reform. First, making painful choices about who gets what from the state (e.g. limiting access to certain treatments) will be an inevitable and at least equally important response to fiscal pressures. The cost-saving potential of making the machinery of government more efficient may have been overstated (although, of course, it is easier to announce public management reforms, with their promise of efficiency savings in the future, than service reductions in the present). Second, rather than attempting to improve public sector performance further, governments are likely increasingly to rely on more service provision by both the private and third sectors.

BOX 4.5 LIMITED EVIDENCE ON THE IMPACT OF INSTITUTIONAL AND MANAGEMENT REFORMS ON EFFICIENCY

Understanding of how institutional and managerial reforms impact technical efficiency in the public sector is limited. A review of empirical evidence uncovered few strong findings, and in each, there are many co-factors to be considered:

- Efficiency does seem to be often associated with the scale of operations, based on evidence collected mainly in the education and health sectors.
- Functional and political decentralisation to sub-national levels can also show efficiency gains.
- Human resource management practices also matter a great deal, with their soft aspects, such as employee satisfaction and morale, being the most important drivers of performance.

Current empirical findings are inconclusive on the impact of ownership, competition and 'agencification'. While private ownership is not a guarantee of efficiency, public ownership does not necessarily lead to inefficiencies either. It is more probable that it is not ownership, but competition that drives efficiency.

Source: Adapted from Van Dooren *et al.* (2007)

Public management reform will undoubtedly continue to play a very significant role in the hunt for efficiency improvements. However, some of the gloss of the first generation of reforms has rubbed off, and there is greater emphasis on the co-factors for successful reform: simple implementation of a standard package is increasingly seen as insufficient (see Box 4.5). There is also growing recognition of the unintended consequences of reform, possibly entailing much larger costs than expected.

Overall, in speculating about the future of public management reforms in the OECD, it seems likely that uncertainty about the actual cost-benefit balance of past reforms will tilt reformers towards more caution and modesty in their future efforts. Perhaps, reformers will pilot reforms more often before scaling them up and target them more carefully towards sectors where they promise to be most beneficial. Reform scepticism may also lead to more scrutiny of the return on resources invested in reforms. Ultimately, however, the public sector is about much more than delivering services efficiently – and its broader political significance in society will ensure that the drive to institute reforms will continue, even if perhaps more cautiously than in the recent past,

SUMMARY

The efficiency-oriented public sector reform movement, which began in the 1980s, has been overtaken by pressures on governmental responsiveness and performance across a wider front. The first generation of reforms improved many services and processes. However, some of the more ambitious reforms failed because of poor design, unintended consequences, new fiscal and societal problems emerging, and the re-emergence of public governance values that go wider and deeper than simply resource efficiency.

Public management reforms are likely to continue throughout the world but the experience of the last two decades suggests that radical reforms may have less chance of success than a more cautious, learning approach and that reforms need to be tailored carefully to the country and sector in which they occur, rather than being 'universal'.

QUESTIONS FOR REVIEW AND DISCUSSION

1   Explain why the public sector reform agenda in OECD countries has changed.
2   Compare the current reform agenda of your national government with the other approaches outlined in this chapter and try to identify which approaches it most resembles.

READER EXERCISES

1   Interview an official, an elected politician or a party official at national or local level in your country, asking them:
    - What do you perceive as the key challenges facing public agencies at present?
    - How do you think they should respond to these challenges?
    - What are the lessons you think can be learnt from past reforms?

55

2   Many of the 'first generation'-type public sector reforms focused particularly on achieving efficiency gains. Choose one public agency in which you are interested and try to find statistical evidence for the extent to which efficiency savings have occurred during the last five years.

3   Check out the public sector reform programme of some other OECD country on the OECD website (www.oecd.org/gov) and compare it with the reform agenda of your own country. Where do you see differences and commonalities?

CLASS EXERCISE

Mapping the reform paths of public sector reforms in your country

Work as a team with some other students on this task:

1   Research sources in the library, on the Internet (in particular OECD), on the public sector reforms in your country and try to identify the three major reform themes.
   ■   For each of these three themes, identify different phases of the reform process (with changing priorities); and
   ■   suggest what factors (economic, social, political) played a role in bringing about this pattern of phases.
2   Present this analysis to your fellow students in the other teams and discuss whether there are consistent patterns across the reforms in the identified reform paths.

FURTHER READING

Jonathan Boston (2000), 'The challenge of evaluating systemic change: the case of public management reform', *International Public Management Journal*, 3 (1): 23–46.

Tom Clark and Andrew Dilnot (2002), *Long-term trends in British taxation and spending*. London: Institute for Fiscal Studies.

Christopher Hood (2005), 'Public management: the word, the movement, the science', in Ewan Ferlie, Laurence Lynn Jr. and Christopher Pollitt (eds), *Oxford handbook of public management*. Oxford: Oxford University Press, pp. 7–26.

Gabriella Legrenzi and Costas Milas (2002), *Asymmetric and non-linear adjustment in the revenue-expenditure models*. Uxbridge: Brunel University.

OECD (2005), *Modernising government: the way forward*. Paris: OECD.

Christopher Pollitt and Geert Bouckaert (2003), 'Evaluating public management reforms: an international perspective', in Hellmut Wollman (ed.), *Evaluation in public sector reform*. Cheltenham: Edward Elgar, pp. 12–35.

Christopher Pollitt and Geert Bouckaert (2004), *Public management reform: a comparative analysis*. Oxford: Oxford University Press.

REFERENCES

Gwyn Bevan and Christopher Hood (2005), *What's measured is what matters: targets and gaming in the English public health care system*. London: ESRC.

Michel Crozier, Samuel P. Huntington and Joji Watanuki (1975), *The crisis of democracy*. New York: New York University Press.

Christopher Hood, Martin Lodge and Christopher Clifford (2002), *Civil service policy-making competencies in the German BMWi and the British DTI*. London: Industry Forum.

Anne Ketelaar, Nick Manning and Edouard Turkisch (2007), *Performance based arrangements for senior civil servants – OECD experiences*. OECD Governance Working Paper. Paris.

Paul C. Light (2006), 'The tides of reform revisited: patterns in making government work, 1945–2002', *Public Administration Review*, 66 (1): 6–19.

Nick Manning and Neil Parison (2003), *International public administration reform: implications for the Russian Federation* (series: Directions in development). Washington: World Bank.

Alex Matheson, Boris Weber, Nick Manning and Emmanuelle Arnould (2006), 'Managing the political/administrative boundary: study on the political involvement in senior staffing decisions and on the delineation of responsibilities between ministers and senior civil servants', unpublished. Paris: OECD.

OECD (2003), *Policies for an ageing society: recent measures and areas for further reform* (Working Paper No. 369). Paris: OECD.

OECD (2005a), *Modernising government: the way forward*. Paris: OECD.

OECD (2005b), *Policy brief – public sector modernisation: open government* (www.oecd.org/dataoecd/1/35/34455306.pdf). Paris: OECD.

OECD (2006), *The challenges of managing government employees in the context of an ageing population in OECD member countries*. Paris: OECD.

OECD (2007), *Measuring government activity*. Paris: OECD.

Christopher Pollitt and Geert Bouckaert (2004), *Public management reform: a comparative analysis*. Oxford: Oxford University Press.

Wallace Sayre (1958), 'Premises of public administration: past and emerging', *Public Administration Review*, 18 (2): 102–5.

Allen Schick (2005), 'The performing state: reflection on an idea whose time has come but whose implementation has not'. Paper prepared for the OECD Senior Budget Officials Meeting in Bangkok, Thailand (www.oecd.org/dataoecd/42/43/35651133.pdf). OECD. Paris

Social and Cultural Planning Office (2004), *Public sector performance: an international comparison of education, health care, law and order, and public administration* (www.scp.nl/english/publications/books/9037701841.shtml). Netherlands: The Hague.

David Stasavage (2006), 'Does transparency make a difference? The example of European Council of Ministers', in Christopher Hood and David Heald (eds), *Transparency: the key to better governance?* Oxford: Oxford University Press, pp. 165–79.

Miekatrien Sterck, Wouter Van Dooren and Geert Bouckaert (2006), *Performance measurement for sub-national service delivery*. Report for OECD. Leuven: Public Management Institute, Katholieke Universiteit.

57

UK Public Administration Select Committee (2003), *On target? Government by measurement*. Fifth Report of Session 2002–3, Vol. I (www.publications.parliament.uk/pa/cm200203/cmselect/cmpubadm/62/62.pdf, accessed 16 May 2008). London: House of Commons.

Wouter Van Dooren, Miekatrien Sterck, Zsuzsanna Lonti and Dirk-Jan Kraan (2007), 'The institutional drivers of efficiency in the public sector', unpublished OECD paper. Paris: OECD.

Max Weber (1956), *Wirtschaft und Gesellschaft* (4th edn). Tübingen: Johannes Winckelmann.

Part II

Public management

The second part of this book explores the main managerial functions that contribute to the running of public services and the management of public sector organizations.

The main management functions considered are strategic management (Chapter 5), marketing (Chapter 6), procurement (Chapter 7), financial management (Chapter 8), human resource management (Chapter 9), information and communications technology (ICT) management (Chapter 10), performance measurement and management (Chapter 11), quality management (Chapter 12), process management (Chapter 13) and inspection and audit (Chapter 14).

While each of these management functions is shown to have acquired greater importance and to have developed increased momentum during the era of New Public Management, each chapter also maps the more recent evolution of these functions within the rather different framework of public governance.

Chapter 5

Strategic management in public sector organizations

Tony Bovaird, Birmingham University, UK

INTRODUCTION

Now everyone wants to have a strategy. To be without a strategy is to appear directionless and incompetent – whether it be a strategy for the organization as a whole, for the corporate centre, for the service delivery units, for consultation with stakeholders, for staff remuneration, for introducing changes to front office opening hours, for office paper recycling . . . Sadly, by the time a word means everything, it has come to mean nothing. So can we rescue any meaning for this much over-used word 'strategy'?

Johnson *et al.* (2008) suggest that we can at least map out the characteristics that distinguish strategic decisions from non-strategic ones (Box 5.1). Thus strategic decisions help to determine what the organization does NOT do (its scope), how well it fits the requirements of its customers and adopts the technologies available to it in the marketplace, what it does particularly well, how well it appeals to its stakeholders, how it balances long- and short-term considerations and how it manages the potential knock-on effects of the narrow-minded and selfish decisions made in separate 'silos' of the organization. In this reading, a decision is strategic if it meets one of these criteria – if not, the decision can be characterized as *operational* or *tactical*, rather than *strategic*. However, 'strategic' should not be confused with 'important' – strategic and operational decisions are BOTH important and both can only be effective if aligned with each other.

LEARNING OBJECTIVES

This chapter is intended to help readers:

- to understand what 'strategy', and 'strategic management' mean in a public sector context;
- to be able to prepare a corporate strategy and/or business plan;
- to understand the difference between strategic management and strategic planning;
- to understand the political dimension to strategy making;
- to understand how strategic management and innovation mutually reinforce each other.

> ## BOX 5.1 STRATEGIC DECISIONS ARE CONCERNED WITH:
>
> ■ scope of an organization's activities;
> ■ searching for fit with the organization's environment through major resource changes or repositing its activities;
> ■ creating opportunities by building on an organization's resources and competences;
> ■ values and expectations of those who have power in and around organization;
> ■ the long-term direction for the organization;
> ■ achieving some advantage for the organization over rivals.
>
> *Source*: Adapted from Johnson *et al.* (2008)

THE BUILDING BLOCKS – 'STRATEGY', 'STRATEGIC PLANS', 'STRATEGIC MANAGEMENT' IN THE PUBLIC SECTOR

So what is 'strategy'? It is perhaps surprising, given how often the word is used, that it has no widely agreed definition. Perhaps we ought to start with an antidote to most definitions, after Karl Weick (1979): 'A "strategy" is an after-the-event rationalization by top management of what they (often wrongly) believe their organization has recently been doing'. While this warns us not to believe everything we are told about strategy, we probably need to develop a more positive definition.

Mintzberg is helpful here. He suggests five different meanings that are often given to the word 'strategy' in management contexts (Box 5.2). These will each be appropriate in different circumstances. Since these meanings are already in wide currency, it would be unwise to insist that only one of these meanings makes sense.

However, when many people think of a 'strategy', they immediately think of a strategic plan (often contained in a written document). The idea of strategic planning is, of course, quite old. Its sources, going back to the nineteenth century, included the town and country planning movement (including the 'worker colonies' of Owen, Cadbury, Salt, Guell, etc., the 'garden cities' of Howard, and the 'machine for city living' of Le Corbusier) and, later, industrial planning, starting in Soviet Russia in the late 1920s and spreading through the Comecon and many other countries since 1945. Ironically, these 'public sector' planning roots then gave rise, from the 1950s onwards, to private sector derivatives in Western countries, particularly budgetary planning and 'manpower' planning, which in turn spread to many public sector organizations. Eventually, the idea of overall corporate plans for an organization, and separate business plans (or 'service plans') for units within the organization, became very strong in both private and public sectors.

However, it is clear that 'strategic management' is more than making and implementing strategic plans. It encompasses, at the very least, the other activities in Box 5.2 – the 'ploy-making' of competitive organizations, the 'pattern-making' of organizations that wish to give a sense of purpose and coherence to their different units and activities, the 'positioning' of the organization to achieve 'fit' between its activities and its environment, and the 'paradigm-changing' activities that try positively to influence the culture of the organization. To this list

BOX 5.2 WHAT IS A 'STRATEGY'?

- **Plan**: some sort of consciously intended course of action, a guideline to deal with a situation.
- **Ploy**: a specific manoeuvre intended to outwit an opponent or competitor.
- **Pattern**: a pattern in a stream of actions.
- **Position**: a means of locating an organization in an 'environment' – the mediating force or 'match' between organization and environment.
- **Perspective/paradigm**: an ingrained way of perceiving the world.

Source: Henry Mintzberg (1987)

of alternative ways of perceiving strategy we might add strategy as 'pull' (or 'stretch') – the focus on improvement of the organization's core competences so that it can do better what it already does well.

Each of these perspectives on strategy is also studied in other fields, as well as strategic management. 'Ploy-making' clearly relates closely to games theory, studied in detail within mathematical economics. 'Paradigm-changing' has been a major theme in organization studies. The definition of strategy as 'positioning' clearly indicates the close relationship between strategic management and marketing strategy (see Chapter 6).

PREPARING A CORPORATE STRATEGY AND BUSINESS PLANS

In this section, we will look at the conventional approach to strategic planning. We can see the corporate strategic plan of an organization as encompassing several constituent parts, which need to be aligned with each other:

- the marketing strategy (to respond to what the environment wants);
- the service production and delivery strategy (to make best use of internal capabilities);
- the financial strategy (to ensure that the necessary finance is available for all resources, including the right level of staffing, necessary for the service production and delivery strategy, and that these financial resources are allocated in the most efficient and effective way possible).

Moreover, each constituent unit of the organization can prepare a 'business plan' (more often called a 'service plan' in the public sector) along similar lines for their part of the organization. In this way, business plans are nested within the overall corporate strategy and should be aligned with it.

This immediately suggests that the contents of the corporate plan may, in large measure, replicate the contents of the organization's portfolio of business plans. However, this would lead to a very cumbersome corporate plan, with little value added. Consequently, the corporate plan often focuses on laying down broad guidelines to which the service or departmental or divisional business plans should conform, at a greater level of detail.

In this section, we look in particular at the preparation and implementation of corporate strategies and business plans, and their relationship to service production and delivery strategies. We leave the detailed consideration of marketing strategies to Chapter 6 and financial strategies to Chapter 7.

In order to prepare this suite of plans, three sets of analyses are necessary:

- analysis of the external environment of the organization;
- analysis of the internal environment of the organization;
- analysis of the strategic options available and their relative merits.

In Chapter 6, we discuss how the external environment can be analysed to help to develop a marketing strategy. In this chapter, we will look in turn at analysis of the internal environment and of the strategic options, before discussing how each of these three analyses can be used in formulating the corporate plan and business plans.

Analysing the internal environment

Here we seek to understand the factors influencing internal stakeholders and the consequent strengths and weaknesses of the organization, compared with other organizations working to serve the same needs and markets.

There are four main elements to this analysis:

- value chain analysis;
- core competence analysis;
- organizational culture analysis;
- competitor and collaborator analysis.

Value chain analysis explores the ways in which the organization creates value for its stakeholders and distributes this value between them. This requires a definition of 'value'. Mark Moore (1995, p. 47) suggests that 'public value' registers

> partly in terms of the satisfaction of individuals who [enjoy desirable outcomes] . . . and partly in terms of the satisfactions of citizens who have seen a collective need, fashioned a public response to that need, and thereby participated in the construction of a community . . .

While helpful, this remains rather vague. We suggest that, typically, 'value-added' in the public sector has several dimensions:

- *user value*;
- *value to wider groups* (such as family or friends of service users);
- *political value* (support to democratic process, e.g. through co-planning of services with users and other stakeholders);

- *social value* (creation of social cohesion or support for social interaction);
- *environmental value* (ensuring environmental sustainability of all policies).

In the private sector, 'value' traditionally referred to the first two items above – the set of benefits to the firm's end users and the returns to its shareholders. However, nowadays there are also pressures for 'corporate social responsibility', which bring the other dimensions of value into play even in the private sector.

Taking this multi-level concept of value, we need to understand how a public sector organization can create value. The model typically used to do this is the value chain, which explores how different core and support activities result in value-added for different stakeholders and how these activities can be reconfigured to improve the strategic capabilities of the organization and thereby increase the value-added; for more detail on this technique, see Chapter 13.

Core competence analysis also explores the strategic capabilities of the organization, as does the value chain, but it focuses on the underlying competences that make the organization particularly useful to its customers. A core competence resides in the organization, not in individuals nor in the technology alone (Box 5.3). There are many different ways in which core competences can be developed – in Box 5.4, some examples of common core competences are illustrated.

BOX 5.3 A CORE COMPETENCE IS . . .

. . . a bundle of skills and technologies that enables an organization to provide a particular benefit to customers.

Source: Hamel and Prahalad (1994, p. 199)

BOX 5.4 SOME EXAMPLES OF CORE COMPETENCES

- *Speed*. The ability to respond quickly to customers and to incorporate new ideas and technologies quickly into services.
- *Consistency*. The ability to produce a service that unfailingly satisfies customers' expectations.
- *Foresight*. The ability to see the environment clearly and thus to anticipate and respond to customers' evolving needs and wants.
- *Agility*. The ability to adapt simultaneously to many different environments.
- *Innovativeness*. The ability to generate new ideas and to combine existing elements to create new sources of value.

Source: Adapted from Hamel and Prahalad (1994)

As in the value chain, a key lesson from the analysis is meant to be that an organization should focus only on those activities for which it has a core competence. Other activities should either be abandoned, or (if they are necessary to deliver value to customers) outsourced. As a corollary, activities where the organization does have core competences should be grown and 'sold on' to other agencies. In this way, core competences become the fundamental building blocks of the organization.

Hamel and Prahalad, writing about private firms, suggest that they should seek to have many core competences. However, organizations in the public sector may not find it possible to have even one core competence, never mind several – because of legislation, they cannot always focus ruthlessly on those activities where they can achieve unique benefits for users and abandon those other activities for which they have no core competences. Consequently, they may have to remain relatively unfocused in their work – with the obvious danger that other, more focused, organizations in the private and third sectors may be able to develop offers to users that are more attractive.

The argument that an organization should focus on those capabilities that give it unique opportunities to add value has become known as the 'resource view of strategy' (Bryson *et al.*, 2007). One key capability in an effective organization is its ability to integrate all the activities in the value chain – this can be a core competence in itself. Consequently, outsourcing of activities to other agencies with superior capabilities in respect of some activities is not unambiguously the right answer, if the organization is poor at integrating externally sourced activities. This argument has often been seized upon, perhaps sometimes too readily, to argue that 'the in-house team may not do some things well, but we are used to working with them'. Clearly, this could lead to complacency in the face of unfortunate levels of inefficiency.

Organizational culture analysis explores the underlying taken-for-granted assumptions and norms in the organization. There are two well-established ways of exploring organizational cultures – one is the 'four cultures' approach of Charles Handy (Box 5.5) and the other is the 'cultural web' of Johnson *et al.* (2008).

The 'four cultures' approach is a valuable way of distinguishing between very different types of organizational culture. However, as Handy himself recognizes, most organizations are likely to have all four cultures simultaneously – e.g. the role culture is likely to predominate in 'steady state' parts of the organization (such as payroll), the task culture is likely to predominate in the innovative parts of the organization (such as new service development), while the power culture is likely to be dominant in those parts of the organization that deal with frequent crisis, where a strong and consistent 'hand on the tiller' is needed (e.g. in public relations or at the very top of the organization).

A more action-oriented approach to the understanding and change of organizational culture is given by the 'cultural web', which suggests the mapping of six different aspects:

1   The *stories* within the organization, e.g. who are the heroes/villains?
2   The *routines and rituals*, e.g. how are regular budget crises handled?
3   The *symbols* of the organization, e.g. who has their own car park space?
4   The *power base* in the organization, e.g. who really makes the decisions?
5   The *structure* of the organization, e.g. hierarchical? How many layers?
6   The *control* system, e.g. how does the organization stop things happening?

BOX 5.5 THE 'FOUR CULTURES'

The *power culture*: all power rests with one individual at the centre of the organization (the spider at the centre of the web, pulling all the skeins) – typical of those organizations dominated by a founder, a major professional figure or a 'conrol freak'.

The *role culture*: all individuals play a clear, standardized role within their own 'silo' of the organization, reporting to a line manager and managing the staff below them in the hierarchy, but they do not exercise initiative and do not communicate with anyone outside of the line management structure – this is typical of large bureaucracies (in both public and private sectors).

The *task culture*: individuals undertake tasks in multidisciplinary, multidepartment groups, in addition to working within a line management structure – this tends to be the culture aspired to by professional staff in public service organizations.

The *person culture*: individuals tend to work alone, with only passing reference to line managers and only working in teams where it suits them – this tends to be typical of academics, small consultancies, research and development staff ('nerds') in technically orientated organizations.

Source: Adapted from Handy (1993)

In summary – the cultural web seeks to establish what the *paradigm* of the organization is – the 'set of assumptions held relatively in common and taken for granted' in the organization (Johnson *et al.*, 2008). An example for a UK government department is given in Box 5.6.

Mapping of the cultural web is, of course, only the beginning. It is necessary for the leaders of an organization to take active steps to change those aspects of the culture that are not appropriate. Typically, they start with the more visible parts of the culture – the structures and control system. However, this is not enough – for culture change to take root, it is necessary to ensure that the stories, rituals and routines and the symbols are altered as well. This is clearly a much harder (and longer) task – it entails winning the 'hearts and minds' in the organization.

Before engaging in such a difficult process, leaders need to be confident that they know what a better culture would look like. Kotter and Heskett (1992) have produced strong evidence (although admittedly mainly from the private sector) that high performing organizations tend to have highly adaptable cultures, which not only respond positively to change but actually celebrate change and seek out innovation. Most studies of the public sector indicate that such attitudes are rare in people and even rarer in organizations as a whole. This possibly remains the single greatest challenge to strategic management in the public sector.

Competitor and collaborator analysis allows us to build on these analyses of the internal environment. Essentially, we need to ask 'How do we compare in terms of value chain and core competences with those rivals we wish to outdo and those collaborators with whom we wish to work'. This allows us to do a 'strengths and weaknesses' analysis of our organization vis-à-vis other organizations in our sector. Once again, as with all elements of an analysis of

BOX 5.6 CULTURAL WEB FOR DEPARTMENT FOR INTERNATIONAL DEVELOPMENT (DFID), UK

Component of organizational culture	Cultural web in 1999	Cultural web after three years of Civil Service Reform Programme (2002)
'Core culture' or 'paradigm'	■ Outward rather than inward looking ■ 'Management will look after itself' ■ '[Many] staff for whom no change would be acceptable, whatever the rationale – all changes resented and resisted'	■ Still outward-looking but conscious now of need to manage itself well ■ Better communications ■ More team-working
Stories	■ When seeking a quality award, cynical reaction by some – just 'trophy hunting'. When it had to be postponed – 'we can't even bag an easy trophy'. When it was finally achieved – 'will just fall back into old ways now they've bagged it' ■ Ability to write good policy papers more important than social and personal skills. 'I don't like to single people out for praise – I don't want others to think I've got favourites'	■ The new Permanent Secretary is 'street-wise' – used to work in DfID. He is more approachable – and he has made it clear that he is annoyed by the way some advisors behave towards one another ■ One management board member appointed from outside because she clearly had better people management skills than inside candidates
Symbols	■ Different treatment of staff in London, Scotland and overseas ■ DfID in Whitehall was 'group of old white men'	■ Improved treatment of in-country appointed staff ■ New, young, non-white Permanent Secretary, who sets example on work/life balance through regular 'long weekends' ■ Open plan offices ■ 'Not as "gradist" as before'
Rituals and routines	■ Disputatious – the debate is valued more than the outcome	■ Staff appraisal is now done very differently, to encourage more development orientation
Power	■ The Department used to feel it was a minor player in the FCO	■ Staff now believe that DfID has significant power on world stage
Structure	■ Very hierarchical, but also very strongly departmentalist	■ Now much more emphasis on teamworking
Control	■ Largely through hierarchical orders to staff, with some monitoring	■ Much more cascading down through the organization of the PSA targets

Source: Adapted from Bovaird (2007b)

the internal environment, this leads to a questioning of how to balance in-house provision with external provision. Where our competitors are better than us, we have the choice of improving, outsourcing or of working with the competitors in 'strategic service delivery partnerships' (which can allow us to use their strengths to make our service offering better). This latter option is often unwelcome in the public sector, especially amongst staff and politicians. However, if the alternative is to continue to do a worse job, then strategic partnering may become seen as desirable. Once again, the most difficult part of the analysis is to ask 'How well will the two organizations gel together in practice – will they achieve synergies working with each other – or will they cause difficulties for each other, so that the partnership is less than the sum of the parts?' As always, this is hard to analyse *a priori* – sometimes the only way to answer this question is to try it out.

Developing and evaluating strategic options

Taken together, the analyses of external and internal factors allow a SWOT (strengths, weaknesses, opportunities and threats) analysis to be compiled for the organization. (It may seem a little cruel that we have taken so long to reach a point that many people feel they can sketch out in five minutes on the back of an envelope, but academic analysis can always make the simple appear much more complex – sometimes fruitfully so!)

The SWOT analysis needs to be turned into a series of strategic options for doing things better in the future – building on strengths, reducing weaknesses, seizing opportunities, countering threats.

The notion of a 'strategic option' is not very clear from the literature – it is often seen as any change that might be made in the existing elements of a strategy. However, a more rigorous approach suggests that a strategic option should be a coherent alternative strategy in itself (Box 5.7).

For an organization to be successful, it must be imaginative at devising a full range of strategic options, so that they can be evaluated and the most appropriate strategic option can be chosen. Of course, this requires imaginative and creative people, who are able to play a

---

BOX 5.7 A STRATEGIC OPTION

This is a connected series of decisions on:

- strategic basis of the organization – ownership, mission, values, scope;
- 'generic strategy' – cost leadership or quality leadership;
- relation of corporate centre to service units;
- 'strategic direction' – consolidation, new services, new markets, or both;
- growth strategy – e.g. 'grow own timber', acquire, buy new, form alliances or partnerships
- competitive tactics;
- desired organizational culture.

role in mapping out these alternative 'futures' for the organization – and such people are not always easy to find, nor do organizations (especially bureaucracies) always allow 'creatives' to play such important roles.

Once a full range of strategic options has been mapped out, they need to be evaluated (unless top management has already decided that it prefers one of them, in which case the evaluation will be more of a 'show trial' for the undesired options). The evaluation process can use three sets of criteria – feasibility, suitability and acceptability – to test out the strategic options before selecting one of them (Johnson *et al.*, 2008).

The *suitability* of the options is typically screened by use of a number of analyses that test if the proposed portfolio of services (for specific target groups) will provide a coherent set of activities, which will provide a good fit between what the external environment requires and the strengths and weaknesses identified in the organization. One such approach is the 'Boston Matrix', which comes from the perspective of the provider side in a public sector organization (Figure 5.1). Here services are ranked by their growth in demand (or need) and by their 'net social value' (which might, for example, be their contribution to meeting the needs of high-priority users, or meeting high-level organizational objectives). Clearly, the services in the 'dead ducks' box are likely candidates for closure, so that more resources are available to grow the 'star' services, repackage and relaunch the 'bread and butter' services, and pilot the 'question mark' services appropriately (so that they either become star services or can be dropped altogether as failed experiments).

The second suitability test is the 'Needs and Provision Matrix', from the perspective of public sector commissioning organizations (i.e. those organizations that decide on what needs to be provided, and for whom, as opposed to organizations that actually do the provision) (Figure 5.2). This suggests that an organization should only make extensive in-house provision where need is high and is not being met by other agencies. This essentially starts from the viewpoint that a commissioning organization must make the most of its scarce resources to encourage the widest possible provision from all agencies in the field, only using its resources for direct provision when all other avenues have been explored.

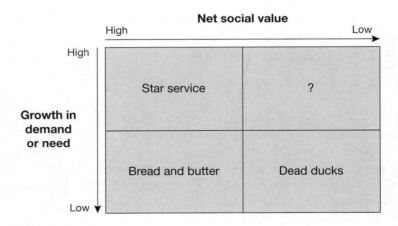

Figure 5.1 Public sector Boston matrix

Need

		High	Low
Provision by other agencies	High	Arrange for targeted provision	No intervention
	Low	Arrange for extensive provision	Encourage provision by others

Figure 5.2 *Need and provision matrix*

Source: Adapted from Walsh (1993)

The *acceptability* of the options needs to be tested against stakeholder objectives, which therefore have to be understood by the organization. In the private sector this would include rate of return on investment, shareholder value added, etc. In the public sector, these objectives are likely to be much more complex – and there are usually many more stakeholders as well. In order to understand the objectives, it is necessary to show the cause-and-effect chain linking high level 'outcome objectives' to the lower level 'service objectives', whose achievement it is believed will contribute to the outcome objectives – i.e. a 'hierarchy of objectives'.

Figure 5.3 illustrates how this might be done in the case of community safety initiatives. The overall map of objectives might belong to the police force, but a more restricted set of

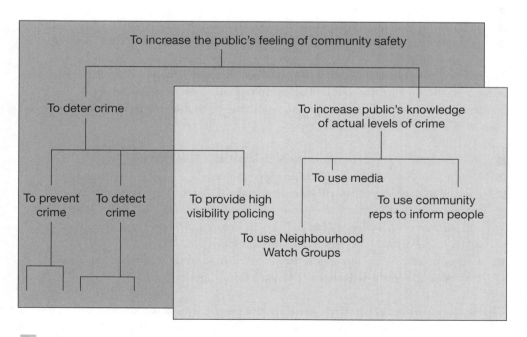

Figure 5.3 *Maps from two stakeholders*

ler box) might apply to a community safety unit in a local
disputed links in the logic of these 'cause-and-effect' chains
es, then there is a need for a more evidence-based approach
Chapter 11).

ncludes financial, technological, staffing and managerial
rwise highly desirable option appears to be infeasible, this
a fight. Most feasibility constraints can be removed or
of energy – or money. Only when the constraint itself has
binding can a feasibility test be accepted as final.

n of the strategic options can be reported in a *Balanced Scorecard*
...., ..96), in order that their relative merits can be assessed. This sets
performance indicators for each of the main organizational objectives, usually grouped under
such headings as 'citizen and user results', 'process improvement results', 'organizational
learning and development results' and 'financial results'. While this technique was originated
for reporting in the private sector, it has now also become popular in public sector organizations
in the UK and USA. (Issues in the use of performance indicators in the public sector are dealt
with more fully in Chapter 11.)

Selecting a strategic option

The analysis and evaluation of strategic options should help a public sector organization to
select its preferred strategic option. This option should spell out three major components:

- a marketing strategy (and associated marketing plans);
- a service production strategy (and associated service delivery plans);
- a resource mobilization and utilization strategy (and associated resource plans).

The components of the marketing strategy are considered in Chapter 6, and the components
of the resource mobilization and utilization strategy are considered in Chapter 8.

The key elements of the service production strategy that emerges from the corporate and
business planning exercises will be:

- a decision on which core competences to maintain and to develop;
- a portfolio of services that will be provided in-house;
- a portfolio of services that will be outsourced;
- a procurement process and protocols, which will ensure that the choice of suppliers
  and partners is transparently fair and that all external providers sign up to the
  achievement of the objectives of the organization;
- a set of objectives and targets that can be monitored to show whether the services
  have been efficiently delivered to the quality level specified.

Clearly, the separation of corporate strategies into the elements of marketing strategy, service
production strategy and resources strategy is artificial and these strategies will often overlap
considerably. Similarly, marketing plans and service delivery plans will often overlap (e.g.

making sure that proper transport arrangements are in place is part of the 'place' factor in the marketing plan, but also part of the 'logistics' factor in the service delivery plan).

JOINING UP STRATEGIES AND 'SEAMLESS SERVICES'

So far we have essentially been discussing the strategy of one public sector organization. In practice, no public sector organization can expect to be successful without close interaction with many other agencies. Most public sector organizations need to work in partnership with others (see Chapter 16).

The complexity of the interactions in the public service supply chain are illustrated in Figure 5.4. This demonstrates how, in the case of one client group, the elderly, there are typically many public agencies that contribute services. Sometimes (but not always), one agency takes the lead in coordinating overall service provision to each client. Further back in the supply chain, of course, all of these organizations have their own suppliers (of equipment, of transport, sometimes of agency staff, etc.).

Figure 5.4 also highlights a facet of supply chains that is usually much more important in the public sector than in the private sector – the service user is often not the sole beneficiary of the service (and in some cases, may not even consider her/himself to be a beneficiary at all). In addition to benefits to the service users, there are also benefits to families, carers, etc., who will often be relieved of some responsibilities because of the services given. Furthermore, there are often benefits to other customers – for example, the experience of 'expert patients' or of enthusiastic day centre users can be used to encourage reluctant clients

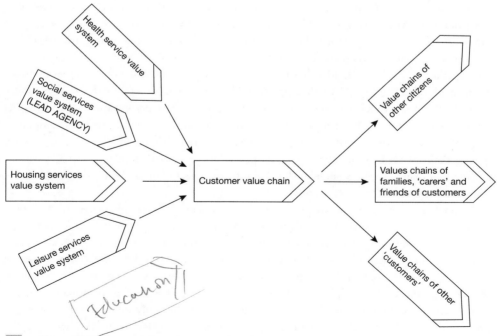

Figure 5.4 The public service supply chain

(for more on this kind of 'user co-production', see Chapter 15). Finally, there may be significant benefits to other citizens, either because they altruistically wish to see people in need being well looked after or because they may feel reassured that they themselves, in turn, will be well looked after in future when they too need such services.

Of course, a supply chain is only as strong as its weakest link. The public sector must ensure that the links between all these value chains are managed, although it may be able to convince others (e.g. voluntary groups) to take on responsibility for managing some of these links.

STRATEGIC MANAGEMENT, STRATEGIC PLANNING AND STRATEGIC THINKING

We have concentrated so far on strategy as 'plan'. This clearly can be a very productive approach. However, it suggests that strategy making is a linear process, based on rational planning – a 'determination of the long-term goals of an enterprise and the adoption of courses of action and the allocation of resources necessary for carrying out these goals' (Chandler, 1962).

In the 1980s, a very different view of strategic management began to emerge, particularly in the work of Henry Mintzberg. Mintzberg suggested (1992) that very few planned, intended strategies actually get implemented – most end up in the rubbish bin. Moreover, many strategies that do get realized were never planned – they might, for example, have been imposed by a dominant political leader or chief executive, or have resulted from an unexpected opportunity that arose. Mintzberg suggested one other type of strategy that has had enormous subsequent influence on the field – 'emergent strategies'. Emergent strategies are those that are grounded in the practice of staff, rather than planned by top managers. They are adopted implicitly, often unseen, because they work better than the official 'planned strategies'.

Of course, not all the emergent strategies that creep out of the woodwork are desirable – it depends on which stakeholder they help. So, for example, public sector staff are sometimes accused of taking a 'job's worth' approach. This is often an emergent strategy, flatly contradicting the explicit customer-oriented strategies of their organization – but it works for such staff (while they get away with it). More sinisterly, corrupt practices sometimes originate as an emergent strategy – e.g. when officials give a licence to a local business more quickly than normal by short-circuiting their procedures and are then offered a small payment as a mark of thanks – this can quickly develop into an expectation (on both sides) that a faster route exists, if a 'back-hander' is given.

Nevertheless, emergent strategies have the potentially desirable characteristic that they are likely to correspond to the needs of the environment in which they emerge. After all, they are generally developed by front-line staff and supervisors who are especially close to service users – Michael Lipsky's 'street-level bureaucrats' (Lipsky, 1980). Experience in many public service redesign initiatives (e.g. the 'business process re-engineering' vogue of the 1990s in the USA and the recent Best Value reviews in UK local government) suggests that it can be extremely difficult to get staff to take part formally in service improvement programmes – thus, emergent strategies that naturally develop from this level of the organization may be all the more valuable.

What are the organizational implications of emergent strategies? Mintzberg suggests that they move the creation of strategy from 'planners' to managers:

> Strategies are not things that are written down periodically, although people do try to write them down. Strategies are things that exist in people's heads; strategic visions cannot easily be written down. So I think managers create the strategy; planners might formalize it.
>
> (Mintzberg, 1992)

Of course, this formalization role of planning is important – it allows an organization to test emergent strategies, once they become noticed. Those that are not in the best interests of the organization can then be stamped out, while those that are valuable can be incorporated into the planned intended strategy and rolled out through the organization.

However, Mintzberg's critique throws serious doubt on the 'plan fetishism' that has long been a characteristic of the public sector and that has perhaps been brought to its apogee by the current UK government, in which not only must every government agency have a strategic plan, but so also must each of its organizational units – and all of these must be 'performance managed' and externally inspected.

STRATEGIC MANAGEMENT IN A POLITICAL ENVIRONMENT

Many of the analytical frameworks used earlier in this chapter are also used in the private sector (although some, like the concept of planning, actually originated in the public sector). It is important that we do not fall into the trap of believing that there is no difference between strategic management in public, private and voluntary sectors. The key differences that spring from the political context in which public sector organizations work include:

- the role of politicians, who often openly clash on major strategic issues;
- the interaction between politicians and other stakeholders, e.g. the media;
- the pressure for 'short-termist' decision-making arising from regular elections.

Strategic management involves difficult decision-making. It normally means *selectivity – not* doing some things – and *focus* – prioritizing the activities and target groups that matter most. This usually annoys some stakeholders. Only if the organization is prepared to weather the adverse comment that selectivity and focus normally bring can it hope to manage strategically. In the private and voluntary sector, selective and focused decisions are often internally controversial but, when the strategy has been selected, all groups can be expected to abide by it and support it in public.

However, the public sector can rarely hope to enjoy the luxury of such public consensus. Opposition politicians often see it as their role to contest publicly, and vocally, almost all strategic decisions made by the ruling group, moreover mobilizing opposition from any groups disadvantaged by the decision.

For strategic direction to be maintained, the ruling group needs to be steadfast in defending its main strategic decisions. However, there are many pressure points by means of which

75

politicians can be driven to make inconsistent decisions or to reverse strategic decisions already taken. These pressures can come from:

- political parties;
- policy networks;
- the civil service or managerial systems;
- professional groups;
- charities or voluntary organizations (at national or local level);
- community groups;
- the media;
- sponsors who provide funding for a party or an individual.

The platforms of political parties are usually designed to take on board the interests of a wide coalition of stakeholders. At worst, this can mean that politicians seek to 'please everyone, all the time'. In these circumstances, strategic management becomes next to impossible. However, even where politicians start out by plotting a clear and principled course, relatively minor changes in the balance of their coalition of stakeholders can demand that they revise their strategies.

The need to maintain political coalitions also explains why highly rational strategies, cooked up by well-informed professionals and backed by top politicians, may still fail because they 'don't go down well on the street'. Since politicians are regularly subjected to this street test, in the form of elections, their strategies are likely to be over-influenced by the short-term and narrow factors that sway voters at a given time (Joyce, 1999).

STRATEGIC MANAGEMENT AND INNOVATION

Finally, it is important to consider the interaction of strategic management and innovation. We stressed above that a healthy organizational culture is, above all, one that is adaptable and that seeks out innovation and change. On the other hand, innovation can be disruptive and even destabilizing to an organization. How can strategic management embed innovative attitudes, balance their potentially damaging effects, and overcome bureaucratic inertia?

Public sector organizations can innovate in many ways, including:

- new services;
- new customers ('target groups');
- new service production processes;
- new procurement processes;
- new partnership arrangements with the rest of the public sector, with the voluntary sector and with the private sector;
- new decision making processes ('addressing the democratic deficit');
- new governance structures and processes;
- new goals and ambitions for the organization;
- new organizational culture.

Given the importance of many of these, 'no change' is normally not an option. However, here, as always, being strategic means being selective and focused. Not all of these innovative directions can be pursued effectively at once – this way madness lies. The UK public sector has often been accused of '*initiativitis*' in recent years because it has not accepted this lesson. So perhaps public sector strategy makers will have to accept that, just as 'no change' is not an option, 'all change' is also not an option.

SUMMARY

This chapter has argued that strategic planning and strategic management are distinctively different. While both are important, strategic management is essential, whereas strategic planning may play a more limited role.

The chapter has considered a range of techniques for understanding the external and internal environment of organizations and for identifying and evaluating strategic options.

It has also emphasized that public sector organizations need to work together with other organizations, in all sectors, if their strategy is to be effective.

They also need to co-plan and co-produce most services with the service users and other citizens, to make the most of the resources in the community.

Political processes are intrinsic to good strategic management in the public sector, but some aspects of political decision making can make it difficult to develop and maintain appropriate strategies in the public sector.

Finally, the chapter has argued that innovation is the lifeblood of good strategic management – and that strategic management must therefore ensure that innovation is embedded with public sector organizations. 'No change' is not an option (but neither is 'all change'!)

QUESTIONS FOR REVIEW AND DISCUSSION

1   How do you think strategic plans in the public sector would differ if they were initially drawn up by politicians and then considered for approval by professionals and managers in the public sector?
2   In what circumstances do you think that realized strategies would be more likely to stem from planned intended strategies than from emergent processes? Why?

READER EXERCISES

1   Find a strategic plan for a public sector organization with which you are familiar. How well has it analysed its external and internal environments? Does it give an indication of the strategic options it considered before it chose its preferred strategy? Does it make clear the evaluation criteria on the basis of which its preferred strategy was chosen?
2   Look through a recent copy of a serious national newspaper. Identify all the references to the 'strategies' of public sector organizations. How many of them meet

the criteria outlined in Box 5.1? Do you think that any of the 'strategies' that do *not* meet the criteria in Box 5.1 are nevertheless genuinely dealing with 'strategic' decisions? If so, how would you amend or add to the criteria in Box 5.1 to allow for this?

CLASS EXERCISES

1 Form into four groups. Each group should prepare a ten minute presentation to argue for ONE of the following propositions:
   - All public sector organizations should prepare and publish detailed strategic plans for all of their activities.
   - Public sector organizations should prepare and publish strategic plans only for their most important activities.
   - Public sector organizations should prepare and publish strategic plans only for those activities that are highly controversial.
   - Public sector organizations should not bother to prepare and publish detailed strategic plans at all, but should rather consult widely on their proposals for specific changes to their activities.

2 In groups, identify some organizations you know, in public, voluntary and private sectors, which have the core competences listed in Box 5.4. Compare your results, identifying any sector differences which appear to emerge.

FURTHER READING

John Bryson (2006), *Strategic planning for public and nonprofit organizations: a guide to strengthening and sustaining organizational achievement* (3rd edn). San Francisco, CA: Jossey Bass.

Gerry Johnson, Kevan Scholes and Richard Whittington (2008), *Exploring corporate strategy: text and cases* (8th edn). Harlow: FT Prentice Hall.

Paul Joyce (1999), *Strategic management for the public services*. Buckingham: Open University Press.

Mark Moore (1995), *Creating public value: strategic management in government*. Cambridge, MA: Harvard University Press.

REFERENCES

Tony Bovaird (2007b), 'Triggering change through culture clash: the UK Civil Service Reform Programme, 1999–2005', in Kuno Schedler and Isabella Proeller (eds), *Organisational culture and the outcomes of public management reform*. London: Taylor & Francis, pp. 221–50.

John Bryson, Fran Ackermann and Colin Eden (2007), 'Putting the resource-based view of strategy and distinctive competencies to work in public organizations', *Public Administration Review*, 67 (4): 702–17.

Alfred Chandler (1962), *Strategy and structure*. Cambridge, MA: MIT Press.

Gary Hamel and C.K. Prahalad (1994), *Competing for the future*. Boston, MA: Harvard Business School Press.

Charles Handy (1993), *Understanding organisations* (4th edn). Harmondsworth: Penguin.

Gerry Johnson, Kevan Scholes and Richard Whittington (2008), *Exploring corporate strategy: text and cases* (8th edn). Harlow: FT Prentice Hall.

Paul Joyce (1999), *Strategic management for the public services*. Buckingham: Open University Press.

Robert S. Kaplan and David P. Norton (1996), *The balanced scorecard: translating strategy into action*. Boston, MA: Harvard Business School Press.

John P. Kotter and James L. Heskett (1992), *Corporate culture and performance*. New York: Free Press.

Michael Lipsky (1980), *Street-level bureaucracy: dilemmas of the individual in public services*. New York: Russell Sage Foundation.

Henry Mintzberg (1987), 'The strategy concept 1: five Ps for strategy', *California Management Review*, 30 (1): 11–24.

Henry Mintzberg (1992), 'Mintzberg on the rise and fall of strategic planning', *Long Range Planning*, 25 (4): 99–104

Mark H. Moore (1995), *Creating public value: strategic management in government*. Cambridge, MA: Harvard University Press.

Kieron Walsh (1993), *Marketing in local government*. London: FT Prentice Hall.

Karl Weick (1979), *The social psychology of organizing*. Reading, MA: Addison-Wesley.

Chapter 6

Marketing in public sector organizations

Tony Bovaird, University of Birmingham

INTRODUCTION

For many years in the 1970s and 1980s, lectures on marketing in the public sector began apologetically with an explanation of why marketing might be important – and generally they adopted a rather defensive standpoint, assuming that many in the audience would be predisposed to be hostile to the concept. This is no longer the case, as the growing literature on public sector marketing attests. However, the suspicion remains that public sector marketing has to demonstrate carefully its role and has to demarcate itself clearly from private sector marketing. This chapter looks at how marketing can contribute to more cost-effective public sector organizations and higher-quality public services.

LEARNING OBJECTIVES

This chapter is intended to help readers:

- to understand the role of marketing in a public sector context;
- to be able to prepare a marketing strategy, and marketing plan for their service or organizational unit;
- to understand how marketing is different in a politically driven organization working on issues with wide-ranging public implications, as opposed to marketing in private firms;
- to understand the limitations of marketing in a public sector context.

THE ROLE OF MARKETING IN A PUBLIC SECTOR CONTEXT

Marketing is often thought of as essentially commercial (i.e. oriented towards making money or, more pointedly, making profits). This clearly is not relevant to most aspects of public services and public sector organizations.

Again, marketing often has rather negative connotations associated with selling, even 'pressure selling'; or of promotion of goods or service, perhaps through 'hype'; or of advertising, perhaps through subliminal influencing. Clearly, if marketing is to play a valuable role in a public sector context, then these negative aspects will have to be transcended.

Fortunately there is no reason to believe that marketing must only be viewed in these pejorative terms. It is quite possible to define marketing in ways that suggest that it could be highly valuable to public sector organizations (Box 6.1). After all, 'markets' are only the arenas in which those needing a service are able to choose alternative providers, either in the public, private or voluntary sector. This is not inherently antipathetical to the public interest. The role of marketing, then, is to mediate between those needing the service and the organization hoping to provide the service. Clearly this can be done efficiently or inefficiently, fairly or unfairly, ethically or unethically, respectfully or insultingly to the potential service user – in all these ways, marketing is no different from other service functions such as production, HR management or finance. Perhaps the sensitivity about the potential for abuse of the marketing role comes from the widespread belief that marketing is the most dishonest and unethical of business functions in the private sector. Whether or not this belief is soundly based need not concern us here (although we might say in passing that private sector marketing has a number of competitors for this distinction – including tricky lawyers, creative accountants and captured auditors, all of whom are regularly in the public eye as a result of major corporate scandals).

To make this clearer, we can contrast the two polar extremes – a *product orientation*, as might typically be evidenced by professionals working in the field who are convinced that they know better than anyone else what service should be provided, and a *market orientation*, such as would be advocated by marketing specialists (Box 6.2).

Clearly, 'customers' in a public sector context include many different stakeholders, all of whose needs require to be considered in public sector marketing. Here we need to refer back to the types of value added in the public sector that were identified in Chapter 5 – value added for users, for wider social groups, for society as a whole ('social value added'), for the polity ('political value added') and for the environment. Marketing can be employed to explore how to increase value added for all the stakeholders involved in each of these ways.

However, there are a number of very different modes in which marketing can be used (Box 6.3). Some of these modes fundamentally seek to serve the user's interest (positive marketing, some variants of anti-marketing), while some seek to serve society's interest (social

BOX 6.1 DEFINITIONS OF MARKETING

'The aim of marketing is to make selling superfluous' (Drucker, 1973).

'Marketing is the establishment of mutually satisfying exchange reationships' (Baker, 1976).

'The strategic business function that creates value by stimulating, facilitating and fulfilling customer demand': proposed new definition, Chartered Institute of Marketing (2007).

BOX 6.2 PRODUCT ORIENTATION VERSUS MARKET ORIENTATION

Product orientation

- Emphasis on getting the 'product' right in professional terms.
- Product is developed first, then there is an attempt to attract customers.
- Organization is inward-looking, its production needs come first.
- Success is measured primarily in terms of professional esteem, with a secondary emphasis on the number of customers attracted.
- And if the service fails? 'We did our best, we produced a really good service – but the market failed – it didn't appreciate us.'

Service orientation

- Emphasis on doing what the customer wants.
- Services are developed to meet expressed wants *and potential wants* in a coordinated way.
- Organization is outward-looking, the customers' needs come first.
- Success is measured primarily by both the number and satisfaction level of customers (i.e. 'quality' as well as quantity).
- Customer is central to everything the organization does (i.e. there is a culture of 'customer obsession').
- And if the service fails? 'We failed to meet the market's requirements.'

BOX 6.3 MODES OF MARKETING

- *Positive marketing*: encouraging target groups to use particular goods, services or organizations because they will meet their needs.
- *Social marketing*: advancing a social, environmental or political viewpoint or cause because it will meet society's needs.
- *Anti-marketing*: encouraging target groups to cease using particular goods, services or organizations, either because it is against their interest or because it is against society's interest.
- *Demarketing*: deterring non-target groups from service uptake.

Source: Adapted from Sheaff (1991)

marketing) and some seek to serve the interests of target users at the expense of non-target users (demarketing).

One of the key issues that emerges from this discussion is 'who is the customer?' There are many potential customers for the public sector, including:

- people currently receiving the service;
- people waiting for it;
- people needing the service but not actively seeking it;
- people who may need the service in the future;
- people refused the service;
- carers of people needing the service (both those receiving it and those not receiving it);
- taxpayers;
- citizens;
- referrers of potential clients of the service.

In the rest of this chapter, we speak of all of these as 'customers', but a proper marketing strategy and marketing plan will normally try to differentiate the needs of each of these different customers and tailor the service to those different needs.

PREPARING A MARKETING STRATEGY AND MARKETING PLANS

In this section, we will consider how marketing strategies and marketing plans can be constructed in public sector organizations.

There is clearly a very strong connection between strategic management and marketing strategy. Indeed a marketing strategy will always be an integral part of the strategy for any organization (or organizational unit such as a service department). The *corporate marketing strategy* will consist of that part of the strategy in which the organization decides:

- which sectors to work in;
- which portfolio of services to provide to users;
- which target groups to provide with these services;
- what objectives and targets can be monitored to show whether the target groups have received the benefits expected from the services.

Clearly, this relates very closely to Mintzberg's concept of 'strategy as positioning'. The corporate marketing strategy responds to what the environment wants. It will be part of the corporate strategy of the organization, complemented by the service production and delivery strategy (to make best use of internal capabilities) (considered in Chapter 5) and the financial strategy (to make best use of all resources) (considered in Chapter 8).

Typically each constituent unit of the organization is expected to prepare a 'business plan' for its part of the overall organization, nested within and aligned to the corporate strategy. Similarly, each business unit is likely to prepare a marketing strategy, which can start from the decisions in the corporate marketing strategy on which markets it is expected to serve and goes into greater detail on the services it intends to produce and the target markets for those services. Finally, the marketing strategy at business unit level needs to be developed into a marketing plan, considering the detailed elements of the 'marketing mix'.

In order to prepare this suite of plans, four sets of analyses are necessary:

- analysis of the internal environment of the organization (considered in Chapter 5);
- analysis of the external environment of the organization;
- analysis of the market segments that the organization might serve; and
- analysis of the market options available and their relative merits.

We will now look at each of the three latter analyses in turn, before discussing how all these analyses can be used in formulating the corporate marketing strategy and business marketing plans.

Analysing the external environment

In analysing the external environment, we seek to understand the factors influencing external stakeholders and the consequent opportunities and threats that face the organization.

There are three main elements to this analysis:

- stakeholder mapping;
- PESTEL analysis and risk assessment;
- 'Five Forces' analysis.

Stakeholder mapping involves identifying the most important stakeholders in the organization and prioritizing them. This is typically done by drawing up a 'stakeholder power/interest matrix' – in Figure 6.1 we have illustrated this with reference to the stakeholders of the DfID, whose organizational culture we considered in Chapter 5. Stakeholders with high power over the organization and high interest in it are clearly critically important (e.g. the UK Foreign and Commonweath Office, the OECD Development Administration Committee, which coordinates most of the world's donor agencies, and the governments of countries receiving aid from the UK, who have to 'play ball' for the aid to be effective) – they should be given central roles in the organization's decision-making and activities. At the other extreme, organizations with neither power over nor interest in the organization can be largely neglected (subject to giving them the level of information that is required by law – and perhaps rather more, just to be on the safe side). This combination often applies to the 'general public', although interest groups to which individuals belong – particularly pressure groups (such as the anti-poverty movement) – will either be in the 'interested, powerful' or 'interested, not powerful' boxes.

However, the lesson from Figure 6.1 is clear – not all stakeholder groups are equal and a public sector organization must decide how to allocate its resources to work most closely with those stakeholder groups that it considers to have priority. Other forms of mapping can be used to help in setting these priorities – but the need for some set of priorities is unavoidable.

85

		Stakeholder Interest	
		Low	*High*
Stakeholder Power	**Low**	**Low priority** General UK public Citizens of recipient countries	**Keep informed** International aid NGOs Anti-poverty movement Media of recipient countries NGOs of recipient countries
	High	**Keep satisfied** HM Treasury UK 'tabloid' media	**Work together to achieve common goals** FCO OECD DAC Recipient country governments UK 'serious' media

Figure 6.1 *Stakeholder power/interest matrix for DfID*

Source: Adapted from original concept by Mendelow (1991)

PESTEL analysis sets out a statement of the main factors that are likely to impact on external stakeholders in the future, separated out into:

- political factors;
- economic factors;
- social factors;
- technological factors;
- environmental and ecological factors;
- legal and legislative factors.

This analysis is notoriously simple to do, to the extent that one can very easily end up with a document that is ludicrously large, detailing all potentially relevant factors. This is clearly of no practical use, so some sort of sieve must be applied to ensure that only the most relevant factors get included in any final document. (However, this still implies that the organization must attempt a very wide and imaginative search for all potentially relevant factors, so that the sieve can be applied to them. Of course, in practice we will expect that organizations – and individuals within them – will display 'blind spots', prejudices and plain ignorance in making this canvas, so that PESTEL analysis cannot ever pretend to be fully comprehensive.) *Risk assessment*, which is the sieve applied to the factors, is clearly a critically important part of PESTEL analysis. There are many different ways of doing a risk assessment, but typically factors are more likely to be included in the PESTEL statement if they score highly on at least some of the following criteria:

- Will the factor have a high impact, if it occurs soon?
- Will the factor have increasing impact over time?
- Is that impact likely to be positive or negative on external stakeholders? (This takes account of the fact that many stakeholders are risk averse, placing more importance on potential costs and losses than on potential benefits and gains.)
- Is there a high probability that the factor will indeed happen in the way forecast?
- Will the factor affect our organization more than other similar organizations that are involved in the same type of activity? (This takes account of the fact that an organization will typically be sensitive to changes in its relative position in relation to other organizations with which it is compared.)

The final piece in the external environment jigsaw is the *'Five Forces' analysis* of Michael Porter. This explores what sectors the organization might like to work in and which sectors it might not. Clearly, it is therefore a model that is relevant for service providing organizations in the public sector, rather than service commissioning organizations.

The Five Forces are:

1 The *threat of new entrants*, which would compete away profit margins.
2 The *threat of substitutes*, which puts a ceiling on the prices that can be charged.
3 The *bargaining power of suppliers* (including the distribution channels), which puts pressure on costs.
4 The *bargaining power of customers*, which puts a ceiling on prices.
5 The *level of competitive rivalry*, which drives down prices.

It was originally applied by Porter to analyse which sectors would be regarded by a private firm as the most competitive – and therefore the least attractive. (Later, Porter was to argue that this was a valid analysis for a firm that wished to be a big fish in a small, local or national pool – but that a firm which really wanted to be a big fish in the global pool was more likely to succeed if it quickly learnt to survive in highly competitive local or national markets.) Such a model may be relevant for some service-providing organizations in the public sector, where they are driven by the need to make target levels of profit (or not to exceed target levels of subsidy). Consequently, we need to adapt it to a public sector context.

In particular, we need to take account of the fact that:

- public sector organizations do not always have a choice which sector they work in (so that this analysis is irrelevant for some organizations, which can only work in certain sectors set out in the legislation, and cannot be applied to some sectors where a particular public sector organization is prohibited from working, either legislatively or politically);
- public sector organizations are not always competitive in their intent; and
- other stakeholders (particularly government) impact on choice of sector.

Consequently, the Five Forces analysis has a different role in environmental analysis by public sector organizations. First, it highlights for providing organizations the sectors in which they are likely to meet strong competitive rivalry. As with private organizations, this is likely to be interpreted as a danger signal: sectors where competitive rivalry is weak will be more attractive.

Second, they need to consider the bargaining power of stakeholders other than suppliers or customers, particularly partners (which might either increase costs or cut revenue) and the likelihood of interference by other levels of government (which again could affect costs or revenue, or might even rule out any work in the sector), since both of these may make a sector less attractive. (Note: these two factors now mean that we are working with a 'Seven Forces' model, but it is highly unlikely that it will become known as anything other than the 'Five Forces' model.)

Third, and rather differently from private sector providers, public sector providers need to consider the collaborative potential of the sector. Since so much of their success will depend on working closely with other bodies – groups representing customers, voluntary organizations filling in gaps in public provision, universities evaluating the cost-effectiveness of alternative service designs – it is important that these different bodies are collaborative in nature and prepared to form effective partnerships (Kooiman, 2003). We will consider this in more depth in the next section, but for the moment it is important to note that public sector use of the Five Forces can – and should – reject using it purely to explore the competitive rivalry of the sector. It is important to ask in relation to each of the Five (or Seven) Forces: How does it affect the sector's ability to work in collaboration?

Analysing market segments

People in different market segments will normally prefer different services or different designs of a given service. The most typical criteria for drawing up market segments in the public sector are demographic (age, household composition), socio-economic (class, socio-economic group, income), economic or social disadvantage (pensioners, unemployed, low income, disability groups, women, ethnic minorities, isolated people, etc.) and geographic (neighbourhood, ward, town, region, etc.). However, more recently there has been greater interest in using such criteria as lifestyle and tastes (often using psychographics). Each of these approaches naturally tends to miss some of the important differences between individuals, although each allows a move away from treating all customers as a mass market. Another form of market segmentation looks at the customers' attitude to the service being provided (unaware, hostile, aware, interested, wavering towards action, tester, occasional user, loyal).

Each of these approaches is useful for a particular form of marketing initiative but the critically important issue is to prioritize between these market segments in order to determine which segments should form the target or priority groups for the public agency. This is one of the fundamental political tasks in any public sector organization.

Analysing market options

The analyses of external factors allow an OT (Opportunities and Threats) analysis to be compiled for the organization, which can help to identify future market options and can in turn be combined with internal analysis of the organization to feed into a full SWOT analysis (see Chapter 5), which can be used to produce a series of integrated strategic options for the organization. These strategic market options should form coherent statements of a market position – a market to be served, a service to be provided and a target market segment for that service. However, it may well be unproductive to try to evaluate these market options on their own. The evaluation of strategy is most likely to make sense when it considers full strategic options that combine market options with internal capabilities and financial/resource options (see Chapter 5). Otherwise, the evaluation is likely to come up with a ranking of market options that is blind to the organization's strengths and weaknesses and resource constraints – this is very likely to lead to the choice of a sub-optimal strategy.

Evaluation of market options should normally not be a desk exercise. It is also possible to do market testing of options, either by trying out some alternatives in pilot studies, analysing the offers made by alternative suppliers or by actually going out to competitive tender and trying an alternative supplier for a period. This is considered further in Chapter 7.

From marketing strategy to marketing plans

The analysis and evaluation of strategic options should help a public sector organization to select its preferred strategic option, including its marketing strategy, with the following key elements:

- a decision on which sectors to work in;
- a portfolio of services that will be provided to users;
- a statement of the priority groups to whom these services are targeted;
- a set of objectives and targets that can be monitored to show whether the target groups have received the benefits expected from the services.

How can this marketing strategy be put into practice? Typically, a marketing plan is prepared that allows the key issues (the 'marketing mix') to be considered and coordinated in detail (Figure 6.2).

These elements of the marketing mix are closely interrelated and therefore need to be planned together, so that they are aligned with each other and support the chosen strategy:

- The *product* (or *service*) needs to be designed with the needs of the customer in mind. Design features need to include not only the core features of the service itself but also the way in which it is delivered, including such 'customer care' aspects as the availability of the service (e.g. opening hours), reliability (e.g. how often is the service defective?) and responsiveness to customers' needs (e.g. does the service take account of differences in gender, age, ethnicity, (dis)ability, etc.?). A key element of service design is market research, which is becoming much more central to public services management, whether conducted by surveys, focus groups or other methods.
- The *promotion* of the service has to be suitable for the target group, so that over time the users become aware of the service, interested in it, keen to use it and then take action to try it out. The mix of promotional methods needs to be carefully thought

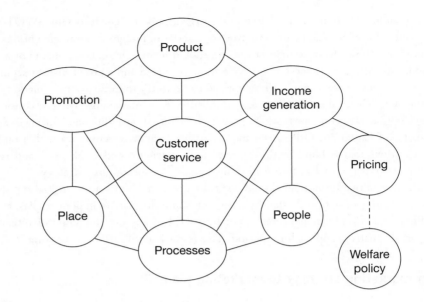

Figure 6.2 *The expanded marketing mix for public services*
Source: Adapted from Christopher *et al.* (1991)

out, including advertising, special sales promotions, sponsorship deals and public
relations campaigns.

- The *place* in which the service is available has to be suitable for the target service user
  (so that it is comfortable to use and is accessible, perhaps through co-location with
  local shopping or other public services, and appropriate transport has to be available
  or be provided – or services can be made available in e-government initiatives, e.g.
  over the Internet or through a call centre).
- The *processes* that are used to assess eligibility and to deliver the service have to be
  clear and understandable for the target group (which includes clear and easy-to-use
  forms, with availability of translation if required) and should be designed to minimize
  time taken and hassle.
- The *people* who supply the service have to be welcoming and empathetic to the target
  group and well trained in giving the service.
- The *income generation* activities of the organization have to be consistent with its principles
  and efficiently organized so that the net income is maximized. Sources of income might
  include fundraising by volunteers, donations, sponsorship, sales of associated services
  (e.g. from a charity shop), merchandising, sales of advertising space or pricing.
- The *prices* that are charged have to be appropriate to the target group's means (which
  will partly be determined by the overall national welfare policy to which the organization
  must conform and to which it contributes), proportionate to the benefits given and
  consistent with the organization's income generation plan. This will sometimes entail
  a concessions system (which may require income assessment procedures, with the
  consequent problems of stigma, deterrence to usage and high costs).

Clearly, there will be considerable overlap between marketing strategies and marketing plans – for example, the decision on the portfolio of services to be offered belongs to both, although it is handled at a finer level of detail in marketing plans. Again, promotion is just one branch of marketing communications, by means of which the organization seeks to keep in touch with its various customers. (This is considered in more detail in Chapter 15, on stakeholder engagement.) Moreover, marketing plans and service delivery plans will often have strong overlaps (e.g. making sure that proper transport arrangements are in place is part of the 'place' factor in the marketing plan, but also part of the 'logistics' factor in the service delivery plan).

MARKETING IN A POLITICALLY DRIVEN ORGANIZATION

Marketing is never easy in any context but it is especially complex in a political environment, where a number of thorny political issues tend to arise.

First, strategic marketing, like strategic management in general, requires clear statements of priorities, particularly about which target groups are priorities for each policy. This means telling many groups that they are NOT priorities – which is politically embarrassing.

Second, promotion of policies and services generally tries to attract customers to use them – but this can be interpreted as 'selling' the ruling group's achievements to the population and can therefore be accused of 'political' or 'spin' motives. Furthermore, the political opposition often feels unconstrained in attacking policies and services as low quality, which can undermine marketing efforts to improve take-up and perceived quality – not something with which private companies normally have to deal.

Third, pricing of services is usually highly controversial and changes of prices tend to be made relatively infrequently, removing the use of a potentially valuable tool in the marketing mix for significant periods (see Box 6.4).

BOX 6.4 PRICING POLICY IN LOCAL GOVERNMENT

In other councils, charges are not reviewed or are simply increased annually in line with inflation, so that charges fail to take account of changing circumstances, e.g. patterns of service use or rapidly rising costs, and charges do not reflect councils' priorities, e.g. that subsidies are targeted toward priority services and communities.

Although 78 per cent of councils identified the views of service users as a major or partial barrier to charging, councils' perceptions of local opposition to charges are not always backed up with robust evidence. The public is more receptive to charging for some services than is often assumed – people believe they get value for money from almost all of the local authority services for which they pay charges and people are more willing to pay charges where they can see what they are getting for their money and have a degree of choice.

Source: Adapted from Audit Commission (2008)

The first of these issues is by far the most important. We might expect, given the rhetoric of the public sector over recent decades, that it has particularly targeted and helped the most disadvantaged groups in society. However, as Le Grand pointed out more than twenty years ago:

> Almost all public expenditure in social services in Britain benefits the better off to a greater degree than the poor . . . [even in] services whose aims are at least in part egalitarian, such as the NHS, higher education, public transport, and the aggregate complex of housing policies.
>
> (Le Grand, 1982)

He goes on to suggest that there persist substantial inequalities in public expenditure per user, in use (standardized by level of need), in opportunity, in access (including cost of access and time taken to get access) and in outcomes. He also suggests that public policies have probably even failed to reduce inequality significantly in many policy areas. These conclusions are likely to have been reinforced by the experiences of the subsequent twenty-five years (Percy-Smith, 2000). If politicians cannot or will not address clearly the need to target public expenditure and public services at the most disadvantaged, then it seems likely that marketing will remain a relatively weak tool for achieving the purposes of public sector organizations – and those purposes will be much harder to achieve.

LIMITATIONS OF MARKETING

While marketing can help public sector organizations to work more effectively to please their customers, there remain significant limitations to its use in the public sector.

First, it is clear that it is often artificial to regard all those who come into contact with the public sector as its customers – certainly prisoners and parents who abuse their children don't fit this description easily. In some cases, the relationship between the state and its subjects is, and is likely to remain, characterized by relations of dominance and punishment rather than exchange and mutual reward. Marketing is less relevant in these circumstances.

Second, the manipulation of public tastes and preferences to make the public sector's services more desirable is questionable in the public sector. This largely rules out some of the approaches of private sector marketing, such as the encouragement of the 'conspicuous consumption of the leisure classes' (Veblen, 1994), or the use of 'the Hidden Persuaders', which create demand for unnecessary services and encourage motives based on 'base desires' such as power, greed and sex (Packard, 1957), or the resort to built-in obsolescence and emphasis on style rather than performance (Nader, 1965).

Third, there are areas where individuals making their own choice will not contribute to the highest good of the society in which they live – whether it be because of spillover effects of their decisions, the poor quality of information on which they act, their lack of under-standing of their own (long-term) best interest, or for other reasons. Where these 'market failures' exist – and it seems likely that there are significant areas of such decision-making in human behaviour – then collective decisions based on political processes will remain superior to individual decisions aided by marketing processes.

In general, then, the balance between marketing and political decision-making as a way of mediating between service users, citizens and service producers is one that will always be hard to find and is likely to shift over time. While marketing may have played too small a role in traditional public administration up to the 1980s, it has perhaps been in danger of encroaching too far in some areas of public policy in the last two decades.

SUMMARY

This chapter has considered a range of techniques for understanding the external environment of organizations and for identifying and evaluating strategic market options. It has also linked these strategies to the marketing plans needed to ensure that they are implemented. It has argued that marketing in a political environment can help to force political decision-making to be more open about its underlying purposes, especially in relation to priority target groups, but marketing must also be sensitive to its limitations when applied in the public domain.

QUESTIONS FOR REVIEW AND DISCUSSION

1   What does 'marketing' mean? What relationship does it have to 'markets'. Why does the term 'marketing' often appear to have a pejorative meaning? Is this justified?
2   What is the relationship between marketing strategy and the marketing mix. When would changes in the marketing mix be so significant that they would amount to changes in the marketing strategy?

READER EXERCISES

1   Consider a public sector organization that you know. Try to identify the main elements of its marketing strategy. Consider one of its services: try to identify the main elements of the marketing mix. Can you suggest some changes to the marketing strategy or the marketing mix that would make this organization more accessible to vulnerable groups?
2   What are the main pros and cons of using an income assessment approach to giving lower prices to disadvantaged groups? How might the net gains from an income assessment system be maximized?

CLASS EXERCISES

1   Divide into groups. Each group should identify the main elements of the marketing mix in the higher education system and propose changes that would help to increase the enrollment of students in this system. Compare notes and identify the reasons behind the main differences in each of the proposals.
2   What are the main limitations of marketing in the public sector? Give examples of these limitations in practice. How might they best be overcome?

FURTHER READING

Alan Andreason and Philip Kotler (2008), *Strategic marketing for nonprofit organisations* (7th edn). Upper Saddle River, NJ: Prentice Hall.

Martin Christopher, Adrian Payne and David Ballantyne (2002), *Relationship marketing: creating stakeholder value* (2nd edn). Oxford: Butterworth Heinemann.

Philip Kotler and Nancy Lee (2006), *Marketing in the public sector: a roadmap for improved performance*, Upper Saddle River, NJ: Wharton School Publishing.

J.J. Lynch (1992), *The psychology of customer care*. London: Macmillan.

Adrian Sargeant (2004), *Marketing management for nonprofit organisations* (2nd edn). Oxford: Oxford University Press.

Rod Sheaff (2002), *Responsive healthcare: marketing for a public service*. Buckingham: Open University Press.

Kieron Walsh (1993), *Marketing in local government*. Harlow: Longman.

REFERENCES

Michael Baker (1976), 'Evolution of the marketing concept', in Michael Baker (ed.), *Marketing theory and practice*. London: Macmillan.

Chartered Institute of Marketing (2007), *Tomorrow's word: reevaluating the role of marketing*. London: CIM (www.cim.co.uk/MediaStore/_Insights/Role%20of%20Marketing%20Agenda%20Paper.pdf, accessed 23 May 2008).

Martin Christopher, Adrian Payne and David Ballantyne (1991), *Relationship marketing*. Oxford: Butterworth-Heinemann.

Audit Commission (2008), *Positively charged: maximising the benefits of local public service charges*. London: Audit Commission.

Peter Drucker (1973), *Management: tasks, responsibilities, practices*. New York: Harper Row.

Jan Kooiman (2003), *Governing as governance*. London: Sage.

Julian Le Grand (1982), *The strategy of equality: redistribution and the social services*. London: Allen & Unwin.

A. Mendelow (1991), Proceedings of the second international conference on information systems. New York, 16–18 December.

Ralph Nader (1965), *Unsafe at any speed: the designed-in dangers of the American automobile*. New York: Grossman.

Vance Packard (1957), *The hidden persuaders*. New York: D. McKay.

Janie Percy-Smith (ed.) (2000), *Policy responses to social exclusion: towards inclusion*. Buckingham: Open University.

Rod Sheaff (1991), *Marketing for health services*. Buckingham: Open University Press.

Thorstein Veblen (1994), *The theory of the leisure class* (1st edn, 1899). New York: Dover Publications.

Chapter 7

Contracting for public services

Andrew Erridge, University of Ulster, UK

INTRODUCTION

This chapter examines the debate surrounding contracting for services and empirical evidence on the effectiveness of UK government policies since 1979. These followed initiatives of the Reagan administration in the USA, and subsequently similar policies have been introduced in countries throughout the world (see Chapter 4).

In general, there has been a shift from competing for contracted services through compulsory competitive tendering (CCT) towards more complex arrangements, which include managing multiple contracts, managing relationships through the supply chain, and developing accountable partnerships. These latter include partnerships with users and communities ('user and community co-production of services'). This chapter will examine the merits of competition and contracting as mechanisms for managing the delivery of externalized services.

LEARNING OBJECTIVES

- To understand the meaning of contracting;
- to understand why contracting for services has been increasing over the past 25 years;
- to be able to identify the pros and cons of contracting out of specific services;
- to understand the links between contracting, competition and collaboration;
- to understand how contracting could be used to pursue the wider socio-economic goals of government.

THE RISE OF CONTRACTING FOR SERVICES: FROM COMPETITION TO PARTNERSHIP?

Competition

We have seen in Chapters 2, 3 and 4 that, in the 1980s and 1990s, many OECD governments, but most notably Mrs Thatcher's government after 1979, were committed to reducing the size and role of the public sector, believing that it was less efficient than the private sector in delivering public services. This led to a fundamental shift away from direct service provision through the hierarchy of public sector organizations towards market-based competition and contractual relationships between public sector organizations and private or non-profit organizations. The ideas of the New Right were successful partly because they succeeded in linking with other influential strands of thought, in particular the growing critique of bureaucracy in the management and organization literature (see Chapter 3).

The ideas of cost reduction (economy) and efficiency were central to the argument in favour of competitive tendering, and a number of subsequent studies (e.g. Walsh, 1991a) described the cost-saving potential of contracting. Government guidance states that 'goods and services should be acquired by competition unless there are convincing reasons to the contrary' (HM Treasury, 1998), and that 'competition is the best guarantee of quality and value for money' (Chancellor of the Exchequer, 1991). Through this policy, it is argued, government can avoid accusations of favouritism and fraud, and the openness of the system will encourage more suppliers to participate, thus increasing competition, which will in turn reduce prices, improve quality and lead to greater innovation among suppliers.

One important policy of the UK government leading to an increase in the contracting out of public services was CCT, which required local authorities and, to a lesser extent, the National Health Service and other public bodies to invite tenders for the provision of public services from private companies. Usually these services had previously been delivered by staff of the organization (the 'in-house' provider), who were now required to compete against outside bidders. This involved setting up a direct service organization (DSO), separate from the client (usually the previous management of the service), which was responsible for the competitive tendering process. As Box 7.1 illustrates, CCT was extended to a progressively wider range of services up to 1992, and rules on the tendering process were tightened. This was mainly because in-house providers won a very high proportion of bids, and the government felt that they had an unfair advantage due to having access to information not available to outside bidders, as well as not being charged in full for common services that were provided centrally by the local authority.

Partnership

While competition was the hallmark of Conservative governments in the UK up until the early 1990s, partnership relations with suppliers were identified as a key element in their 1995 White Paper *Setting New Standards*. This sought to develop a new approach to supply relations, which had been characterized previously by short-term competitive tendering procedures. The White Paper (HM Treasury, 1995, p. 13) states that:

BOX 7.1 COMPULSORY COMPETITIVE TENDERING IN LOCAL GOVERNMENT: SERVICES COVERED AND MAIN POLICY CHANGES

Services covered

- 1980: construction, buildings, highways;
- 1988: building and street cleaning, catering, grounds maintenance, vehicle repair;
- 1989: maintenance of sport and leisure facilities;
- 1992: cultural facilities, e.g. theatres and libraries; construction related, e.g. architecture, engineering; corporate, e.g. administrative, legal, financial, personnel and computing; clerical, e.g. police support.

Policy changes in 1992

- Client-contractor split reinforced (1992);
- specified time periods for each stage in tendering process (1992);
- restriction on costs allowed to be offset by in-house bids (1992).

Departments will work together with suppliers to secure improvements in the performance of both parties. Although they will press suppliers to reduce cost and improve quality, they will recognise that mutually satisfactory relationships are in the interests of both sides and will avoid an unnecessarily adversarial approach.

By emphasizing cooperation and collaboration, UK policy initiatives set out to change the nature of the procurement function and of the relationship between government departments and suppliers. By moving away from the competitive market model represented by CCT, partnership working with suppliers can build social capital, leading to reduced transaction costs, increased outputs and improved outcomes (e.g. greater social cohesion). Social capital, according to Woolcock (1998), is a complex resource that encompasses the 'norms and networks facilitating collective action for mutual benefit' (p. 155). Social capital research (see Erridge and Greer, 2002, pp. 504–7) suggests that increased interaction and exchange can:

- lead to the development of trust and the creation of norms and sanctions that reduce transaction costs;
- improve access to resources among network members;
- create identity resources that build a sense of 'belonging' and shared action;
- have positive ripple effects within society by encouraging participation and creating greater social cohesion.

Since 1997, UK Labour government policies have reinforced this more participative, collaborative approach, with CCT replaced by Best Value, the expansion of the PFI through

PPPs, and an approach to contracting that facilitated the effective delivery of more complex services.

In relation to issues such as the environment or quality of life for disadvantaged groups, network relationships have provided an opportunity for interested stakeholders to work together more closely and set out common and clear objectives to address community problems. For example, collaborative supply relations have facilitated close engagement between the government departments, registered charities, and local schools and communities in the implementation of local environmental projects. Under this arrangement, partnership stakeholders collaborate to share information, set up performance measures, report on the progress of environmental projects and disseminate good practice in an effort to improve the environment in local communities. Similarly, the government's home energy efficiency scheme established interdependent working relationships between Buying Solutions (part of the Office of Government Commerce), government departments, local councils and Help the Aged to improve the quality of life for disadvantaged groups. By addressing such complex and diverse issues, trusting relationships have encouraged the sharing and coordination of information regarding performance and quality standards, facilitated common strategies between stakeholders, and encouraged cooperative action in working towards a collective goal (Erridge and Greer, 2002, p. 517).

The scope and nature of service contracting

The UK public sector spent about £150 billion (13 per cent of GDP) in 2003–4 on procuring a wide range of goods and services, all the way from commodities such as pens and paper, to big construction projects such as schools and hospitals, and complex human services, such as fostering – of this, local government accounts for £40 billion, health for £18 billion, defence £17 billion and central government about £15 billion (Simms, 2006; HM Treasury, 2007). Taken together, this procurement expenditure accounted for about one-third of 'total managed expenditure', the government's favoured measure of public spending. However, only £26 billion of it – around 5.8 per cent of 'total managed expenditure' was accounted for by 'third party public service provision' (i.e. by external service providers).

CHOOSING BETWEEN PUBLIC, VOLUNTARY OR PRIVATE SECTOR SUPPLIERS

The increase in contracting for services that were previously delivered directly by public sector organizations reflects a partial move away from the predominant form of service delivery before 1979 through the internal bureaucracy to alternative forms of delivery. The outcomes of market testing for a central government department or agency service, or of a CCT exercise for a local authority or NHS service, could be as follows:

- retain the service in-house;
- contract out to a private sector contractor;
- contract out to a voluntary sector provider;
- a 'mixed economy' of provision involving in-house, voluntary and private sector providers.

In a recent report, Entwistle *et al.* (2002) summarized the arguments for and against internal service provision as shown in Box 7.2.

BOX 7.2 THEORIES OF INTERNAL AND EXTERNAL SERVICE PROVISION

Transaction cost economics

In an extensive body of work, Oliver Williamson has argued that the make-or-buy decision should be determined by the comparison of the transaction costs of internal versus external provision. It is cheaper to buy one-off services – such as building a school – than it is to maintain all of the necessary construction staff and plant in-house. On the other hand, in-house provision is well suited to services that are provided frequently, that involve a non-trivial degree of uncertainty and that need significant transaction-specific investments.

Principal-agent theory

Donahue (1989) points out that successful contracting requires that the agents tasked with performing a particular function can be readily controlled by their principal (the client). This requires that exact specifications can be drawn up, outputs easily measured and inadequate suppliers quickly replaced. It is this logic that informed CCT. Donahue cites waste collection as exemplifying the benefits of contracting, concluding that: 'Contractors chosen by fair and honest bid contests typically out-perform public monopolies' (p. 68).

Contestable markets

Many of the criticisms of public providers hinge upon the absence of competitive forces, which allows public providers to be inefficient monopolies. From this perspective, the remedy is clear – the public sector should, where possible, create competitive pressures by giving service users as wide a choice as possible from a broad range of alternative providers, giving rise to a mixed and vibrant economy of provision. Contracting-out per se would simply replace public monopolies by private monopolies. This is the reasoning that underpins the New Labour government's objective of encouraging public sector organizations to create and manage markets in which existing suppliers find their position contested by new suppliers.

Functional matching

The fourth perspective suggests that the public, private and voluntary sectors are good at doing different things. Based on a clear understanding of the different strengths of the different sectors, public agencies can allocate functions to the most suitable sectors.

Source: Adapted from Entwistle *et al.* (2002, pp. 10–11)

The above theoretical considerations suggest that internal providers have an advantage in the provision of services where:

- future needs and priorities cannot be predicted with certainty, so that any service specification undertaken now is likely to need significant variations in the future;
- outputs are diffuse and difficult to measure, so that the degree of achievement of any output-based specification is difficult to determine;
- the service will require assets that will be under-employed if only used for in-house provision;
- flexibility and responsiveness, local knowledge and the exercise of political judgement are required.

CHOOSING BETWEEN COOPERATION AND COMPETITION

Even though traditionally UK public procurement policy has reflected the competitive approach, the keywords in the current UK approach to public procurement are 'quality', 'value for money' and 'sustainability': 'The challenge is to meet the public's demands for increasingly high quality public services at good value for money and in a sustainable way' (HM Treasury, 2007). In the public sector, the definition of these three keywords is far from straightforward (see Chapters 11 and 12). Value for money is essentially a balancing act between cost and quality, and can only be properly determined by taking into account the nature of the contract, stakeholder aspirations and resources available.

The means by which value-for-money is to be achieved is a source of much debate. Domberger and Jensen (1997) found that the search for economic efficiency through competition could reduce cost and improve quality of public services. However, Walsh (1991a) suggested that this was not because of competition per se but mainly because increased attention was being paid to quality through monitoring, explicit inspection and emphasis on standards.

Caldwell et al. (2005) argue that there are many examples of contractual or tendering conditions impeding competitive markets, ranging from irregular tendering patterns locking suppliers out of markets to disjointed contractual practices encouraging suppliers to over-extend themselves. They suggest that this challenges public procurement contractual approaches towards being able to reward suppliers for *excellence* rather than just for *volume*. Moreover, they argue that managing public markets for competitiveness means managing key supplier relationships and that these cannot be managed serially, contract by contract – there is a need to look beyond choosing the 'best supplier' for individual contracts, and instead to examine how to manage suppliers within a portfolio of market relationships.

The move away from purely competitive approaches towards more collaboration is long-standing – it was foreshadowed in a 1995 UK White Paper, which stated that procurement strategy should: 'combine competition and co-operation in an optimum way' (HM Treasury, 1995, p. 37). The policies of the Labour government since 1997, while retaining of necessity the element of competition to comply with regulatory requirements, have reflected this increased emphasis on collaboration through partnership with the private and voluntary sectors. The NHS internal market was abolished to be replaced by a more collaborative process of commissioning for services between primary care consortia, trusts, and private and voluntary providers. Best Value was announced as the replacement to CCT in local government and required a process of service review, consultation with stakeholders and competition on a voluntary rather than compulsory basis. Partnering with the private sector was pursued more vigorously, especially through PPPs, to fund infrastructure capital projects (e.g. London Underground) and service delivery (e.g. the provision of customer services to Liverpool City Council by BT).

The European Commission has pushed both competitive and collaborative approaches. Competition has been a central element of its public procurement policies, including the Services Directive, which aims to break down barriers to cross-border trade in services between EU member states, so that service providers, particularly small and medium-sized enterprises, will find it easier to set up business and offer services in other member states and to provide services across the boundaries of member states.

However, the EU has also promoted a more collaborative approach – it now suggests that there should be greater dialogue between purchasers and suppliers, arguing that a more cooperative approach can reduce costs through working with suppliers to identify inefficiencies in the supply chain, while improved supply market intelligence and a better use of resources can lead to commercial gains without competition. This 'competitive dialogue' approach attempts to combine the advantages of competition and collaboration by allowing 'market testing' at the early stage of the service design and procurement process, while getting the advantages of close collaborative working with the final shortlist of potential partners, before making the final procurement decision.

PUBLIC-PRIVATE PARTNERSHIPS FOR SERVICES DELIVERY

PPPs, whether conventionally financed out of public expenditure or privately financed under the PFI, have increasingly become the vehicle for providing the infrastructure to deliver government policy through, for example, the building and equipping of schools, hospitals, transport systems, water and sewerage systems. However, there is no uniform pattern of provision, with a mixed economy of provision between public, private and voluntary sectors being adopted as appropriate for each project.

Bovaird (2006) analyses three case studies to illustrate how market relationships have changed in a multi-stakeholder procurement environment, each representing one form of the new procurement approaches that are emerging (Box 7.3):

- relational contracting
- partnership procurement
- distributed commissioning.

The move to PPPs has not been without its costs in procurement terms. Caldwell *et al.* (2005) argue that one effect of the rapid expansion of PPPs has been to increase the impediments to competition, particularly in 'common markets' such as construction, information technology and communication systems and consultancy – and public service commissioning needs to develop competencies in unravelling the interconnections between provider consortia.

BOX 7.3 CASE STUDIES ON STAKEHOLDER RELATIONSHIPS IN PPPS

Relational contracting for Revenues and Benefits service: consultants of the company Unisys were encouraged to work informally with staff working in the Revenues and Benefits section of the London Borough of Harrow to identify barriers to more effective and efficient working and to explore staff reactions to different options for change. A bottom-up approach was adopted, which allowed a new approach to emerge that built on existing knowledge bases in the department, was consistent with the most positive aspects of department culture and that allowed local priorities to be incorporated in the resulting systems. Simultaneously, the consultants came to recognize new ways of solving problems by marrying their technical expertise with the service knowledge held by front-line staff. The contract was simply to improve the quality of the service while making savings – it did not revolve around the delivery of a fixed specification.

Partnership procurement of Dudley Community Health Unit: The original idea of the Primary Health Trust and the local authority was 'Let's build a local Mental Health Unit'. It then became a 'one-stop shop' for all primary health services in the local area, so that the business case was health-driven. Later the concept was extended to incorporate social services and the local library and was developed as a PFI project. Mill Group was chosen as the preferred developer and facility manager because it agreed to be flexible. In spite of the complexity of this joint procurement process, the building was completed on time, on budget and on specification. At no stage did a 'variations management game' emerge. Nevertheless, with hindsight, the underlying concept was probably under-ambitious – in this co-location model, the services are 'next door' to each other, rather than being truly joint and seamless, in their commissioning and delivery.

Distributed commissioning: A local Community Trust took advantage of the redevelopment of old military barracks in the rural village of Caterham, which had long-standing housing and social problems. The Trust managed to broker a planning agreement with the private developer, who was suspicious at first that the arrangement was an attempt to lower densities and profit margins on the site, but eventually agreed to contribute over £2 million for social facilities and believed it had made a bigger profit on the development than if it had gone for traditional middle income housing. The Community Trust has used its funds to establish a range of economic, social, educational, cultural and sports facilities on the site and to manage them so that they respond to wider community needs in the area (including a skate park, community theatre group, craft workshops, sports teams, etc.). The Trust also negotiates with major service providers in the area on behalf of villagers. Local villagers, initially suspicious of swamping by 'incomers', have played a major part in the evolution of the new community activities, which have significantly improved the quality of life for local villagers. In this way, the commissioning of local public services has been distributed to a local group of people, rather than simply being decided by the local council.

Source: Adapted from Bovaird (2006)

INTERNATIONAL DEVELOPMENTS IN CONTRACTING FOR PUBLIC SERVICES

While the above examples are based upon the UK, there is evidence that, as with other aspects of the New Public Management, the use of contracting and PPPs has grown internationally, involving broadly similar approaches in most cases, although the drivers differ in each country, and the processes are adapted to the particular constitutional, legal and governance arrangements of each country.

A particularly interesting example of the changing use of contracting for public services is given by France, where the tradition of contracting out local public services has been predominantly one of partnership and cooperation rather than competition and antagonism (West, 2005). However, in recent years this traditional approach, based on the bilateral values of trust and cooperation, has been challenged by a new discourse of local public services governance, which emphasizes detailed contract planning and close contract monitoring. West (2005) argues that this reveals the beginning of a shift in the governance of public service exchange relationships from relatively noncontractual and bilateral to relatively contractual and trilateral. It may mark a move away from the protection of public sector providers, as French contractors increasingly bid for contracts under the EU Directives. It also reflects increasing concern with the vulnerability of the traditional 'partnership' arrangements to corrupt practices (Hall, 1999). Moreover, the greater use of contracting for public services across EU borders has resulted in frequent investigations by the European Commission and occasional critical judgements by the European Court of Justice, but rarely penalties to match the offence.

A further spur for PPP working has been provided by the Office of Management and Budget (OMB) which in 2001 announced a new requirement that all US federal agencies should consider 5 per cent of their (civilian) posts for potential outsourcing by the end of 2002, an extra 10 per cent by the end of 2003, and half by the end of 2005 (Smith 2003). Smith suggests (p. 290) that, on average, cost reductions of over 30 per cent are achieved through the process, 'managed competition', which is being used to do this (although it is less clear what has happened to the quality of the services provided in these contracts). Smith reports that audits undertaken by the General Accounting Office have shown that contractor failures resulting from the managed competition process have been relatively infrequent.

Contracting for wider socio-economic goals of government

At present, policy on contracting, through the structures and procedures mentioned above, partly reflects the market model supported by public choice theorists but also new arrangements of co-production between public, private and nonprofit sectors. Self (1993) argues that the market model is inconsistent with the public interest on three grounds:

1   Public choice encourages the individual to maximize economic opportunities and personal wealth, whereas public interest requires identification or sympathy with others' needs.
2   Political liberty cannot be treated as the dependent variable of a strong, autonomous market system; rather a balancing of the roles of the state and the market is required.

3   The market system makes no distinction between individuals' 'wants', and common 'needs' essential for a tolerable life.

Of course, there is always a danger that the dominant voices heard in supply chain debates will be commercial interests, usually large, powerful corporations which may ignore other issues, such as environmental damage created, unfair employment conditions or the exploitation of poorer producers. This suggests that public sector organizations should provide moral leadership by incorporating this broader social dimension into contracting decisions.

The socio-economic dimension of public procurement involves 'any purposeful action intended to improve the social welfare of the whole or part of the same population' (Fernandez Martin, 1996, p. 39). Policy areas that tend to be considered include unemployment, social exclusion, protection of minorities, income distribution, economic development, particularly in relation to small firms, and environmental policy.

There are a number of methods through which the objectives of these policies could be achieved. Contractual clauses may be included, requiring contractors to comply with wider government goals such as combating discrimination on grounds of sex, race, religion or disability. For example, in the UK, companies bidding to run the £300 million New Deal programme to help disadvantaged groups had to prove their commitment to 'work-place diversity'. Set-asides overcome market inequalities by allowing only certain sections of the economy (e.g. small firms) to tender for contracts and thus increase competi-tiveness. Prompt payment policy protects smaller firms and subcontractors in particular against larger customers' opportunistic behaviour by providing that payment be made within thirty days. 'Green' sourcing protects natural resources and the environment in which citizens live. Coote (2002) argues that the purchasing policy of the NHS could influence health and sustainable development by encouraging local suppliers and helping to regenerate and support the economies of disadvantaged neighbourhoods. It could also choose goods and methods of production and distribution that are likely to safeguard health and the environment.

Opponents of the use of procurement for socio-economic purposes have argued that the outcome is likely to be extra or hidden costs and therefore policy should remain market based (see McKinstry quote). However, as we have already discussed, given that the market model is flawed, there is a moral imperative for governments to ensure that the public interest is served. An example of a successful use of public procurement to promote employment is presented in Box 7.8.

> . . . the truth is that contract compliance involves a vast, costly expansion of state bureaucracy, since it requires an army of inspectors, advisors and officers to ensure its iplementation. By focusing on ideology rather than quality and value, it is bound to reduce efficiency.
>
> *Source*: Leo McKinstry (2006)

BOX 7.8 THE NORTHERN IRELAND UNEMPLOYMENT PILOT PROJECT

Northern Ireland has historically suffered from much higher levels of unemployment than other regions of the UK. The new 2002 Public Procurement Policy in Northern Ireland included a pilot project that was seen as an opportunity to redress this imbalance by taking advantage of the high level of public sector infrastructural investment and procurement of goods and services in the region. A condition was included in selected contracts for construction and services requiring contractors to submit a social policy statement and employment plan, outlining how they would meet the requirement actively to seek to employ people from the long-term-unemployed target group. On award of contract, the winning contractor was required to implement the proposals. The pilot project was monitored over a two year period from July 2003 to July 2005, and a final evaluation report was submitted in September 2005.

The pilot project led to the recruitment of fifty-one new employees from the target group, of whom forty-six were retained by the contractors. Those who have left employment will have benefited from their experience of work. The creation of these jobs was achieved with very little additional direct cost. The overall 'project cost per job created' during the evaluation period was £900,000, against a construction industry benchmark of £1 million.

The employment plan process has quickly become an embedded part of the culture of contracting with government amongst construction contractors, those most involved to date. The survey issued to all contractors at the end of the pilot project showed that almost two-thirds believed that the inclusion of the employment plan as part of the contract did not dissuade them from tendering for the contract. The procedures generally operated successfully, although there were a small number of instances of non-compliance. The Water Service provides an example of best practice, with four projects within the pilot, resulting in thirteen people from the target group being employed at a project cost per job created of £0.72 million. There was clearly commitment to the pilot from the top of the organization, project managers were fully informed and committed, arrangements for regular monitoring reports were agreed with contractors, and arrangements were made by contractors to link up with an FE college to provide potential employees.

Source: Adapted from Erridge (2007)

SUMMARY

This chapter has found that, for all of the radicalism of some governments around the world, policy on contracting has not resulted in a massive transfer of service provision from the public to the private sector. Where services are delivered by the private sector, there is some evidence of savings and improved quality, but these must be weighed against higher transaction costs, incidences of contractor failure and inequality effects on public sector employees.

105

The UK Labour government since 1997 has pursued partnership with the private sector, adopting a more collaborative approach but backed by an increase in inspection and audit (see Chapter 14). While there is therefore a common recognition of the necessity of using private sector expertise and finance, the difference perhaps lies in the Labour government's greater respect for a public sector ethos, and recognizing the distinctive contribution that public sector employees can make. However, this attitude does not persist where these employees are felt to be resistant, or where the services they provide are deemed to have failed (whether schools, hospitals or local authorities). In these cases, the Labour administration has proved equally, if not more, prepared to intervene than its predecessors, based upon ever more prescriptive performance targets.

This suggests that the core problem that recent governments in the UK and elsewhere have sought to address through contracting is the perceived failure of public agencies to manage the delivery of public services efficiently and effectively. Increasingly, the solution is being found in a mixed economy of public, private and voluntary provision.

There are some key areas where we cannot yet be sure of the lessons emerging on contracting out and partnership working, and where, therefore, further research is needed. These include, in particular:

- Can a more collaborative approach be developed through amending the European Directives and UK rules and regulations on procurement policy?
- What are the drivers, forms and outcomes of contracting, in particular PPPs, in different countries with varying constitutional, legal and governance arrangements?
- How can socio-economic goals be pursued through contracting while retaining the focus on best value for money and collaboration with the private sector?

QUESTIONS FOR REVIEW AND DISCUSSION

1   Should social and employment rights be protected through the contracting process by the insertion of relevant clauses in contracts? What are the benefits and risks of allowing such concerns to be embedded in contracts?

2   Why is it easier to operate market-based contracting approaches for simple repetitive services than for complex, professionally based activities? Discuss which services fall into these categories in (1) a major metropolitan local authority in your country, and (2) an executive agency of central or regional government in your country.

3   What are the main factors that make local authorities reluctant to contract out services to the private sector? What steps do you consider central government might take to encourage local government to make more use of effective opportunities for contracting out?

READER EXERCISE

Select at least three articles on using private sector contractors or private finance to provide public services that have recently appeared in quality daily or Sunday newspapers. What arguments and/or evidence do they provide in relation to the issues discussed in this chapter?

CLASS EXERCISE

Identify in class some public services that have been contracted out. In groups, discuss the extent to which the contracting out of these services has more successfully met the needs of:

■ those for whom the service is provided;
■ the providers (i.e. the managers and employees);
■ the government's political and managerial goals.

FURTHER READING

Tony Bovaird (2006), 'Developing new relationships with the "marke"' in the procurement of public services', *Public Administration*, 84 (1): 81–102.

Nicholas Deakin and Kieron Walsh (1996), 'The enabling state: the role of markets and contracts', *Public Administration*, 74 (1): 33–48.

Simon Domberger and Paul Jensen (1997), 'Contracting out by the public sector: theory, evidence and prospects', *Oxford Review of Economic Policy*, 13 (4): 67–79.

John Donahue (1989), *The privatization decision*. New York: Basic Books.

Andrew Erridge (2007), 'Public procurement, public value and the NI Unemployment Pilot Project 2', *Public Administration*, 85 (4): 1023–43.

HM Government (2007), *UK Government Sustainable Procurement Action Plan*. London: DEFRA.

REFERENCES

Tony Bovaird (2006), 'Developing new relationships with the "market" in the procurement of public services', *Public Administration*, 84 (1): 81–102.

Nigel Caldwell, Helen Walker, Christine Harland, Louise Knight and Jurong Zheng (2005), 'Promoting competitive markets: the role of public procurement', Special edition on public procurement, *Journal of Purchasing and Supply Management*, 11 (5/6): 242–51.

Chancellor of the Exchequer (1991), *Competing for quality: buying better public services*. London: HMSO.

Anna Coote (ed.) (2002), *Claiming the health dividend. Unlocking the benefits of NHS spending*. London: King's Fund.

Simon Domberger and Paul Jensen (1997), 'Contracting out by the public sector: theory, evidence and prospects', *Oxford Review of Economic Policy*, 13 (4): 67–79.

Tom Entwistle, Steve Martin and Gareth Enticott (2002), *Making or buying? The value of internal service providers in local government*. London: Public Services Network.

Andrew Erridge (2007), 'Public procurement, public value and the NI Unemployment Pilot Project', *Public Administration*, 85 (4): 1023–43.

Andrew Erridge and Jonathan Greer (2002), 'Partnerships and public procurement: building social capital through supply relations', *Public Administration*, 80 (3): 503–22.

Jose M. Fernandez Martin (1996), *The EC public procurement rules: a critical analysis*. Oxford: Clarendon Press.

David Hall (1999), *Privatisation, multinationals, and corruption*. London: Public Services International Research Unit, University of Greenwich.

HM Treasury (1995), *Setting new standards: a strategy for government procurement*, Cm 2840. London: HMSO.

HM Treasury (1998), *Comprehensive spending review on efficiency in civil government procurement expenditure*. London: HMSO.

HM Treasury (2007), *Transforming government procurement*. London: HMSO.

Leo McKinstrey (2006), 'Sign here – you know this is good for you: private contractors everywhere must now prove their devotion to the new creed of political correctness', *The Times*, 27 April 2006.

Peter Self (1993), *Government by the market?* London: Macmillan.

Sir Neville Simms (2006), *Procuring the future: Sustainable Procurement National Action Plan: recommendations from the Sustainable Procurement Task Force*. London: DEFRA.

Arthur Smith (2003), 'Public-private partnership projects in the US: risks and opportunities', in Akintola Akintoye, Matthias Beck and Cliff Hardcastle (eds), *Public-private partnerships: managing risks and opportunities*. Oxford: Blackwell.

Kieron Walsh (1991), *Competitive tendering for Local Authority services*. London: Department of the Environment.

Karen West (2005), 'From bilateral to trilateral governance in local government contracting in France', *Public Administration*, 83 (2): 473–92.

Michael Woolcock (1998), 'Social capital and economic development: toward a theoretical synthesis and policy framework', *Theory and Society*, 27 (2): 151–208.

Chapter 8

Financial management in public sector organizations

James L. Chan, University of Illinois, Chicago, USA and
Xuyun Xiao, Peking University, China

INTRODUCTION

The importance of money to government may be obvious, but good public financial management is often taken for granted. This chapter will discuss how the changing roles of public management alter government's financial management systems. These systems are analyzed in terms of their underlying conceptual models. It will be argued that, as government has evolved from a hierarchical bureaucracy to an organization with multiple stakeholders and eventually to a node in an institutional network, the tasks of public managers have been transformed from direct control to balancing the interests of stakeholders (see also Chapter 1). Corresponding to these stages of evolution are the classical model, the NPM (new public management) model and the governance model based on the original insights of Barnard (1968, originally 1938) and Simon (1945). These models are described and compared, along with the key issues faced by practice and research.

Public financial management (PFM) faces several identity issues. First, governments are urged to adopt best practices. But there are few guidelines for assessing PFM quality. Since PFM is a service function, what is its value to clients, and who are these clients? Furthermore, how much resource should be spent on quality improvement? The second issue is whether it is appropriate for government to uncritically emulate private sector practices. Third, what is the proper boundary of PFM? Does "public" include only core governmental agencies? Or does it encompass government-owned nonprofit institutions and business enterprises? Finally, finance often involves the creative search for financing alternatives; this may be antithetical to prudent and routine management. Therefore, how much weight should be given to the "finance" and "management" aspects of PFM? These issues are resolved differently in various PFM systems, which are analyzed in terms of three conceptual models below.

LEARNING OBJECTIVES

This chapter will look at the following key issues:

■ changes of government's financial management systems and their underlying conceptual models;

■ the context of each of the models discussed;

■ their contents;

■ the supporting discipline of each of the models.

THE THREE MODELS

The classical model

There are two cardinal rules in the classical PFM model: (1) a government should balance its budget, and (2) a government unit should not overspend its appropriations. These rules are codified in laws and regulations. In the United States, most state and local governments operate under balanced budget laws. Even though the federal constitution does not require a balanced budget, it does stipulate that "No money shall be drawn from the Treasury, but in consequence of Appropriations made by Law, and a regular Statement and Account of the Receipts and Expenditures of all public Money shall be published from time to time" (Constitution of the United States, Article I, Section IX, Clause 7). In conformity with this provision, there are statutes and regulations on budget preparation, approval and execution, and eventual cash disbursement by the Treasury. Financial management makes budgetary resources available to officials to carry out authorized purposes.

PFM is often described in terms of revenue collection and spending. There is, however, no general agreement about the scope of financial management. The revenue side is often slighted, with more attention paid to public expenditure management. Here, budget specialists think that financial management starts after a government agency receives appropriations – legal authorization to enter into contracts or make cash outlays. As such, financial management is an invisible bureaucratic function uninvolved in policy decision-making and largely unaffected by budgeting approaches. As PPBS, ZBB and mission budgeting come and go, financial management ensures organizational stability and continuity by following standard operating procedures – see Box 8.1.

BOX 8.1 BUDGETING APPROACHES . . .

■ PPBS (planning, programming, budgeting system): favored in the 1960s to stress longer time horizon and detailed specification of activities.

■ ZBB (zero-based budgeting): a 1970s antidote to incremental budgeting, requiring the justification of every dollar requested.

■ Mission budgeting: a 1990s reincarnation of PPBS, relating resource requests to goals.

These procedures dictate how transactions are handled. Whereas the budget embodies substantive decisions – who gets what, how much and when – financial management dutifully carries out spending policies. While specific procedures differ from one jurisdiction to another, they generally entail some or all of the following steps: (a) annual appropriations are divided into quarterly allocations, (b) contractual commitments are approved and made, (c) goods and services are received, and (d) payments are made. These transactions are recorded in the budgetary accounting system in terms of the use of appropriations, and in the financial accounting system in terms of effects on assets (economic resources), liabilities (obligations for goods/services received), and revenues and expenditures/expenses (increases and decreases in net resources, respectively).

In addition, there are some specialized functions such as investment management and debt administration. Interested readers are referred to textbooks (e.g. Mikesell, 1995) and manuals for practitioners (e.g. Allen and Tommasi, 2001).

Sound financial management is easier said than done. This is the case anywhere, but especially so in developing countries. The situation is abysmal in the poorest nations:

> What is budgeted is often not disbursed, and what is disbursed often does not arrive. Salaries go unpaid for months, operating funds do not materialize, and government debts remain unsettled. At the same time, the executive branch makes unbudgeted expenditures throughout the year. These loose practices make public spending data extremely spotty – and the data that does exist is often inaccurate or even falsified.
>
> (Thomas, 2001, p. 39)

For all its contributions to the smooth functioning of government, the classical PFM model cannot solve two problems: intentional budget deficits and operational inefficiency. Governments can run deficits by deliberately pursuing fiscal policies that cause spending to exceed revenues. They do so in order to achieve macroeconomic objectives (e.g. stimulating production and employment) or for political reasons (e.g. placating interest groups). In that case, even the most competent financial management cannot hope to raise enough revenue or reduce sufficient expenditure to compensate for such "deficits by design." Nor can the faithful execution of the law necessarily achieve economy and efficiency. Finance-related laws usually do not usually deal with performance issues. Furthermore, a mentality of legal compliance is not conducive to creative thinking or actions to lower cost and increase efficiency. The NPM model of financial management arose to deal with these inadequacies of the classical model.

The "New Public Management" model

In the idealized NPM model, the distinction between public management (as distinguished from administration) and business management is blurred to the point that private sector practices are urged upon government. Government bureaucracies turn into strategic business units competing with each other, and citizens become customers. The budget-maximizing bureau chiefs are reformed into cost-conscious and revenue-hungry entrepreneurs. Performance and results – not inputs – are stressed. Government officials follow, not the laws

111

of specific jurisdictions, but the universal rules of the marketplace: economy and efficiency. A business-like government naturally uses private sector management techniques.

Accounting-based tools figure prominently in "new public financial management" (NPFM), a term coined by Olson *et al.* (1998). NPFM takes a number of strong normative positions. It insists that accounting principles, preferably set by professional groups independent of government, should be used in budgeting. Double-entry recording should replace the single-entry system. Accrual accounting is offered as an alternative to the cash budget (see Case Example 8.1). The government's financial picture should be presented as a whole to the public. The full costs of government services should be calculated as a basis for setting prices for both public and internal services. Outputs and outcomes should be measured, compared with benchmarks, and verified by value-for-money audits.

That is the rosy scenario NPFM offers to government. Yet, despite extensive experimentation in a half dozen countries over two decades, a "globally standardized NPFM system" still does not exist, as there is "no one way of understanding NPFM" (Olson *et al.* 1998, p. 437). Though billed as a global movement, the above practices have made the most headway only in the English-speaking developed countries. There the accounting profession, led by chartered accountants or certified public accountants, enjoys a high degree of independence

CASE EXAMPLE 8.1 **THE USE OF ACCRUAL ACCOUNTING IN THE UK**

In business (including state-owned enterprises), accrual accounting requires recognition of revenue only after delivery of goods and services and expenses – costs of resources used and debts incurred – are matched against the revenue to arrive at a period's income. Applying this method to the core public sector, where taxes are levied to finance collective goods jointly consumed by the public, is highly problematic. Accrual accounting also refers to the recognition and reporting of various rights (assets) and obligations (liabilities).

In the UK, since 2000 all financial planning in central government has been done on the basis of accrual accounting (or "resource accounting", as it is called). Instead of departments having separate cash budgets for "current" and for "capital" expenditure, they have a consolidated expenditure limit, calculated by making estimates of the likely current costs and capital costs over the budget period (now typically three years). All assets which are used by the department are charged for, to exert pressure on their economical usage. Departments have much more freedom to decide the balance between capital and current expenditure (but this is still constrained, as capital expenditure usually has to be financed through public private partnerships, such as the Private Finance Initiative). This system also allows the clear separation of the "programme budgets" which are used to provide goods and services to users (e.g. the levels of benefits payments made to claimants), and the "running costs" which are the managerial costs of administering the programmes.

Source: HM Treasury (2000a)

and wields considerable power as arbiter of what constitutes full disclosure to the public. Either directly or in alliance with others, accountants and auditors formulate or heavily influence auditing and accounting principles for corporations, non-profit organizations and the public sector. These principles encourage (indeed, mandate) transparency of financial matters to the public gaze. Internally, cost-cutting and revenue-enhancement opportunities are identified (see Case Example 8.2).

The above stories illustrate the way "new public managers" deal with financial problems. They act like entrepreneurial businessmen, turning cost centers into revenue or profit centers. They master the concept of opportunity costs and eagerly make use of otherwise idle resources. They think "outside the box" by defying conventions and offering creative solutions. Instead of following rules, they make the rules.

NPFM has the potential to energize an ossified bureaucracy, but there are several problems with it. First, it does not address the core issue in government. In the final analysis, government exists to take care of the consequences of market failure, doing those things for which business lacks incentives or which it is not equipped to handle. Besides its peripheral agencies and activities (which can be and have been privatized), the government promotes general welfare by providing collective goods and financing them through general taxation. Equity rather than

CASE EXAMPLE 8.2 **TURNING COST CENTERS INTO REVENUE CENTERS**

Osborne and Gaebler, the champions of "reinventing government", encouraged governments to be entrepreneurial. For example:

- The Milwaukee Metropolitan Sewerage District turned 60,000 tons of sewage sludge into fertilizer every year and sold it for $7.5 million.
- Phoenix earns $750,000 a year by selling methane gas from a large wastewater treatment plant to another city for home heating and cooking.
- The St Louis County Police, after developing a system for officers to telephone in their reports, licensed the software to a private company and earned $25,000 for every new user.
- The Washington State ferry system in the early 1980s earned $1 million new revenue a year through re-tendering its food service contracts; more than $150,000 a year by selling advertising spaces in its terminal building; and another $150,000 a year by allowing duty-free shops on its two international boats.
- Paulding County, Georgia, rented extra beds in its jail to other jurisdictions for $35 a night to handle their overflow, generating $1.4 million in fees with $200,000 in profit.
- Some Californian police departments reserved motel rooms to serve as weekend jail cells for convicted drunken drivers at $75 a night.

Source: Adapted from Osborne and Gaebler (1993, p. 197)

efficiency, economy or even effectiveness is the ultimate criterion in public or political decision-making in a democracy. As Case Example 8.3 shows, purely economic approaches such as "payment by results" have their limits in a political public sector context.

Second, the worst bureaucracies are often pitted against the best-run corporations, thus creating a distorted comparison. As the collapse of Enron (the giant American energy-trading company) and Andersen (one of the former Big 5 international auditing/consulting firms) and subsequent corporate scandal shows, all is not well in the business world and the auditing profession. Indeed, the principles of democratic government – separation of powers, checks and balances – might well help reform corporate governance. Third, in its extreme form, NPFM may be as unsustainable as previous radical reforms. It elevates administrative discretion at the expense of legislature power. It promotes the ethos of the business-minded accountants against the politically savvy policy analysts. It does not appreciate the primacy and resilience of budget rules in government. It fails to recognize that cost cutting could only go so far: below the fat lie the bones – the core government institutions to which the public turns in time of crisis and turmoil. What is needed is a governance model that recognizes the respective roles, competences and advantage of government, civic society and businesses.

The Barnard-Simon governance model

The roots of governance may be traced to an organization theory pioneered by Chester Barnard and Herbert Simon. Instead of profit maximization for stockholders, Barnard (1968, originally 1938) argued that the manager's function was to motivate the contribution of everyone who holds resource needed to carry on the business. Simon (1945) applied Barnard's insight to government in his landmark *Administrative Behavior*. He views an organization – government or business – as being in equilibrium when its managers succeed in balancing the contributions from, and the inducements given to, its stakeholders (see Table 8.1, for examples). Given their knowledge of input-output relationships, managers are keenly aware of the complementarity and substitutability of the resources held by different stakeholders. Their essential

CASE EXAMPLE 8.3 **"PAYMENT BY RESULTS" IN UK HOSPITALS**

Like the previous Conservative government, the UK Labour government after 1997 tried again and again to improve the performance of health care by introducing competition between hospitals. For example, in April 2005, the then health minister John Hutton intended to extend the use of "payment by results" to 70 per cent of a typical hospital's general income, in which health service funds follow the patient and hospitals received a fixed sum for each course of treatment. However, after trials of the new hospital payment scheme found evidence of manipulation through "gaming", the reform plans were scaled back to 30 per cent of most hospitals' activity.

Source: Adapted from *Financial Times*, 11 January 2005

Table 8.1 *Government as a coalition of stakeholders*

Stakeholders	Contributions (benefits to the organization)	Inducements (costs to the organization)
Voters	Legitimacy	Public services to individuals and for general welfare
Taxpayers	Tax dollars	Public services to individuals and for general welfare
Customers	Fees	Specific goods and services for personal use
Grant givers	Financial resources, mandates[1]	Services to target or general population
Bond holders	Financing (for fixed periods)	Interest payments, principal repayment
Vendors	Goods and services	Payments or promises of payments
Employees	Services, skills, ideas	Compensation and benefits (current and future), non-financial benefits
Governing boards, oversight bodies	Authority, policy guidance, monitoring of performance	Power, prestige, services to constituency, likelihood of re-election, achievement of personal agenda
Managers	Skills in negotiation, persuasion and implementation	Salary, promotion, career advancement

Note: 1 From higher levels of government, to allow grants to be used in specific ways, and policies as conditions of the grant.

Source: Adapted from Chan (1981)

task is to maintain a critical mass of the inputs in the right amounts that will be necessary for the organization's ability to deliver services. In this regard, what makes financial management critical is that it controls money – the currency for acquiring a wide variety of other resources. The organizational role of the financial manager is to keep the score of finance-related exchanges, advise management on the terms of those exchanges, and monitor financial performance of all the parties concerned.

Barnard and Simon focused on individual organizations. However, the solution of many complex societal problems requires the cooperation of a network of public and private institutions (see Chapter 13). For example, in the 1999 fiscal year, the federal government in the United States spent only 5.2 percent of its total expenditures itself in direct provision of goods and services; over 70 percent was spent through "indirect government" or "third-party government" (Salamon, 2002). In such a situation, to be effective government has to empower others, rather than exercising direct control (see Kickert and Koopenjan 1997, for elaboration). In addition to minding the government's own finances, public financial managers keep a watchful eye on the viability of the institutional network and its participants. Such a role is not unlike that of an organization's financial managers, who monitor its creditors and debtors alike. This similarity has led us to name the governance model of public financial management after Barnard and Simon.

115

Table 8.2 Tools of government

Tools	Product/activity	Producer or provider	Recipient
Direct provision	Both public and private goods and services	Public agency by government employees	Service recipients, both individuals and organizations
Contracting	Goods and services with attributes of private goods	Contractors (business and nonprofit organizations)	Service recipients, mostly individuals, could be organizations
Grants	Goods and services: public or private goods	Grantee: lower level of government, non-profit organizations	The public or specific individuals
Direct loans	Credit facility, loan, borrowed money, financing	Public agency approving the loans	Individuals, businesses, other governments, non-profit organizations
Loan guarantees	Promise to make principal and interest payments in case of default of borrower	Public agency making the promise	Individuals, businesses, other governments, non-profit organizations
Insurance	Promise to pay for losses incurred	Public agency	Individuals or businesses
Regulation	Rules and regulations	Public agency	Individuals and organization subject to jurisdiction

Source: Adapted from Table 1-5 of Salamon (2002, p. 21)

Working through others provides government with more tools (Table 8.2). Besides direct provision of goods and services, government could enter into contracts with, or give grants to, business and non-profit organizations. It could provide loans, loan guarantees or insurance coverage. Even less directly, it issues regulations to influence others' behavior. Compared with taxation and spending, these are more complex contractual arrangements. They all have financial implications. Grants, loans, guarantees and insurance are financial transactions. Regulations may seem relatively inexpensive to government (other than administrative costs), but they do impose compliance costs on the regulated. In all these relationships, there exist a set of claims and obligations that bind the government and its network partners. An important function of government financial managers is to help structure contracts with network participants and monitor their contractual performance.

COMPARATIVE APPRAISAL OF THE MODELS

After discussing the models underlying public financial management individually, it is time to bring them together for comparison and appraisal in terms of their context, contents and supporting analytical disciplines.

As a service function, the role of financial management is heavily influenced by its environment. Specifically, the nature of the entity being managed and the higher-level manager tend to affect what financial managers do (Table 8.3). In a bureaucracy headed by a director bent on strong control, the financial manager follows rules and carries out orders. The same approach will not work if the financial manager works for a business-minded task-master who is constantly looking out for cost-cutting opportunities. Furthermore, a manager in the self-centered mode of NPM has to change his/her mind-set when confronted with the need to weave together a network of similarly self-interested institutions. The new environment calls for the ability to see others' perspective, an essential skill in successful negotiations.

Its different roles in altered contexts have serious implications for the content of public financial management (Table 8.4). Financial managers are rewarded for their contributions to conformity (classical model), short-term efficiency and economy (NPM model) and long-term effectiveness and equity (governance model). Consequently, they think of what is managed differently, and monitor different aspects of financial performance.

Table 8.3 Context of public financial management

	Classical model	NPM model	Governance model
Entity	A hierarchical bureaucracy in a government with separate powers and checks and balances	A mission-driven and cost-conscious strategic business unit	An organization interacting with others in a network of public, civic and business institutions
Image of the general manager	A budget-maximizing civil servant obsessed with legal compliance and financial control	A public entrepreneur focusing on customer satisfaction, raising revenues and cutting costs	A savvy executive knitting and maintaining an institutional network to deliver services
Primary role of financial management	Implementing fiscal policies on revenue, expenditure, borrowing and investment	Searching for potential revenues and least-cost method of service delivery	Securing financing in order to keep intact the organizational and network coalitions

Table 8.4 Contents of public financial management

	Classical model	NPM model	Governance model
Goals and performance criteria	Legal and contractual conformity	Efficiency, economy	Effectiveness and equity
Object of management	Organizational units and sub-units	Services, activities	Multilateral institutional relations
Key financial variables and tools	Revenues, expenditures, investments and debts	Full cost recovery, cost savings and incremental revenues	Revenues, expenditures, grants, contracts, loans, loan guarantees, insurance, regulations

Public financial management – in the broad sense – is aided by budgeting, accounting and auditing (Table 8.5). The input and control orientation in the classical model gives way to the mission-driven output budgets favored by the NPM model. The macro-perspective of the governance model requires a more encompassing (i.e. global) budget to see how resources are allocated to various service providers. Similarly, rule-based budgetary and financial accounting would not be appropriate for the NPM model; what is needed is the ability to analyze costs in support of management decisions. The multiple contractual arrangements in the governance model require keeping track of many claims and obligations. By the same token, the scope of auditing is broadened to encompass non-financial aspects of performance.

SUMMARY

Scholars of public management have over time changed their views of what a good government is. A good government used to be an efficient bureaucracy that faithfully executed public policy. More recently, advocates of "New Public Management" endow a good government with an entrepreneurial spirit that treats citizens as customers (who care more about outputs and outcomes than inputs). Now a good government plays its part in a larger institutional network. These shifting perspectives have in turn redefined the ideal public administrator/manager. She used to fight to enlarge her agency's share of the budget pie; now she cuts costs and searches for new revenues, and builds strategic alliances. In service of the new public manager, the financial staff person has to acquire new skills. It is not enough for him to know how to keep the books correctly; he has to spot opportunities for cost savings and revenue enhancements. Better still is a financial wizard who can leverage others' strengths and defeat competitors. In order to integrate the diverse finance functions, governments have appointed chief financial officers (CFOs) with expanded authority and responsibility. If the rise – and occasional spectacular fall – of corporate CFOs is any guide, public financial management will be anything but dull as governments seek to tackle their fiscal problems with rigor and creativity.

Table 8.5 *Supporting information services*

	Classical model	NPM model	Governance model
Budget	Departmental, line-item input budgets	Mission-oriented budgets with output/outcome orientation	Global budgets
Accounting	Budgetary accounting, financial accounting	Product/service costing, differential costs and benefits	Accounting for claims and obligations
Auditing	Compliance and financial audits	Operational audits: economy, efficiency	Audits focusing on outputs, outcomes, effectiveness and equity

QUESTIONS FOR REVIEW AND DISCUSSION

1   What gave rise to the three models of public financial management?
2   What are the salient features of the three models of public financial management?
3   In what ways is the classical model necessary but insufficient for governments in the contemporary world?
4   In what ways may the adoption of the NPM and Barnard-Simon governance model be regarded as reforms – changes for the better – as against mere changes?

CLASS EXERCISES

1   Should poor countries be exempted from the financial management requirements discussed in this chapter? Which one of the models discussed in this chapter is more appropriate for developing countries? Why?
2   Write the job descriptions of the following government officials: chief finance officer, budget director, comptroller, treasurer, internal auditor.
3   A local government health department operates a community mental health center. The center's basic occupancy costs (e.g. rents, utilities) are paid by the local government. However, its services are financed by grants. Currently, there are two programs. The clinic is financed by a multi-year state grant, and the community outreach program is paid by a federal grant. Today the center's executive director received three letters. The health department wants to reduce the center's budget by 20 percent. The state is cutting its grant by 30 percent, and the federal grant program is being phased out in two years. Advise the executive director what to do and how to go about it.

FURTHER READING

Richard Allen and Daniel Tommasi (eds) (2001), *Managing public expenditures. A reference book for transition countries*. Paris: OECD.

Robert D. Behn (2001), *Rethinking democratic accountability*. Washington, DC: The Brookings Institution.

John L. Mikesell (1995), *Fiscal administration*. Belmont, CA: Wadsworth.

REFERENCES

Richard Allen and Daniel Tommasi (eds) (2001), *Managing public expenditures. A reference book for transition countries*. Paris: OECD.

Chester I. Barnard (1968, originally 1938), *The functions of the executive*. Cambridge, MA: Harvard University Press.

J. L. Chan (1981), 'Standards and issues in governmental accounting and financial reporting', *Public Budgeting & Finance,* 1 (1): 55–65.

HM Treasury (2000a), *Government accounting 2000: a guide on accounting and financial procedures for use of government departments.* London: HM Treasury.

Walter J.M. Kickert and Joop F.M. Koopenjan (1997), 'Public management and network management: an overview', in Walter J. M. Kickert, Erick-Hans Klijn and Joop F. M. Koopenjan (eds), *Managing complex networks: strategies for the public sector.* London: Sage, pp. 35–61.

John L. Mikesell (1995), *Fiscal administration.* Belmont, CA: Wadsworth.

Olov Olson, James Guthrie and Christopher Humphrey (1998), *Global warning: debating international developments in new public financial management.* Oslo: Cappelen Akademisk Forlag.

David Osborne and Ted Gaebler (1992), *Reinventing government. How the entrepreneurial spirit is transforming the public sector.* Reading, MA: Addison-Wesley.

Lester M. Salamon (2002), *The tools of government.* Oxford: Oxford University Press.

Herbert A. Simon (1945), *Administrative behavior.* New York: Free Press.

Melissa A. Thomas (2001), 'Getting debt relief right', *Foreign Affairs,* 80 (5): 36–45.

Chapter 9

Human resource management in the public sector

Sylvia Horton, University of Portsmouth, UK

INTRODUCTION

The public sector is very labour intensive – around 70 per cent of the budgets of most public organisations are spent on staff. The management of human resources has high priority not only because of the cost but also because human resources are the agents of all government activities. There are currently over five million people employed in the UK public sector, which represents more than 20 per cent of all official employment.

There have been significant changes in the way people are managed in the public sector over the last twenty-five years around the world. Just as public administration and government have been giving way to new public management and governance, so traditional personnel management has given way to human resource management (HRM). This chapter examines the reasons for that change and its effect on how public officials are currently managed. Finally, it highlights some of the major issues confronting HRM in the public sector today, first in the UK and then internationally.

LEARNING OBJECTIVES

■ To identify the functions of people management in the public sector;
■ to compare and contrast traditional personnel management and HRM;
■ to examine some of the HRM issues facing public organisations today.

PERSONNEL MANAGEMENT FUNCTIONS

Personnel management is essentially about getting, retaining and developing the people skills that are required by organisations to enable them to achieve their objectives. It involves job design, recruiting and selecting staff to fill the jobs, motivating them to perform at the standards required and training and developing them to ensure they have the skills and competencies required and are equipped to cope with change. It also involves designing and administering reward systems; dealing with discipline and grievances; and ensuring that organisations operate within the regulatory frameworks set down by the law.

BOX 9.1 CLASSICAL DEFINITION OF PERSONNEL MANAGEMENT

Personnel management is directed mainly at the organisation's employees: finding and training them, arranging for them to be paid, explaining management's expectations, justifying management's actions, satisfying employees' work related needs, dealing with the problems and seeking to modify management action that could produce unwelcome employee response. Although . . . a management function, it is never totally identified with management interests . . . there is always some degree of being in between the management and the employees, mediating the needs of the each to the other.

Source: Torrington and Hall (1987, p. 14)

The latter now features very prominently in the work of personnel managers, as there is a great deal of employment and health and safety legislation, which has emanated from national governments and the European Union in the last twenty-five years.

Personnel management is contingent upon a range of environmental factors including:

- the ownership, sector, size, tradition and stage of development of an organisation;
- the political, economic, social, technological, international and legal contexts;
- the degree of stability or turbulence of the environment;
- the philosophy of people management held by senior executives;
- the competence and capacity of the organisation to resource people effectively.

The world of work has changed dramatically during the last fifty years (see Box 9.2) and it is clear that the competitive environment has been a major driver of that change. In the private

BOX 9.2 CHANGES IN THE WORLD OF WORK

- End of the 'career for life' – job mobility and new career patterns.
- Perceptions of job insecurity.
- Flexible modes of employment.
- Feminisation of the labour market.
- Globalisation and internationalisation of goods, services, finance, information and workers.
- Continuing demographic and labour market changes – ageing workforce.
- New skills profile, educated labour force and rising expectations.
- ICT revolution including e-commerce and e-government.
- The emerging knowledge economy.

sector the ever-changing environment of global competition, new technology and changes in attitudes and expectations of people as consumers and as workers have been met with new *mantras* such as 'sustainable competitive advantage', 'added value', 'core competencies', 'strategic capability' and 'employer of choice'. In the public sector the driving force is always political but today's public sector is all about efficiency, effectiveness and 'public value', concepts which are giving rise to many thorny (and contested) issues within the systems of governance that are emerging. In particular, the management of people is converging across organisations and national boundaries, although there are still significant differences between public and private organisations and between different countries which reflect contingent variables.

THE STRUCTURE OF PUBLIC SECTOR EMPLOYMENT IN THE UK

Public employees are those employed by government bodies. Their status and some important aspects of their conditions of service vary from one part of the public sector to another. Central government in the UK employs 570,000 civil servants. Historically, and still today, they are servants of the Crown and subject to rules and regulations made by government or executive order. They also have a special code of conduct (see www.cabinet-office.gov.uk), which involves being loyal to the government of the day, irrespective of its political composition, and not divulging any information unless authorised to do so (see also Chapter 21). The Cabinet Office has overall responsibility for coordinating national human resources policies as well as specific responsibility for the whole civil service. Northern Ireland has a separate civil service, which is based on law, like most civil services throughout the world.

There are nearly three million people employed by local authorities in the UK, in some 400 occupations, including teachers, social workers, planners, architects, engineers, surveyors, managers and administrators. Over one million doctors, nurses, paramedics, managers and administrators work in the National Health Service (NHS) in over 500 hospital and primary health trusts in England and in Local Health Boards in Wales, Scotland and Northern Ireland. Police officers and civilian staffs are employed by forty-three separate police authorities in England and Wales, eight in Scotland and by the Police Force of Northern Ireland. There are also a variety of non-departmental public bodies (NDPBs), each employing their own staff. Within this myriad of public bodies there is no common personnel system – each service has its own policies that are applied across all its employing bodies. In contrast to the public sector framework in other countries, the staff of these organisations (local government, NHS, police and NDPBs) do not have civil service status. The number of public officials declined after 1979, but their numbers have been rising again since 1997 (see Table 9.1).

TRADITIONAL PUBLIC SECTOR PERSONNEL MANAGEMENT

The traditional system of personnel management (TPM) in the UK public sector evolved slowly from the mid-nineteenth century but was well established by the 1950s. It was characterised by distinctive institutions and practices, which were broadly universal (see Box 9.3).

Table 9.1 UK public sector employment 1979–2005, selected years

Year	Civil service	Local government	NHS	Total
1979	738,000	2,997,000	1,152,000	7,449,000
1984	630,000	2,942,000	1,223,000	6,900,000
1994	555,000	2,642,000	1,201.000	5,290,000
1997	516,000	2,728,000	1,197,000	5,166,000
2000	516,000	2,776,000	1,285,000	5,290,000
2004	570,000	2,889,000	1,476,000	5,751,000
2005	570,000	2,929,000	1,531,000	5,848,000

Source: Adapted from Economic Trends, 1995, and Office of National Statistics, 2005

BOX 9.3 CHARACTERISTICS OF TRADITIONAL PERSONNEL MANAGEMENT IN THE UK

- An administrative personnel management function.
- A paternalistic style of management.
- Standardised employment practices.
- Collectivist patterns of industrial relations.
- A model and good practice employer.

Source: Farnham and Horton (1996a, p. 80)

Personnel policies were determined by politicians and senior civil servants and administered by the respective organisations. Recruitment procedures, pay, conditions of service and all personnel regulations were centrally determined. There was little discretion left to line managers or personnel specialists. The Treasury had overall responsibility for public expenditure and personnel and set down the general policies. The style of management was paternalistic, and this was reflected in concern for the welfare of employees and the expectation that they would be treated fairly and equitably. Employment practices, covering recruitment, pay and conditions, were very closely regulated. Recruitment was open and competitive using clearly prescribed examinations, tests and interviews. There were standard contracts, that provided for continuous, life-long employment and generous pension rights, although some public services, such as the NHS, local government and education, had large numbers of part-time workers. National pay structures had incremental scales and automatic increases of salary each year. This meant that, whatever part of the country or whatever department they were working in, public employees were paid the same, according to their grade and length of service. They also received the same holidays, sick leave and pension rights.

Pay and conditions were determined by collective bargaining and joint regulation and union membership was very high, ranging from 60 to 90 per cent throughout the public sector.

BOX 9.4 WHAT MAKES A 'GOOD EMPLOYER'

The Good Employer should ensure that it . . .

■ offers satisfactory rewards – pay, pensions and security;

■ provides a worthwhile job and the means to do it so that in the short-term the individual can give of his/her best and in the long-term can have opportunities for advancement;

■ provides a good working environment;

■ shows consideration towards staff and respects their aspirations and needs;

■ provides security and a sense of common purpose.

Source: Civil Service Department (1975, p. 8) (Crown copyright)

Government was considered to be a 'good' employer (see Box 9.4) and to set an example to the private sector as a 'model' employer. Central government offered fair wages and, from the 1950s, equal pay for women. It was the first to provide occupational pensions and to gradually reduce working hours. This commitment to being a good employer was not always practised consistently. Moreover, it was not simply altruistic – these practices were aimed primarily at attracting and retaining the best-qualified staff and people with a public service motivation. This remains a major concern today in an increasingly competitive labour market environment.

Until the 1970s there were no professional personnel managers. The personnel administrators (or 'establishment officers') had very limited discretion in the interpretation and the application of standardised policies, and line managers had very few personnel responsibilities. In the civil service, for example, the recruitment of all staff was done through centrally organised competitions run by the Civil Service Commission. Pay and conditions of service were standardised to ensure uniform treatment throughout the country and to avoid competition. A national service existed in which policies and procedures were consistently and uniformly applied.

FROM TRADITIONAL PERSONNEL MANAGEMENT TO HRM

During the 1970s these personnel practices came under attack. This was part of a more fundamental ideological attack on welfare Keynesianism and 'big government' in the context of creeping globalisation and the changing international economic environment (Farnham and Horton, 1993). Public services were condemned as overstaffed, inefficient, supplier-led and unresponsive to public needs or demands. Public sector trade unions and professional associations were seen as over-powerful and able to force up wages and to push for continuous growth of the public sector, causing public expenditure to rise and draining resources away from the private sector. Other criticisms were that rewards were not linked to performance or productivity and public services were dominated by either generalist administrators or professionals and were not managed like the private sector. Since the 1980s the public services in the UK have been transformed and TPM has been replaced by HRM.

BOX 9.5 CORE IDEAS COMMON TO HRM MODELS

1   People are an organisation's most important resource and the key to its success.

2   People are an asset, and investment in 'human capital' is good business. The capital must be maintained and developed to ensure the full exploitation of its potential value.

3   Human resources strategy must be integrated with business strategy to ensure the achievement of organisational goals and objectives.

4   Employees must be committed to the organisation's mission, goals and objectives and to its values to ensure 'business' success.

5   The right to manage is legitimised by the need for the organisation to survive in competitive environments and to achieve its goals and objectives.

HRM is sometimes used as a loose synonym for personnel management, but here it is used to denote a distinctive approach to managing people. It has its origins in the writings of US scientific management and human relations theorists in the first half of the twentieth century (Mullins, 2005), but in its current form it emerged in the late 1970s in the USA. It is essentially a business-oriented approach to managing people. There are a number of HRM models that either describe or prescribe how human resource policies should be/are integrated with strategic business planning to create or reinforce an appropriate organisational culture and to gain the commitment of staff to the goals and objectives of the organisation (see Beardwell and Holden (1994) for a discussion of the models).

Storey (1995) identifies two approaches to HRM that he defines as 'hard' and 'soft'. 'Hard' HRM focuses on strategy and the utilisation of human *resources* and concentrates on head counts, costs and performance. It is rational, calculative, business-centred and rooted in managerial concerns for efficiency and economy. Staff represents a cost to be minimised and controlled, rather than an asset to be valued. In contrast, 'soft' HRM regards human resources as a vital investment and focuses on people-centred policies such as staff development, training, communication, motivation and leadership. Evidence suggests there is an attempt in UK public services to balance the two, although external environmental factors appear to determine which strategy is foremost at any one time.

THE PROCESS OF CHANGE

The process of change from TPM to HRM in the public services has been incremental, but today all public services have HR Directors and HR strategies and reflect many of the characteristics outlined in the HRM model above. In contrast to the highly centralised, standardised, cost-oriented, ad hoc and pragmatic approach of TPM, which was short term, employee-centred and separated from other aspects of policy, HRM is decentralised, 'business'-oriented, steered from the centre but locally managed. The fragmented organisations that make up today's public services are more open and diverse, and their HR policies and practices reflect, in many ways, the private sector on which they are increasingly modelled.

The process by which they have been transformed can be divided into several stages and illustrates some of the significant changes in the way that people are now managed.

Downsizing and the introduction of performance management

The aim of UK governments during the 1980s was to reduce the size of the state and public expenditure. They privatised many public utilities and forced cuts in manpower in the civil service by imposing strict budgets and manpower ceilings. Performance management was introduced, requiring every department to decide what business they were in, what their goals and objectives were, how they were going to achieve them and what standards and criteria they were going to apply to assess their efficiency and effectiveness. At the level of individual members of staff, annual appraisals were used for setting objectives and targets and assessing performance. In 1986 the government imposed performance-related pay (PRP) and required central government departments and agencies to phase in its implementation and link it to individual performance appraisals. Performance management was gradually introduced into all other parts of the public sector, and tight financial and performance targets were set by central government for them to achieve. New financial systems, involving the delegation of budgets, saw the creating of 'line managers', accountable for the way the budgets were spent and achieving the targets set for them, including savings on staffing costs.

Structural re-engineering

A report by the Efficiency Unit (1988) stated that improvements in the management of the civil service were being impeded by its over-centralised structure and the size and complexity of its departments. It recommended that all executive activities should be hived off from departments, set up as agencies and run by chief executives with extensive delegated managerial authority (see also Chapter 17). Between 1988 and 1997, over 150 agencies were created (James, 2003). From 1996 they were given full control of all personnel matters, which meant they could decide who to recruit, what types of contract to offer, how to train, develop and assess their staff and what reward systems to apply. Personnel management was now highly decentralised and could reflect the particular needs of each organisation. Differences in structures, policies and procedures produced a very complex and fragmented civil service but gave departments and agencies great flexibility.

Structural re-engineering was not confined to the civil service but occurred throughout the public sector. For example, local authorities were compulsorily required openly to tender for contracts to provide manual services, thus exposing them to the market. As a result authorities rationalised their internal structures, introduced purchaser-provider splits and delegated personnel responsibilities. They were also subject to financial cutbacks designed to force them to review their activities and their wage bills.

Total quality management

During the 1990s public organisations were exposed to total quality management (TQM). The Citizen's Charter (Prime Minister's Office, 1991) set down quality standards for all parts of the public sector and required them to produce charters and benchmarks against which the quality of their services could be judged by service users, internal management and central government departments. The private sector became the benchmark for developments in performance and quality management; in 1996 the Cabinet Office adopted the European Business Excellence Model, later called the EFQM Excellence Model, against which civil service departments, and all other public organisations, were required to test their management processes, including their personnel management (see also Chapter 12). In order to develop customer-oriented behaviour, public officials were often trained in 'customer-first' practices, required to wear name badges and to work in more open environments. The public was now seen as customers and consumers of public services and not subjects or citizens.

Investors in People and competency management

All these developments have had an effect on personnel. The public services have been managerialised since 1979, and management skills and competencies have assumed great importance in selecting and developing public officials. Moreover, investing in people to ensure they have the knowledge, skills and abilities to do their jobs has also been given high priority (see Case Example 9.1).

Competency management is an integrated set of activities concentrated on implementing and developing competencies of individuals, teams and organisations in order to realise the mission and the goals of the organisation and improve the performance of its staff. It is a particular approach to identifying, attracting, developing and rewarding the competencies necessary to realise the mission, goals, objectives and targets of the organisation (Horton, 2006, p. 63). The use of a competency approach and competency frameworks is now widespread throughout the public services (CIPD, 2001; Farnham and Horton, 2002; Horton, 2006). Many claims are made for competency management, and it is a key characteristic of contemporary HRM, but there is still very little empirical evidence that it delivers what is claimed or that it adds value to the organisation. In Box 9.6 you can see the six main competencies identified in the competency framework use within the Senior Civil Service.

CASE EXAMPLE 9.1 **THE HRM STANDARD INVESTORS IN PEOPLE**

In the reception area of many public agencies in the UK you can now see a plaque stating that their HRM policy has been accredited by the organisation Investors in People (IiP). This is the national standard against which organisations assess their policies and practices in managing people. It was launched in 1991 by the Department of Employment as a means of encouraging national training and development. The IiP process is linked to advanced HR development strategies and ensures that training and development reinforce corporate objectives, business plans and performance targets.

For further information, see www.investorsinpeople.co.uk (accessed 16 May 2008).

> ## BOX 9.6 THE COMPETENCY FRAMEWORK FOR THE SENIOR CIVIL SERVICE: LEADERS FOR RESULTS
>
> This framework is used in the selection of the top civil servants and in identifying areas for training and development.
>
> - Giving purpose and direction: creating and communicating a vision for the future.
> - Making a personal impact: leading by example.
> - Thinking strategically: harnessing ideas and opportunities to achieve goals.
> - Getting the best from people: motivating and developing people to achieve high performance.
> - Learning and improving: drawing on experience and new ideas to improve results.
> - Focusing on delivery: achieving value for money and results.
>
> *Source*: Farnham and Horton (2002, p. 41)

Developments in HRM continued under the Labour government elected in 1997. Its *Modernising Government* (Cabinet Office, 1999a) agenda was committed to continual improvement in public services and ensuring that public officials were capable of delivering its policies of modernisation and reform. New emphasis was placed on creativity, radical thinking and embracing collaborative working. Civil servants were required to be more risk-taking and innovative, and the government would provide incentives for innovation and excellent service delivery (Cabinet Office, 1999a). *Reform of the Civil Service* (Cabinet Office, 1999b) had six themes reflecting a new HRM approach. These included better and more integrated strategic and business planning (including HR planning); sharper performance planning; strong leadership, with a clear sense of purpose; greater diversity; more openness; and a better deal for staff. These same themes permeated the government policies for the rest of the public sector.

The latest development in HRM is the introduction of a new *Professional Skills in Government* programme, which is designed to ensure that all civil servants have the requisite skills and competencies to fill the jobs at every level, and it is mirrored by training offered at the National School of Government. Local government, the NHS, education and the police all have their own HR strategies for ensuring that their staffs have the skills and competencies required in the twenty-first century and the leadership to steer their organisations.

INTERNATIONAL TRENDS IN PUBLIC SECTOR HRM

Many of the trends identified in UK public services can also be seen in other OECD countries (Demmke, 2004; Farnham and Horton, 1996b, 2000, Farnham *et al.*, 2005; Pollitt and Bouckaert, 2004; OECD, 2005a). Throughout the OECD many HR practices for public servants are becoming more like those in private organisations.

A number of OECD countries have changed the legal status and employment conditions of civil servants (a process termed 'normalisation' in the Netherlands). Similarly, in Italy the

129

'privatisation' of public sector employment since 1993 meant aligning the employment conditions, which have traditionally been governed by separate rules, with those in the private sector. The same reform is currently under way in Portugal. However, most Eastern European countries have modelled their civil service system on the German system, which still foresees life-time employment for the core civil service within a public law framework.

Other changes, including flexible working patterns (Nomden, 2000) and flexible pay (White, 2000), are now widespread. The distinction between career- and position-based civil service systems is blurring as countries are opening up their public services to recruit people with specialist skills on short-term employment contracts, career civil servants are being seconded to private organisations and there is far more voluntary exit at mid-career stage (Demmke, 2004). Further, many OECD countries have been experimenting with PRP, although only a handful of countries have adopted an extended, formalised PRP policy (Denmark, Finland, Korea, New Zealand, Switzerland and the UK) (OECD, 2005a). Clearly, experiences with PRP have been mixed. Even though PRP is a very attractive idea for many governments, some schemes have had design and implementation problems with negative effects on staff motivation. In particular, performance assessment is inherently difficult in the public sector (see Chapter 11).

There is also some weakening of the collectivist cultures of public services, as trade union membership is declining in many countries, although that trend is less evident in the Scandinavian countries and Germany, where there is a long tradition of partnership and co-determination, and in countries such as Belgium, where trade unions are closely linked to political parties.

CASE EXAMPLE 9.2 **PERFORMANCE-RELATED PAY IN THE UK CIVIL SERVICE**

In an evaluation of the Civil Service Reform Programme, involving interviews with a wide range of civil servants in four departments in 2002 and 2005, it was clear that PRP was widely disliked ('like bald men scrambling over a comb', one respondent commented), although for an inventive array of different reasons. No issue in the Civil Service reform agenda was so widely or so strongly held to undermine the basic principles of effective working in the civil service or said to have resulted in so much unnecessary effort. One top manager summed up the current PRP system in his organisation as 'irrelevant to our core concerns, divisive within teams and unfair in the sense that the highest gains do not go to those staff who contribute most to the effective working of the organization'.

Interviewees, at all levels, suggested the need for more freedom to experiment with reward approaches that would recognise team effort and that would not rely so much on monetary compensation. While team working can be and often is rewarded (usually by non-monetary mechanisms) below the level of the Senior Civil Service (SCS), a number of interviewees insisted that there was little or no incentive for it within the SCS.

Source: Adapted from Bovaird and Russell (2007, pp. 314–15)

Clearly, while it is possible to identify common trends in OECD countries, HR systems are still very different.

KEY GOVERNANCE ISSUES IN HRM

All countries are currently faced with a number of pressing HR issues. One is the *ageing of the population and the work force*. This is creating pressure for changes in service delivery and HRM. In addition to changing demands for health, pensions and social services over the next ten to fifteen years, around 20 per cent of the public sector workforce will be retiring, and by 2040 it is estimated there will be only one person in the workforce for every retired person. This has resulted in the OECD undertaking research into 'good practice' in managing government employment in the context of an ageing population (OECD, 2007).

A second issue facing HRM is that of *diversity*. All countries are faced with pressures to examine their diversity strategies to ensure that their public services do not discriminate on the grounds of gender, ethnicity, religion, sexual orientation and now age (see also Chapter 20). Diversity is intended to move HR systems away from an emphasis on representation of groups to an emphasis on individual worth and contribution to the organisation. In particular, in the UK recent civil service reforms have strongly focused on diversity issues by asking for 'a dramatic improvement in diversity' (Bovaird and Russell, 2007, p. 310). However, what often happens in practice is examined in Case Example 9.3.

CASE EXAMPLE 9.3 **DIVERSITY MANAGEMENT IN THE UK CIVIL SERVICE**

The field of *diversity* was regarded by virtually all [those interviewed in our four civil service case studies] as critically important and, in each organisation, it was stressed that substantial efforts were being made to improve both employment and user profiles (relative to the population profiles of the relevant catchment areas). . . . However, diversity – interpreted in terms of both staff composition and service delivery – was not a high profile element in any of the change programmes studied, with the exception of [the Health and Safety Executive] which had been in the vanguard of moving from 'equal opportunity' policies to 'diversity management'. . . . There was no suggestion from any of our interviewees that the diversity drive had so far threatened the tradition of civil service recruitment and promotion on meritocratic principles – although a small number expressed concerns that this might happen at some stage in the future, if the current drive continued and was successful. [In the Department for International Development] there was general pride in the fact that ethnic diversity had been achieved at the very top – but staff in all case studies pointed out that many top managers were still 'Oxbridge types'. Overall, there was general consensus that momentum had grown in tackling this issue since the start of the [the Civil Service Reform Programme] but progress continued to be patchy.

Source: Bovaird and Russell (2007, p. 314)

A third issue is *Leadership*. The OECD and its member states now recognise the need for leadership in rapidly changing and modernising public organisations. They accept that leaders can be developed and trained and have evolved strategies and policies to raise the profile of leaders and leadership throughout their public services (see also Chapter 18). In the UK, centres of excellence in leadership have been established for all parts of the public sector, including local and central government, health, defence, education and police (Horton and Farnham, 2007). Similar leadership programmes are mushrooming in other OECD countries, albeit, in many cases, quite traditional management training hides behind the new label. Despite an absence of definitive empirical evidence indicating the critical relationship between leadership and performance, and the difficulty in measuring the strength of this relationship, it is becoming increasingly accepted that appropriate leadership is a key ingredient in the effective performance of individuals, groups, organisations, regions and even nation states in the contemporary world (Bolden, 2004).

SUMMARY

HRM is a key area of management. If the HR policies are not right then public organisations will not attract the human resources they need to perform the functions of government and deliver the services that government has promised the electorate. In our modern system of governance it is not only those employed in public organisations but also those in the voluntary and private organisations, in partnerships or contracted to deliver the services who are important. There are clear trends towards convergence of HR practices, both nationally and internationally, but there are contextual factors that impose limits on the extent of that convergence.

QUESTIONS FOR REVIEW AND DISCUSSION

1   What do you understand by HRM and how, if at all, does it differ from personnel management?
2   Why do you think HRM was introduced in the UK? Against which criteria would you judge its success?
3   What are the key HRM issues facing governments today in your country? Do they differ between levels of government?

READER EXERCISES

1   Why do you think people are attracted to the civil service and local government? Do you think the reasons have changed in recent years?
2   What are the functions associated with HRM? Think about the links between them and how a competency framework can be used to integrate them.
3   What purposes can staff appraisal serve? What are barriers to these purposes being successfully achieved?

CLASS EXERCISES

1   In two groups identify the main characteristics of either traditional people management (TPM) or new people management (HRM). In a plenary session discuss the major similarities and differences.
2   Working in 4 subgroups representing (a) a local authority, (b) a NHS Trust, (c) a civil service agency or department, and (d) a police authority, research the HR policies of each type of organisation. In the plenary session, the groups should compare and discuss their respective HR policies.
3   In groups discuss the following two questions and feed back into a whole class discussion:
    ■   In what ways is the world of work changing compared with twenty years ago and what changes do you envisage over the next twenty years?
    ■   What are the implications of the changing world of work for employees, managers and for the HR professionals within public organisations?

FURTHER READING

Tony Bovaird and Ken Russell (2007), 'Civil service reform in the UK, 1999–2005: revolutionary failure or evolutionary success?', *Public Administration*, 85 (2): 301–28.

Christoph Demmke (2004), *European civil services between tradition and reform*. Maastricht, Netherlands: European Institute of Public Administration.

David Farnham and Sylvia Horton (2000), *Human resources flexibilities in the public services*. Basingstoke: Macmillan.

Sylvia Horton, David Farnham and Annie Hondeghem (eds) (2002), *Competency management in the public sector: European variations on a theme*. Amsterdam: IOS.

OECD (2005c), *Performance-related pay policies for government employees*. Paris: OECD.

REFERENCES

Ian Beardwell and Len Holden (1994), *Human resource management: a contemporary approach*. Harlow: FT Prentice Hall.

R. Bolden (2004), *What is leadership*? Exeter: Leadership South West.

Tony Bovaird and Ken Russell (2007), 'Civil service reform in the UK, 1999–2005: revolutionary failure or evolutionary success?', *Public Administration*, 85 (2): 301–28.

Cabinet Office (1999a), *Modernising government*, Cm 4310. London: Stationery Office.

Cabinet Office (1999b), *Reform of the civil service*. London: Stationery Office.

CIPD (2001), *Competency frameworks in UK organisations* (Research report). London: CIPD.

Civil Service Department (1975), *Wider issues review*. London: HMSO.

Christoph Demmke (2004), *European civil services between tradition and reform*. Maastricht, Netherlands: European Institute of Public Administration.

133

Efficiency Unit (1988), *Improving management in government: the next steps* (Report to the prime minister). London: HMSO.

David Farnham and Sylvia Horton (1993), *Managing the new public services*. Basingstoke: Macmillan.

David Farnham and Sylvia Horton (1996a), *People management in the public services*. Basingstoke: Macmillan.

David Farnham and Sylvia Horton (1996b), *New public managers in Europe*. London: Macmillan.

David Farnham and Sylvia Horton (2002), 'HRM competency frameworks in the British civil service', in Sylvia Horton, David Farnham and Annie Hondeghem (eds), *Competency management in the public sector: European variations on a theme*. Amsterdam: IOS, pp. 33–47.

David Farnham, Annie Hondeheim and Sylvia Horton (2005), *Staff participation and public management reform: some international comparisons*. Basingstoke: Palgrave Macmillan.

HMSO (1991), *The citizen's charter. Raising the standard*. London: HMSO.

Sylvia Horton (2006), 'Competencies in people resourcing', in Stephen Pilbeam and Marjorie Corbridge (eds), *People resourcing: contemporary HRM in practice*. London: FT Prentice Hall.

Sylvia Horton and David Farnham (2007), 'Turning leadership into performance management', in Rainer Koch and Pat Weller (eds), *Public governance and leadership*. Wiesbaden: Gabler Edition, Wissenschaft Deutscher Universitäts-Verlag, pp. 429–55.

Oliver James (2003), *The executive agency revolution in Whitehall*. Basingstoke: Palgrave.

Laurie Mullins (2005), *Management and organisational behaviour*. London: Prentice Hall.

Kohn Nomden (2000), 'Flexible working patterns in European public administration', in David Farnham *et al.* (eds), *Human resources flexibilities in the public services*. London: Macmillan, pp. 280–97.

OECD (2005a), *Modernising government: the way forward*. Paris: OECD.

OECD (2007a), *Ageing and the public service: human resource challenges*. Paris: OECD.

Christopher Pollitt and Geert Bouckaert (2004), *Public management reform: a comparative analysis* (2nd edn). Oxford: Oxford University Press.

John Storey (1995), *Human resource management: a critical text*. London: Routledge.

Derek Torrington and Laura Hall (1987), *Personnel management*. Hemel Hempsted: Prentice Hall.

Geoff White (2000), 'Pay flexibility in European public services: a comparative analysis', in David Farnham *et al.* (eds), *Human resources flexibilities in the public services*. London: Macmillan, pp. 255–79.

Chapter 10

Managing ICTs in public sector organizations

Christine Bellamy, Nottingham Trent University, UK

INTRODUCTION

It was in the early years of the 1990s that governments throughout the developed world first became seriously interested in the potential contribution of information and communications technologies (ICTs) to transforming public services and governance (Bellamy and Taylor, 1998). Since then, we have seen huge changes in these technologies and in the ways they are used. ICTs are no longer elite technologies, available only to those with special training and know-how. Innovations such as those listed below have focused policymakers' minds on how governments should change in order to take advantage of the pervasive presence of these technologies amongst the citizens they serve:

- the extraordinary growth of the Internet and World Wide Web;
- public acceptance of plastic card technology and the important shift to online shopping; and
- the advent of third-generation (3G), multi-function mobile phones, hand-held gadgets such as iPods and BlackBerries, and digital interactive TV (DTV).

Just as business has learnt to exploit e-commerce, so government and public services have been obliged to learn how to exploit the capabilities associated with e-government and e-democracy.

Many commentators have expressed the hope that the wise use of ICTs will help to restore the legitimacy of political institutions and public services, by increasing their accessibility, responsiveness and comprehensibility and allowing citizens to engage with them more easily and influentially. It is widely recognized, however, that this hope is likely to be frustrated if the use of electronic channels to deliver public services and promote democratic engagement creates new forms of social exclusion, by encouraging an ever-widening 'digital divide' between people with access to new technologies – and the skills and confidence to use them – and those without. Digital government will also miss its marks, if citizens do not trust digital technologies or fear that governments will abuse personal information carried on public service information systems. For their part, public services also need increasingly robust guarantees about the identity of citizens, if online transactions are not to be plagued by fraud.

Thus, investing in the right technologies and getting them to work reliably is only part of the challenge posed by ICTs: information-age government also requires the establishment of effective policies for social inclusion, privacy and identity management. In this chapter, we will examine these issues in the context of current government policies and practices.

LEARNING OBJECTIVES

- To be aware of the changing understanding of the significance of ICTs, and their implications for public service delivery and democratic practice;
- to understand the need for active policies to minimize the 'digital divide';
- to understand the crucial importance of protecting personal data and managing identity.

THE STRATEGIC SIGNIFICANCE OF ICTS: FROM A FOCUS ON TECHNOLOGY TO A FOCUS ON INFORMATION

Governments have used computers on a significant scale for non-military, administrative purposes only since the early 1970s. The marked interest in joining up computers via electronic networks dates from the 1980s, and it was later still, with the arrival of the Internet in the mid-1990s, that governments began to develop e-channels for exchanging information with citizens. Digital technologies are relative newcomers to the toolbox of governance. Nevertheless, they are tools that fit very well with the strategic aspirations of twenty-first century governments to transform public service delivery. These aspirations have their intellectual roots in two sets of literature developed in the late 1980s and early 1990s. Their influence in government reflects a (largely) one-way transfer of ideas from private to public sector, and reflects the important shift from a preoccupation with *technology* as a strategic resource to a growing interest in *information* and its strategic exploitation.

The relationship between technology and business strategy

The first set of ideas deals with the relationship between ICT and strategic management (for example, Scott Morton, 1991). Its main purpose was to persuade managers that technology should cease to be regarded simply as a tool for *implementing* business strategy. Rather, the new information and communications capabilities associated with ICTs should be used to *shape* strategy. New, more speedy and direct ways of communicating with customers and suppliers would allow better intelligence about the market to be collected and exploited, new distribution techniques to be developed and new supply chains to be constructed. Managers should ask not *'how can ICT help me do my business?'* but *'how can I best do business now that I have ICT?'* This literature also tended to follow a 'technological determinist' approach: i.e. it assumed that technology was a key driver for change, and that businesses that failed to recognize the strong 'economic imperative of ICT' would fail in an increasingly competitive world.

Re-engineering processes – towards joined-up electronic services

This second set of ideas has directly influenced the discourse through which e-government continues to be discussed (Davenport, 1993). It critiques the highly fragmented departmental structures associated with traditional bureaucracies and asserts that new information systems fail mainly because they replicate this fragmentation, with the result that customer data remain imprisoned in departmental 'silos', preventing organizations from responding flexibly and holistically to customers' needs. Business process re-engineering (BPR) advocates, instead, that business processes and bureaucratic structures should be *fundamentally* re-engineered (see Chapter 13). First, processes should be integrated *horizontally* (i.e. between departments), to build up a full picture of a customer's needs, preferences and transaction history. Second, BPR advocates *vertical* integration between supply, production, distribution and consumption. For example, processing a welfare claim effectively depends on the quality and timeliness of data lodged by the claimant. It follows that inviting customers to input data themselves – perhaps over the Internet – is not only cheaper and faster but likely to increase accuracy. 'Direct' services, in the manner of 'direct' banking or insurance services, are, therefore, both cost-effective *and* better. Costs and red-tape could be reduced still further, if basic personal data (name, address, gender, date of birth, marital status, for example) are *shared* between information systems across government rather than collected separately by each department. Indeed, many governments worldwide are becoming interested in developing a central register of residents and citizens, or at least a virtual one, ensuring that basic data about citizens are consistent across government. This register would be updated as citizens navigate key 'life events', such as being born, getting married, becoming employed, moving house or entering into residential care.

TRANSFORMING GOVERNMENTS FOR THE INFORMATION AGE: DEVELOPING ELECTRONIC SERVICE DELIVERY

In the mid to late 1990s, many countries developed plans for e-government, beginning with the highly influential National Performance Review (Office of the Vice President, 1993) published by the Clinton Administration in the USA. The plans for Australia, Canada, Estonia, Singapore, South Korea, the UK, the USA and the Scandinavian countries are often considered to be the most successful. All of them place a great deal more emphasis on electronic service delivery (ESD), especially via the Internet, than on other applications of ICTs, including e-democracy.

Governments tend to use websites most intensively to publish information for public services customers. Many sites also provide forms for customers to download, and most now offer facilities to make payments, apply for services or licences, or register property ownership or important life events: indeed, the ability to conduct transactions online is a key criterion by which the European Union benchmarks member states' prowess in e-government. The study *Government on the Internet* (Comptroller and Auditor-General, 2007) reveals, for example, that British citizens could apply and pay for a driving licence, apply for, be offered and accept a university place, file their annual tax return, file company accounts and obtain a real-time forecast of their state pension, although they could not yet apply online for social security

137

benefits. Overall, this report estimated that around 25 per cent of public services in EU member states could be completed online, with Sweden offering most and Latvia, least. Other important surveys are the EU's Benchmarking Report (Capgemini, 2007) and the annual *Global E-Government Report* (West, 2007).

It is important to recognize that the growing availability of online transactions is not, of itself, an indicator of enhanced service quality: some information-age services are better delivered through other channels, especially the phone. Services for the sick, the poor and elderly people – such as social security, health and advice services (for example, the British medical helpline, *NHS Direct)* – need to be mediated by appropriately trained human beings in call centres or in real-world offices. Other groups in the population, in particular young people, are much more likely to access public services through the Internet as Case Example 10.1 demonstrates.

In other words, one important issue for the management of digital-age services is the development of 'channel strategies' offering the best mix of delivery modes to meet the needs of different groups of citizens.

This point brings us to a key question: how best to use the flexibilities offered by ICTs, to shift from the one-size-fits-all approach hitherto adopted by public bureaucracies, to one that tailors services to the needs of different segments of the population, such as the elderly,

CASE EXAMPLE 10.1 **COUNSELLING ON SEXUALITY ISSUES FOR YOUNG PEOPLE**

Stradanove (www.stradanove.net/, accessed 16 May 2008) is a website for young people, managed by the city of Modena on behalf of the region of Emilia-Romagna in Italy. The initiative started in 1997 when the regional government passed a new law relating to the 'promotion and coordination of policies oriented towards young people' (Law 21/96) and set up a budget to implement it. Since then, this regional budget has been reduced, and the local authority is currently looking for new resources to sustain the initiative. The website is visited daily by thousands of users from all over Italy and abroad. The information on the website is provided by a team of young volunteers, supported by experts who can also provide advice online. The content on the site has two themes: practical information (work, sex, personal safety, drugs, studies, travel, etc.) and current 'what's on?' information (music, cinema, theatre, books, etc.) and 'what's up?' (news, new techologies, etc.). *Stradanove* has demonstrated that a public agency can provide high-quality advice through the Internet very successfully. It has also triggered new ways of using public services that were previously impossible. A significant example concerns sexual behaviour. While young girls and couples typically are happy to seek regular counselling on a face-to-face basis, young men are much more reluctant to do so. Since this counselling has been available on the website, many young men have made use of it.

Source: www.govint.org (accessed 16 May 2008, see interview section)

students, farmers, the unemployed or owners of small businesses. One approach is to use electronic networks to join up back-office systems, so that departments can be physically reconfigured to enable the services used by the same client group to be co-delivered. For example, the British Department of Work and Pensions (www.dwp.gov.uk, accessed 16 May 2008) has been reorganized into three 'businesses' that deliver DWP services to people of working age, pensioners and the disabled, respectively. The most ambitious example of this approach is the Australian agency *Centrelink*, which was hived off from the Australian Department of Social Security in 1997 (www.centrelink.gov.au, accessed 16 May 2008). *Centrelink* not only administers all social security benefits to its various 'client groups', but also delivers services to them on behalf of ten other government departments. An increasing range of these services are now delivered online.

In the digital age, ICTs can also enable the clustering of services through front-offfice, one-stop electronic outlets aimed at different sections of the population, regardless of the configuration of back-office departments, and this may be easier to achieve than radical organizational change. Thus, many e-government strategies focus heavily on creating one-stop 'portals'. For example, the British government's portal for business (www.businesslink.gov.uk, accessed 16 May 2008) offers businesses access to a growing range of transactions and information relating to a wide range of matters, including tax, employment policy, environmental policy and health and safety regulations. Indeed, the development of a flagship portal for government has formed a critical plank in the strategies of world-leading countries. This approach enables government to establish a well-known, trusted brand for all its electronic public services, thus increasing uptake of services and public confidence in electronic channels. For example, *Directgov* is now the official brand of e-government in Britain. Its portal (www.direct.gov.uk/en/index.htm, accessed 16 May 2008) offers access to a huge range of services, which are presented partly by 'product group' (for example, services relating to motoring, employment and 'environment and greener living') and partly by 'client group' (for example, services for young people, over 50s and parents). In this way, it is hoped that the wide and confusing variety of public services will become easier to use. Indeed, an important function commonly ascribed to web technologies is to mask the underlying complexity of the machinery of government in contemporary states, making them more comprehensible and accountable to their citizens. Grappling with such complexity may, however, be easier said than done. *Directgov* is the third attempt to design a clear, branded, single portal for British public services. Its present format is the result of a lot of hard thinking – and much trial and error – regarding the best way of representing a government system composed of a vast range of departments, agencies and ad hoc bodies and of several tiers of government, including local authorities and the devolved administrations in Scotland, Wales and Northern Ireland. In contrast, the online portal of the Australian state of Victoria – one of the early movers in e-government (see Case Example 10.2) – shows what can be done by forceful leadership operating in a simpler governmental system, serving a much smaller population. Readers may also be interested to explore the functions and service clusters offered by other leading government portals, for example the Canadian Government portal at www.servicecanada.gc.ca (accessed 16 May 2008), and the US Federal Government portal at www.usa.gov (accessed 16 May 2008).

CASE EXAMPLE 10.2 **THE PORTAL OF THE AUSTRALIAN STATE OF VICTORIA: WWW.VIC.GOV.AU**

In the middle of the 1990s, the Australian State of Victoria decided to invest heavily in the development of e-government, as a way of providing cost-efficient, modern public services for a small population spread over a large geographical territory. Since then, Victoria has become one of the acknowledged leaders in ESD. The development of ESD was assisted by a number of factors, including:

■ strong political leadership – in the form of a new premier strongly committed to e-government;

■ effective project management – in the form of an energetic project manager operating with clear lines of accountability;

■ a population that was willing to engage with new technology.

A key feature is the extensive and well-designed portal. This portal now clusters services mainly by the relevant department (having apparently abandoned its previous policy of organizing, in part, by life events such as giving birth). Its strongest feature is the availability of facilities to undertake a wide variety of online transactions with public services: to make payments, apply for services and comply with various registration requirements online. The portal is also designed to offer links to other relevant services when each facility is used: for example, accessing the page to apply for a 'senior card' provides links to other services for elderly people.

Source: www.vic.gov.au (accessed 16 May 2008)

DEVELOPING ONLINE DEMOCRACY

If information is power, then ICTs offer huge opportunities to remove many of the barriers to accessing information and participating actively in public life. The democratic potential of ICTs seems, therefore, to be immense, but writers on e-democracy have disagreed strongly about its likely impact. There are three main scenarios. ICTs could:

■ help reinvigorate representative democracy, by enabling citizens to engage more actively with electoral processes and institutions;

■ help establish more direct forms of democracy, by obviating the need for elected representatives to mediate between citizens and government;

■ reinforce the power of existing political elites, by giving them more powerful tools for political marketing and spin.

Chadwick's book on *Internet Politics* (2006) illustrates the wide variety of e-democratic initiatives that have taken place over the last few years, but most commentators agree that, thus far at least, there is little evidence that new models of democracy are being institutionalized into the fabric of Western states. On the contrary, research suggests that Internet technologies are being tamed by political elites (Margolis and Resnick 2000), and, as we have seen, governments' attention has been more strongly focused on ESD rather than on the health of the wider political system. Nevertheless, there are encouraging signs that e-democracy is claiming some place, at least, on formal policy agendas. In Britain, for example, factors as diverse as the establishment of the new assemblies in Scotland and Wales and worryingly low election turnouts, especially among young voters, have stimulated growing, if patchy, interest in the use of ICTs to strengthen representative democracy.

British national government policy favours a twin-track approach to e-democracy. (OGC/ Office of the e-Envoy, 2002). One track is designed to 'modernize' the electoral system, for example by introducing remote electronic voting (RVEM) via the Internet or via mobile phones, which, the Government believes, would update the image of democratic politics, particularly among the young (Ministry of Justice, 2007). A report evaluating RVEM (Pratchett, 2002) led to some pilot projects (see the reports at: www.electoralcommission.org.uk/ elections/pilotsmay2007.cfm, accessed 16 May 2008). This work confirmed that a number of difficult problems still need to be solved before RVEM can more widely used. The main issues relate to:

- supervision – ensuring that voting in places other than polling stations is private and free;
- security – protecting systems from hacking, viruses, technical failure and commercial failure of IT suppliers;
- fraud – protecting the election against systematic and deliberate attempts to corrupt results;
- privacy – protecting the secrecy of votes, once cast and counted;
- public confidence – persuading voters to trust e-voting.

The second track aims to exploit ICTs to increase public participation in policy-making (see also Chapter 15). Since 1997, the British Government has introduced comprehensive arrangements for public consultations, that mandate the use of electronic media (see: bre.berr.gov.uk/regulation/consultation, accessed 16 May 2008). However, at the time of writing, *Citizenspace* (the space provided for public consultation and online discussions on an earlier version of the British government portal) had been removed, and Directgov appeared to be more focused on providing facilities for consumer complaints about inadequate local government services than for public engagement in national policy. More aggressive uses of the Internet for public engagement are to be found, instead, on the prime minister's website (www.number10.gov.uk, accessed 16 May 2008), where citizens can initiate or sign a petition to the PM, engage in web-chats with ministers, connect to the government's presence on *Youtube*, access policy briefings and watch videos about current issues, while the British Parliament site (www.Parliament.uk, accessed 16 May 2008) offers live video-feeds of debates both in the chambers and committees. Sub-national governments (local authorities and devolved administrations in Scotland, Wales and Northern Ireland) also experiment with online e-democratic initiatives: some are described in Case Example 10.3.

CASE EXAMPLE 10.3 **E-DEMOCRACY IN BRITISH GOVERNMENTS: SOME EXAMPLES**

■ www.camden.gov.uk (accessed 16 May 2008) – the website of the London Borough of Camden, which provides facilities for involvement in local decisions, for example, by providing an online consultation board, lists of public meetings and the opportunity to sign up for consultation alerts.

■ www.wales.gov.uk (accessed 16 May 2008) – this dual-language site provides formal minutes of all the Assembly's committees, along with information about public meetings and events, and details of public consultations being undertaken by the executive of the Welsh Assembly. Facilities for online feedback are also provided. Readers may be particularly interested in the Welsh national ICT strategy at www.cymruarlein.wales.gov.uk/ (accessed 16 May 2008).

■ www.scottish.parliament.uk (accessed 16 May 2008) – the Scottish Parliament is still the only national assembly in the UK to offer advanced facilities for online petitions. Citizens can create a petition, publicize it, invite signatures, submit it to the Parliament and join in online discussion.

MANAGING KNOWLEDGE IN THE INFORMATION AGE

'Knowledge management' (KM) has, in the last decade, become recognized as an increasingly strategic function in contemporary businesses and services (Davenport and Prusak, 1998). Its perceived importance stems from the distinction between:

■ facts and figures held in computer systems and manual files (data);
■ ordering of data into resources imbued with meaning and relevance (information);
■ constructing shared and explicit understandings of how information can be applied to solving problems and getting things done (knowledge).

KM involves 'knowing what an organization knows'. It depends on the insight that bringing better knowledge to bear on social or organizational problems may be less a matter of collecting yet more data, and more to do with exploiting the vast quantities of data already held on information systems as a result of day-to-day transactions with customers and suppliers. KM therefore involves understanding how these data can be transformed into resources that are fully valued and used, in ways that enable the organization systematically to learn and develop its business.

KM has huge implications for public management. In the course of carrying out their business, contemporary public services collect data from more or less all people who are citizens of, or who are resident in, a country. These data could, if appropriately managed, form an incomparable resource for policymakers and managers. They could help managers understand much more about their customer base (for example, who actually claims the welfare benefits to which they are entailed?) or about the incidence of particular social problems (e.g. in which neighbourhoods are most crimes actually committed and at what times of day?), so that resources can be more effectively targeted, policies refined and the impact of interventions monitored. Patients' medical records could throw considerable light, for example, on the epidemiology of disease, and data in social services, school, medical and police records could help us better understand why some neighbourhoods or people become socially excluded or suffer disproportionately from crime.

It is not surprising, therefore, that there is growing interest in data management techniques, such as:

- data matching – comparing data sets to identify cases with particular parameters (for example, matching social security and personal tax records to identify people who might be claiming benefits while undertaking paid employment; or matching benefits records with census data to identify elderly people who are not taking up welfare benefits to which they are entitled);
- data mining – analysing data already held on operational systems to yield new management or policy information (for example, analysing records of educational institutions to uncover access trends; or mapping the incidence of crimes against geographic information systems to identify hotspots on which to focus crime reduction initiatives).

INFORMATION SHARING: THE 'WICKED ISSUE' FOR E-GOVERNMENT?

It can be seen that many high-value applications of such techniques depend on bringing data together from several services or agencies. Thus knowledge management reinforces the current emphasis on joined-up government (Perri 6 *et al.*, 2002; Perri 6, 2004), which is encouraging frontline agencies to develop multi-agency approaches to addressing social problems, and especially to fight terrorism and crime. The events in New York on 11 September 2001 also stimulated interest in harnessing electronic data in the war against international terrorism. For example, in 2002 the European Parliament passed legislation allowing member states to require commercial Internet service providers to retain customer data (such billing and service usage data) for up to seven years, against the grain of data protection principles requiring that personal data should be disposed of as soon as practicable. However, an attempt by the (then) British Home Secretary considerably to extend his powers to intercept Internet traffic was temporarily withdrawn, as a result of worries aroused by the spectre of electronic surveillance.

Despite such worries, the British Government has taken an increasing number of legislative powers to share information between services to help fight such evils as social security fraud, child abuse, organized crime, anti-social behaviour and illegal immigration. In some cases, these powers include rights of access to the files of private organizations such as banks and building societies. In 2002, a report on *Privacy and Data Sharing* published by the British Cabinet Office (PIU, 2002) made nineteen proposals for new legal powers to share data between government agencies and beyond. Some, such as a proposal for automatic data exchange between the vehicle licensing agency (DVLA) and insurance companies, would simply streamline administration, but most were aimed at promoting inter-agency collaboration to reduce social ills: for example, it was proposed to share data to identify cases where children are at risk of social exclusion or deal with those who fail to attend school. Two years later, the government's strategy for *Transformational Government. Enabled by Technology* (Cabinet Office, 2005) placed huge emphasis on information sharing as a tool for achieving 'citizen-centric government' – government that focuses holistically on solving citizens' problems, regardless of the boundaries between departments or disconnections between information systems. At the time of writing in early 2008, however, the government had failed to come up with clear principles for resolving the tension between imperatives to share personal information and imperatives to safeguard privacy and ensure the confidentiality necessary to deliver services effectively, especially in socially sensitive fields. A high-level 'vision statement' was published in 2006 (www.dca.gov.uk/foi/sharing/pubs.htm, accessed 16 May 2008), prompting much talk in the media about the 'big brother state'. A cabinet committee, established to publish a detailed implementation plan, failed to do so. Information sharing looked set to become one of the 'wicked issues' in British government: too important to drop, but too contentious on which to act. Meanwhile, the government's problems were exacerbated by a widely publicized report for the Information Commissioner, which, he said, demonstrated that Britain was 'sleepwalking into the surveillance society' (Surveillance Studies Network, 2006).

SOME KEY ISSUES

This discussion begins to show why achieving e-government goes to issues beyond the relatively simple problems associated with technological innovation and organizational change, though even these problems cannot always be solved successfully, as experience in the UK and elsewhere has painfully shown (Cabinet Office, 2000). E-government strategies depend, too, on the assumption that citizens will be willing and able to use electronic channels, that they will trust governments to use personal information responsibly, and that governments can protect online transactions from fraud and other attacks. As the British Government's strategy recognizes, 'Information sharing, management of identity . . . and information assurance are therefore crucial' (Cabinet Office, 2005: para 10). The remainder of this chapter will be devoted to explaining why.

DATA QUALITY AND DATA PROTECTION

The exploitation of personal data held by public services for the purposes described above assumes that these data are accurate, up to date and complete; if this is not the case, then governments risk committing great injustices, ones that could bring public services into considerable disrepute. For example, sentencing an offender on the basis of an inaccurate criminal record, charging the wrong man for paedophilia or accusing an upright citizen of social security fraud may cause the individuals involved untold anguish and harm. This is one reason for the critical importance of effective data protection regimes. In the EU, data processing is regulated by principles originally derived from the European Convention of Human Rights (which establishes a right to privacy) and elucidated in the European Parliament's Data Protection Directive (95/46/EC). The Directive has been domesticated into the law of member states, where its implementation is monitored by national data protection registrars, for example the UK's Information Commissioner. Most public services also publish codes of practice on data protection and data sharing based on the eight European principles of data protection, which can be consulted in Schedule One of the UK's Data Protection Act at www.dataprotection.gov.uk (accessed 16 May 2008).

It will be seen that these principles require people who control personal data to process them 'fairly', and to ensure that data processing is 'proportionate' to the purposes for which it is undertaken: they would ask, for example, whether it is 'proportionate' to keep copies of the DNA of the whole population because a tiny minority of us are predatory paedophiles. Where possible, the consent of the data 'subject' should be obtained, and data should not be shared for purposes that are incompatible with those for which they were originally collected (the so-called 'finality principle'). These principles seem clear enough, but data protection law is, in practice, a minefield. As we can see from the references above to social security fraud, crime and terrorism, the right to privacy cannot be absolute: data protection law therefore requires managers in public services to make judgements about what processing *is* proportionate and when the need for consent or the finality principle *can* properly be overridden by the wider public interest. There is, unsurprisingly, considerable anxiety about the DPA in Britain today, both among managers who have to exercise such judgements, and among commentators who consider the Act either too lax or too restrictive.

AUTHENTIC IDENTITY AND PROTECTING PRIVACY

The issue that is proving even more intractable is the authentication of identity online: public services need to know that they are dealing with the right person and are aware that identity theft is increasing fast. In the late 1990s, the European Union's plans assumed that member states would lead in authenticating identity, mainly by strengthening national identity card schemes. Although such cards are compulsory in only a few European countries (notably, Belgium, Germany, Greece and Luxemburg), cards are carried voluntarily by citizens in most other countries in the EU and, with the exception of Denmark (Hoff and Rosenkrands, 2000), have not proved particularly contentious. Identity cards have not however been used in the USA, Canada, Australia or in Britain (except in time of total war), and these countries have thus far declined to become the monopoly authenticator of personal identity. Thus the British Government has tried, not very successfully, to induce the private sector to make a market in authenticating identity, for example by selling 'digital signatures' (e.g. to authenticate transactions on the British Government's secure registration service at www.gateway.gov.uk (accessed 16 May 2008)). In 2002, however, the Government broke radically with long tradition, and consulted the public about plans for a national identity card scheme backed by a citizens' register (Home Office, 2002). Legislation was passed in 2006, but these plans are very controversial, and at the time of writing the timescale for implementation was not considered to be entirely firm.

ACCESS AND EQUALITY – CLOSING THE DIGITAL DIVIDE

E-government strategies also assume that the public will have the resources, the understanding and the skill to access electronic networks. The success of e-government depends, therefore,

145

on the effectiveness of strategies to address the 'digital divide'. In Britain, this issue is being addressed in two main ways. First, the Government is committed to near universal access to the Internet, and hopes that this will be achieved as much by the rapid dissemination of 3G phones and DTV as by the spread of personal computers. To stimulate the market, the UK was an early mover in liberalizing the telecommunications industry and issuing franchises for 3G phones. Perhaps as a result, Britain is among the leading nations for access to the Internet and to DTV (Comptroller and Auditor-General, 2007).

Second, significant effort is being devoted to extending opportunities and support for people to get online. The Government has financed projects for households in socially deprived areas to try out DTV and has set up a network of UK Online Centres throughout the country, offering Internet access, IT training and advice about education and job search facilities. Most of these centres are being located in FE colleges and community centres, and all public libraries are being linked to a network offering similar facilities. UK Online is also being supported by a series of initiatives to place networked computers in all schools and to train children in e-citizenship. Similar initiatives are being taken in other countries, often by municipal governments. Case Example 10.4 features an extract from an interview with the then Head of the Information Office in Tampere, Finland, in which he discusses measures taken to address the digital divide.

CASE EXAMPLE 10.4 **MEASURES TO ADDRESS THE DIGITAL DIVIDE AT MUNICIPAL LEVEL: THE CASE OF TAMPERE, FINLAND (EXCERT FROM AN INTERVIEW)**

Mr Seppälä: It is evident to the City of Tampere that traditional service delivery must also be maintained into the future because there will continue to be a 'digital divide'. But we have also taken action to deal directly with the 'digital divide'. In particular, we offer training for citizens in various ways. For example, the City of Tampere has founded an Internet café with rather low charges for users and it has also set up 70 free Internet access points in libraries, schools and universities. The City of Tampere also has an Internet bus which travels around the city and which various social groups and associations can rent for training courses. In 2004 we also subsidized the start-up of a computer shop where citizens can get advice on PCs and professional help for software and hardware problems. It is becoming increasingly evident that all these measures are having some real impact. For example, when we introduced on-line applications for evening classes in 2001, there was not much take-up. Now 70 per cent of all applications are made on-line. A similar development has been taken place in our health-care centre where more and more appointments are made on-line. This shows that our citizens have become used to on-line services.

Source: www.govint.org (accessed 16 May 2008, see interview section)

SUMMARY

This discussion points to a rapidly changing agenda, one that raises serious issues for citizens and their political representatives, as well as for public service managers. The focus is no longer on managing technological innovation to cope with well-defined tasks. Rather, the emphasis is shifting onto the wider political significance of technologically enhanced methods of processing information and exploiting knowledge. The chapter has also raised important issues of principle, including ones that go to the heart of the meaning of such concepts as privacy and equality in contemporary citizenship. The exercises that follow are therefore designed to stimulate thinking and debate about these crucial issues.

QUESTIONS FOR REVIEW AND DISCUSSION

1 Assuming that facilities become available, what would be the main benefits and barriers for *individual citizens* in (a) voting in local elections over the Internet or (b) taxing a car online. What steps could public services take to maximize trust in using such facilities among a wide cross-section of the population?

2 Why have governments become more interested in e-democracy in recent years, and by what criteria would you judge its success?

3 Why have governments become more interested in sharing personal information between public services in recent years? What benefits and dangers are there (a) *for citizens* and (b) *for governments* if this practice is extended?

4 Why should governments be worried about the 'digital divide'. How would you assess attempts to address it, either in your own country or in Tampere, Finland?

READER EXERCISES

1 Visit at least some of the portals cited in this chapter and also the website of your own local or municipal authority. Make a note of the main features offered by these sites, and also take note of the ways in which services are clustered (for example, are they organized according to the department administering a service, by 'product group', by 'client group' or by 'life event'). In the light of your notes, what would you consider to be the best site, and why?

2 Visit the websites listed in Case Example 10.3. How would you rate their contribution to the enrichment of democracy in the UK? Give reasons for your ratings.

3 Make a list of the government services that hold files containing your own personal data. Make another list showing which files you would, and which you would not, consent to be shared with other agencies, and why? In the light of these lists, consider whether there are sufficient safeguards in place to protect your privacy.

CLASS EXERCISES

1   Organize a formal debate on the proposition that 'this House supports national identity cards and believes that it should be compulsory for all citizens to carry one'.
2   Organize a class discussion to explore the circumstances in which it is right for governments to cross-match sensitive personal data (such as social security records, bank accounts, criminal records held on a central police service computer or medical records) without the consent of the data subject. Get a rapporteur to make a note of your main conclusions.

FURTHER READING

Probably the most comprehensive text on the significance of the Internet for students of politics and public management is:

Andrew Chadwick (2006), *Internet politics: states, citizens and new communications technologies.* Oxford: Oxford University Press (Chapters 4, 8 and 10 are particularly relevant to discussion in this chapter).

For a discussion of joined-up government:

Perri 6, Diana Leet, Kimberley Seltzer and Gerry Stoker (2002), *Towards holistic governance. The new reform agenda.* Basingstoke: Palgrave (especially Chapters 2 and 7).

For a review of international progress in e-government:

Sandford Borins, Kenneth Kernaghan, David Brown, Nick Bontis, Perri 6 and Fred Thompson (2007), *Digital state at the leading edge.* Toronto: University of Toronto Press.

The classic studies of the surveillance society are:

David Lyon (1994), *The electronic eye. The rise of the surveillance society.* Cambridge: Polity Press.

David Lyon (ed.) (2003), *Surveillance as social sorting. Privacy, risk and digital discrimination.* London: Routledge.

For an interesting history of the changing ways in which a state uses personal information:

Edward Higgs (2004), *The information state in England.* Basingstoke: Palgrave Macmillan.

Other:

Barry N. Hague and Brian Loader (1999), *Digital democracy.* London: Routledge.

Office of the e-Envoy (2000), *UK online action plan.* London: Cabinet Office.

REFERENCES

Christine A. Bellamy and John Taylor (1998), *Governing in the information age.* Buckingham: Open University Press.

Cabinet Office (2000), *Successful IT: modernising government in action* (The McCartney report). London: Cabinet Office.

Cabinet Office (2005), *Transformational government. Enabled by technology*, Cm 6683. London: HMSO.

Capgemini (2007), *Benchmarking the supply of online public services* (http://ec.europa.eu/information_society/newsroom/cf/itemlongdetail.cfm?item_id=3634, accessed 16 May 2008).

Andrew Chadwick (2006), *Internet politics: states, citizens and new communications technologies.* Oxford: Oxford University Press.

Comptroller and Auditor-General (2007), *Government on the Internet: progress in delivering information and services online*, HC 529 2006–7. London: Stationery Office (www.nao.org.uk/publications/nao_reports, accessed 16 May 2008).

Thomas H. Davenport (1993), *Process innovation: re-engineering work through information technology.* Boston, MA: Harvard Business School Press.

Thomas H. Davenport and Laurence Prusak (1998), *Working knowledge: how organisations manage what they know.* Boston, MA: Harvard Business School Press.

Jens Hoff and Jacob Rosenkrands (2000), 'When democratic strategies clash: the citizen card debate in Denmark', in Jens Hoff, Ivan Horrocks and Pieter Tops (eds), *Democratic governance and new technology.* London: Routledge, pp. 101–8.

Home Office (2002), *Entitlement cards and identity fraud. A consultation paper*, Cm 5557. London: HMSO.

Michael Margolis and David Resnick (2000), *Politics as usual. The cyberspace 'revolution'.* London: Sage.

Ministry of Justice (2007), *The governance of Britain*, Cm 7170. London: HMSO.

Office of the Vice President (1993), *From red tape to results. Creating a government that works better and costs less.* Report of the National Performance review. Washington, DC: US Government Printing Office.

OGC/Office of the e-Envoy (2002), *In the service of democracy. A consultation paper on a policy for electronic democracy.* London: Office of Government Commerce/Office of the e-Envoy.

Perri 6 (2004), 'Joined-up government in the western world in comparative perspective', *Journal of Public Administration Research and Theory*, 14 (1): 103–38.

Perri 6, Diana Leet, Kimberley Seltzer and Gerry Stoker (2002), *Towards holistic governance. The new reform agenda.* Basingstoke: Palgrave.

PIU (2002), *Privacy and data sharing: the way forward for public services.* London: Cabinet Office, Performance and Innovation Unit.

Lawrence Pratchett (2002), *The implementation of electronic voting in the UK.* London: Local Government Association.

Michael Scott Morton (ed.) (1991), *The corporation of the 90s. Information technology and organisational transformation.* Oxford: Oxford University Press.

Surveillance Studies Network (2006), *A report on the surveillance society.* Wilmslow: Information Commissioner's Office.

Darrel M. West (2007), *Global e-government 2007.* Providence, RI: Brown University (www.insidepolitics.org, accessed 16 May 2008).

Chapter 11

Performance measurement and management in public sector organizations

Geert Bouckaert, Catholic University of Leuven, Belgium and
Wouter Van Dooren, University of Antwerp, Belgium

INTRODUCTION

> *Sir Humphrey*: Minister, you said you wanted the administration figures reduced, didn't
> you? *Jim Hacker*: Yes. *Sir Humphrey*: So we reduced the figures. *Jim Hacker*: But only
> the figures, not the number of administrators. *Sir Humphrey*: Well of course not. *Jim
> Hacker*: Well that is not what I meant. *Sir Humphrey*: Well really Minister, one is not
> a mind-reader, is one? You said reduce the figures, so we reduced the figures.
>
> (Yes Minister 2.1 'The Compassionate Society')

Performance management is both about measurement and management, about information
and action (Hatry, 1999; Morley, Bryant and Hatry, 2001). The aim of this chapter is to
explore the concept, the potential and the practice of performance measurement and
management in public sector organizations.

LEARNING OBJECTIVES

This chapter will look at the following key issues:

- the evolution of performance measurement and management in the public sector;
- the key concepts in performance measurement;
- the key concepts in performance management;
- some traps and lessons learned in performance management.

THE EVOLUTION OF PERFORMANCE MANAGEMENT

The New Public Management (NPM) actively emphasizes the significance of performance
measurement as a management tool in government (OECD, 1997a). Indeed, accurate
performance information is needed for the implementation of management instruments such

as performance pay, performance contracts or performance budgets (Hatry, 1999). However, NPM did not originate the idea of measuring government performance. In both Europe and the United States, there had already been long-standing performance measurement initiatives (Bouckaert, 1995a). As early as 1949, the first Hoover Commission in the United States aimed at shifting the attention of the budget from inputs towards functions, activity cost and accomplishments. This increased influence of civil servants cumulated in the development of planning and management approaches such as the Planning, Programming and Budgeting System (PPBS), management by objectives (MBO) (see Chapter 5) and zero-based budgeting (ZBB) (see Chapter 8).

In the late 1980s and early 1990s, there was a new emphasis on performance management, mainly because of rising fiscal deficits in government but often also inspired by ideologies of keeping the state as small as possible (see Chapter 3). In this phase, the main objective of performance measurement was to identify how to increase efficiency and/or to cut spending. By the mid- and late 1990s, government performance was increasingly seen as a key component of the competitive advantage of national economies and a contributory factor in overall societal performance. Minimizing the public sector was no longer the dominant public management reform strategy (Pollitt and Bouckaert, 2004). Outcomes and quality concerns gained importance in many countries (see Chapter 12). For example, in 2000 the UK central government removed the Compulsory Competitive Tendering (CCT) regime in local government and replaced it with a Best Value approach, in which the quality of services has to be assessed (see Case Example 11.1).

Thus, the focus of performance measurement and management has changed through time in accordance with the dominant understanding of what constitutes 'government performance'. In times of shrinking public budgets and a discourse of 'less government', as in the 1980s, performance measurement and management tends to focus on inputs and efficiency. More recently, the decline in trust of public institutions has pushed performance measurement systems towards measurement of quality-of-life indicators and the quality-of-governance (see Chapters 12 and 15). In this respect, performance measurement and management are children of their time, with a new generation emerging roughly every decade.

KEY CONCEPTS IN PERFORMANCE MEASUREMENT

The input-output model of performance measurement

This section will look at how different types of performance can be measured. There are a number of levels at which performance measurement can operate – it may refer to the measurement of inputs, outputs or outcomes, and it may focus on economy, efficiency or effectiveness. We can integrate these concepts in an input-output model of the policy and management cycle – see Figure 11.1 (Bouckaert et al. 1997).

The input-output model gives a systemic overview of the aspirations of an organization (field 1). These are general 'end purposes' that are usually derived from the organization's mission statement or general policy documents. The next step in the policy cycle is to infer more operational objectives from these general strategic guidelines (field 2). Next we enter the management cycle, i.e. the daily operations of the organization. The management cycle consists of the inputs that go into the organization, the activities for which the inputs are used

CASE EXAMPLE 11.1 **THE MOVE TO BEST VALUE IN THE UK**

The 'Best Value' initiative was introduced in English local government in 1997 to replace the much-hated CCT legislation, first as a pilot initiative, then as a statutory duty from 1 April 2000.

In practice, 'Best Value' meant (DETR, 1999a):

- Every part of the council's budget had to be reviewed at least once every five years.
- Every review had to apply the '4Cs' methodology to the service or the cross-cutting issue, consisting of the following steps:
  - Challenge the need for the service and the way it is carried out.
  - Consult with all relevant stakeholders.
  - Compare the performance of the service with other providers.
  - Compete – test the competitiveness of the service.
- As a minimum level of comparison, each council had to compare its performance with other comparable councils against each of the 'best value performance indicators' (of which there were over 100 in every authority and far more in the largest local authorities). These indicators included some that measured inputs, volume of activity, volume of output, productivity levels, unit costs, number of users, percentage of schoolchildren passing exams at 16 and 18, user satisfaction levels, reliabilty levels, numbers of complaints, etc. – in other words, the whole spectrum from inputs to outcomes and from efficiency to quality.
- Each local authority had to publish a plan to improve its performance significantly. Initially, these plans had to ensure that, within five years, each service would have reached the performance level that the upper quartile of authorities achieved in 2000. (In 2002 this was amended to give more emphasis to 'stretch targets' agreed by each local authority with government departments across a range of priority issues.)

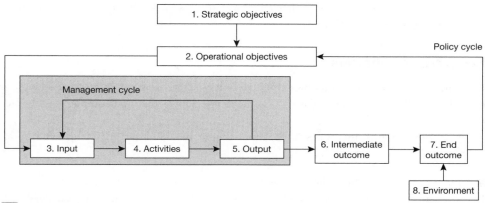

Figure 11.1 *The policy and management cycle*

Source: Bouckaert *et al.* (1997)

and the outputs that are realised by these activities *(fields 3, 4 and 5)*. Personnel, infrastructure, finance and premises are some typical inputs. With these inputs, activities are undertaken. For example, a school will organize lessons and a library will shelve books that may be lent out. The activities result in outputs (e.g. number of students passing exams or number of books on loan). Management should be concerned that the inputs yield the right amount and quality of outputs by organizing the activities in the best possible way. Therefore, the manager's feedback loop focuses primarily on inputs and outputs *(from field 5 to field 3)*.

> The number of patients treated and discharged from a mental hospital (output indicator) is not the same as the percentage of discharged patients who are capable of living independently (outcome indicator).
>
> *Source*: Cited in Hatry (1999, p. 15)

When the outputs, i.e. the policy and management products, leave the internal organization, they have impacts on society and the world in general. The crucial question is whether and what outcomes result from the outputs. A sharp distinction must be made between outputs and outcomes. Outcomes are events, occurrences, or changes in conditions, behaviour or attitudes. Outcomes are not what the programme or organization itself did, but the consequences of what the programme or organization did.

We can make a distinction between intermediate outcomes and end outcomes *(fields 6 and 7)*. This is a pragmatic but important division between the ends ultimately desired and the interim accomplishments that are expected to lead to those end results (although, of course, they may not) (Hatry, 1999, p. 15). Since a long time may elapse between the delivery of outputs and the occurrence of the end outcomes, the causality between the output and end outcome may be difficult to establish. The impact of societal environment *(field 8)* should be assessed. The policymaker must be concerned that the desired outcomes are achieved. The policymaker's feedback loop is the confrontation of the outcomes with the objectives *(fields 1 and 2)* which closes the circle. Of course, this clear-cut distinction between the policy and management cycles is valuable for analytical purposes but it does not exist in reality. In making their decisions, managers need policy guidelines and political decisions on the allocation of resources, while policymakers in turn need information on the feasibility of outputs and thus, expected outcomes.

Performance indicators

Performance indicators are variables that tell us how close we have come to reaching our objectives. Different kinds of indicator can be derived from the input-output model – see Box 11.1.

The combination of the boxes in the input-output model allows us to formulate ratio-indicators.

- *Economy* is the cost divided by the input, e.g. the cost per employee, the costs per office.
- *Productivity* is the output divided by one specific input, e.g. bus hours on the road per employee (for public transport), shop or restaurant closures per inspection (for food inspection), crimes cleared up per police officer per day.

BOX 11.1 A TYPOLOGY OF PERFORMANCE INDICATORS

■ **Input indicators**: e.g. number of employees, money spent, number of hospital beds, number of public buses.

■ **Output indicators**: e.g. number of pupils taught, number of discharged patients, vehicle miles.

■ **Intermediate outcome indicators**: e.g. new knowledge, increased skills, number of recovered patients, user satisfaction with services.

■ **End outcome indicators**: e.g. increased grades achieved in schools, reductions in unemployment, increased health and well-being.

■ **Societal environmental indicators**: e.g. age structure, economic indicators such as growth of GDP.

■ *Efficiency* is the output divided by (an index of) all of the inputs. Usually the only index of all inputs that is available is cost, which leads to the specific efficiency indicator of *unit cost* (e.g. cost per discharged patient, cost per crime cleared). Since *all* the costs of all the inputs used to obtain an output need to be calculated in financial terms, this can only be properly calculated if the organization has a high quality analytical financial system.

■ *Effectiveness* is outcome divided by output, e.g. number of complaints received about dirty streets per kilometre of streets that receives regular cleaning.

■ *Cost-effectiveness* is outcome divided by cost, e.g. cost per unemployed person moving into employment.

Performance standards

A performance measurement system that focuses on the different steps in the input-output model should provide an organization with sufficient information to plan, monitor and evaluate both policy and management. The next step is to lay down standards that establish how well (or how badly) the organization is performing. A minimum standard is a value of a performance indicator that must be met.

Standards may be set in different ways:

■ Politicians, for example, are sometimes tempted to set a popular standard as a symbol of how good their policies are, rather than as a yardstick for performance. The Kyoto standard for CO_2 emissions may be one high profile example.

■ Another method is to use a scientific norm, e.g. for the maximum quantities of dioxin allowed in the food chain.

■ Mostly, however, the standards are set by comparison, usually either between time periods or across organizations. Time series analysis compares past performance with current performance. Cross-section analysis compares the organization with other organizations. Naturally, a comparison that combines both time series and different organizations will yield the most information.

The process of comparing performance across organizations is known as *benchmarking*. Where benchmarking is used to derive 'league tables', it requires a high degree of comparability between the organizations to be compared – otherwise the comparisons are likely to be regarded as unfair (especially by those shown in a bad light). This is all the more serious if these league tables trigger government action – e.g. intervention by a higher level of government or loss of budgets. However, such comparisons do not tell us why the differences occur and, moreover, they may often leave out the most interesting comparisons – e.g. with high performing organizations that are not 'comparable' on most dimensions, but where their high-performance is potentially transferable.

Statistical techniques for performance measurement

Several techniques might enhance the analytical capacity of the organization to understand its performance. *Stochastic Frontier Analysis* is a statistical technique by which the service production function is estimated from a priori specified parameters, while allowing for some variation by the inclusion of random variables. Techniques such as *Data Envelopment Analysis* and *Free Disposal Hull* are also useful tools for comparing organizational performance both in time and place, while controlling for external variables. These are non-parametric methods, which implies that the optimal production function is determined by the data. These techniques have been applied to public sector services to compare public sector services such as fire services, local civil registry offices, hospitals, schools, prisons and courts, police forces, etc. (e.g. Bouckaert, 1992; HM Treasury, 2000b).

KEY CONCEPTS IN PERFORMANCE MANAGEMENT

Performance measurement only becomes valuable when it is followed by management action – it is only justified if it is used (see Case Example 11.2). Performance management can be broadly defined as 'acting upon performance information'. In this section we will examine some of the most important functions of performance information in public sector management. Performance information can be used for different purposes – in the policy cycle, for accountability purposes or in financial management (considered in Chapter 8 rather than here).

The policy cycle consists of four steps, i.e. policy preparation, decision, implementation and evaluation. Performance information may be used in all the different steps of the policy cycle. Analysis of predicted performance (against the background of past performance) can help in the development of better-thought-out policies. Objectives are formulated, performance indicators are deduced from the objectives, and targets are set. Next, performance information may be used by management to monitor whether the policy is on track. The value of monitoring will be highly dependent on the timeliness and frequency of the measurement effort. Finally, performance information may be used in policy evaluation.

156

CASE EXAMPLE 11.2 **CITISTAT IN US CITIES**

One way for a mayor to think about CitiStat might be as follows:

> A city is employing a CitiStat performance strategy if it holds an ongoing series of *regular, periodic meetings* during which the mayor and/or the principal members of the mayor's leadership team plus the individual director (and the top managers) of different city agencies *use data* to analyze the agency's past *performance*, to establish its next *performance* objectives, and to examine its overall *performance* strategies.

This characterization is not a very demanding one. Given, however, that these meetings are 'ongoing', 'regular' and 'periodic', one subtle feature of citiStat is often missed by casual observers: this ongoing discussion of performance involves much persistent follow-up on past performance deficits and previous commitments to fix specific problems, as well as follow-up on decisions, commitments and established expectations for future performance improvements. The key aspect of this way of thinking about public management is the clear, express, detailed focus on performance.

Source: Adapted from Behn (2007, pp. 7–8)

Performance measurement provides a bird's-eye view, upon which action might be taken. However, it should be noted that more than performance information is often needed for an evidence-based policy cycle. While performance information may help to trigger in-depth examination of why performance problems (or successes) exist (Hatry, 1999, p. 160), causal models and more qualitative research are generally needed to carry out such examination. This implies that effective performance management sometimes needs more information than routine performance measurement can supply.

Performance information in the form of targets can play a role in any of the four stages of the policy cycle. Targets are a specific value of a performance indicator to be reached by a specific date. (For 'SMART' objectives and targets, see Chapter 12.) The UK public sector has become especially famous for its fixation with targets (although since 2005 the UK government has signalled its desire to reduce the number of targets imposed on public agencies and is – slowly – attempting to implement this decision). While targets have the advantage of providing more clarity to front-line staff and middle managers, they can generate gaming, which can not only waste resources but also render the whole information system unreliable (Bevan and Hood, 2007).

Performance management can also be used for accountability purposes. Different accountability relationships exist between stakeholders (see Box 11.2). Performance information can be used so that stakeholders can hold each other to account for how well they have each performed their assigned responsibilities.

BOX 11.2 A TYPOLOGY OF ACCOUNTABILITY RELATIONS

Accountability of government to citizens and society: Government is responsible for a range of public services and other activities within society. Performance information may be a useful tool to enhance its responsiveness towards society and its citizens/clients. Until now this process of interaction has usually been unilateral, e.g. performance indicators have been published in the annual reports of governments and their agencies. However, this accountability may be more effective if citizens are involved in the performance measurement process in general and particularly in the definition of the indicators.

Accountability of the administration to politicians: The administration oversees the implementation of policies decided upon by politicians – it can therefore be required to demonstrate its performance level to politicians. Indeed, administrators themselves often demand the chance to provide performance information to politicians – often because it may offer an organizational defence against the irrationality (as they see it) of political decisions. However, if performance information is to influence politicians, it must be tailored to their interests and needs. Canadian civil servants, for example, recently took an initiative to make performance information more useful for parliamentarians by focusing on societal and quality of life indicators (Bennett *et al.*, 2001).

Accountability of decentralized agencies to central departments: A third accountability relationship exists between central government departments (e.g. Ministries, regional or local offices of national government) and decentralized or devolved bodies (e.g. executive agencies of central government). Government, even when it operates more at 'arm's length', remains responsible for the outputs that are produced by its agencies, although how the agencies produce these outputs is no longer its concern. Consequently, performance information becomes crucial in the steering of these decentralized or devolved bodies. Indeed, in the case of a genuine devolution of responsibilities to an agency, the performance information captured in the management contract becomes the single most important tool for steering and direction. The *Next Steps* agencies in the United Kingdom, for instance, were set up under the terms of a framework agreement with their 'home' government department. Each year a Public Service Agreement, with performance targets, and a Service Delivery Agreement are negotiated between the government department and the Treasury, and one element of this relates to the performance of the executive agencies sponsored by that department (see Chapter 17). The achievement of these targets is taken very seriously by all the parties concerned, not least because failure could influence the Treasury's attitude to future budget changes. Similarly, performance indicators can be used in inter-governmental relations, for example where central government exercises control on local authorities through the Audit Commission's Best Value indicators in the UK (Audit Commission, 2000). (This approach is not relevant, of course, in the many countries where local self government is protected from central intervention by its constitutional position.)

Accountability of individual employees and teams to the top management: Performance information finally may be used to hold internal organizational units or individuals to account for how they discharge their responsibilities. Performance management in this case can help to motivate personnel to search for improvements (Hatry, 1999). Of course, this assumes that many employees are motivated by the desire to produce good results – then the mere provision of performance information combined with more freedom to organize their activities should provide them with sufficient scope to improve. However, on occasion, additional incentives are often used. Monetary incentives ('performance pay') are probably the most notorious example. Although performance pay exists in many public sectors (OECD, 1997a), it remains controversial – it is said to be disruptive of teamwork, insulting to professionals who believe themselves to be in 'public service' and difficult to calculate because so many external factors impact on the performance of any individual or team (Bovaird and Russell, 2007).

PERFORMANCE REPORTING: THE BALANCED SCORECARD

Everyone wants their performance to be measured ('How was I?'), but most people are much more nervous about having their performance reported. This paradox indicates to us the deepest challenge of performance management – performance measurement is a natural human impulse but performance reporting is subject to deep and difficult obstacles that make it highly suspect.

So far, so obvious. At this point, along came Kaplan and Norton (1996). Their fundamental insight was that performance reporting is multifaceted. There is no one way of representing performance – the 'balanced scorecard' they recommended included results areas for financial, customer, internal process and innovation/growth results. Furthermore, they soon realised that this approach, based on performance indicators and targets, needed to be tied to a understanding of the cause-and-effect relationships of strategic objectives, which they labelled the 'strategy map' (Kaplan and Norton, 2004).

Moreover, 'what good looks like' tends to differ substantially between different stakeholders (see Chapter 5), so that the balanced scorecard can represent the perspectives of a variety of key stakeholders (although, interestingly, Kaplan and Norton themselves don't take this approach). The balanced scorecard approach in the London Borough of Barking and Dagenham takes this approach. It is divided into results areas from five perspectives, illustrated in Figure 11.2, in each of which there are a range of strategic objectives. For each objective there is at least one performance indicator, which is reported regularly to the top management of the authority.

The balanced scorecard approach quickly took off in the private sector and is now widespread in the public sector around the world (Neely *et al.*, 2006).

SOME TRAPS AND LESSONS IN PERFORMANCE MANAGEMENT

Performance measurement provides interesting possibilities for enhancing public sector management and policy-making (Bouckaert and Halligan, 2008). However, it also contains some traps.

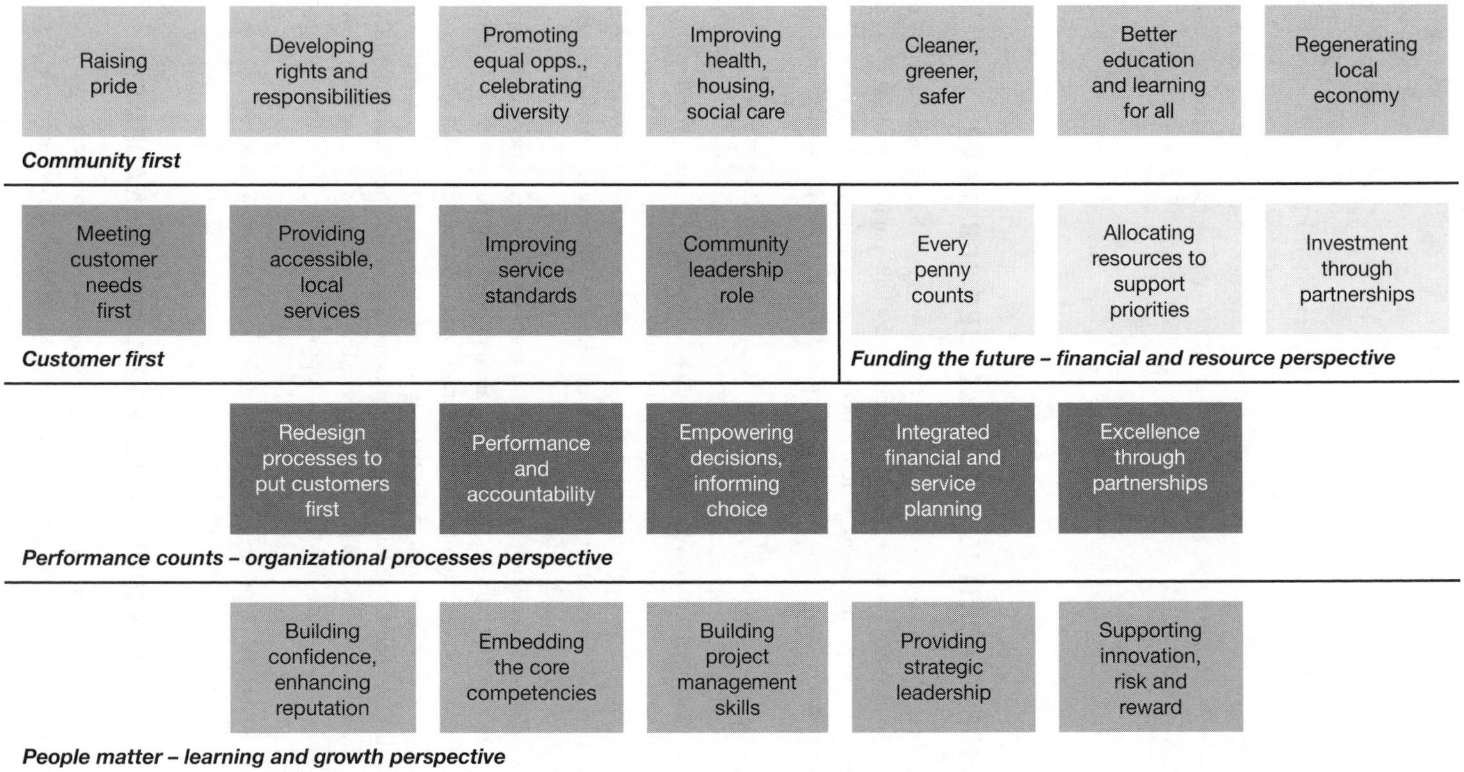

Community first

| Raising pride | Developing rights and responsibilities | Promoting equal opps., celebrating diversity | Improving health, housing, social care | Cleaner, greener, safer | Better education and learning for all | Regenerating local economy |

Customer first

| Meeting customer needs first | Providing accessible, local services | Improving service standards | Community leadership role | Every penny counts | Allocating resources to support priorities | Investment through partnerships |

Funding the future – financial and resource perspective

Performance counts – organizational processes perspective

| Redesign processes to put customers first | Performance and accountability | Empowering decisions, informing choice | Integrated financial and service planning | Excellence through partnerships |

People matter – learning and growth perspective

| Building confidence, enhancing reputation | Embedding the core competencies | Building project management skills | Providing strategic leadership | Supporting innovation, risk and reward |

Figure 11.2 *Strategy map for balanced scorecard in LB of Barking and Dagenham*

Source: Adapted from a presentation by John Tatam given in Lithuania, 2006, with permission

Lack of interest of politicians and/or citizens. The ownership of performance management initiatives usually lies within the administration. Politicians and the public often appear uninterested in the performance information that is provided – until things go wrong. One response to this frustrating situation is to tailor performance measurement to the demand, implying that citizens and politicians should become involved in defining performance indicators that interest them.

Vagueness and ambiguity of goals. This is often inherent in politics, and indeed may well be politically rational: making objectives and indicators clearer and more concrete might lead to political conflict, in those situations where different stakeholders have different values and expectations. However, managers usually desire clarity of goals in order to maintain strategic direction. The tension between these political and managerial requirements may often be irresolvable.

Targets without goals. Goals are important, but without targets they may have little meaning for operational managers. However, the opposite is also true – targets alone are dangerous, as managers need to have an understanding of the organizations' aspirations when they find themselves in those difficult situations where they have to choose between targets. While the UK may have greatly over-emphasized the importance of targets, without enough attention to goals, the public sector in many other countries has given insufficient attention to the usefulness of targets in focusing managerial action.

Games playing. Sometimes organizations have an interest in portraying a flattering image of themselves. Of course, performance information can be functional or dysfunctional for an organization in this respect – some performance information may be very discomforting. Consequently, where some performance targets are especially important in public relations terms, organizations may be tempted to cheat in their performance reporting (Bevan and Hood, 2007).

It appears likely that the risk of data corruption is higher when organizations see performance measurement as imposed externally. Local government, for example, tends to see, and resist, central government attempts at control through performance measurement and reporting exercises. Schools confronted with league tables may 'teach for the test' rather than to impart knowledge. Reported crime detection rates may be increased by spending more time getting convicted criminals to confess to their past crimes rather than trying to solve current crimes. The performance figures of a drug offenders' rehabilitation agency may be raised by directing activity towards the easy cases and refusing to accept the more difficult cases. All of these abuses can be partly tackled by effective data auditing, a common approach to safeguard the accuracy, reliability and comparability of performance information. However, when incentives are high, abuse may become more ingenious to escape detection.

SUMMARY

This chapter suggests that performance management is possible, but not easy. Performance measurement and management in the public sector have evolved over time, with many ups and downs – they now attempt to cover a much wider range of concepts than forty years ago, from inputs through outputs to outcomes and addressing issues of economy, efficiency, effectiveness and quality. There remain significant difficulties but important lessons have been learnt.

Performance measurement is only useful if it improves policy or management. Clearly, performance data must be reliable and should cover the dimensions of performance that really matter. Performance management has often been considered to be about the 'hard' data, whereas quality management is often considered as a 'soft' management issue (see Chapter 12). Yet the focus on costs and efficiency at the expense of service quality can be dangerous, as the CCT regime in the UK showed. Indeed, the Citizen's Charter in 1991 can be seen as an implicit admission by the UK government that the emphasis on the 'three Es' – economy, efficiency, effectiveness – had been overdone. There is now an understanding in the UK, and in many other OECD countries, that performance management has to go hand in hand with quality management.

Finally, performance management is probably especially necessary in a turbulent organizational environment. Let us suggest a proof *ex absurdum:* if an organization does not measure its performance, it will only tentatively understand what its impact in society is, and consequently its ability to respond appropriately will erode. Therefore, it is important to develop performance measurement systems in order to know at least a little more and to develop performance management systems in order to have a little more control over performance.

QUESTIONS FOR REVIEW AND DISCUSSION

1 What are the main types of performance that need to be measured and reported in the public sector? Who cares about these performance measures – and why do they care?
2 How can an organization decide whether its performance management system produces benefits at least as great as the costs it imposes?

READER EXERCISES

1 Take an annual report from a public agency with which you are familiar. Identify the performance indicators reported in it. Classify them according to the categories in Figure 11.1. Do you think that the balance between these types of performance indicator is appropriate for this agency?
2 Take one of the performance indicators identified in the previous reader exercise. Consider how an individual, a unit or a whole organization might find ways of influencing the reported level of that indicator in order to make their work look more successful. For each of these possible abuses, suggest ways in which that kind of behaviour could be made less easy or less likely to succeed.

CLASS EXERCISES

1 Identify a case currently in the media where a public agency appears to have been changing its practices or its reporting approach in order to improve its 'league table'

position, without necessarily improving its actual level of performance. Discuss how the performance measurement and reporting system might be changed in order to make such behaviour less likely in the future, while still producing useful information for the stakeholders who wish to hold this agency to account.

2   Discuss how your class, your tutor and your college assesses performance – of students, of staff and of the organization as a whole. What are the major limitations in this performance assessment? How could they be tackled?

FURTHER READING

Geert Bouckaert (1995b), 'Improving performance measurement', in Arie Halachmi and Geert Bouckaert (eds), *The enduring challenges of public administration*. San Francisco, CA: Jossey-Bass, pp. 379–412.

Geert Bouckaert and John Halligan (2008), *Managing performance, international comparisons*. London: Routledge.

Hans de Bruijn (2002), *Managing performance in the public sector*. London: Routledge.

Harry P. Hatry (1999), *Performance measurement: getting results*. Washington, DC: Urban Institute Press.

REFERENCES

Audit Commission (2000), *Aiming to improve: the principles of performance measurement*. London: Audit Commission.

Robert Behn (2007), *What all mayors would like to know about Baltimore's CitiStat performance strategy*. Washington, DC: IBM Center for the Business of Government.

Carolyn Bennett, Donald G. Lenihan, John Williams and William Young (2001), *Measuring quality of life: the use of societal outcomes by parliamentarians*. Ottawa: Office of the Auditor General of Canada.

Gwyn Bevan and Christopher Hood (2007), 'What's measured is what matters: targets and gaming in healthcare in England', *Public Administration*, 84 (3): 517–38.

Geert Bouckaert (1992), 'Productivity analysis in the public sector: the case of fire service', *International Review of Administrative Sciences*, 58 (2): 175–200.

Geert Bouckaert (1995a), 'The history of the productivity movement', in Arie Halachmi, Marc Holzer (eds), *Competent government: theory and practice. The best of public productivity review, 1985–1993*. Burke, VA: Chatelaine Press, pp. 361–98.

Geert Bouckaert and John Halligan (2008), *Managing Performance, International Comparisons*. Routledge, London.

Geert Bouckaert, Tom Auwers, Wouter Van Reeth and Koen Verhoest (1997), *Handboek Doelmatigheidsanalyse: prestaties begroten*. Brussels: Ministry of the Flemish Community.

Tony Bovaird and Ken Russell (2007), 'Civil service reform in the UK, 1999–2005: revolutionary failure or evolutionary success?', *Public Administration*, 85 (2): 301–28.

163

DETR (1999a), *Local Government Act 1999: Part I, Best value* (Circular 10/99). London: Department of Environment, Transport and the Regions.

Harry P. Hatry (1999), *Performance measurement: getting results*. Washington, DC: Urban Institute Press.

HM Treasury (2000b), *Improving police performance: a new approach to measuring police efficiency*. Public Services Productivity Panel Report No. 4. London: HM Treasury.

R. Kaplan and D. Norton (1996), *The balanced scorecard: translating strategy into action*. Boston, MA: Harvard Business School Press.

R. Kaplan and D. Norton (2004), *Strategy maps*. Boston, MA: Harvard Business School Press.

Elaine Morley, Scott P. Bryant and Harry P. Hatry (2001), *Comparative performance measurement*. Washington, DC: Urban Institute Press.

Andy Neely, Mike Kennerly and Angela Walters (2006), *Performance measurement and management: public and private*. Cranfield: Cranfield School of Management.

OECD (1997a), *In search of results: performance management practices*. Paris: OECD.

Christopher Pollitt and Geert Bouckaert (2004), *Public management reform: a comparative analysis* (2nd edn). Oxford: Oxford University Press.

Chapter 12

Quality management in public sector organizations

Tony Bovaird, University of Birmingham, UK and
Elke Löffler, Governance International, UK

INTRODUCTION

What is the likelihood that two or more strangers would have the same view when it comes to deciding what is a high quality service and what isn't? We might assume that people would give different weights to different attributes of a given service before forming their judgement (Bovaird and Halachmi, 1999, p. 145). So, while it might be easy to agree on the absence of quality, it is likely to be a more complex task getting agreement on what exactly quality is.

Yet a definition of quality is likely to be important – without it, we will lack a language in which to discuss quality inside and outside the organization. And it makes us vulnerable to those manipulative managers who launch so-called 'quality initiatives' simply to disguise some deeply unpopular decisions in the organization, because who can be against quality?

For many public agencies, the simple route has been to identify 'quality' with the implementation of quality assurance systems such as ISO standards, the European Foundation for Quality Management (EFQM) or the Common Assessment Framework (CAF). This chapter will explore these approaches and how we can use them for improving the quality of a service.

We also explore the wider dimensions of quality, including quality of life and quality of governance – typically, politicians, the media and citizens are more interested in these concepts than in technical quality assurance tools. This implies a shift in interest from quality of service in a single agency towards quality assessment by multiple stakeholders of the outcomes from partnerships.

LEARNING OBJECTIVES

This chapter will address the following objectives:

- to identify differences of quality management in the public and private sectors;
- to review key issues with quality assessment in the public sector;
- to explore the major quality assurance systems used in the public sector;
- to examine key obstacles to, and success stories in, quality improvement in the public sector;
- to extend the concept of quality to quality of life and governance processes.

DIFFERENCES OF QUALITY MANAGEMENT IN THE PUBLIC AND PRIVATE SECTORS

Quality management, as with many government reforms, has its roots in the private sector. As always, careful thought has to be given to the issues arising from the transfer of private sector management principles to the public sector.

First, most quality management approaches, including total quality management (TQM), have originally been developed for the manufacturing industry. Yet, goods and services have very different characteristics. For example, standardization is a key element of quality in mass-produced goods, whereas service quality in personal services often means variability in order to meet different customer needs (Gaster, 1995, p. 36–44).

Second, there is an absence from the private sector TQM vocabulary of many of the key concerns that have characterized debates about the provision of public services. For example, the TQM literature rarely refers to 'citizens' or even to 'communities'. Its vocabulary is one of clients, customers, consumers and users (Pollitt and Bouckaert, 1995, pp. 6ff.). However, unlike companies, public agencies cannot choose their customers – they often have to serve a rather large set of stakeholders with diverging interests. Moreover, the relationship of public service agencies to their customers is often one of rationing services and saying 'no' (Beale and Pollitt, 1994, p. 205), rather than simply trying to please them, which places a fundamental limit upon the concept of 'user responsiveness'.

Third, even though many politicians like to pay lip service to quality, other issues, such as tax levels, are also important to them. In particular, politicians know that not all voters are service users. Therefore, service quality is unlikely to become the sole parameter for judging excellence in a public organization.

This does not mean that (private sector) quality concepts do not work in a public sector setting – but they clearly have to be adapted to fit that setting.

WHAT WE MEAN BY 'QUALITY' AND HOW CAN WE MEASURE IT

As the context and drivers of public policy have changed over time (see Chapter 2), the meaning of quality has also changed. Bovaird and Löffler (2003) have distinguished five key concepts of quality during its evolution as a concept:

- quality as *'conformance to specification'* (a meaning deriving from an engineering perspective and from the 'contract culture');
- quality as *'fitness for purpose'* (or 'meeting organizational objectives', essentially deriving from a systems perspective);
- quality as *'aligning inputs, processes, outputs and outcomes'* (deriving from the strategic management perspective);
- quality as *'meeting customer expectations'* (or 'exceeding customer expectations', deriving from consumer psychology);
- quality as *'passionate emotional involvement'* – quality as that 'which lies beyond language and number' (the social psychology approach).

We can therefore say with confidence that there is no agreed definition of quality. It seems likely that organizations will find it difficult to bring about substantial quality improvement until they have fastened upon one definition of quality – whichever of the above five options they choose. Trying to run with two or more of these definitions in a single organization is likely to make the quality management process confusing and unconvincing – not only for front-line staff and service users but also for top and middle managers and for politicians. Having no definition of quality within the organization is equally bad – it means that quality remains a fuzzy concept and cannot be operationalized or assessed.

Once quality is defined, using one of the above approaches, it becomes possible to analyse certain aspects of quality, even using quantitative methods in some cases. Scholars as well as practitioners have made various attempts to find a quality measure that can capture several dimensions of quality, incorporating the views of different stakeholders (employees, customers, etc.). Yet, relying on a single quality index is always risky for management (Bouckaert, 1995c, p. 26). First, a quality index is not at all transparent, as the different dimensions of quality are hidden. Second, it also allows for deficient dimensions to be compensated – for example, customer service may be traded off against additional features of a product. Such compensation is inappropriate if some stakeholders require minimum achievements of specific quality dimensions.

Given that quality is a multidimensional concept, it needs to be assessed over a whole set of dimensions instead of relying on a sole index – see Box 12.1.

For example, the quality of a public swimming pool may be assessed on the basis of water temperature, availability of flumes and wave machines, opening hours, conformance to clean water norms, friendliness of staff and perception of the safety of the facility.

The definition of a set of quality dimensions is only a first step in the process of quality measurement – they have to be made operational with quality indicators.

BOX 12.1 CHARACTERISTICS OF SERVICE QUALITY

For services, the following quality dimensions influence a customer's view of quality:

- tangibles
- reliability
- responsiveness
- competence
- courtesy
- credibility
- security
- access
- communication
- understanding the customer.

Source: Zeithaml *et al.* (1990, p. 23)

Typically, quality indicators can be categorized as quantitative versus qualitative and subjective versus objective.

Objective indicators have the useful characteristic that they can be independently verified. However, it is often hard to quantify them – e.g. it is hard to construct an objective quantitative indicator measuring the comfort of waiting rooms in public agencies. Even though quantitative indicators such as the room temperature, the number of seats and the size of the waiting area may give some hints about the basic conditions of the waiting room, more qualitative information on its cleanliness, level of noise, decorative state, availability of private areas for confidential discussion, and 'atmosphere' would be much more useful in allowing service providers to decide whether it embodied the appropriate quality level. Moreover, we would normally like to ask the users of the service about their perceptions of these characteristics – a waiting room may look good to designers but be hated by the local mothers with young children who use it.

Subjective indicators measure the perceptions or expectations of people about some dimension (or overall level) of quality. Once we start to explore user attitudes and satisfaction levels, we find, rather ironically, that significant quantification is usually possible – e.g. in the waiting room example, we can summarize the proportion of users who are satisfied (and dissatisfied) with the overall quality of the waiting room, the proportion of users who think that the temperature is comfortable, the decor is attractive, etc.

Ideally, a sound set of quality indicators should include both quantitative and qualitative indicators, and both objective and subjective factors. In particular, we would suggest that no approach to assessing quality should contain only quantified or only objective factors – such assessments seem likely to miss some essential aspects of what we mean by 'quality'.

For measurement to be meaningful to managers, it will often be valuable to set targets for these quality indicators (see Chapter 11). In quality assessment, these targets will have to cover dimensions that cannot be objectively quantified. This is critically important – quality assessment must be more than just number crunching. Typically, it will involve subjective assessments (e.g. user satisfaction surveys) or objectively determined checklists of features (such as conformity to ISO 9000 standards), which cannot be aggregated into a single number. This can be frustrating for 'hard-nosed' analysts – but it is not surprising: by definition, quality cannot be reduced to quantity!

SMART?

'SMART objectives' are often recommended for public services – Specific, Measurable, Achievable, Realistic and Time-related – but this just turns them from objectives into targets. (HM Treasury in the UK now insists, after decades of misusing them, that they should be called 'SMART targets'!) Moreover, quality targets, which are often valuable to managers, cannot be reduced just to quantifiable measures – they have to retain a 'qualitative' element if they are to be valid.

WHO KNOWS ABOUT QUALITY?

This discussion leads to an important admission – different stakeholders 'know' different things about quality, and this has to be built into any quality management system. In Table 12.1, we look at whether quality is privately experienced, or socially experienced, and whether what we mean by 'quality' in a particular context is simple or complex to specify. As can be seen, these dimensions lead to very different conclusions – sometimes users are likely to be the best arbiters of quality (where the service experience is essentially private, with few social knock-on effects, and where it is relatively simple to gauge its quality dimension). In other situations, however, we might well come to the conclusion that professionals or politicians might be the best arbiters. Finally, in very complex services, with important knock-on effects, then we might well conclude that no one stakeholder group is likely to be a sound arbiter of quality – here it is likely that all stakeholders will need to be involved in the quality assessment process.

We might furthermore conclude that it is unwise to exclude any stakeholders from the quality assessment process, since they are all likely to believe that they understand aspects of quality which the other stakeholders neglect – and they will be reluctant to acquiesce to any quality assessment in which their voice was not heard. This is especially likely to be true of service users, since they often have an intense experience of what the service means to them and they will be reluctant to believe that others can fully understand their perspective.

CITIZEN AND SERVICE CHARTERS: STATING QUALITY STANDARDS

The essential idea behind citizen's charters, as introduced in the UK under the Prime Minister John Major, was that 'the citizen must be told what service standards are and be able to act where service is unacceptable' (HMSO, 1991: 4). The basic principles of the UK citizen's charters were:

- information and openness
- choice
- courtesy and helpfulness
- well-publicized complaints procedures
- value for money.

The Conservative government's concept of citizen's charters in 1991 considered the market as the point of departure, with the purpose of increasing competition and choice for individual citizens – note the singular in *citizen's* charter! The basic mechanism for quality improvement was meant to be pressure from service recipients on service producers. However, this is just one possible mechanism by which charters could work – the very first citizens' charters in the UK actually originated in Labour-dominated councils in the late 1980s, directed at meeting people's needs as recipients of services, and recognizing their rights as citizens (Gaster, 1995, p. 98).

169

Table 12.1 Who knows about quality?

	Quality is privately experienced	Quality is socially experienced
Quality is simple to specify	Users know about quality	Politicians know about quality
Quality is complex to specify	Professionals know about quality (together with users)	No one group knows about quality – politicians must act as referee between different views

Source: Adapted from Kieron Walsh (1991b)

In 1991, explicit promises about service standards were made in specific charters such as the Parent's Charter for schools, the Patient's Charter for the health service, and Tenant's Charters for public housing. By 1997, there were over forty charters for ministries and over 10,000 local charters (including those issued by councils and NGOs).

The first citizen's charters were devised without much involvement of the public, and many standards were minimum standards, rather than 'best practice'. Moreover, most users had little awareness of the charters, except the Patient's and Passenger's charters (Beale and Pollitt, 1994, pp. 215, 219). However, if we judge the success of the Citizen's Charter only by the interest of citizens, we miss the point. The Citizen's Charter enabled interest groups representing different types of user to prove more clearly and rigorously that the service in which they were interested was not meeting its promises.

> A charter's promises can incorporate several different types of quality standard:
>
> - 'hoped-for standards' (often politically promoted);
> - 'minimum' standards;
> - assured or guaranteed standards (with compensation).

The Labour government of Tony Blair relaunched the charter idea in 1998 under the new label 'Service First' but eventually lost interest in it and focused its national customer service efforts through the Charter Mark programme (see this volume, p. 173). Paradoxically, after interest in charters waned in the UK, the charter idea took off in many other countries, often following quite closely the UK model. Some countries, such as Italy and the Netherlands, went even further, introducing financial compensation in cases of failure to meet the standard.

By 2007, charters in the UK were on the rise again, particularly for public transport, social services and housing, although they are now voluntary. There is also a new generation of charters for services that have been decentralized below council level, called neighbourhood charters or community compacts (CLG, 2008).

CASE EXAMPLE 12.1 **THE SERVICE CHARTER OF LELYSTAD IN THE NETHERLANDS**

The community of Lelystad believes it is important to deliver good services to its citizens. That is why the local authority has decided to develop a service charter. Its motto is: 'YOU go first!' Since February 2006 the local authority guarantees to service users a waiting time no longer than 20 minutes.

If the local authority does not live up to its promises, citizens can complain. If they have to wait longer than 20 minutes at any service desk, the local authority will compensate them with a gift voucher for €10. For citizens, this is compensation for having to wait, while for Lelystad it is a stimulus to make sure that next time the council manages to deliver service within 20 minutes.

Source: Adapted from Löffler *et al.* (2007, p. 65)

MAJOR QUALITY ASSURANCE INSTRUMENTS IN THE PUBLIC SECTOR

Since the search for the most appropriate set of quality indicators is time-consuming and requires long experience with performance measurement and consultations with different stakeholders, 'ready-off-the peg' quality assurance (QA) systems have become popular in recent years in the private and (with some time lag) in the public sector. Their purpose is to 'assure', i.e. to guarantee, that a stated level of quality will be achieved in the organization.

For those quality managers trained as engineers, the implementation of a QA system is often considered as the solution to all quality problems within an organization. Yet the introduction of any quality assurance system is only meaningful if the agency already has in place clearly stated quality standards (e.g. service charters) and effective performance and quality management systems. Otherwise, there is very little to assure and no means of assessing how well it is being delivered. It is rather like buying expensive house insurance without checking whether the house has any value. In the absence of these foundations, there must be a suspicion that ISO certifications and EFQM accreditation have simply become a trophy hunt to bring glory to top management, rather than a search for quality improvement.

We will now explore the basic objectives and structure of several quality assurance systems – ISO standards, Charter Mark, EFQM and CAF. The characteristics of these QA approaches arise partly from the different definitions of quality that they addess. *ISO standards* are particularly relevant for assuring processes and suggesting process improvements, which means that they often fit well with a definition of quality that focuses on 'conformance to specification' or 'fitness for purpose'. The *EFQM* and *CAF* are good for assuring the alignment between the 'enablers' and the results of an organization. The UK *Charter Mark Scheme* focuses strongly on customer service and 'meeting or exceeding customer expectations'. None of these approaches takes account of the wider impacts of the organization's activities – this is the strength of the *GI Governance Test,* which is about how to assure quality of life and good governance principles in public service networks (see Chapter 15).

The ISO 9000 Series and third party certification

ISO is the International Organization for Standardization, which is a federation of national standards bodies, and which is responsible for preparing international standards.

For details, see www.iso.org

The ISO 9000 series is an internationally recognized standard for quality assurance. The standard outlines how quality systems should be set up in organizations where a contract between seller and buyer requires the demonstration of a supplier's ability to supply to mutually agreed requirements.

Not surprisingly, the standardization approach has its roots in manufacturing and in the military sector in the USA from the 1940s. (It reached the UK public sector, through the Ministry of Defence, in the 1960s but took decades to become more widespread.)

It is apparent that the main focus of the ISO system is on contracting situations. The recommended QA system consists of compliance with twenty-three elements of 'good' quality management, which will allow an organization to formulate and deliver contracts at an appropriate and agreed standard. However, more recently ISO 9004 has been developed to adapt this approach to situations in which contracts are not put in place, e.g. in some approaches to TQM.

The establishment of a quality assurance and management system along ISO 9000 guidelines involves considerable costs, particularly in paperwork systems that clearly document all procedures in the organization. In view of this investment, organizations typically want to have their compliance to ISO 9000 standards to be verified. Independent, so-called 'third party' (i.e. external) certification offers the possibility of using quality as a marketing tool – indeed, the desire to expand into new markets where their reputation is unknown or to protect existing markets where an external threat is perceived are common motivations for an organization seeking certification under ISO 9001. This applies both to private service providers wanting to bolster their chances of winning public contracts by displaying their 'quality badge' and also to 'in-house' public sector providers who want to demonstrate to their client department (and politicians) making procurement decisions that they are 'competitive' in quality terms with potential private sector rivals.

In Autumn 2000 a revised version of the ISO 9000 series was published by ISO (see www.iso.org/iso/pressrelease.htm?refid=Ref1152). The ISO Technical Committee recommends that organizations adopt this new ISO 9001:2008 standard, which specifies requirements for a basic quality management system for any organization. The practices described in ISO 9004:2000 may then be implemented to reach higher levels of quality. Essentially, the revised versions of ISO 9000 since 2000 locates ISO closer to quality excellence models. There are also more specific ISO standards, such as ISO 14001 for environmental management systems and the OHSAS 18001 standards for health and safety management systems.

Finally, there is a further UK QA approach based on assessable standards, namely Investors in People, a national standard setting out the requirements for good practice in training and development of staff to achieve organizational goals. The degree of overlap between Investors in People and ISO 9000 is significant – indeed, in the late 1990s there was experimentation in the UK public sector on joint assessment between these two schemes (Cabinet Office,

1999c). Because of its more limited scope – basically staff development – and its greater flexibility, it has become more popular than ISO 1900 in the UK public sector.

The Charter Mark scheme

The Cabinet Office launched Charter Mark in 1992 as an external certification programme to foster customer service in the UK public sector. Although closely linked to the Citizen's Charter initiative of the time, it is not necessary for public agencies applying for the Charter Mark to have a charter. However, the assessment criteria were closely based on the six Charter principles (see above). Typically, the Charter Mark badge is awarded for three years. In 2003, the Charter Mark criteria were revised and promoted as a self-assessment tool, as well as for certification (see www.cabinetoffice.gov.uk/chartermark).

After an independent review of the Charter Mark scheme, a new standard – the Customer Service Excellence (CSE) standard – was launched in 2008. It is intended to act as a driver of continuous improvement, a tool for developing skills, an independently assessed means of validating achievement and a way to capture best practice and feed lessons back to government. It requires the demonstration of *personalization* (services designed around the needs of the public, including hard-to-reach groups), *collaboration* (with citizens), *workforce skills* (linking public service reform and staff training), *leadership and commitment* (to customer focus, from top management to the front-line) and *accountability* (to communities and individuals).

> *Customer satisfaction* is defined as the difference between customer expectations and perceptions of actual performance. Therefore, decreasing satisfaction may stem either from increasing customer expectations or growing perceptions of bad service.
>
> *Source*: Adapated from Zeithaml *et al.* (1990)

Quality excellence models: EFQM and the CAF

Quality excellence models may be used for self-assessment or as the basis of external assessment. Most quality excellence models have been developed first for the private sector and have been transferred to the public sector. In Europe, they clearly cluster around two core models – the 1999 version of the EFQM Excellence Model (previously known as the Business Excellence Model, which in turn was partially adapted from the Malcolm Baldrige Award in the USA), and the Common Assessment Framework of the European Member States (CAF).

The EFQM Excellence Model (see www.efqm.org), on which a number of Western European national quality award schemes have been based (see Löffler, 2001), has become a widely used self-assessment instrument in the UK and Scandinavian countries, but an organization can also call in external assessors to judge their 'level of excellence' against the model. The assessment framework is a scoring matrix called RADAR – results, approach, deployment, assessment and review – driven by a set of in-depth questions in relation to each of the five enablers and four results areas.

173

At present, EFQM offers two certification processes: a first level 'Committed to Excellence' label, which requires the applicant organization to carry out a self-assessment process and to demonstrate the implementation of at least three improvement plans during a site visit of an EFQM assessor. There is also a more demanding 'Recognized for Excellence' accreditation with the option to go for a 3, 4 or 5 star recognition. And, last but not least, private and public organizations may take part in the European-wide EFQM Excellence Award, which is run on an annual basis.

> The EFQM Excellence Model includes the following key elements:
>
> - leadership
> - policy- and strategy-making
> - people management
> - partnerships and resources
> - processes
> - people results
> - customer results
> - 'impact on society' results
> - key organizational results.
>
> The first five of these factors are labelled 'enablers' (essentially critical success factors), and the last four are the performance results.

Over time, EFQM has also introduced more specific Excellence Frameworks which focus on topical issues such as Knowledge Management, Corporate Social Responsibility and Risk Management.

The Common Assessment Framework (CAF) has been promoted as a 'light' version of the EFQM Excellence model, specifically designed for public organizations starting on the quality journey. The first two versions of CAF explicitly stressed how much easier the self-assessment approach was under CAF. However, the current (2006) version has adopted the EFQM RADAR approach, while still giving public agencies the option of using the simplified assessment method. Consequently, the sole remaining key difference from EFQM is that the CAF criteria can be downloaded without any charge from the CAF Centre Internet site (www.eipa.eu).

At present, the CAF Centre offers no accreditation, although there are demands from the CAF community for this. Currently, the EFQM 'Committed to Excellence' Scheme is normally prepared to recognize self-assessment processes based on the CAF.

QUALITY MANAGEMENT INITIATIVES

Many managers take the view that quality needs to be measured and controlled (sometimes even going as far as to use the old maxim 'If you can't measure it, you can't manage it'). We believe this is going much too far. Even though measurement and quality control (more realistically 'quality shaping') are important tools for improving quality in public administration, they are only part of the process. Experience in the UK – where there are more inspectors, auditors and regulators than taxi drivers (Hood *et al.*, 1998) – suggests that a strong focus on measurement and monitoring can easily create a new bureaucracy in the public sector without much improvement in public services (Travers, 2007). We have to acknowledge that, ultimately, not all aspects of quality can be measured, and that *sensing* quality, with determination to follow up and correct those areas where it feels inadequate, is at least as important as gathering 'objective' evidence.

But how can quality improvement be put into practice? Does it really need high commitment from the top, as many quality gurus believe, or can quality management be implemented as a bottom-up approach? Case Example 12.2 suggests that implementation depends strongly on the existence of 'champions' at all levels of the organization.

CASE EXAMPLE 12.2 **THE COURTS SERVICE, UK**

A new Chief Executive took over in the Courts Service in 1998, with a mandate to produce major improvement in the Service. He immediately appointed an experienced change consultant, who had worked with him previously, to carry out a benchmarking exercise. It was seen as important that her work should be seen as credible, independent and 'owned' as far as possible by staff, many of whom (including all the directors) were interviewed during the exercise. The EFQM Excellence Model was used as a framework for the analysis. Strengths and weaknesses ('areas for improvement') were highlighted.

The two main strengths identified were the 'can do' culture – staff were willing to work long hours to solve delivery problems – and staff commitment – staff cared about quality, results and customer service. The 'areas for improvement' were built into a comprehensive action plan, with nine 'strands', including strategic planning, leadership, putting people first, focusing on customers and the needs of the business, developing internal and external partnerships, centre/field relationships, resourcing and targeting for success, and IT to support the business and communications. 'Strand leaders' were appointed to lead developments in each of the nine strands, generally comprising one senior member of HQ and one senior member of field staff. They were supported by cross-cutting steering groups, with people from HQ and the field, and were empowered to take the issue forward however seemed best, as long as it helped develop the new organizational culture and included consultation with people from throughout the organization.

A Change Manager was appointed from internal staff, who was supported by the external change consultant. The programme was publicly launched in early 1999, with a series of events involving about 1,000 staff. The Chief Executive also visited about eighty locations in his first year, which made him and the programme very visible.

The benchmarking exercise was repeated by the same consultant in late 2000, again based on the EFQM Excellence Model. It found that many improvements had already occurred, particularly in strategic planning, leadership development (a top priority in the first phase), internal communication and the achievement of Charter Marks. Local improvements had often been driven by local staff who had accepted the role of 'change champions'.

However, the exercise highlighted that more still needed to be done on customer service, project and programme management, implementing the IT strategy, managing external relationships, and involving more staff at every level.

Source: Adapted from Bovaird and Gaster (2002)

It will be interesting to see how the quality management initiative of the Courts Service evolves as practice tells us that quality initiatives are difficult to sustain. Often they are simply imposed from above, sometimes through engagement of an external consultant, and seen as an 'add-on' process', irrelevant to 'the staff who do the work'. As Lucy Gaster (1995, p. 9) stresses, quality management has to be embedded within an organization's values, otherwise it is bound to fail. Another good example of such a transformed public agency is the Federal Office of Administration (*Bundesverwaltungsamt*) which started its quality journey more than ten years ago.

So getting the systems right – developing quality assessment systems and providing staff training in customer service – is only one aspect of implementation: when moving from public service quality to governance quality, the negotiation of values with different stakeholders becomes a crucial issue for quality management.

CASE EXAMPLE 12.3 THE FEDERATION OFFICE OF ADMINISTRATION (FAO) IN GERMANY

The quality improvement activities in FAO have been strongly driven by the Vice-President, Giso Schütz, who started the implementation of a quality management system back in 1996. The quality management system was developed in-house, initially within just one department but then throughout the whole organization. The process started with the definition of a vision statement for the whole organization. About 30 members of staff, from all levels of the hierarchy and interest groups, were involved and there was also extensive consultation with the other 2,000 staff members, to achieve a clear understanding of where the organization would go in the future.

As a staff survey showed, the time and resources invested into communicating the new vision were well spent – most staff welcomed the change from a bureaucratic organization to a modern service provider. Of course, there were initially also some sceptics, who thought that the vision could never become a reality. These doubts quickly faded away when staff began to receive 'thank you' letters from service users, soon followed by international recognition, when FAO was showcased at the first European Quality Conference in Lisbon in 2000. Furthermore, the Bertelsmann Foundation nominated FAO as one of the best-run public agencies in Europe. The improvements achieved included, for example, the reimbursement of travel expenses within 48 hours (maximum), compared with weeks. Today, hardly any members of staff talk explicitly about quality any more in the Agency – it has become internalized and part of the code of conduct shared by all staff. Consequently, FAO continues to lead innovations in e-government, and its innovations are now being imitated by other federal agencies. However, Herr Schütz is not afraid of competition from imitators – he believes that this can only drive his agency to stay at the leading edge of innovation.

Source: Adapted from Löffler (2006)

FROM QUALITY OF PUBLIC SERVICES TOWARDS QUALITY OF LIFE

There is empirical evidence that many citizens who are reasonably satisfied with the quality of the public services that they receive are, at the same time, cynical about, and mistrustful of, government, Parliament and the civil service (see CCMD, 1998). This indicates that there is no linear relationship between service quality and trust.

From this wider perspective, an excellent public agency is not simply one that has the characteristics of an excellent service provider. It must also be excellent in the way in which it discharges its political and social responsibilities to its constituency (see Chapter 15).

As a consequence, quality indicators should not only focus on measuring service quality as provided by an individual organization, but also the quality of services provided by the overall service system, and the overall quality of life in a specific area. Quality of life indicators will therefore be needed for a wide range of dimensions of the quality of life – for example, those measured by the Audit Commission (Box 12.2) and others such as the quality of life at work, the quality of culture, arts, entertainment, sports and other aspects of leisure, the quality of lifelong learning, etc.

Moreover, a high-quality public administration must not only be able to increase customer satisfaction with public services but also build trust in public administration through transparent processes and accountability and through democratic dialogue. In order to do so, conventional business concepts of quality, which regard public agencies as service providers and citizens as customers, must be enriched by a political concept of quality that perceives public agencies as catalysts of a responsible and active civic society, through activation of citizens and other stakeholders.

BOX 12.2 KEY QUALITY OF LIFE INDICATORS OF THE AUDIT COMMISSION

The indicators used in a pilot of the Audit Commission included the following thirteen themes:

- combatting unemployment;
- encouraging economic regeneration;
- tackling poverty and social exclusion;
- developing people's skills;
- improving people's health;
- improving housing opportunities;
- tackling community safety;
- strengthening community involvement;
- reducing pollution;
- improving management of the environment;
- improving the local environment;
- improving transport;
- protecting the diversity of nature.

Source: Audit Commission (2002a, p. 7)

BOX 12.3 QUALITY INDICATORS FOR GOVERNANCE PROCESSES

- Strength of political institutions – voting, party membership, activism.
- Strength of civic institutions – membership, volunteering, office-holding, fundraising, donations.
- Strength of sharing and collective behaviour – environmental protection, social care, crime prevention, sharing of household work.
- Achievement of equity and equality – of opportunity, income, outcome, etc.
- Respect for diversity, tolerance of difference.
- Level of openness and transparency in organizations – in public, voluntary, private sectors.
- Levels of honesty and integrity in public domain.
- Ability of the community to manage itself and meet needs not met by the state.

Source: Bovaird *et al.* (2003)

This is likely to be the focus of the development of quality management in the new era of public governance. In Box 12.3 we suggest some of the areas in which future quality indicators will need to be developed in order to assess the quality of local governance processes – and many of these will also be relevant at national level to assess the quality of public governance in a country as a whole. One approach to such an assessment of public governance, the GI Governance Test, is illustrated in Chapter 15.

SUMMARY

Not so long ago, quality was regarded as a topic that was essentially subjective and therefore not amenable to rational analysis – it was assumed that it was essentially 'a matter of opinion'. In recent years, many different ways have been found to bring the discussion of quality management into the centre of managerial decision-making.

However, although there are now many useful tools and techniques available to examine quality in the public sector, it is essential that we remember that the essence of quality lies beyond that which can be described or measured. Consequently, we need to leave a space, in all our quality management systems, for the appropriate use of judgement and subjective assessment. The study of management is now much richer because this is better understood and accepted than it used to be.

In the future, we are likely to see discussions of 'organizational excellence' being extended beyond assessment of the quality of services towards assessment of the quality of life outcomes to which public organizations and their partners contribute, and assessment of the quality of public governance processes.

QUESTIONS FOR REVIEW AND DISCUSSION

1   Consider the approach to quality which suggests that its appreciation lies beyond language and quantification (the approach that believes that quality involves 'passionate emotional involvement'). Are there any public services where this might be the most appropriate approach, in your view? If this approach were taken to quality management in one of these services, how do you think the achievement of better quality could be ascertained?

2   What are the arguments for using more than one approach to defining quality in an organization? How do you think the organization could avoid confusion in its subsequent quality management initiatives?

READER EXERCISES

1   Consider the different approaches to quality accreditation. Find a public agency in your area that has won accreditation under one of these schemes. Do you think that this has made any obvious difference to the quality of the service which it provides? If yes, think about how you have assessed the quality of service in your own mind – what definition of quality have you used? If no, think through the possible reasons why the accreditation process has not made a difference?

2   Take the example of a public organization with which you are familiar. Consider how the elements of the EFQM Excellence Model or the CAF might be applied to this organization? Are there any other dimensions of 'excellence' in the organization that you think are not captured in this model?

CLASS EXERCISES

1   How do you think quality should be defined in a university or college? Given this definition, how do you think it ought to be measured? What dangers do you think might emerge from such a measurement process? How would you suggest that they be minimized?

2   Divide into groups. Each group should look at one or two service charters and suggest ways in which their achievement could be assessed – either quantitatively or qualitatively or both. Groups should then critique each other's suggestions in a plenary session.

FURTHER READING

Lucy Gaster (1995), *Quality in public services: manager's choices.* Buckingham: Open University Press.

Christopher Pollitt and Geert Bouckaert (eds) (1995), *Quality improvement in European public services. Concepts, cases and commentary.* London: Sage.

Christopher Pollitt, Geert Bouckaert and Elke Löffler (2007), *Making quality sustainable: co-design, co-decide, co-produce, co-evaluate.* Finland: Ministry of Finance.

179

REFERENCES

Audit Commission (2002a), *Quality of life: using quality of life indicators.* London: Audit Commission.

Valerie Beale and Christopher Pollitt (1994), 'Charters at the grass-roots: a first report', *Local Government Studies,* 20 (2) (summer): 202–25.

Geert Bouckaert (1995c), 'Measuring quality', in Christopher Pollitt and Geert Bouckaert (eds), *Quality improvement in European public services. Concepts, cases and commentary.* London: Sage, pp. 20–8.

Tony Bovaird and Lucy Gaster (2002), 'Civil service reform: evaluation'. Unpublished case study for Cabinet Office.

Tony Bovaird and Arie Halachmi (1999), 'Community scorecards: the role of stakeholders in performance assessment', in Arie Halachmi (ed.), *Performance and quality measurement in government: issues and experiences.* Burke, VA: Chatelaine Press, pp. 145–55.

Tony Bovaird and Elke Löffler (2003), 'Evaluating the quality of public governance: indicators, models and methodologies', *International Review of Administrative Sciences,* 69 (3): 313–28.

Tony Bovaird, Elke Löffler and Jeremy Martin (2003), 'From corporate governance to local governance: stakeholder-driven community score-cards for UK local agencies?', *International Journal of Public Administration,* 26 (8 & 9): 1–24.

Cabinet Office (1999c), *Quality schemes task force.* Report. London: Cabinet Office (http://archive.cabinetoffice.gov.uk/servicefirst/2000/taskforce/report.htm, accessed 25 May 2008).

CCMD (1998), *Citizen/client surveys: dispelling myths and redrawing maps.* Ottawa: Canadian Centre for Management Development.

CLG (2008), *Communities in control: real power, real people,* Cm7427. London: Stationery Office.

Lucy Gaster (1995), *Quality in public services: manager's choices.* Buckingham: Open University Press.

HMSO (1991), *The citizen's charter,* Cm 1599. London: HMSO.

Christopher Hood, Colin Scott, George Jones, Oliver James and Tony Travers (1998), *Regulation inside government: waste-watchers, quality police and sleaze busters.* Oxford: Oxford University Press.

Elke Löffler (2001), 'Quality awards as a public sector benchmarking concept in OECD countries: some guidelines for quality award organisers', *Public Administration and Development,* 21 (1): 25–47.

Elke Löffler (2006), 'Lessons from Europe: innovations in public sector quality', in Ministry of Public Administration (ed.), *Good practices in Slovenian public administration.* Ljubljana, Slovenia: Ministry of Public Administration, pp. 25–36.

Elke Löffler, Salvador Parrado and Tomás Zmeskal (2007), *Improving customer orientation through service charters: a handbook for improving quality of public services.* Paris: OECD, Ministry of the Interior of the Czech Republic and Governance International.

Christopher Pollitt and Geert Bouckaert (eds) (1995), *Quality improvement in European public services: concepts, cases and commentary.* London: Sage.

Max Travers (2007), *The new bureaucracy: quality assurance and its critics.* Bristol: Policy Press.

Kieron Walsh (1991b), 'Quality and public services', *Public Administration,* 69 (4): 503–14.

Valarie A. Zeithaml, A. Parasuraman and Leonard L. Berry (1990), *Delivering service quality: balancing customer perceptions and expectations.* New York: Free Press.

Chapter 13

Process management in public sector organizations

Kuno Schedler and *Utz Helmuth*, University of St Gallen, Switzerland

INTRODUCTION

With the increasing popularity of quality management in the private sector, business processes and their optimization have become an important issue for business. But does this also apply for the public sector, which is subject to different demands and restrictions from business? Business process thinking has indeed found its way into the public sector. In this chapter, we will show that it offers many advantages – in particular, it helps to eliminate wasteful activities inside organizations and to redesign processes so that they add more value for the organization's external customers, especially users. However, radical approaches to improving process management continue to be a challenge for traditional work patterns and hierarchical structures in public agencies.

LEARNING OBJECTIVES

■ To understand what a process is.
■ To distinguish different processes from each other.
■ To learn how processes are measured and optimized.
■ To understand the challenges which process management entails for public management.

THE PARADIGM CHANGE FROM A HIERARCHIAL TO PROCESS-ORIENTED ORGANIZATION

Let us think of the classical organization paradigm: as with companies, public agencies were traditionally organized in a top-down manner. This form of organization, typically described as a *hierarchical structure*, is marked by a pronounced internal orientation, as well as long communication and decision-making chains. Work tasks are typically delegated by line managers from top to bottom, and decisions are presented for authorization from bottom to top.

The major advantage of hierarchical organizations is that all parties involved know what they have to do — e.g. in army chains of command. This form of organization, however, suffers from two decisive disadvantages: First, decision-making times are relatively long, and, second, internally focused staff are not responsive to customers, nor much interested in their needs and preferences. Their working world exists inside rather than outside the organization.

In view of the increased competition faced by many public sector organizations since the 1970s, they have increasingly taken up various private sector approaches to environmental analysis, such as SWOT analysis and Porter's value chain analysis. In these approaches, the organization is not viewed as a hierarchical alignment of individual functions of a company but rather as a production process. Organization functions are assigned to the production process as primary or support activities. This new perspective has considerable organizational consequences. The vertical view of the organization (top-down line management) has changed into a horizontal view (input-output relationships) (see Figure 13.1). This organizational form is called a *process-oriented organization*.

Following the establishment of process thinking in many companies in the 1980s, a second wave in the 1990s, particularly influenced by Champy and Hammer (1993), promoted the idea of a *re*-engineering of processes to make them more customer-oriented (so-called *business process reengineering*). In the following, we will use the simplified term 'process management'.

This private sector discourse must be adapted appropriately before it can be transferred to a public sector context, as public agencies are subject to quite different requirements and regulation. From a legal perspective, for instance, there may be situations where it is necessary, at least formally, to organize a public agency on hierarchical lines. Elected politicians, for example, may believe that only the subordination explicit in hierarchy can ensure that they are able to control the administration. However, such considerations may conflict with the pressures to more process-driven approaches, arising from the financial pressures to use resources more efficiently, and the consequent pressure on public agencies to prioritize efficient service delivery (see Chapters 2 and 11) and quality management (see Chapter 12).

Of course, most public agencies provide services, rather than manufactured goods. Here, the development of information and communications technology (ICT) stands public

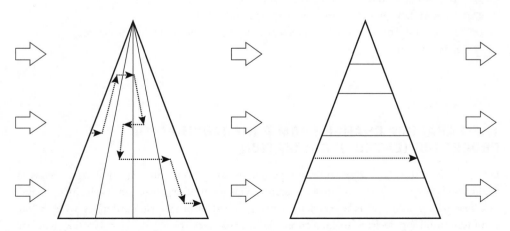

Figure 13.1 *90° rotation from hierarchical to process-oriented organization*

organizations in particularly good stead, because information and data processes typically constitute the core of the 'production process' in a service. Through the development of uniform communication protocols, data and database standards, the triumphal march of ICT is smoothing the way for a business process orientation in public agencies (see also Chapter 10). First, different departments in different locations can now access the same data simultaneously. Second, electronic data management considerably reduces decision making and process throughput times. Furthermore, through the Internet, customers can link up to processes within public agencies and receive services directly, without having to go through other intermediaries or other interfaces, which can greatly speed up and streamline the service that the public service organization offers to its customers.

The nature of a process

What exactly is a process? Let's have a look at this more closely. In terms of the process organization outlined earlier, one can visualize a business process as a recipe for achieving results in organizations. As in a cook-book, it documents in a step-by-step fashion who has to undertake which activities in an organization in order to achieve a particular goal. A process proceeds chronologically from input to output, i.e. from the provision of resources to the

> ### WHAT IS A BUSINESS PROCESS?
>
> 'The logical organization of people, materials, energy, equipment, and procedures into work activities designed to produce a specified end result.'
>
> *Source*: Pall (1987)

delivery of the service. The fundamental components are 'events as triggers' and the activities that follow them. These activities are often assigned to organization functions (also called organizational 'roles').

When looking at a public organization, different types of process can be observed. It is useful to make the distinction between core processes and support processes (Porter, 1985). A *core process* in an organization is one that makes a *significantly higher* contribution to the *perceived* customer benefit than is the case in a potentially competing organization. *Support processes*, by contrast, have more unspecific, supportive functions and do not need to be produced in one's own organization – they could be outsourced (see Chapter 7).

This distinction, originally developed for the manufacturing industry, can be transferred to the public sector, as shown by the value chain of a hospital (Figure 13.2). Processes such as the treatment of patients can be considered as core processes, while the facility management of a hospital can be seen as a support process.

However, in the public sector, process analysis is not based only on efficiency arguments. In many cases, the shape of processes is predefined by legal norms. These guarantee legal rights of citizens in their contacts with the government. For example, most processes related to building applications include time limits for possible legal objections. Shortening these 'waiting times' may be seen as better process management but it also involves potentially sensitive reductions in citizens' ability to mount a well-reasoned objection. A significant part of perceived 'public value' (see Chapter 5) arising from public sector processes often lies

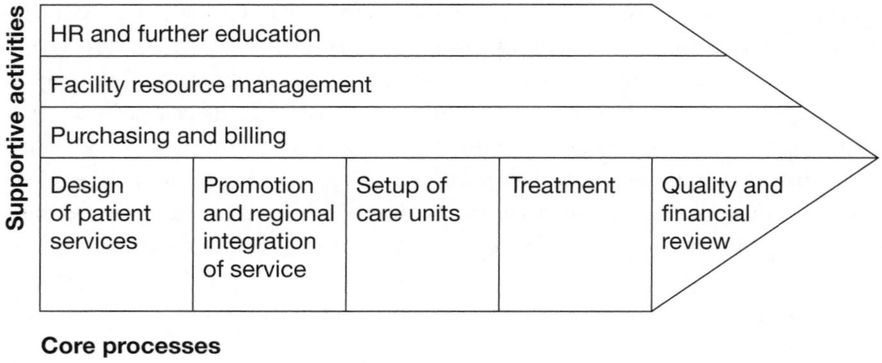

Figure 13.2 *Value chain of a hospital*
Source: Adapted from Porter (1985)

precisely in this intertwining of organizational action and existing laws, rules and norms. In many cases, this means that certain government processes cannot easily be privatized or outsourced. For example, in most European countries it is considered impossible to privatize criminal courts, as only the state is seen as a legitimate guardian of the norms underlying the operation of court processes.

Lenk (2007) suggests a further distinction between well-structured *production processes* (e.g. dealing with a tax return) and open-ended *decision-making processes* (e.g. dealing with a planning application). The latter grant considerable degrees of freedom to administrative officers. Both sets of processes occur in public agencies, but only the former is suitable for full process mapping and standardization. Moreover, in decision-making processes, team-based working may be preferable to sequential process cycles, and the ICT approach may need to take this into account, e.g. the setting up of a virtual round-table or discussion forum for the architects and planners involved in processing a planning application.

The process chain needs to consider the interaction between the parties concerned, e.g. different professional groups, managers and citizens. In public services, it is rarely appropriate to model the supply chain as simply a vertical, continuous sequence of activities linking suppliers to their customers. Often service users and other citizens are involved in several stages of the 'supply chain', e.g. in co-designing or co-managing or co-delivering certain activities (see Chapter 15). Consequently, customers and other stakeholders of public agencies need to be modelled in separate strands (or 'swimming lanes', as we shall call them later).

Analysing a process

The first step in process analysis is the recording of processes. This helps not only to identify weaknesses in processes, and the potential for optimizing them, but in documenting them for quality assurance or for replicating them elsewhere.

The second stage is to consider alternative process chains for achieving the same customer benefits. This can be done by reconfiguring existing processes or by *de novo* analysis (e.g. in business process re-engineering). A key element of service redesign is to determine the information that is required for the analysis. Returning to the metaphor of the cook-book, different dishes and preparation methods have to be chosen, depending on whether a dish is intended for a vegetarian, child or sick person. Table 13.1 provides an overview of possible information to be considered in the recording and analysis of processes. In determining the relevant information, the intended objectives and target groups of the process are key. Managers who want to bring about a radical improvement in the efficiency of a process require different information to the supervisors who are responsible for making the process run smoothly. However as most processes in public administration involve several organizational units, comprehensive information is usually not at hand and often has to be collected in advance or through special investigation.

For the recording of information, a combination of written survey and interviews has proved to be of value. Questionnaires help to establish in a structured manner the basic features of a process, such as the people involved, activity sequences and information flows. In a second step, the person doing the recording should have the opportunity to clarify potential ambiguities with the staff concerned.

Such a multiplicity of recorded information inevitably leads to the question of how this information can be meaningfully reproduced. A simple description in text form, as in a cooking recipe, quickly reveals serious limitations. An alternative is provided by the graphical depiction of business processes, introduced by Fritz Nordsieck (1932) at the beginning of the 1930s. In particular, process sequence and parties involved are immediately apparent from such an illustration. Through formal symbols, rules and abstractions, further information can be depicted in these business process diagrams. Moreover, such diagrams aid comparisons between business processes. The audience being addressed should be taken into account – highly formalized business process diagrams designed to help the software programmer will probably not be understood by top managers. A remedy to this problem is provided by subsets, which allow different levels of detail to be shown to different stakeholders. A subset represents a window into the underlying process, using a selection of the information available.

In Figure 13.3, such a subset is illustrated for the process of passport application in a Swiss city. It uses the internationally accepted methodology of the non-proprietary standard *Business Process Modelling Notation* (BPMN). For purposes of modelling, BPMN uses flow objects,

Table 13.1 *Information dimensions for the structured recording of processes*

Feature of the process	Information that is likely to be required
Parties involved in process	Internal organization units, customers, other external parties
Resources and events used in the process	Input, output, activities, media, data, ICT, environmental conditions in which the process is carried out
Sequential aspects	Sequence of activities, frequencies of different activities, throughput times for different activities
Quality of the process	Importance of the process for the value-added to the customer, frequency of service failures or customer complaints or need for customer revisits/retreatment

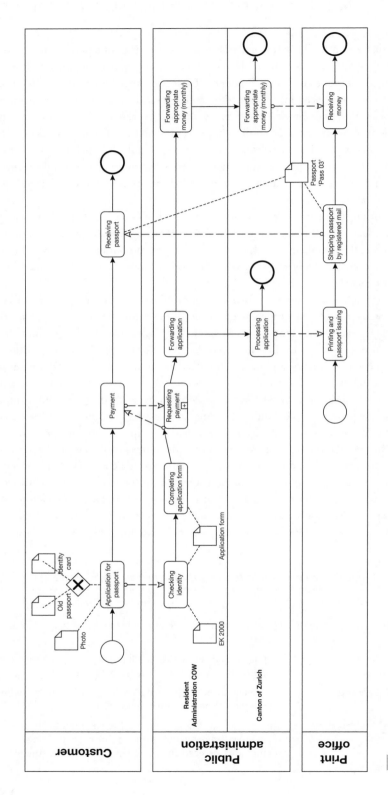

Figure 13.3 Process map for application for a Swiss passport in the City of Winterthur

connecting objects and artifacts. *Flow objects* describe *what* is happening: In the form of circular *events*, they describe the start, interruption and end of a process. Rectangular *activities* stand for the tasks in a process ('open letter') and show sub-processes (marked by an '+'). Diamond-shaped *gateways* mark the diverging and converging of processes. *Connecting objects* join flow objects through arrows. Unbroken arrows indicate the process flow, broken arrows indicate information flows between different organizations, and broken lines represent associations. Finally, the example also shows *artifacts* in the form of *data objects*, which are used to describe more closely data used by activities. These are symbolized by a sheet of paper with the upper right-hand corner folded over. The various parties involved are separated from one another by 'swimming lanes' (within an organization) or 'pools' for different organizations (cf. Fig. 13.3).

Optimizing a business process

The third stage in process analysis is process optimization – choosing the right option for process improvement. Every optimization is inevitably normative. The chosen goal provides the line of attack for the optimization procedure. Such goals can take very different shapes according to the stakeholder concerned. While politics normally insists on its primacy ('the administration should push through its policies'), the general legal framework demands that decisions of the administration should above all be correct in terms of the law and the law should be the same for all. Customers, too, push for their own needs ('decisions should be made as quickly as possible and should take into account our special circumstances'). The definition of the goal of process optimization is therefore a decision about which diverging interests often contend, so that these interests have to be weighed up against each other.

In the following, we will concentrate on four *business management optimization dimensions*: the internal organizational dimensions of (1) effectiveness and (2) efficiency, and the environmentally-influenced dimensions of (3) adaptivity (or 'fit') to the legal framework or environment and (4) customer benefit of the process (see Figure 13.4).

Effectiveness describes the degree to which a goal is achieved. Imagine the example of a street cleaning programme – this is said to be effective if the city streets appear clean. (For a production process, the key indicator of effectiveness would often be the 'defect' rate.) *Efficiency*, by contrast, measures the input–output ratio (see Chapter 11). If Team A is able to clean an area in one week using nine workers while Team B requires ten workers, Team A is more efficient than Team B. What is then important is the interplay of both factors: the work of the two teams can only be fully compared if one brings in how well they clean the streets (effectiveness). If the streets of Team A constantly have to be recleaned, owing to frequent complaints from residents, then the performance of Team B might, on balance, be judged the better.

An indicator that reflects both the effectiveness and the efficiency of a process is the *total throughput time*. This incorporates not only the actual processing, but also post-processing times that are caused by quality failure, appeals, etc. The total throughput time may be lengthened, for example, if a file remains untouched for too long (since additional clarification has to be asked for), or if a decision is contested owing to flaws in the process. However, it is important that cases that in one sense are lower priority should not be completely

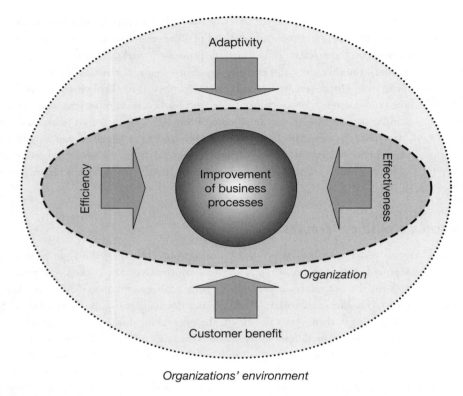

Figure 13.4 *Dimensions influencing the optimization of business processes*

overlooked. The demand for efficiency is itself subject to the efficiency paradigm: reorganizing processes is costly and should be subject to efficiency considerations, too. Consequently, putting in significant resources to optimize a very rare process is likely to be less efficient than optimizing one with a high number of cases, especially if those cases relate to high priority groups. It is not surprising that services such as tax collection or issuing of driving licences tend to be the most successfully transferred to online platforms, as they exhibit the quantities necessary for efficient reform. In addition, the Accenture (2006) public sector survey shows that, in many countries, the utilization of e-government services offered by government is lagging clearly behind Internet penetration and even in the countries categorized as developed, only 16 per cent of respondents regularly use e-government services.

The example of street cleaning above also shows why quality management is so inherently linked with process management. An effectively cleaned street requires good quality management in order to achieve the goals of cleanliness. Optimized processes inevitably require advanced quality management processes. Conversely, techniques of process management such as clear documentation of processes (inherent in the implementation of ISO norms) are important building blocks in successful quality management (see Chapter 12). Table 13.2 cites several process-oriented process optimization initiatives that are well suited to the public sector.

BOX 13.1 EXAMPLES OF INEFFECTIVE AND INEFFICIENT PUBLIC PROCESSES

Ineffective processes:

■ strong variance in the service quality;

■ unusually high death rate (health care);

■ high crime rate (police and public safety organization);

■ poor results in the OECD Pisa study (school system);

■ low place in research rankings (university system);

■ high number of successful appeals or complaints against administrative decisions (e.g. for a planning authority).

Inefficient processes:

■ high number of activities which have to be redone;

■ arbitrary process flow due to unclear responsibilities;

■ fourteen signatures needed for each draft (responsibilities too spread out);

■ work that is not value-adding (double examinations in health care);

■ outmoded teaching methods (getting all students to write out standard notes);

■ delays in treating high-priority cases (no triage system when customers register);

■ unnecessarily expensive purchasing (e.g. due to corruption).

Table 13.2 *Overview of process optimization approaches*

Initiatives	Implementation
Omit	Seek and cancel unnecessary work steps
Standardize	Standardize work steps with comparable content, thus making them transferable
Improve use of resources	Are all resources used in such a way that the total throughput time is reduced? Are any areas under-capitalized, thus causing generally higher costs through uneconomical maintenance measures (e.g. outdated ICT equipment or transport fleet)?
Replace with other processes	Does it make sense to replace a process with another, thus avoiding duplicate work?
Do activities in parallel	Reduce the process duration for the customer through the simultaneous processing of several sub-processes
Outsource	Transfer processes that are uneconomical and/or do not reach a critical number of cases to other administrative units or external service providers
Avoid doubling back	Implement quality measures so that post-processing becomes superfluous
Collaboration	For complex, non-sequential decision-making processes, structure collaboration such that the relevant stakeholders are integrated from the outset

Although shortcomings in, and potential improvements to, processes may be obvious to external observers, in organizations there appears to be a fatal tendency for sub-optimal processes to creep in. As the contrast between self-assessment and external assessment usually shows, the internal perception of an organisation is quite different to that of an external observer. In this way, sub-optimal business processes can become a 'blind spot' within an organization. Even when the 'blind spots' are detected, a solution may be some way off – organizations can become locked into fatal routines, they can become mired in competitive wrangling, and many other, quite natural social patterns of behaviour can cause or prolong poor business processes. Established procedural models for business process optimization can be a great help in tackling this, as shown by Case Example 13.1 at IBM, covering the billing process, a mass process that also frequently appears in the public sector.

When considering optimization, the question inevitably arises of the extent of change that is acceptable in the organization. Are there unchangeable rules or 'sacred cows' that cannot be touched? The technique of business process engineering is so controversial precisely because it designs changes at the drawing board, and is therefore detached from the established business culture and the constraints that this imposes. However, diverse demands are placed on the organization and its processes by the environment – and it can be dangerous for the organization to preserve its 'sacred cows' and refuse to respond to these environmental pressures. As in the IBM case study, the success of processes is not merely determined by their effectiveness and efficiency, but also by the *adaptivity* of those processes. Optimized processes are of no use if the organization's environment is changing, unnoticed, and now calls for entirely different services. Process-oriented organizations therefore have to design their processes to take into account the dynamic needs of customers and other stakeholders, in a sustainable fashion. This means that organizations need *dynamic capabilities* – those capabilities that equip the organization to adapt all other organizational capabilities quickly and appropriately to changing circumstances. We have to be realistic, though, and admit that this adaptivity is often harder for public agencies, in spite of repeated and heartfelt efforts for reform, because there are so many limitations at the *political level* that lie outside the influence of public managers.

Limitations to process optimization

In federal countries such as Australia, Austria, Germany, Switzerland and the USA, or states with relatively autonomous regions such as Belgium and Spain, the scope for action between central, regional and local levels of government tends to be clearly legislated. Processes that cross jurisdictions cannot be optimized at the stroke of a pen – no matter how attractive the potential process improvement (e.g. partnership procurement, virtual team-work) may be. In such countries, process improvement can therefore be constrained by the constitution. Nevertheless, there are normally mechanisms for inter-jurisdictional working – and where these are insufficient, the option of constitutional change is sometimes a long-term possibility.

The range of action in most public agencies – aside from major national efforts such as the recent reforms of the federal system in Germany – focuses mainly on the level of the administrative unit. Nevertheless, there are now many efforts to optimize processes across public agencies, for example, inter-municipal cooperation has become a big issue in Germany,

CASE EXAMPLE 13.1 **PROCESS OPTIMIZATION AT IBM**

At the beginning of the 1980s, IBM had difficulties in keeping its internal processes abreast of a continually changing environment. An example of this was outgoing invoices. Although 96 per cent were correctly drawn up from the outset, 54 per cent of the total work time of the department flowed into quality assurance methods to stop the other 4 per cent from occurring. However, this only enabled the final quota of correct invoices to rise to 98.5 per cent. The overriding goal therefore had to be to prevent the errors from the outset instead of using a considerable amount of resources to rectify mistakes retrospectively. The company faced this challenge with a quality management offensive. One key factor seen as critical to success was the improvement of work processes. A process methodology was developed and implemented to integrate fundamentals of quality management into the processes.

This quality management system focused on the following features of every process:

- Ownership should be clearly assigned.
- Process/sub-process should be defined and documented.
- Supplier/customer relationships and requirements should be identified.
- Quality measurements and control points should be established.
- Process simplification should be undertaken.
- Defect prevention methodology and statistical methods should be utilized.

After designating ownerships, processes were then evaluated on the following scale:

5: The current process is either ineffective and flawed or the 'foundations of quality management' are *not* implemented.

4: Although the current process has weaknesses on the operational or control level, these can be rectified in the near future. The 'foundations of quality management' are implemented.

3: The current process fulfils the 'foundations of quality management', is effective in that it covers the customer demands and for the most part does so efficiently and under control.

2: In addition to the requirements of the third step, considerable process improvements were carried out, expressed in measurably improved results. Possible changes in the company environment are evaluated, and corresponding internal process adaptations at least firmly planned.

1: In addition to the requirements of the second stage, the process is evaluated from the perspective of the customer and is practically free of errors.

Furthermore, changes in the functional and first-level management as well as at the employee levels were implemented. This process orientation, together with the strict process evaluations, improved the billing process and related quality measures.

Source: Adapted from Kane (1986, pp. 24–33)

Switzerland, the UK and the USA, as this allows very small local authorities to save resources by pooling processes.

Of course, such process change within partnerships meets lots of difficulties in practice. At the organizational level, the first step in optimization – the determination of one party as responsible for the overall process, the *process owner* – is difficult, or even impossible. At the technical level, there is the inherent problem that very different approaches and standards are already established, which even in the long term can only be rationalized with great difficulty (e.g. very different interface channels between the organizations and service users). This argument, however, should not be misunderstood as a general objection to efforts towards optimization in the public sector. Rather, we must beware of unrealistic expectations (e.g. that partners' services can be 'joined up seamlessly' within a year or two), and be alert to the dangers inherent in their practical implementation (e.g. assuming that some parts of processes are mandatory, however inefficient or ineffective, and therefore ignoring them in the optimization dialogue).

The discussion in recent years surrounding ICT interoperability between different administrations and between administrations and their customers has demonstrated the many difficulties obstructing the consistent design of cross-organizational processes – for instance, non-uniform communication protocols or the lack of signature infrastructures, meaning that data need to be printed out and re-entered at successive stages in the process. Federal states tend to be at a disadvantage here, as the degree of freedom of individual administrative levels is particularly high. Nevertheless, this is not an insuperable obstacle – initiatives such as 'eCH.ch' or 'KoopA ADV' in the very federally organized states of Switzerland and Germany are attempting to counteract this trend, coming to joint definitions of uniform services, establishing uniform communication standards and joint regulation of ICT investment projects.

Finally, the perceived *customer benefit* needs to be central to process improvement, a concept that is increasingly gaining in importance in the public sector. An example of this is the widespread attempt to provide single contact points for citizens to deal with public agencies in their area, with e-enabled know-how, such as contact centres ('call centres'), one-stop shops on the Internet, citizen bureaus and centralized inward investment promotion agencies (e.g. www.ukinvest.gov.uk). Thereby, customer benefit is not limited to economic perspectives: when, in Australia the first one-stop shops were created in the 1970s, their main purpose was to enable social welfare recipients to receive the help they were entitled to – without having to know all the administrative responsibilities and red-tape requirements.

Process change as a challenge

If processes in public institutions are changed, then the managers are faced with a great challenge. Each existing system defines routines, power and responsibilities to which the employees have become accustomed. If this system changes, this initially triggers uncertainty, as both the managers and the employees cannot completely foresee what the future system will bring for them. This raises the question of how social processes that are triggered by process optimization can be managed.

Empirical investigations into the management of change processes unfortunately do not provide a consistent picture, although it appears that participatory management tends to have

CASE EXAMPLE 13.2 **PROCESS OPTIMIZATION OF PUBLIC PROCUREMENT IN THE STATE OF NORTH RHINE-WESTPHALIA**

The public procurement portal for the awarding of contracts of the state of North Rhine-Westphalia (www.evergabe.nrw.de) in Germany provides an example of a process optimization on the micro level in a highly regulated sector. The Internet platform allows the publication and downloading of tender documents and electronic submission of bids. It is intended to realize the four dimensions of process optimization discussed previously – efficiency, effectiveness, adaptability and customer benefit.

The process places very high-quality demands on the organizations involved, as they have to adhere to comprehensive form requirements, confidentiality and encoding requirements laid down by the EU and the German Federal Government. The public agencies could be liable for substantial damages if they do not comply with the agreed procedures (e.g. by sending incomplete documentation), and prospective contractors can be excluded from the tender if they do not conform to the procedures. Both the administration and the companies concerned therefore have considerable interest in an optimization that helps to avoid potential errors in the tender process.

The solution adopted, as shown in Figure 13.5, resulted in considerably reduced costs for both sides. Instead of searching in many publications for suitable tenders, as was previously the case (1), the bidders are now automatically informed about suitable tenders via email. The fee for the duplication of documents is dropped (2). The bidder merely authenticates himself/herself once (3) in order to download the tender documents (4). This saves not only the fee, but also a great deal of time. In the non-digital procedure, by contrast, bidders had to wait for the contractor to check that payment had been received (5), copy the tender documents (6), check that everything was complete (7), where necessary rectify (8) and finally send the documents (9). In addition, the placing of bids is facilitated as it ensues electronically (10), thus sparing the postage time and enabling the bidder to gain confirmation in real time that the bid has been submitted within the prescribed time. In addition, the public agency can now make electronic comparisons of the bids (11).

This process optimization has demonstrated that both sides can benefit from a shortening of the procurement deadlines, which can reduce the duration of the whole process by up to 20 per cent. Moreover, both the parties concerned can make considerable savings because, as shown in the process diagram, they can reduce their inputs.

positive effects on performance and job satisfaction – albeit to a more limited extent than is commonly assumed (Wagner, 1994). Thomas and Davies (2005) showed, in a qualitative study in the British public service, that employees may boycott changes in work organization during the introduction of New Public Management, if they do not understand the background to the changes. The authors believe that resistance by employees is brought about not only by changes that they see as unfounded and pushed through by management – i.e. as their

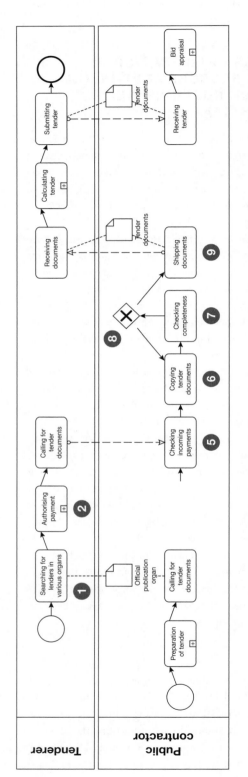
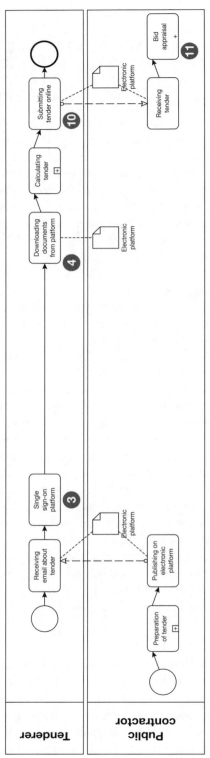

Figure 13.5 *Process optimization in awarding contracts in North Rhine-Westphalia (Top: Old procedure; Bottom: Optimized electronic procedure)*

reaction to perceived repression – but above all by feeling that their identities are being called into question by the change. Conversely, in an investigation into the introduction of a new computer system in a British authority, Symon (2005) points out that the resistance, although damaging for the employer, can in itself create a sense of identity for those affected.

SUMMARY

Process management provides a new angle to the traditional, hierarchical view of public administration. From this 90° shift in perspective, organizational action is analysed as steps towards the creation of public value – steps that cross organizational units and hierarchical levels. Optimizing processes in public administration leads to greater efficiency and effectiveness, but also to better quality. There are, however, certain limits to the potential scope for reorganizing, determined by legal requirements that guarantee the democratic and/or legal rights of citizens and others affected.

Traditionally, bureaucracies have been seen as machine-type organizations with strict intra-organisational boundaries and task divisions. Modern public management, however, is multilayered, multidisciplinary and collaborative. Public managers are challenged to structure their organizations along lean processes that allow for responsive, cost-effective and timely government services. Administrative processes are clearly one area that continues to harbour great potential for optimization – and the struggle to find ways of achieving this has been at the heart of many public sector reform programmes around the world in the last twenty-five years.

QUESTIONS FOR REVIEW AND DISCUSSION

1   Distinguish between activities, processes and services. How are they related to customer benefit?
2   How do process maps relate to strategy maps (Chapter 6)?
3   Why do democratic and legal requirements limit the potential for process optimization?

READER EXERCISES

1   Think of the last activity that you undertook with a public agency (e.g. making a passport application, applying for a grant or social insurance benefit). Can you think of any ways in which the process could have been made more efficient? More effective? Faster? Why do you think those improvements have not already been introduced?
2   Find an article in a local or national newspaper or magazine about problems arising from changes taking place in a public sector organization. Examine the article to find evidence of whether process changes have played a role in generating these problems.

195

CLASS EXERCISES

1   Divide into groups of four to six people. Each group should identify one key process of your university/school that leads to an important end result which a student has to undertake as part of his or her studies (e.g. passing an exam, submitting high quality assignments, making job applications, etc.). Draw up a process map for this process and suggest ways in which the process might be improved to add value to students and to the administration of the programme. Each group should present its findings in a plenary session to the other groups.

FURTHER READING

James Champy and Michael Hammer (1993), *Reengineering the corporation*. New York: Harper Business.

Richard B. Chase, F. Robert Jacobs and Nicholas J. Aquilano (2007), *Operations management for competitive advantage* (11th international edn). Boston, MA: McGraw-Hill, Chapter 5.

Klaus Klaus and Roland Traunmüller (2002), 'Preface to the focus theme on e-government', *EM – Electronic Markets*, 12 (3): 147–8.

Robert MacIntosh (2003), 'BPR: alive and well in the public sector', *International Journal of Operations & Production Management*, 23 (3): 327–44.

Edoardo Ongaro (2004), 'Process management in the public sector: the experience of one-stop shops in Italy', *The International Journal of Public Sector Management*, 17 (1): 81–107.

Karl E. Weick and Robert E. Quinn (1999), 'Organizational change and development', *Annual Review of Psychology*, 50: 361–86.

REFERENCES

Accenture (2006), *Leadership in customer service: building the trust* (www.accenture.com).

James Champy and Michael Hammer (1993), *Reengineering the corporation*. New York: Harper Business.

Edward J. Kane (1986), 'IBM's quality focus on the business process', *Quality Progress*. Milwaukee, WI: American Society for Quality, pp. 24–33.

Klaus Lenk (2007), 'Reconstruction public administration theory from below', *Information Polity*, 12 (4): 207–12.

Fritz Nordsieck (1932), *Die schaubildliche Erfassung und Untersuchung der Betriebsorganisation*, Stuttgart: C.E. Poeschel.

Gabriel A. Pall (1987), *Quality process management*, Englewood Cliffs, NJ: Prentice Hall.

Michael Porter (1985), *Competitive advantage*. New York: Macmillan.

Gillian Symon (2005), 'Exploring resistance from a rhetorical perspective', *Organization Studies*, 26 (11): 1641–63.

Robyn Thomas and Annette Davies (2005), 'Theorizing the micro-politics of resistance: new public management and managerial identities in the UK public services', *Organization Studies*, 26 (5): 683–706.

John A. Wagner III (1994), 'Participation's effects on performance and satisfaction: a reconsideration of research evidence', *The Academy of Management Review*, 19 (2): 312–30.

Chapter 14

Scrutiny, inspection and audit in the public sector

John Clarke, Open University, UK

INTRODUCTION

Although publicly provided services have always been subject to forms of scrutiny, the emergence of new organisational forms and structures of service provision in recent years has made scrutiny an increasingly significant feature of their governance and management. In particular, the move towards more fragmented, dispersed and 'arm's length' structures of provision has led both central and local government to enlarge and enhance their repertoire of forms and practices of scrutiny.

Since the 1980s, we have experienced a period of innovation and reform in the organisational systems of providing public services (see Chapters 2 and 4). While such changes have been uneven internationally, some key elements of reform (towards the de-monopolisation of public sector organisations; the move towards marketisation and privatisation of service provision and an enthusiasm for the model of New Public Management) have attained international currency (see Chapter 4).

THE 'POLITICS OF ORGANISATIONAL DESIGN'

The rise of anti-statist and pro-market political projects has been accompanied by a 'politics of organisational design'. This politics has systematically challenged notions of the public (public interest, public services, public spending and public sectors) in order to 'liberate' private interests and markets from the growth of the state in the second half of the twentieth century (Clarke, 2004; Newman and Clarke, 2009). Although states have not been swept away, the programmes of reform in many countries have marketised, privatised and broken up public services in pursuit of the innovation, efficiency and choice promised by market advocates.

In this chapter, I explore the view that the reform of public services has driven an expansion of forms of scrutiny (particularly those of inspection and audit) and has simultaneously led to a blurring of boundaries between audit, inspection, organisational design and consultancy.

The purposes and processes of scrutiny have become complicated in the effort to govern a dispersed system of public provision at a distance. Expanded scrutiny – what Power has called the 'audit explosion' (1993, 1997) – emerges in this process of reform, and its continued spread has been driven by the problems of managing the organisational forms and relationships created by the reform process.

This chapter will explore the development of scrutiny, the changing forms and meanings of scrutiny, and the arguments about the necessity, desirability and effectiveness of such processes.

LEARNING OBJECTIVES

This chapter will look at the following key issues:
- the conditions leading to the recent 'audit explosion' in the public sector;
- new practices of audit;
- changing roles of scrutiny agencies and processes;
- the challenges to scrutiny of public sector organisations.

LEVELS AND NEW FORMS OF SCRUTINY

Until the 1980s, the archetypal organisational form of public service provision was that of the professional bureaucracy, in which hierarchical administration of policies and resources left spaces for professional autonomy, judgement and practice (Clarke and Newman, 1997). Combined with the governmental processes of representative democracy, such systems contained particular models of accountability and scrutiny.

These centred on vertical chains of accountability through the levels of the bureaucracy to senior officials and upwards to elected politicians (at local, regional or national level). They were supplemented by norms of administration and professional practice, often embodied within ethical codes of conduct that were supervised by professional disciplinary bodies such as the medical model of professional self-regulation (see Chapter 21). In some cases they were also subject to professional inspection to evaluate and advise upon standards of practice (e.g. in teaching, social work and policing, see Hughes *et al.*, 1996). Finally, the professional bureaucracies were typically subject to the practice of audit (in its traditional accounting meaning) to ensure that financial probity and good practice were being pursued in the handling of public funds.

The late twentieth-century reforms of public service organisation disrupted these systems of accountability and scrutiny in two main ways. First, they fragmented and dispersed the organisations of service provision through the multiple strategies of decentralisation, marketisation, and privatisation, thus dislocating the possibilities of internal, vertical and hierarchical systems of control and scrutiny. The resulting complexity of organisational forms of public service provision – decentralised, semi-autonomous organisations linked in shifting webs of competitive and collaborative relationships, and subject to mixes of vertical and horizontal pressures for responsiveness and accountability – posed new problems of how to scrutinise service providers.

Second, however, public choice theorists and advocates wove a compelling story out of the inadequacies, problems and frustrations of professional bureaucracies around the issue of trust. The combination of representative democracy and professional bureaucracy rested on assumptions about the effective articulation of the public interest through political representation, administrative neutrality and professional disinterest (Clarke and Newman, 1997; Dunleavy, 1991). Such critics argued that none of these assumptions held – and that politicians, bureaucrats and professionals were better viewed as fundamentally venal, self-interested and seeking to maximise their own power, resources and status. Although public choice thinkers certainly did not invent mistrust of, and challenge to, the practices of public service organisations, they did organise them into a coherent case for the dismantling of such institutions. In particular, this story of mistrust demanded new forms of discipline and scrutiny to supplement the introduction of market forces.

NEW PRACTICES OF AUDIT

Audit has historically meant the practice of scrutinising financial control processes and financial decision-making, as in the work of the National Audit Office (NAO) in the UK (see also Pollitt *et al.*, 1999) and national and regional audit courts in other OECD countries. The practice of fiscal scrutiny – the role of audit in its accountancy meaning – is concerned to verify the accuracy of financial statements and to check whether money has been spent for the purposes declared. In this narrow sense, audit is an effort to ensure sound financial management (see Chapter 8), and to stop fraud and corruption (see Chapter 21). The need for such financial scrutiny was reinforced in the 1980s by rising anxiety about public spending and, from a different perspective, by the drive towards 'businesslike' methods in public agencies, with the attendant dangers of financial malpractice. The establishment of organisations and procedures of financial scrutiny is still high on the agenda in other European countries such as Spain and is currently regarded as a critical issue in Central and Eastern European countries.

While internal audit generally retains these characteristics, in more recent years the practice of external audit in relation to public services has come to include a much wider range of evaluative and normative functions, most evidently in the work of the Audit Commission in the UK – see Case Example 14.1.

This shows that the Commission has significantly extended the role of external audit, from its traditional concern with the accuracy of accounts and whether public bodies were acting within their legal remit. VFM audit involves an assessment of service performance, often contesting professional judgements in a way that did not occur when audit was confined to narrower financial and legal concerns.

The expansion of the meanings and practices of external audit is a significant process in the context of UK governance and is echoed in some other national settings (see Pollitt *et al.*, 1999). In the UK, the Audit Commission's VFM studies have linked questions of accounting, evaluation, the identification of 'best practice', issues of organisational design, and management consultancy (Clarke *et al.*, 2000). That is, the Commission became an agency

CASE EXAMPLE 14.1 **THE GROWTH OF THE AUDIT COMMISSION SINCE 1983**

The Audit Commission was established in 1983 to appoint and regulate the external auditors of local authorities in England and Wales, paralleled by the Audit Commission for Scotland. Some of these auditors are part of the district audit service, while others are private firms that win the tender to do the external audit for the relevant public agencies. In 1990, its role was extended to include the National Health Service (NHS). The Audit Commission's functions in local government have grown to include carrying out value for money (VFM) studies and the collection and audit of national statutory performance indicators for councils, police and fire authorities. In 2000, the Government placed a duty on all local authorities to achieve best value in their activities, and the Audit Commission was charged with scrutinising local councils' best value performance plans and carrying out inspections of their best value reviews. In 2002, the Audit Commission took on the task of undertaking a Comprehensive Performance Assessment (CPA) for each local authority, updated regularly. From 2009, this will be replaced by a Comprehensive Area Assessment (CAA), based on the level of achievement of the Local Area Agreement (LAA) in the area of each upper tier local authority (i.e. county or unitary authority). Under the CAA approach, most local authorities (and their partners) will be subject to 'risk-based' assessments, i.e. they will only have a full assessment if the initial, desk-based assessment suggests that there are substantial risks of non-achievement of LAA targets or other national and local strategic objectives.

More information about the Audit Commission is available at www.audit-commission. gov.uk.

of policy and organisational innovation, prescribing best practice, identifying dangerous deviations and divergences, advising on the most effective organisational systems, structures and cultures, and propounding the need for better management of public services. This expanded audit role can be seen also in many other countries – e.g. the Canadian Office of the Auditor General – see Case Example 14.2.

Although not the focus of this chapter, a parallel blurring of boundaries can be observed in the large private sector accounting firms, which developed policy and management consultancy practices alongside (and sometimes interleaved with) their audit work.

NEW ROLES OF EXTERNAL AUDIT AGENCIES

This development of external audit means displacing or co-opting professional knowledge bases. *Displacement* implies that they are subordinated to the specification of 'quality' by politicians or managers. *Co-option* implies that the professional knowledge bases are integrated into the VFM audit or policy evaluation model, e.g. through processes of peer review.

The achievement of improved organisational performance has been increasingly viewed as the province of 'good management' rather than professional standards. The pursuit of 'quality',

CASE EXAMPLE 14.2 **THE NEW ROLES OF THE AUDITOR GENERAL OF CANADA**

The Auditor General's responsibilities were clarified and expanded in the 1977 Auditor General Act, which enacted a broader mandate to examine how well the government managed its affairs, in addition to its continuing role of scrutinising the accuracy of financial statements. However, the important principle was maintained that the Auditor General does not comment on policy choices, examining only how those policies are implemented (as in the case of the UK National Audit Office and Audit Commission).

The Act directs the Auditor General to address three main questions:

■ Is the government keeping proper accounts and records and presenting its financial information accurately? This is called 'attest' auditing. The auditor attests to, or verifies, the accuracy of financial statements.

■ Did the government collect or spend the authorised amount of money and for the purposes intended by Parliament? This is called 'compliance' auditing. The auditor asks if the government has complied with Parliament's wishes.

■ Were programmes run economically and efficiently? And does the government have the means to measure their effectiveness? This is called 'value-for-money' or performance auditing. The auditor asks whether or not taxpayers got value for their tax dollars.

In December 1995 the position of Commissioner of the Environment and Sustainable Development was established within the Office of the Auditor General and an obligation was placed on government departments to publish annual sustainable development strategies (a linking of activities that is usual among national audit bodies).

Source: Adapted from material currently and previously available on the website of the Auditor General of Canada, www.oag-bvg.gc.ca/

'excellence' or 'standards' means that evaluative agencies have come to colonise organisational terrain that was previously the province of professional expertise (see also Kirkpatrick and Martinez-Lucio, 1995). Different public services have seen different accommodations between professional expertise and evaluative agencies. Hughes and his colleagues (1996) have suggested that the emergent external audit-and-inspection regimes that operate in different welfare fields vary partly as a result of the relative power of the different professional groups. Box 14.1 illustrates three different types of UK inspection agency.

The development of evaluation has been partly marked by a *shift from compliance to competition*. The evaluation of performance has centred on producing comparative information (e.g. 'league tables') through which organisations are judged in terms of their relative success in achieving desired results. Hood *et al.* (1998, pp. 14–17) talk about these processes as involving a 'hybrid' of oversight' and 'competition'.

The proliferation of types and agencies of external audit and inspection suggests that governments continue to have problems coordinating public provision. In particular, the fragmented and dispersed organisational systems developed during the past twenty years pose

BOX 14.1 THREE TYPES OF UK INSPECTION AGENCY

HEFCE (Higher Education Funding Council for England, with parallel agencies in Scotland, Wales and Northern Ireland) is a body that regulates higher education provision, combining funding, target setting and evaluation (such as the five yearly Research Assessment Exercise that evaluates and grades research quality of all subjects in all UK universities). The Funding Councils were originally responsible for Teaching Quality Assessment, but controversies over method and process led to the establishment of a further body – the Quality Assurance Agency – to evaluate teaching standards.

Ofsted (Office for Standards in Education) was established in 1988 to set and assess standards in schools. It inspected schools (and local education authorities that are responsible for some schools), provided evaluations of performance, produced 'league tables' of comparison between schools, and formed judgements on the 'best' approaches to teaching and school management. Ofsted was renamed the Office for Standards in Education, Children's Services and Skills in 2007 and brought together the experience of four formerly separate inspectorates, to inspect and regulate care for children and young people, and inspect education and training for learners of all ages.

The **CSCI** (Commission for Social Care Inspection) was launched in April 2004 as the single independent inspectorate for all social care services in England. It incorporated the work previously done by the Social Services Inspectorate (a long-established 'professional' inspectorate, originally staffed by experienced social workers and social work managers who carried out inspections and engaged in professional support and development); the SSI/Audit Commission Joint Review Team and the National Care Standards Commission (NCSC). However, CSCI was given a much wider remit than its predecessor organisations, and its creation was a significant milestone for social care. Paul Snell, CSCI's Chief Inspector, appointed in July 2006, said: 'Our job is to make sure that services are relevant and personal to the people who use them: give people choice; give people voice; give people dignity; and most importantly safeguard and promote their rights and welfare.' From 1 April 2007, the responsibility for regulating children's social care services was transferred from CSCI to Ofsted. Recently, the government announced that, subject to legislation, from April 2009 a new single body responsible for regulating both adult social care and health, the Care Quality Commission, will be established.

distinctive problems of control. There are also continuing arguments about whether external audit and inspection agencies are the most effective or appropriate method of coordination. The 'high cost/low trust' mix of external scrutiny poses questions about value and efficacy; while the competitive, intrusive and interventionist mode of scrutiny creates potentially antagonistic relationships (between provider organisations; between providers and external scrutiny agencies and between provider organisations and government). 'Audit', in its most general sense, has become the focus of controversy about whether it promotes better public services, and whether it is the best way to promote better public services (Downe and Martin, 2007).

THE INTERNAL RESPONSE: LOCAL GOVERNMENT SCRUTINY PANELS

In the Local Government Act 2000, new arrangements defined a scrutiny role for elected members of councils in holding council executives ('cabinets') to account. Moreover, they laid out a role for councillors in scrutinising the work of other agencies providing local services. There is now a clear distinction between the role of the council's cabinet in proposing and implementing policies, and the role of non-cabinet members in reviewing policy and scrutinising cabinet decisions. Councils have to set up 'overview and scrutiny' arrangements, generally through panels of elected members (but sometimes with coopted members of the community), which under the Act have the power to summon members of the cabinet and officers of the authority before it to answer questions, and are able to invite other persons to attend meetings to give their views or submit evidence. (Interestingly, the 2000 Act does not give to council scrutiny panels the same powers in this respect that Parliamentary Select Committees have.)

These scrutiny powers to consider matters not the responsibility of the local authority, but affecting its area or its inhabitants, were extended by the Health and Social Care Act 2001, enabling local government scrutiny of local health services. Scrutiny panels have increasingly sought to review issues affecting the wider community interest, rather than just internal services and issues.

In practice, the current powers and resources for council overview and scrutiny have not ensured adequate status for it within councils, so that it is still regarded as a relatively 'toothless' element of the overall scrutiny of local services and decisions. On the other hand, this does suggest that councils have not been prepared to shackle their decision-making processes by setting up a 'shadow' process internally to mimic the expected activities of external audit and inspection. Whether or not these internal scrutiny processes will ever be sufficiently strong to convince central government that external scrutiny can be relaxed is still unclear.

CHALLENGES TO EXTERNAL SCRUTINY

In this section, I explore three areas of challenge to the regime of expanded external scrutiny of public service provision. The first deals with problems about the methods of external scrutiny and evaluation; the second with problems of representing the 'public interest' in external scrutiny processes; and the third examines challenges about the necessity and desirability of external scrutiny as a means of controlling public services.

Methodological problems of evaluation

There is a growing literature that explores the political, organisational and methodological problems associated with evaluation (e.g. Boyne, 1997; Cutler and Waine, 1997; Pollitt, 1995) (see also Chapter 22). The methodological problems concern the reliability and replicability of the knowledge that 'audit' produces. The technical notion of audit (in its accounting sense) aimed to produce reliable knowledge of organisations' financial performance and financial systems. Other forms of evaluative scrutiny (both internal and external) have

205

been criticised for using less robust methodologies. Such controversies came to a head over Ofsted school inspections in the late 1990s in the UK. External scrutiny organisations have tended to accept that there have been methodological problems, but that they will be overcome in the next, methodologically improved, round of evaluation. Other methodological problems concern the difficulty of identifying the causal variables associated with performance change (Pollitt, 1995).

The organisational consequences of the 'audit explosion' form a second focus of concern. Systems of evaluation, it is suggested, distort organisational performance, making it focus on what is being measured: 'what is counted is what gets done'. It is argued that public service organisations are typically multiple stakeholder and multi-objective organisations, but audit processes tend to focus on a limited number of objectives, usually those currently highly valued by central government (Bevan and Hood, 2007). In a different way, audit and inspection have had consequences for audited organisations in that they require them to divert scarce resources into the process of being evaluated (Power, 1993). Data have to be collected (often in new formats for different scrutiny agencies). Documentation and systems have to be made to conform to auditing requirements. On-site 'visits' have to be prepared for, stage-managed and performed. The outcomes of inspections, audits and evaluations have to be managed (particularly in relation to valued stakeholders). The 'audit explosion' has multiple costs – both in the creation and maintenance of the audit agencies, and in the organisations being audited. This is much more the case for external scrutiny than for internal scrutiny processes, essentially because the external reputation of the organisation stands to be damaged much more by an unfavourable report from an external source.

Third, it has been a consistent point of criticism that public services were poorly documented, producing little reliable information about their performance other than accounting for 'inputs'. As a result, organisations have been required to produce auditable information about their activities, with a steadily increasing emphasis on outputs and outcomes (the effects produced by the organisation's activities). Such information would allow the organisation to be evaluated both intrinsically and comparatively (i.e. is it efficient, and is it more or less efficient than similar organisations?). These demands for auditable organisations have been framed by discourses of accountability and transparency – against the suspicion of 'producer domination' of organisational choices. While both internal and external audit and service review processes have demanded the increased 'auditability' of information, for most public service organisations the externally imposed burden has been the driving force, pushing internal audit and review to 'shadow' the actual or expected demands arising from external scrutiny.

This concern with producing evaluative information creates a number of subsidiary dilemmas (at the intersection of the organisation and the auditing agency, whether internal or external):

- To what extent can the objectives of the organisation be clearly and simply specified – e.g. what is a school for?
- To what extent is the performance of the organisation measurable – e.g. do exam results measure school success?
- To what extent is organisational performance a closed system in which outcomes reflect the effect of organisational activity – who or what else contributes to 'results'?

■ To what extent can comparability be guaranteed between organisations – what unmeasured or unmeasurable factors within or outside organisations may differentiate organisational performance?

Each stage of evaluation involves potentially contested processes of social construction. There are potential conflicts over the definition of objectives; over the choice of indicators; over the attribution of causal effects; and over how comparison is effected. More substantively, however, the construction of these evaluative processes requires an organisation that produces auditable information.

The representation of public interest in scrutiny agencies and practices

There have been many political controversies surrounding the rise of external scrutiny, which involve questions of social and political 'independence'. A different way of putting this is to ask what biases may enter into the systems of 'independent' evaluation? There are at least three possibilities that have been raised by critics. The first concerns social biases about the public interest: whom do external 'auditors' and 'inspectors' have in mind when they see themselves as *representing the public*? Given the arguments over 'representation' in political life and public services (about the composition of organisational bodies in relation to the social composition of the nation), this is likely to become an increasingly significant question. Like the judiciary and magistracy, scrutineers may be scrutinised in terms of their ability to represent the diversity of the public's social composition and interests.

There are other controversies about the social biases of scrutiny that centre on the 'enthusiasms' of external auditors and inspectors within the sphere of organisational and occupational controversies. Can external auditors or inspectors lay claim to know the 'one best way' in the face of contested choices that may be rooted in organisational, occupational or local-political knowledges and imperatives? Much of the controversy that surrounded Ofsted's role in schooling in the UK centred on its dogmatic insistence on one approach to teaching. Such partisan enthusiasms call the supposed independence of evaluation into question.

Finally, there are questions about the 'political' independence of external scrutiny agencies. They typically occupy an ambiguous constitutional space, created by government but 'at arm's length' from it. The precise arrangements vary between countries and between different sorts of agency (see Pollitt *et al.*, 1999; Hood *et al.*, 1998). But the increasing involvement in performance (rather than merely financial) evaluation aligns the agencies more directly with assessing organisations against current government policies and targets. Similarly, the blurring of boundaries between evaluation, consultancy and prescription narrows the distance between evaluation and government, creating possibilities for critics to challenge the claimed independence of external scrutiny agencies. The shift away from the traditional audit function to being one of the key elements of the new governance implicates external scrutiny agencies more directly in the business of government politics, policy and control.

None of these challenges has halted the rise of external scrutiny processes. Indeed, they are typically dismissed as the defensive complaints of 'producer interests' unwilling to make themselves 'transparent' and 'accountable'. Nevertheless, they represent important political issues for the future development of governance relationships.

207

The necessity, desirability and effectiveness of scrutiny processes

Scrutiny processes are inherently 'low-trust/high-cost' models for controlling public services and they tend to be shaped by centralist assumptions and orientations. This is true of both internal and external scrutiny processes, although it normally more characterises external scrutiny. As a result, scrutiny processes accentuate some tendencies in the new governance, but restrict or even repress others. External scrutiny, in particular, fits less readily with diversification, innovation and participatory models of local governing of services. It is also more difficult to adapt to forms of network and partnership working, producing problems of overlap, integration and multiple 'ownership'.

However, external scrutiny seems likely to remain a favoured tool of central governments in the context of fragmented and dispersed systems of service provision. It may be that the most severe challenge to it emerges not from the public service sector, but from the misfortunes of audit in the private/corporate sector. The recent (2002) spectacular failures of audit to uncover or report fraud and malpractice in major corporate enterprises (e.g. Enron), and the blurring of lines between audit, consultancy and management in the activities of large accounting firms, have called 'audit' into question as an effective governance mechanism. Arguments have raged about the causes of such failures (weaknesses of the US model; bad management; overly 'cosy' relationships between auditors and auditees and so on). Similarly, arguments about how audit might be put right proliferate – including the inevitable sugges-tion that 'auditors need to be audited' (*Financial Times*, 3 July 2002). Whether such problems will have implications for the organisation of scrutiny in its various forms in the public sector remains to be seen.

SUMMARY

In this chapter I have tried to sketch the development of scrutiny systems as part of the new governance of public services. I have emphasised the appeal of processes of external audit, inspection and evaluation as a means of government's exercising 'control at a distance' in dispersed and fragmented systems of service provision. I have suggested some of the instabilities and sites of potential challenge associated with the 'audit explosion', particularly those associated with the expansive blurring of roles towards organisational or management consultancy on the one hand and towards prescriptions of organisational practice on the other. As such, external scrutiny processes are likely to remain a site of potential tension in the relationships between governments, public service organisations and the public. Much of this is likely to be concentrated in increasingly fractious relationships between central governments (committed to the reform of public services) and service providers (trying to lessen the 'burden' of scrutiny and concentrate limited resources on service provision). The balance of external scrutiny – whether it intensifies or moves to what is sometimes called 'light touch' – is likely to depend on whether relationships of trust can be reconstructed around the triangle of public, government and public services. In the absence of such trust relationships, the 'audit explosion' is likely to continue.

QUESTIONS FOR REVIEW AND DISCUSSION

1   What conditions drove the 'audit explosion' in relation to public services?
2   What role do 'scrutiny' agencies play in the new governance?
3   To what extent does the practice of 'audit' distort organisational performance?
4   What challenges does the expansion of scrutiny face?
5   Is there a 'crisis of audit'? What are the implications for the scrutiny of public services?

READER EXERCISES

1   Obtain a report from an external scrutiny agency. To what extent is it shaped by any of the issues discussed above?
2   How many forms of scrutiny has the organisation in which you work (or in which someone you can ask works) experienced in the last two years? What are the different forms of scrutiny?
3   Talk to someone who has recently experienced external audit, inspection or evaluative scrutiny in their work. What are they key features of their experience? Do they connect to any of the issues discussed above?

CLASS EXERCISES

In small groups, consider the questions about audit and control below.

1   *Auditing public services*:

   ■   To what extent can the objectives of the organisation be clearly and simply specified – e.g. what is a school for?
   ■   To what extent is the performance of the organisation measurable – e.g. do exam results measure school success?
   ■   To what extent is organisational performance a closed system in which outcomes reflect the effect of organisational activity – who or what else contributes to 'results'?
   ■   To what extent can comparability be guaranteed between organisations – what unmeasured or unmeasurable factors within or outside organisations may influence organisational performance?

2   *Controlling public services*

   ■   How might governments evaluate the provision of public services if they did not use external audit, inspection and other scrutiny agencies?
   ■   How might relations of trust be constructed between publics, governments and public services?

209

FURTHER READING

John Clarke, Sharon Gewirtz, Gordon Hughes and Jill Humphrey (2000), 'Guarding the public interest: auditing public services', in John Clarke, Sharon Gewirtz and Eugene McLaughlin (eds), *New managerialism, new welfare?* London: Sage/Open University.

Howard Davis and Steve Martin (eds) (2008), *Public service inspection in the UK*. London: Jessica Kingsley Publishers.

James Downe and Steve Martin (2007), 'Regulation inside government: processes and impacts of inspection of local public services', *Policy and Politics*, 35 (2): 215–32.

Christopher Hood, Colin Scott, Oliver James, George Jones and Tony Travers (1998), *Regulation inside government: waste-watchers, quality police and sleaze busters*. Oxford: Oxford University Press.

Michael Power (1997), *The audit society*. Oxford: Oxford University Press.

REFERENCES

Gwyn Bevan and Christopher Hood (2007), 'What's measured is what matters: targets and gaming in healthcare in England', *Public Administration*, 84 (3): 517–38.

George Boyne (1997), 'Comparing the performance of local authorities: an evaluation of the Audit Commission indicators', *Local Government Studies*, 23 (4): 17–43.

John Clarke (2004), *Changing welfare, changing states*. London: Sage.

John Clarke and Janet Newman (1997), *The managerial state: power, politics and ideology in the remaking of social welfare*. London: Sage.

John Clarke, Sharon Gewirtz, Gordon Hughes and Jill Humphrey (2000), 'Guarding the public interest: auditing public services', in John Clarke, Sharon Gewirtz and Eugene McLaughlin (eds), *New managerialism, new welfare?*. London: Sage/Open University.

Tony Cutler and Barbara Waine (1997), *Managing the welfare state*. Oxford: Berg.

James Downe and Steve Martin (2007), 'Regulation inside government: processes and impacts of inspection of local public services', *Policy and Politics*, 35 (2): 215–32.

Patrick Dunleavy (1991), *Democracy, bureaucracy and public choice*. London: Harvester Wheatsheaf.

Christopher Hood, Colin Scott, George Jones, Oliver James and Tony Travers (1998), *Regulation inside government: waste-watchers, quality police and sleaze busters*. Oxford: Oxford University Press.

Gordon Hughes, Robert Mears and Christopher Winch (1996), 'An inspector calls? Regulation and accountability in three public services', *Policy and Politics*, 25 (3): 299–313.

Ian Kirkpatrick and Miguel Martinez-Lucio (eds) (1995), *The politics of quality in the public sector*. London: Routledge.

Janet Newman and John Clarke (2009), *Publics, politics and power: remaking the public in public services*. London: Sage.

Christopher Pollitt (1995), 'Justification by works or by faith? Evaluating the new public management', *Evaluation*, 1 (2): 133–54.

Christopher Pollitt, Xavier Girre, Jeremy Lonsdale, Robert Mul, Hilka Summa and Marit Waerness (1999), *Performance or compliance? Performance audit and public management in five countries*. Oxford: Oxford University Press.

Michael Power (1993), *The audit explosion*. London: Demos.

Michael Power (1997), *The audit society*. Oxford: Oxford University Press.

Part III

Governance as an emerging trend in the public sector

The third part of this book focuses explicitly on governance as an emerging trend in the public domain. It examines a number of themes central to public governance, and suggests how they are interlinked with public management and how these themes may evolve in the future, if public governance continues to acquire increasing importance.

Chapter 15 examines the relationship between governance and government. It suggests that the growing interest in public governance has arisen at least partly because of the modern necessity for governments to work in partnership with and to co-manage networks of external stakeholders.

The subsequent chapters explore how public policy makers and managers have moved from being largely concerned with the management of public organizations to working within partnerships and networks (Chapter 16), and through agencies and decentralized management systems (Chapter 17), how the role of leaders has been reconceptualized as distributed between different layers of the organization and between organizations (Chapter 18), how public agencies are finding new ways to engage with citizens and other stakeholders (Chapter 19), the changing agenda for management of equalities (Chapter 20), new concerns with and approaches to ethics and standards of conduct in public sector organizations (Chapter 21), and evidence-based approaches to developing and refining policy and practice in the public domain (Chapter 22).

Chapter 15

Public governance in a network society

Elke Löffler, Governance International, UK

INTRODUCTION

There is a fast-increasing academic literature on public governance, public policy networks and network management in the public sector – and new variations on these ideas keep being invented – but much confusion remains about these concepts and, for most practitioners, they don't mean much at all. Does this mean that concepts of good governance are simply the invention of political scientists and are of little importance in practice?

I want to argue that the reality is quite the opposite. As this chapter will show, public decision-making and the production of public services have undergone fundamental changes in the last fifteen years or so. This is partly because we now have a more fragmented state, with far more public agencies (see Chapters 2, 4 and 17). It is also partly because citizens now expect different types of information (see Chapter 11), better communication (see Chapter 6) and, in some limited (but very vocal) cases, are keener to engage in public decision-making processes (see Chapter 19). Perhaps most important of all, it has come about because of 'wicked' policy problems, which make coordination and joint working a key for all agencies and managers working in the public domain (see Chapter 16).

As a result, public agencies no longer just have to be good at getting their internal management systems right – financial management, human resource management, ICT and performance management – but they also have to manage their most important external stakeholders well in order to achieve the desired policy outcomes and a high quality of public services. In other words, network management has become a key competence of public agencies.

LEARNING OBJECTIVES

This chapter will help readers:

- to distinguish key concepts in public governance;
- to identify the most important stakeholders in public governance;
- to understand network management as a specific mode of public governance;
- to understand how the role of government is changing from the role of service provider towards the role of co-producer.

SORTING IT ALL OUT: KEY GOVERNANCE CONCEPTS

Like most concepts in social sciences, governance is not a new term. Indeed, the term governance was first used in France in the fourteenth century where it meant 'seat of government' (Pierre and Peters, 2000, p. 1). The term became much more popular when the World Bank 'reinvented' governance in a World Bank Report of 1989 (see Box 15.1). The use of the term governance by the World Bank signalled a new approach to development that was based on the belief that economic prosperity is not possible without a minimum level of rule-of-law and democracy. At the same time, use of the seemingly apolitical term 'governance' was valuable in preventing criticism that the World Bank was trying to interfere in the political decisions made by debtor countries.

Today, governance has become a highly topical issue for international organizations – the United Nations, OECD and the Council of Europe all produce policy-relevant advice and research related to various governance issues. For example, the Council of Europe recently endorsed a Strategy on Innovation and Good Governance at local level, which aims at mobilizing action by national and local authorities through a public commitment to 12 Principles of Good Democratic Governance. In particular, this new initiative hopes to improve public governance through external certification for public agencies – the European Label of Innovation and Good Governance (see the 2007 Valencia Declaration, www.coe.int/t/e/legal _affairs/local_and_regional_democracy/Main_Bodies/Conference_Specialised_Ministers/ Valencia_2007/MCL-15(2007)5final_EN.pdf). Such initiatives indicate the topicality of 'good governance' but, at the same time, it is interesting to observe that a previous, high-profile European governance initiative, widely promoted in a White Paper on Governance (European Commission, 2001) has now been 'archived'.

In contrast to the enthusiasm for governance in the world of international organizations and national agencies dealing with developing countries, the concept of good governance is

BOX 15.1 DEFINITIONS OF GOVERNANCE

The exercise of political power to manage a nation's affairs.

(World Bank, 1989, p. 60)

Governance is the process whereby societies or organizations make important decisions, determine whom they involve and how they render account.

(Canadian Institute on Governance (www.iog.ca))

Public governance is how an organization works with its partners, stakeholders and networks to influence the outcomes of public policies.

(Governance International, UK (www.govint.org))

The pattern or structure that emerges in a socio-political system as a 'common' result or outcome of the interacting intervention efforts of all involved actors. This pattern cannot be reduced to [the outcome produced by] one actor or groups of actors in particular.

(Kooiman, 1993, p. 258)

given much less priority by most old European member countries. Clearly, governments find it more congenial to recommend good governance to others than to deal with uncomfortable governance issues themselves. Nevertheless, governance crises such as corruption scandals or street riots in ethnically mixed areas put public governance firmly on the political agenda. For example, the UK government gave a high profile to the Nolan Public Standards Committee after issues of 'sleaze' in public life achieved a high media profile (see Chapter 21). We can also observe the emergence of a wide range of new think tanks and consultancy organizations aimed at fostering governance in the public domain.

Many governmental and non-governmental organizations have also focused on the attributes that they believe constitute 'good governance' (see Box 15.2).

It might be thought that the multiplicity of views on what constitutes governance in a positive and normative sense make it a less than useful concept. However, almost all definitions contain some common elements which show that governance (Bovaird and Löffler, 2002):

- assumes a multiple stakeholder scenario where collective problems can no longer be solved only by public authorities but require the cooperation of other players (citizens, business, voluntary sector, media, etc.) — and in which practices such as mediation, arbitration and self-regulation may often be even more effective than public action;
- recognizes the importance of both formal rules (constitutions, laws, regulations) and informal rules (codes of ethics, customs, traditions) but assumes that negotiation between stakeholders seeking to use their power can alter the importance of these rules in specific situations;

BOX 15.2 DEFINITIONS OF 'GOOD GOVERNANCE'

Good governance has eight major characteristics. It is participatory, consensus oriented, accountable, transparent, responsive, effective and efficient, equitable and inclusive and follows the rule of law. It assures that corruption is minimized, the views of minorities are taken into account and that the voices of the most vulnerable in society are heard in decision-making. It is also responsive to the present and future needs of society.

(United Nations Economic and Social Commission for Asia and the Pacific
(www.unescap.org/pdd/prs/ProjectActivities/Ongoing/gg/governance.asp))

Five principles underpin good governance and the changes proposed in the EU White Paper: 'openness, participation, accountability, effectiveness and coherence'.

(White Paper on European Governance
(http://europa.eu.int/comm/governance/index_en.htm))

Good governance has to be defined as context-specific. Given that it is impossible fully to implement all desirable governance principles at the same time stakeholders need to agree on strategic governance priorities.

(Governance International, UK (www.govint.org))

- no longer focuses only on market structures as steering mechanisms, as in conventional 'New Public Management' approaches, but also considers hierarchies (such as bureaucracies) and cooperative networks as potential facilitating structures in appropriate circumstances;
- does not reason only in terms of the logic of ends and means, inputs and outputs, but recognizes that the characteristics of the key processes in social interaction (transparency, integrity, inclusion, etc.) are likely to be valuable in themselves
- is inherently political, concerned as it is with the interplay of stakeholders seeking to exercise power over each other in order to further their own interests – and therefore cannot be left to managerialist or professional decision-making elites.

The big challenge in practice is how to bring about 'good governance'. The definitions above make it clear that it cannot be achieved by good government alone. For example, in order to reduce crime it is important that the police service has sufficient resources, that it is efficiently managed and that it behaves in a fair and honest way and avoids racial and gender discrimination. If these prerequisites are not in place, crime levels can get out of hand in particular areas and inappropriate police responses may easily result in riots and an increase in lawlessness. However, the long-term solution to the problem of crime may not be within the power of the police or achievable even by means of better designed interventions on the part of government or other public sector organizations. At the root of the problem may be insufficient integration of immigrants, insufficient work and stimulating leisure opportunities for young people or simply a high rate of unemployment in a particular area. In this case, good governance requires the cooperation of all relevant stakeholders in tackling the underlying problem. This is likely to include actions by various public agencies such as schools, NHS and local authorities – but also by community organizations, etc. As Case Example 15.1 shows, the police may even involve business in order to become more effective in tackling crime.

CASE EXAMPLE 15.1 **POLICE TRAIN SHOP ASSISTANTS TO CUT SHOP-LIFTING**

In the London Borough of Camden, police officers gave six staff members of two local stores from the Dixons group of electrical products the same training as the Metropolitan Police's 765 part-time officers under a pilot scheme. The trial was judged to be highly successful. Antony Rumming, 22, a Dixons team leader in Camden, said that the training had helped him to catch twenty potential fraudsters in the last year. 'It helps knowing what they are going to do and the patterns involved' he said. A recent survey estimated that retail crime costs the industry £2.25 billion annually. The police have already announced further measures to give civilians special roles in major investigations, including murder inquiries.

Source: Adapted from *The Guardian*, Saturday, 30 October 2004

So governments may be no longer necessarily the central actor but only one actor in the policy process (Scharpf, 1978). As Rod Rhodes (1997, p. 57) puts it: 'the state becomes a collection of inter-organizational networks made up of governmental and societal actors with no sovereign actor able to steer or regulate. A key challenge for government is to enable these networks and seek out new forms of co-operation'.

In other words, the importance of public governance does not so much pose the question of 'how much state?' but rather 'which state?' – where we have to deal with the state as the interaction of multiple stakeholders, each of whom has some public responsibility to influence and shape decisions in the public sphere.

Moreover, the move from government to governance requires all stakeholders to play a much more imaginative role in shaping the decisions in their communities or policy networks. This is exemplified in relation to local governance in Table 15.1.

IMPORTANT STAKEHOLDERS IN PUBLIC GOVERNANCE

If governance is much more than government, does this mean that governments no longer have an important role to play in local politics and service delivery? Or, as the public governance experts Jon Pierre and Guy Peters (2000) ask provocatively: 'Does government still matter'?

Such questions are misguided, as they consider governance issues out of context. More meaningful governance questions are rather: When does government still matter? What functions could public agencies share with other stakeholders – and which can they not share? What are the roles of different stakeholders, including the public sector, in solving different problems in society?

The concept of stakeholders originally just included people who have a stake (or share) in a particular issue, service or organization – i.e. those who are *affected* in some way by the actions of the organization. However, the concept of stakeholder is nowadays usually widened to cover also people whose actions *affect* the organization concerned. Stakeholders can be groups of people, organisations, or individuals.

Typically, public governance issues are likely to involve the following key stakeholders (amongst others):

- citizens (as individuals);
- community organizations that are loosely organized;
- non-profit organizations (including charities and major Non-Governmental Organizations), who are often quite tightly organized;
- business;
- media;
- public agencies (e.g. different levels of government/Parliament, including international levels);
- elected politicians;
- trade unions.

It is obvious that the stakeholders who are most important in any public governance issue will vary, depending on the policy area, the geographic area or the community concerned.

219

Table 15.1 *The move from local government to local governance*

Local government needs to consider not only . . .	. . . but increasingly
Organizational leadership	Leadership of networks and partnerships
Developing organizations	Developing communities
Ensuring policy coherence across organizational departments and services	Ensuring policy coherence across organizational and sectoral borders and levels of government as well as over time (sustainable development)
Creating a set of values and a sense of direction, which leaves room for individual autonomy and creativity for mid-level managers and employees	Creating a set of values which are consistent with the expectations of citizens, companies, partners and other stakeholders
Policy and strategy	'Politicking': balancing strategic interests
Focus on the needs of customers	Activating civil society (through information, consultation and participation) in local policies and management
Separation of politics and administration	Governance as a process of interaction between elected officials, politically appointed officials, ad hoc advisors, career civil servants and external stakeholders
Annual plans, concentrating on current expenditure	Long-term plans, incorporating activity plans, capital budget plans and asset management for the whole community
People management	Management of the labour market and its implications
Increasing labour productivity through efficiency drives	Improving staff contribution to all the goals of the organization
Getting staff to focus on quality of service	Getting staff to focus on quality of life, in terms of quality of service outcomes for users and other stakeholders and also quality of working life for fellow staff
Motivation through more objective evaluation systems and more flexible pay systems	Motivation by allowing staff to contribute a wider range of their skills and aptitudes to the work of the organization and the community
Recruiting and retaining qualified staff through transparent hiring processes	Recruiting, training and promoting staff in ways that increase the diversity of the public service in terms of gender, ethnicity, age and disabilities
Making better use of staff resources within the organization	Making better use of staff resources by increasing mobility within the public sector and also between other sectors and other areas
Resource management	Resource and knowledge management
Budget formulation as a top-down exercise (with fixed ceilings on total expenditures)	Preparation of local budgets with active participation of city councillors, including community representatives
Measurement of unit costs for performance improvement and performance monitoring	Measurement of money and time costs of the organization's activities, as experienced by both the organization and its stakeholders

Local government needs to consider not only . . .	. . . but increasingly
Resource management	Resource and knowledge management
Transparent financial reporting	'Fiscal transparency' to communicate with external stakeholders (business, citizens, media, etc.) on the value-for-money of activities
Improving technical efficiency	Improving social efficiency, including equitable distribution of budgets and services
Making ICT available to all staff for efficiency-enhancement purposes	Generating and sustaining new knowledge through knowledge management, both for staff and for other stakeholders interacting with the organization (including making ICT available to all stakeholders to improve effectiveness)
Processes	Internal and external relationships
Internal improvement processes ('business process re-engineering')	Improved management of processes beyond organizational borders, including intergovernmental relations and constraints
Competing for tendered tasks	Managing multiple contracts and supplier relationships; building and maintaining accountable partnerships, with users, communities and other organizations where appropriate (co-production of services with users, communities and other stakeholders)
Measurement of objective and subjective results	Measurement of multidimensional performance
Reporting systems based on needs of public managers and government oversight bodies	Publishing of performance information based on the needs of stakeholders in the community (social, ethical and environmental reporting)
Benchmarking results, internal processes or organizational performance against other local authorities	Involving stakeholder groups in the definition of performance standards and measurement of performance against results achieved in other communities
Use of performance information for control purposes	Encouraging innovation and learning at multiple levels (individual, organizational, networks)
Improving the functioning of the local authority	Developing good local governance
Improving the internal efficiency of local authorities	Improving the external effectiveness of local authorities and improving the local outcomes and the quality of life
Increasing user satisfaction in relation to local services	Building citizen trust in local government through transparent processes and accountability and through democratic dialogue
Serving the community by producing policies, services and knowledge (community leader)	Enabling the community to plan and manage its own affairs and co-produce its own services (community developer)

Source: Adapted from Bovaird and Löffler (2002, pp. 21–3)

In order to solve 'wicked' policy problems successfully it is important to identify the most relevant stakeholders – one powerful way to do this is by drawing up a stakeholder power-interest matrix (see Table 6.1 in Chapter 6). The first step is to brainstorm all stakeholders who are believed to have a stake in the organization concerned, or to be affected by the organization's actions. The second step is to allocate these stakeholders into one of four categories by determining:

- their power over your organization/service/project (Are they powerful enough to do your organization harm? Or are they so weak that your organization does not care much what they think about your organization?);
- the interest they have in your organization/service/project.

The position of stakeholders in the matrix helps managers to understand how best to engage with them.

Clearly, not all stakeholders are equally important and relevant in relation to a given action by the organization. This insight may seem contradictory to the governance principle of 'equal treatment'. However, the fact is that effective governance requires priority setting, including deciding which of your stakeholders matters most to any decision that has to be taken in a given situation.

NETWORKS AS A SPECIFIC MODE OF PUBLIC GOVERNANCE

For some academics, public governance refers to 'self-organizing, inter-organizational net-works' (Rhodes, 1997, p. 53). Yet, as Pierre and Peters (2000, pp. 14–26) point out, although networks have become an increasingly important aspect of public governance, they are only one specific mode of public governance. There are also other governance mechanisms that remain significant in the public, private and voluntary sectors. In particular, these include:

- hierarchies
- markets
- communities.

This means that public governance not only involves cooperation but also competition and conflict management. The key governance issues are not simply how to develop and maintain networks, but which governance mechanisms are appropriate in which context.

However, we must ask: what do we mean by 'networks'? In general, policy networks consist of a variety of actors who all have their own goals and strategies but who are dependent on each other to achieve the desired public policy outcomes. There is no single actor who has enough power to ensure the achievement of the policy outcomes himself/herself. Obviously, the operation of networks will differ depending on the distribution of power and the institutional context, which determines incentives or obstacles for cooperation (Kickert and Koppenjan, 1997, p. 41ff). One famous categorization of policy networks comes from Rhodes (1997) (see Table 15.2). Policy communities are at one end of the continuum and involve close relationships between a limited number of participants, while issue networks

Table 15.2 The 'Rhodes typology' of policy networks

Type of network	Characteristics of network
Policy community/ territorial community	Stability, highly restricted membership (usually including strong political links), vertical interdependence, limited horizontal articulation
Professional network	Stability, highly restricted membership (usually with very weak political links), vertical interdependence, limited horizontal articulation, serves interest of profession
Intergovernmental network	Limited membership (usually including political representatives), limited vertical interdependence, extensive horizontal articulation
Producer network	Fluctuating membership (usually with weak political links), limited vertical interdependence, serves interest of producer
Issue network	Unstable, large number of members (usually including political representatives), limited vertical interdependence

Source: Adapted from Rhodes (1997, p. 38)

are at the other end and involve loose relationships between many participants with fluctuating interactions.

As the public sector has become more fragmented and the boundaries between public, private and non-profit sectors have become more blurred, the nature of networks has changed. In the UK, functional policy networks based on central government departments have expanded to include more actors, most notably from the private and voluntary sectors (Rhodes, 1997, p. 45). At the same time, the number of networks has increased significantly.

As a result, the implementation of public policies has had to adapt, placing more emphasis on the need for integration and coordination. Hierarchical, top-down policy-making typically does not work in networks, particularly as they have no obvious 'top'. In the academic literature, network management is seen as consisting of two major elements (Kickert and Koppenjan, 1997, p. 46):

- direct management of interactions within networks (so-called *game management*);
- influencing the institutional arrangements in order to improve conditions for cooperation indirectly (so-called *network constitution*).

If public policies are the result of the interactions ('games') between several actors with different goals and perceptions, improvements in public policies can be achieved through the effective management of these games. Klijn and Teisman (1997) identify three key network management strategies to improve the game management and the network structuring – see Table 15.3.

Given that the actors of a network have different goals and perceptions, there is a need to create some degree of alignment between the perceptions of different actors in relation to what needs to be done, which resources can be used, and the circumstances in which certain actions are acceptable. This process of identifying similarities and differences in actors' perceptions and the opportunities that exist for goal convergence is referred to as 'convenanting'. Whether or not a network achieves the jointly agreed outcomes depends on

223

Table 15.3 Key network management strategies

	Perceptions	Actors	Institutional arrangements
Game management	Convenanting	Selective (de)activation	Creating and implementing rules of the game
Network constitution	Reframing perceptions	Formation of new networks	Changing the rules of the game

Source: Adapted from Klijn and Teisman (1997, p. 106)

whether or not it includes all those actors who possess indispensable resources and also those actors who have the power to undermine achievement of the network's goals, if they have been left out (see Scharpf, 1978). Last but not least, actors have to agree on institutional arrangements that facilitate the coordination of their activities. These arrangements may be highly formalized (e.g. convenants between different levels of government) or informal (e.g. agreements on working procedures within project teams).

In contrast to the game management strategies, changing the constitution of existing networks involves longer-term strategies. Where different actors with indispensable resources are unwilling to cooperate, or even to communicate with each other (as has happened sometimes, e.g. in Belfast or in Jerusalem), it may be necessary to engage in activities to change the perceptions of these actors. In other cases, there may be a need to reconstitute a network and to bring in new actors. This is typically a problem in citizens' consultation exercises, which are often dominated by 'the usual suspects'. In many cases, minorities and 'inarticulate' groups find it hard to get a platform and to make known their perceptions (see Chapters 19 and 20). Furthermore, existing institutional arrangements may prove to be weak in protecting the interests of the actors of a network. For instance, in e-government the major players may be 'techies', fascinated by the technology requirements to make e-government work, and 'marketeers', driven by the desire to promote government services online to their current users. In this case, a serious digital divide can open up, in which non-users of ICT services (often very vulnerable people who are actually high-priority clients of the services concerned) are seriously disadvantaged in the debate about service design and service delivery mechanisms (see Chapter 10).

THE CHANGING ROLE OF GOVERNMENT FROM SERVICE PROVIDER TOWARDS CO-PRODUCER

While developments in public governance have alerted us to the importance of multi-stakeholder approaches to most public issues, there is still great uncertainty about the relative role of different stakeholders in improving quality of life, solving the 'wicked problems' in society and ensuring that public governance processes are improved. We cannot yet be clear about 'what works, where and when' in addressing these issues. It is important, therefore, that we make appropriate use of the evidence available, and take steps to improve that evidence on public governance (see Chapter 22).

224

In the absence of clear evidence, experimentation may be revealing – indeed public agencies increasingly recognize that they have to work with their key stakeholders at all stages of the policy cycle in order to improve services and outcomes. In practice, this means that public agencies have to:

- co-design their services and policies together with their users and other key stakeholders;
- co-manage their resources with other partners;
- co-deliver their services with users and their communities;
- co-assess their services with their key stakeholders.

This means that policy-making is no longer seen as a purely 'top-down' process but rather as a negotiation between many interacting policy systems. Similarly, services are no longer simply delivered by professional and managerial staff in public agencies, but rather co-produced by users and their communities. User and community co-production can be defined as 'the provision of services through regular, long-term relationships between professionalized service providers (in any sector) and service users or other members of the community, where all parties make substantial resource contributions' (Bovaird, 2007, p. 847).

While parts of the private sector have already been involving users for a long-time in co-delivery of services (e.g. self-service supermarkets, bank cash withdrawal machines) and service design and testing, e.g. of computer software, co-design of services and policies is now becoming increasingly common in the public sector. Local authorities in the UK now even have a duty 'to inform, consult and involve users', and consultation has become a new industry (see Chapter 19).

What is much less common is the involvement of the public in decisions on the use of public resources. Typically, professionals and elected politicians do not trust citizens to be able to make such complex decisions – which, of course, overlooks the fact that all of us have to make very complex financial decisions in our own life, such as buying a house or a car. Moreover, many elected representatives consider the involvement of citizens in budget issues as a threat to their power. However, the UK is the first country where central government has taken an active approach towards participatory budgeting (PB) and has pushed local authorities (see Case Example 15.2) to give voters a direct say on public spending, e.g. in the form of community chests (see also www.participatorybudgeting.org.uk). In other European countries, some local authorities have been following the Porto Alegre example in Brazil, inviting citizens to have a say on how to allocate financial resources on public services or investments, often in rather more far-ranging approaches than has so far been the case in the UK.

Interestingly, Switzerland provides a longstanding example (since 1848) of a country where citizens are not only consulted on public budgets and tax issues but even have the last word! As Table 15.3 shows, citizens in a town such as Baar have a very large range of opportunities to play a real part in decisions affecting their town, their county (*Kanton*) and their country. However, such examples of direct democracy are still rare around the world.

When it comes to the involvement of users and citizens in public service delivery there is a lot more co-production going on than one might at first assume (Löffler *et al.*, 2008). By definition, in service systems the client appears twice, once as a customer and again as part

CASE EXAMPLE 15.2 **PARTICIPATORY BUDGETING IN THE BERLIN BOROUGH LICHTENBERG**

Berlin-Lichtenberg (*c*.256,000 inhabitants) is one of the twelve boroughs of the city-state of Berlin. (Berlin is not only a capital city but also one of the sixteen *Länder* in Germany). Like the other boroughs, it has a number of its own responsibilities, such as the running of old people's homes and kindergartens, and a number of responsibilities that have been transferred to it by the Greater Berlin Council (e.g. payment of child benefits). These latter responsibilities are not part of the PB process at borough level.

Since the local government elections in 2002, Lichtenberg Borough Council has had a Left Party majority (the successor of the former communist party of the German Democratic Republic). The mayor volunteered to introduce PB in her borough in late 2005 and got all-party agreement to launch it. Previous (failed) examples of PB in Germany suggest that all-party backing is a key success factor, as it keeps the concept of PB out of party politics and prevents it being abandoned as changes of political power occur.

The total budget of Berlin-Lichtenberg amounts to about €500 million and consists of about 300 services. By 2008, citizens have already been involved in three rounds of decisions on how to prioritize current spending of about €30 million on those services that are borough responsibilities. It is planned also to include investment spending in the 2009 budget cycle.

The discussions and voting take place in citizen assemblies at neighbourhood level but people can also vote by Internet and post. This mix of media has been important in reaching out to different groups of citizens.

Source: Adapted from interview at www.govint.org

Table 15.4 *How often a citizen of Baar could vote (December 2001 to December 2004)*

Level of government	Number	Type of election
Votes at federal level	38	Ballot box
Votes at *Kanton* (county) level	7	Ballot box
Votes at municipal level	47	Ballot box
Municipal assemblies in Baar	13	Municipal assembly
Total	105	

Source: Figures provided by Jürg Dübendorfer, former mayor of the town of Baar

of the service delivery value chain. Sometimes, service professionals 'do the service for the customer' (e.g. a surgeon performs an operation on a patient). However, service professionals often play solely an 'enabling' role, so that the client actually performs the service task (e.g. by taking a medicine or adopting a diet as prescribed by medical staff). Here the client becomes a co-producer of the service. Typical private sector examples include the software improvement through users identifying the 'glitches' or flight booking over the Internet. In the public sector, citizens take the role of co-producers when they join in with recycling schemes and take action to save energy in their home. There is also more and more co-delivery of public services, involving volunteers and members of communities. One such co-delivery scheme that has been rolled out nationally is the UK Expert Patients Programme (EPP) (see Case Example 15.3).

CASE EXAMPLE 15.3 **THE UK EXPERT PATIENTS PROGRAMME RUN BY VOLUNTEER TUTORS**

The programme aims at providing a six week course for people with chronic or long-term conditions. The course is delivered by trained and accredited tutors who are also living with a long-term health condition. It aims to give people the confidence to take more responsibility and self-manage their health, while encouraging them to work collaboratively with health and social care professionals. The EPP does not provide health information or treatment, nor does it address clinical needs. Course topics include healthy eating, dealing with pain and extreme tiredness, relaxation techniques and coping with feelings of depression.

The data from approximately 1,000 EPP course questionnaires showed that, four to six months after completing the course:

- GP consultations decreased by 7 per cent;
- outpatient visits decreased by 10 per cent;
- A&E attendances decreased by 16 per cent;
- pharmacy visits increased by 18 per cent.

In addition to this, key research findings from a randomized trial carried out by the National Primary Care Research and Development Centre found that course participants have:

- improved partnerships with doctors;
- increased confidence to manage their condition;
- improved quality of life and psychological well-being;
- increased energy;
- a high level of satisfaction with the course.

Source: www.expertpatients.co.uk (accessed 15 May 2008)

Recent literature suggests that the concept of co-production is now relevant not only to the service delivery phase of services management but can extend across the full 'value chain' of service provision, including monitoring and evaluation activities (Bovaird, 2007). But given that evaluation is still considered as something of a threat in the public sector, and often does not take place at all if not imposed by central government or the European Commission (see Chapter 22), the involvement of citizens in an evaluation exercise is often considered even more daunting. Nevertheless, even professional auditors have to acknowledge that 'citizen inspectors' can bring in a different perspective that can add value to the reports done by professionals. For example, in the UK, tenants of social housing are recruited to work as 'tenant inspection advisors', joining the Audit Commission inspection teams that assess the quality of social housing providers, in order to ensure that inspection remains clearly focused on the customer's experience of housing services. A real bottom-up initiative that goes even further is the citizen inspectorate in Bobigny in France, which audits the local authority and publishes regular reports that are presented to the mayor in a public meeting (see interviews, www.govint.org).

ASSESSING PUBLIC GOVERNANCE

One way in which the quality of public governance can be assessed in practice is shown by a case looking into the quality of local governance in social housing estates in Carrick, a district council in the south-west of England. The methodology allowed the measurement of the gap between what local stakeholders expected and the performance of local agencies, both in terms of *quality of life* (against four key dimensions, namely liveable environment, community safety, health, social well-being and disability issues, and education and training) and *principles of public governance* (including transparency, partnership working, sustainability and honest and fair behaviour). These dimensions of quality of life and principles of governance were selected as high priority in discussions with the Board of Carrick Housing and were subsequently confirmed in focus group discussions.

The core of the methodology was discussion in twelve focus groups with different stakeholders, centring around one quality of life issue and one governance principle, selected as particularly relevant to that focus group. Four key questions were addressed to each focus group in relation to each topic:

- the current *state* (e.g. 'How safe do you feel on your estate?');
- the *trend* (e.g. 'Has safety on this estate improved or got worse in the couple of years?);
- *proposals* (e.g. 'What do you think communities and organisations in your area can do to deal with the community safety problems you have identified?');
- *commitment* of participants ('What would YOU be prepared to do in order to help these proposals to get implemented?').

The results of the discussions about the current state of the quality of life and governance issues are shown in Figure 15.1. The multi-stakeholder assessment process provided greater insights than is available from most measurement approaches and also brought the stakeholders

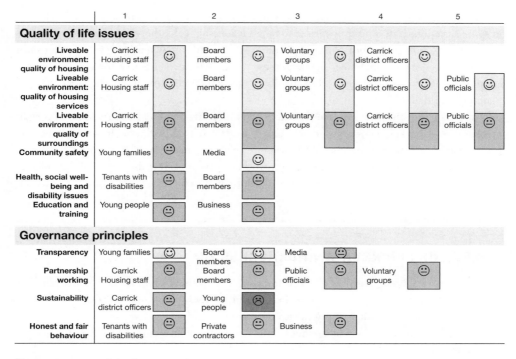

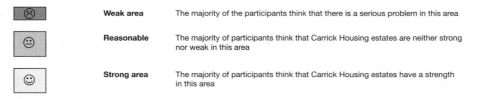

Key to present situation

☹ Weak area	The majority of the participants think that there is a serious problem in this area
☺ Reasonable	The majority of participants think that Carrick Housing estates are neither strong nor weak in this area
☺ Strong area	The majority of participants think that Carrick Housing estates have a strength in this area

Figure 15.1 *Scorecard of quality of life and implementation of governance principles in Carrick public housing estates*

Source: Bovaird and Löffler (2007), unpublished annex

into the process in such as a way as to increase their commitment to find solutions to the problems identified.

SUMMARY

This chapter has stressed that the concepts of 'governance' and 'good governance' are contestable, but that they are central to an understanding of the way in which government and the public sector relate to their society.

Government is not enough, since governance is enacted by many other stakeholders. However, good governance in society and in the polity will usually require good government.

The key question for government is, which role should it adopt in which context? Whereas in some situations it may be appropriate to take a leadership role, there may be other contexts in which stakeholders do not trust government sufficiently, or where government does not have the necessary competence. In such cases, it may be more effective for government to adopt the role of a co-producer and to enable users and their communities to be *part* of service planning and delivery.

The other question for government (and any other stakeholder) is to choose the right mechanism – market, hierarchy or network – to deal with a problem. In some cases, the problem at stake can be solved through market mechanisms; in other cases, the problem should be delegated to groups in the community or other networks. But there are still problems, such as national defence, that are best dealt with by hierarchies.

QUESTIONS FOR REVIEW AND DISCUSSION

1   What does 'good governance' mean for you? Try to think of a number of attributes of good governance and how each of them could be operationalized in order to allow you to assess the quality of public governance.
2   Describe how network management differs from the management of hierarchical organizations.

READER EXERCISES

1   Choose an organization with which you are familiar (e.g. your college or your employer). Undertake a stakeholder analysis for that organization by identifying all the stakeholders who have affected it or may be affected by it. In a second step, decide who are the stakeholders to whom most attention needs to be paid by allocating them into a power-interest matrix.
2   Think of one key public policy area that concerns you. What are the main mechanisms by which non-governmental stakeholders can influence the outcomes? What are the main ways in which their influence could be strengthened?
3   Take a copy of a serious newspaper (note: be careful, this exercise could reveal a lot about you!) and identify the major public governance issues that are surfaced in its stories (e.g. transparency, integrity or honesty of staff in public agencies; engagement of non-governmental stakeholders in policy decisions; ability to work in partnership with other agencies; etc). Do the stories suggest any mechanisms by which these governance issues might better be tackled?

CLASS EXERCISES

1   Identify in class an important 'wicked' public policy problem that affects your quality of life (such as high pollution in your city, high levels of crime in your neighbourhood, discriminatory behaviour against the group to which you belong,

etc). In groups, discuss which stakeholders are likely to be most successful in solving this problem. Then discuss the obstacles that exist to giving this stakeholder the power needed to allow them the opportunity to implement their solution. In the class plenary session, compare your analyses.

2　In groups, discuss which stakeholder(s) should take the lead in producing a healthier population in your city, and why. Compare your answers in a plenary session of the class.

FURTHER READING

Tony Bovaird (2007), 'Beyond engagement and participation – user and community co-production of public services', *Public Administration Review*, 67 (5): 846–60.

Tony Bovaird and Elke Löffler (2002), 'Moving from excellence models of local service delivery to benchmarking of "good local governance"', *International Review of Administrative Sciences*, 67 (1): 9–24.

Jon Pierre and B. Guy Peters (2000), *Governance, politics and the state*. New York: St Martin's Press.

Gerry Stoker (2004), *Transforming local governance: from Thatcherism to New Labour*. Basingstoke: Palgrave Macmillan.

REFERENCES

Tony Bovaird (2007), 'Beyond engagement and participation – user and community co-production of public services', *Public Administration Review*, 67 (5): 846–60.

Tony Bovaird and Elke Löffler (2002), 'Moving from excellence models of local service delivery to benchmarking of "good local governance"', *International Review of Administrative Sciences*, 67 (1): 9–24.

Tony Bovaird and Elke Löffler (2007), 'Assessing the quality of local governance: a case study of public services', *Public Money and Management*, 27 (4): 293–300

European Commission (2001), *White Paper on European Governance.* Brussels: Commission of the European Communities (http://europa.eu.int/comm/governance/white_paper/index_en.htm, from 1 May 2008).

Walter J.M. Kickert and Joop F.M. Koopenjan (1997), 'Public management and network management: an overview', in Walter J.M. Kickert, Erick-Hans Klijn and Joop F.M. Koopenjan (eds), *Managing complex networks: strategies for the public sector*. London: Sage, pp. 35–61.

Erik-Hans Klijn and G.R. Teismann (1997), 'Strategies and games in networks', in Walter J.M. Kickert, Erick-Hans Klijn and Joop F.M. Koopenjan (eds), *Managing complex networks: strategies for the public sector*. London: Sage, pp. 98–118.

Jan Kooiman (ed.) (1993), *Modern governance: new government–society interactions*. London: Sage.

231

Elke Löffler, Salvador Parrado Diez, Tony Bovaird and Greg Van Ryzin (2008), *'If you want to go fast, walk alone. If you want to go far, walk together': citizens and the co-production of public services*. Birmingham: Governance International.

Jon Pierre and B. Guy Peters (2000), *Governance, politics and the state*. New York: St Martin's Press.

Rod Rhodes (1997), *Understanding governance. Policy networks, governance, reflexivity and accountability*. Buckingham: Open University Press.

Fritz W. Scharpf (1978), 'Interorganizational policy studies: issues, concepts and perspectives', in K.I. Hanf and Fritz W. Scharpf (eds), *Interorganizational policy-making: limits to coordination and central control*. London: Sage, pp. 345–70.

World Bank (1989), *Sub-Sahara Africa. From crisis to sustainable growth: a long-term perspective study*. Washington, DC: World Bank.

Chapter 16

Partnership working in the public domain

Tony Bovaird and *John Tizard*, University of Birmingham, UK

PARTNERSHIPS – LOVED AND HATED?

This chapter looks at partnership working in the public domain, particularly (but not exclusively) between public sector and private sector organisations. So, be careful – this topic can damage your health. There is probably no other issue in this book which is so prone to turn previously quiet, gentle citizens into apoplectic fire-breathing ideologues. A tip for starters, therefore – before you finally make up your mind about the issues considered here, read the chapter, dip into the further reading and do the exercises. And along the way, observe your own reactions, and ask yourself what exactly is it that drives most of us to feel passionately about these issues. In that way, there is a good chance that the energy you release will generate some light, and not just heat!

LEARNING OBJECTIVES

This chapter is intended to help readers:

- to understand the different types of partnership that are found in the public domain;
- to understand their benefits and limitations; and
- to probe under the surface of partnerships to see the level of 'jointness' which they exhibit.

PARTNERSHIPS – LOVE THEM OR HATE THEM?

Now, everyone wants to work in partnership. You might think it has always been so, but this would be very wrong. Until very recently – certainly until the early 1990s – it was very common for public agencies (and local authorities and central government departments in particular) to be inward-looking and to assume that their core task was to get right their *own* business, leaving others alone to see to *their* businesses similarly. And, if this inbred way of thinking was in the public sector for so long, surely it is right to be suspicious of whether the recent outbreak of 'partnerships' and 'joined-up government' is always as 'joined up' as it might on the surface appear. This chapter will explore how and why the move to partnership has occurred, and whether it is always as thorough-going as it appears.

First, let us admit that there are a huge number of different types of partnership in the public sector. For example, the concept includes public-public partnerships, and partnerships between the public and private sectors, the public and third sectors and, even more complicated, between the public, private and third sectors. Indeed, we can even see some examples of private-third sector partnerships to deliver public services.

Furthermore, we can classify public partnerships in a number of ways, including:

- *relationships* — which can vary between 'loose' (e.g. in an informal network), politely coordinative, genuinely collaborative, fully power-sharing, and purely contractual (although there is a question whether the latter is a 'real' partnership);
- *economic basis*: supply-side (e.g. to get cost advantages or market power), demand-side (e.g. to improve service commissioning) or mixed demand/supply-side partnerships (e.g. to boost the economy of a city or region);
- *policy objectives* (e.g. promoting economic productivity, empowering clients and the disadvantaged, tackling social inclusion).

One particular type of partnership has been the focus of particular attention over the years — public-private partnerships (PPPs). The 'private' element of this concept is variously interpreted as covering *only* the 'private for profit' sector or the 'non-public' (both for-profit and not-for-profit) sector. In this chapter, we focus particularly on this latter type of partnership. Since they originally became fashionable in the USA and UK around thirty years ago (Bovaird, 2004b), the concept of PPPs has been strongly promoted by many people but also faced several sources of animosity, both conceptual and practical.

Why people like partnerships . . . and why they don't

There are lots of reasons why some people are enthusiastic about the potential for partnerships (Box 16.1).

BOX 16.1 PARTNERSHIPS ARE LIKED BY ORGANIZATIONS BECAUSE . . .

- They help organizations to tackle 'wicked problems' they could not address successfully their own.
- They allow sharing of expertise and other resources.
- They allow gaps to be filled in the services on offer to users.
- They allow joint risk-taking and experimentation, so that organizations can learn what works and what doesn't.
- Working with partners, especially from other sectors, may give access to organizational cultures and experiences that encourage learning in ways not otherwise available.

234

BOX 16.2 PARTNERSHIPS MAY BE SEEN UNDESIRABLE BECAUSE . . .

- They may lead to fragmentation of structures and processes;
- . . . and this may lead to blurred responsibilities and accountabilities.
- *Staff* may lose their jobs or experience worse conditions of service within the new partnership.
- *Politicians* may fear losing control over policy-making and service decisions.
- *Service users and citizens* may fear becoming objects of a profit-making calculus rather than a public service ethos.
- *Voluntary organizations and NGOs* may be reluctant to swop their independence and critical roles, just to become public service providers.

Source: Adapted from Bovaird (2004a)

However, as Box 16.2 shows, there are counter arguments . . .

In the cut-and-thrust of debate within different contexts, the proponents of each set of arguments have learnt from each other and partly changed their positions. For example, many proponents of the public sector now advocate more risk-taking and innovation within public sector organizations, to obviate the need for cumbersome cross-organizational arrangements to respond to new needs and technologies. On the other side, legislation and regulation in the UK now provide some protection of employment rights for transferred and newly recruited staff, to respond to staff concerns about PPPs.

THE CONTEXT: THE INTERNATIONAL EMERGENCE AND GROWTH OF PPPS

Public-public partnerships are a relatively recent phenomenon. They are associated with the 'joined-up government' movement in the UK (late 1990s), the 'whole of government' approach in Australia (after 2000) and the 'franchise government' movement in the US (1990s). Public-private partnerships, by contrast, have a long international provenance. As we shall see, France has a strong claim to be the historical home of PPP working, and the US has had PPPs since the 1930s. However, it was only in the 1970s that PPPs began to attract much wider notice internationally as an alternative to the two main sectors (Fosler and Berger, 1982). In this section, we will therefore focus on the development of PPPs across the world.

The story of PPPs in the modern era starts in the US. In 1938, the federal government created a partnership, between the public sector and the private market to produce housing in urban areas, which was highly effective. After 1945, a series of federal housing and development programmes relied primarily on private developers to rebuild the inner cities, using public subsidies to stimulate private development: 'within the US, public-private cooperation [led by elite, business-dominated groups] has always formed the touchstone for urban redevelopment policy. Local government never played the major role of British local authorities in housing provision and industrial development' (Fainstain, 1994, p. 115).

235

Further PPPs for urban regeneration sprang up in the 1960s and 1970s (Fosler and Berger, 1982), e.g. through the Urban Development Action Grant, which Blakely (1994, p. 154) described as 'the most powerful stimulus for downtown restoration ever devised'. Most large US cities redeveloped large parts of their downtowns in revitalization projects, supported through federal government transfers and loan guarantees – famous examples were the ports of Baltimore and Boston, which subsequently influenced European examples such as Bristol, Liverpool and Barcelona.

During the 1970s, federal government reduced its financial support and withdrew from its oversight role, forcing localities to turn to the private sector for funding of major projects. As local authorities became increasingly entrepreneurial, they moved from their traditional role as regulator to co-investor (Fainstain, 1994: 115). In a famous critique of the 'urban growth coalitions' behind these PPPs, Logan and Molotch (1987, p. 62) suggest that:

> The people who use their time and money to participate in local affairs are the ones who – in vast disproportion to their representation in the population – have the most to gain or lose in land use decisions. Local business people are the major participants in urban politics, particularly business people in property investing, development and real estate financing.

Consequently, the US urban development case emphasizes how important it is not only to ask 'PPPs for what?' but also to ask 'PPPs for whom?'

While the US public sector has a long history of contracting out to the private sector such activities as waste disposal, highways construction and maintenance, facility and building management and repair, ambulance services, vehicle fleets, and professional services such as architecture, engineering and legal advice, these services were often externalized on the basis of standard contracts. However, more genuinely collaborative PPPs have also occurred in the US and, in recent years, have become important in transportation, water and many aspects of social policy.

Rosabeth Moss Kanter (1994) has highlighted the growing role of leading companies in the US in the social sector – in public schools, welfare-to-work programmes and inner city redevelopments. For instance, the 'Pathways to Independence' training programme, which Marriott International ran in partnership with government and non-profit sectors in thirteen US cities after 1991, focused on honing the job and life skills, and job habits, of welfare recipients, who were guaranteed a job when they completed the programme. A private third sector partnership is exemplified by BankBoston with its First Community Bank, launched in 1990 to target newcomers to the banking system, such as inner city residents, working mainly with community organizations in New England.

In more recent years, there has been increasing interest in PPPs around the world, for a variety of reasons. Moreover, major international financial institutions, such as the IMF, World Bank and European Bank for Reconstruction and Development have also been supporting and promoting PPPs.

PPP growth has sometimes been dramatic. Indeed, PPPs are now written into legislation in many countries (for example urban policy legislation in the UK and USA, into national industrial policies in France, and into economic development policies in Italy, the Netherlands and the UK).

236

The partnership-influenced urban development programmes in the US in the 1960s were closely observed in Europe but did not inspire immediate copying. However, by the 1980s there was a flood of PPPs in almost all EU countries and in many sectors. There are few patterns observable in this remarkable change-round – it seems that the route travelled in each EU country was significantly different, although the destinations had strong similarities.

Many PPPs at the local level in the EU are transport projects, while many others deal with urban development, as in the US. Others typically deal with environmental issues, technology innovation and knowledge development (and ICT) (Teisman and Klijn, 2000). The mechanisms used for PPPs differ greatly throughout Europe. Spain, Portugal, Finland and Holland have the most advanced PPPs of the PFI-type (Ball, 1999). The use of build-operate-transfer contracts (or variants such as build-operate-own) is also quite popular in Europe as a technique by which consortia of constructors and financiers can be become involved in financing, constructing, operating and maintaining major infrastructure (Li and Akintoye, 2003). However, these are not always 'partnerships' in the full sense, as many operate essentially on contract management lines.

In the EU the notion of partnership has become one of the organizing principles of the Structural Fund programmes. This EU notion of 'partnership' refers to a broad local alliance between public authorities, private organizations, 'the social partners' and the population. As the years have gone by, the Commission has increasingly required the partnership principle to be taken into account in applications for joint funding from Europe. It now encourages PPPs in virtually every field and is willing to support them not only from the Structural Funds but also from a wide range of smaller initiatives (e.g. Resider, Konver or Interreg).

In practice, however, the main focus has been on trans-European networks (TENs) and, to a lesser extent, energy and telecommunications networks. More recently the EC has also prioritized projects centred on employment creation and on education and training (Jones, 1999, p. 295).

Indeed, since the 1980s there have been a number of world-renowned PPPs in transport in Europe – the Channel Tunnel, the Oresund connection between Denmark and Sweden and some transnational high-speed railways and stations. Some of these are concessions, with the return for the private investor coming from customer payments. In other forms of service and infrastructure, PPP payments to the private sector are made by the public sector client partner.

Nevertheless, the role of the EU should not be overstated. Its projects make up only a small number of the PPPs in most member states and have not noticeably catalyzed the major PPP developments in those states. Furthermore, its own competition rules have proved a barrier to the development of partnership working in some cases. All EU member states, however, have to follow EU legislation when developing and managing PPPs.

France is often claimed to be the European country with the most experience in operating PPPs – since the seventeenth century many canals and bridges have been built by granting concessions, and this system still continues in much of the transport network. Moreover, many more public services such as water, sewage, refuse collection and treatment, urban transport, mass housing, and facilities for culture, sports and social affairs have been operated by private companies since the nineteenth century. Famous examples include the water companies Compagnie Générale des Eauxs (called Vivendi since 1998) and the Lyonnaise des

Eaux (now called Suez), which have not only survived but, from the 1980s onward, have led the international movement to bring the private sector into water services. By far the most important institutional form of private involvement in public services in France is the Société Économie Mixte (SEM), dating from 1926, when local authorities received a general power to run local services, either directly or through financial participation in firms (Burnham, 2001, p. 51). For much of the post-war period they have been the main vehicle for the planning and construction of housing and other development. The local authority retains majority control and funding but involves other partners – historically the major player being the public sector bank, *Caisse des Dépôt et Consignations* (CDC).

Burnham (2001, p. 49) estimates that in 2001 there were about 1,215 SEMs in existence and about one-third of local authority investment was made through a SEM. About a quarter of these were constructing, maintaining or managing buildings; another quarter were active in urban redevelopment; and the rest were building or operating public services such as transport, cable neworks or car parks, or distributing electricity. SEMs have the advantage of allowing the fragmented and small French communes to garner economies of scale in service provision, unlike in-house providers.

In spite of this long experience with private sector involvement in public service provision, Le Galès and Mawson (1994: 64) conclude that there has been little experience in France of the type of collaboration that has developed in the UK in recent decades. They suggest that, in general, at the local level, mayors provide the main source of local leadership and do not wish to share it with private partners. However, perhaps the main reason is that PPPs have been institutionalized in France, mainly through the SEMs, in which the public sector has a significant degree of control and influence compared with the private sector.

Since 1945 a long tradition has developed in Germany of state partnership with the private sector – evidenced, for example by large-scale state shareholding in major industrial enterprizes such as Volkswagen, Lufthansa, VEBA, VIAG at the national level, and RWE at the regional level. Some of these shareholdings still remain, while others have now been liquidated. This is a very different PPP model to the more usually recognized public service and/or infrastructure projects. The move to a more partnership-oriented involvement of the private sector started in the 1970s. PPPs have been particularly common since the mid-1980s, initially in urban renewal and major transportation facilities (Sack, 2003). In the 1990s, PPPs became everyday practice, extending into energy supply, refuse disposal, transport and telecommunications, sport and leisure, social housing and car park provision. By 2000, over half of medium and large local authorities had entered into partnerships with private ICT providers. By 2002, over half of German cities were implementing PPPs (in some cases, in PFI-type projects). However, the growing partnership working in personal social services is still largely dominated by public-non-profit arrangements. In the UK, over 800 formal PFI-type PPPs are currently operational (2008).

THEORETICAL RATIONALE OF PARTNERSHIPS

In understanding the role of partnerships in the public sector, we need to examine the very different conceptual frameworks that are frequently used to examine inter-organizational behaviour in the public sector and private sector.

Traditional economic analysis argues that resource allocation is most 'efficient' when it is arranged through markets in which potential suppliers compete with one another to cut costs and to attract customers by improving the quality of the goods or services. When applied to the public sector from the 1980s onwards, this analysis gave rise to experiments in privatization, outsourcing and internal market mechanisms for the provision of public services. Competition between providers was seen as key to these cost and quality benefits being achieved. There has been a strand of thinking in UK government policy since the 1980s that emphasizes the value of competition, rather than collaboration.

However, in the NPM approach, commissioners or purchasers of services in the public sector were also seen to have the potential for economies of scale or economies of scope if they worked with one or more other agencies – e.g. economies of scale from buying in bulk through purchasing consortia for the purchase of paper, furniture, etc., or economies of scope through the sharing of some expertise, e.g. specialist music teachers, consumer fraud enforcement staff, etc. Such partnerships were seen by economists as potentially efficient.

Consequently, NPM approaches accept that partnerships can sometimes play a useful role, but partnership working must be scrutinised very carefully, to ascertain if it masks anti-competitive behaviour. Where private partners are brought in to provide public services, the public sector may be suspected of simply wanting to raise maximum revenues by granting monopolies to private firms (as was certainly the case with some of the UK privatizations in the Thatcher era, albeit subject to some regulation of pricing and terms of service).

Some loose ends in the economic analysis of these propositions did give some concern, even at the time when NPM was gaining ground in the public sector. For example, some public choice theorists continued to be sceptical of any argument for public sector intervention in markets, and therefore saw PPPs as only 'half-way' solutions, preferring outright privatization.

More importantly, transaction cost analysis (Williamson, 1975; Walsh, 1995) argued that, where contracts were complex, the high costs of designing, letting, monitoring and enforcing these contracts meant that organizations might well be better off undertaking many activities in-house (even where they were relatively bad at these activities) unless relational contracts could be set up. Relational contracts rely on trust (rather than the purely economic incentives in traditional or 'transactional' contracts) and form the basis for long-term relationships. They can apply at the level of strategic partnerships, but also at the level of outsourcing small-scale services to sub-contractors – the basic criterion for moving to a relational contract is whether the transaction costs of detailed, specification-based contracts outweigh the likely benefits of such a relationship.

This analysis suggested that traditional public sector contracting had often been fundamentally misguided, leading to confrontational contracting that was based on the mutual attempt to take advantage of the other party (see Chapter 7). It suggested a new partnership-based approach to contracting, in which both parties would find it advantageous to find ways of helping each other to be more successful. This approach, though, had little time for PPPs where it could not be demonstrated that there was a complementarity of resources – in particular, it was highly suspicious of those UK PFI schemes that appeared only to be proposed because private sector funding was made mandatory by public sector financing rules ('marriage for money'), rather than because there was any natural match between the different expertises brought by the public and private sector 'partners'.

Meanwhile, emphasis in the strategic management literature on strategic alliances, joint ventures and consortia (Bovaird, 2004a) reinforced the importance of partnership and collaborative working, as opposed to competitive behaviour (although they can also provide opportunities for 'cost dumping' and 'benefits raiding'). This literature suggested that partnerships can contribute to competitive (or collaborative) advantage by:

- providing *economies of scale* (and perhaps critical mass) in the provision of services;
- providing *economies of scope* (i.e. the ability to exploit more fully the complementary capabilities in the partner organization) in the provision of services;
- providing *opportunities for mutual learning* between the partners (in the long-term dynamic process of interaction between the partners).

It may be that only when all participants have become expert in achieving 'collaborative advantage' with their partners is it likely that the partnership as a whole will be able to gain competitive advantage against other rival partnerships (Huxham, 1993). This has been the aim of some UK PPPs, in which local authorities have joined forces with major private sector suppliers of business services (such as contact centres, financial processing centres, etc.) with the hope that the PPP will win business from surrounding local authorities (and other public agencies) so that the costs of the service fall, giving significant benefits to the local authority concerned and higher profits to the private partner.

From the mid-1990s, the emerging public governance paradigm reinterpreted key strategic management concepts in NPM:

- *Decision-making has to become shared* within partnerships, which implies trust-building and capacity-building activities, so that different members of the partnerships and networks play their agreed roles.
- *Accountability has to become shared* within partnerships, so that both democratic accountability of politicians and managerial accountability are reinforced, not undermined, by the shared responsibilities for partnership activities.
- *Goals and plans have to become coordinated and integrated*, so that partners have to show sensitivity towards each other's goals, which may change over time. (This is not the quite same thing as having 'shared' goals – as long as their goals are complementary, a successful partnership can exist between partners who have quite different goals.)
- *Extensive relationship contracting should be used, rather than in-house provision or transactional contracts with external providers,* so that there is less emphasis on 'clear divisions of labour for actors' and more on partnership working (see Chapter 7).
- *Management of the strategic change process should be joint,* typically in the form of cross-agency teams and project groups.

In summary, the mode of strategic management in public governance has to change from attempting to impose strategic control on stakeholders towards the negotiation of overall strategies within which decisions of partners will mutually influence each other, in a process of strategic experimentation and diversity.

240

ASSESSING THE BALANCE BETWEEN COSTS AND BENEFITS FROM PARTNERSHIP WORKING

The evidence on the success of partnership working is still rather scant. The UK Treasury reported in 2003 that PFI 'helps ensure desired service standards are maintained, that new services start on time and facilities are completed on budget and that the assets built are of sufficient quality to remain throughout their life'. However, other critics have asserted that PFI has been cumbersome, slow, unresponsive to the needs of public sector clients and inflexible, given that PFI contracts usually last for very long periods.

In a world that recognizes the importance of good governance, and not just the efficient delivery of public services, the requirements placed upon the working of partnerships will necessarily be rather more demanding than under the NPM paradigm. Where partnerships are attempting to solve 'wicked problems', their success criteria cannot sensibly be restricted to the efficiency with which they produce their outputs or even how well each partner is able to improve its performance against its own objectives – although both of these remain important. Partnerships are therefore likely to have a first tier of objectives (and PIs) that highlights outcomes, such as quality of life improvements. Of course, partnerships are often reluctant – just as individual partners are – to take responsibility for achievements in areas in which they have relatively little control over outcomes. However, there is little point in moving to partnerships if they are not going to accept the need to demonstrate whether they have made better or worse the problems they are addressing.

A further corollary of the public governance perspective is that performance should be judged at the level of the partnership, rather than simply at the level of the agency. Asking each individual partner to account for its contribution to the partnership, and whether it is getting 'value for money' from these contributions is highly dangerous – it is like separating out the roots of a plant to see which is contributing most to the health of the plant, a process that may itself actually kill the plant. It is more appropriate that partners should be held to account for whether the partnership itself is working successfully and whether the agency might do more to contribute to its success.

Moreover, a full evaluation of partnerships must not only cover the degree of achievement of the partnership's objectives and solution to the 'wicked problems' they are facing, but whether their working has been based on principles of good governance.

GOVERNANCE OF PARTNERSHIPS

Partnerships must not only help to deliver the objectives of the public sector and solve the 'wicked problems' with which they are faced, but their working has to be based on principles of good governance. In Table 16.1 we set out some of the differences, from a governance perspective, which we would expect to see between genuinely collaborative partnerships (between any organisations, whatever their sector) and those relationships which simply involve the 'partners' respecting the contracts to which they are legally committed.

Obviously, the emphasis between the criteria by which good governance is judged may vary from partnership to partnership. The criteria highlighted in Table 16.1 have been selected as the 'lowest common denominator' from the approaches to good governance that have been advocated by major international and multinational agencies in recent years.

241

Table 16.1 *Partnerships from a governance perspective*

Governance principles	Transactional contractual relationships	Collaborative partnerships
Citizen engagement	Consultation with citizens and other stakeholders	Participation of citizens and other stakeholders in decision-making
Transparency	Limited to areas where stakeholders have a 'need to know' in order to monitor the contract – and, even then, limited by 'commercial confidentiality'	Open book working in respect of all partners (including user and citizen representatives, where appropriate) as a critical element of building trust
Accountability	The contractor must account to the purchaser in line with all performance reporting procedures agreed in the contract, particularly in relation to budgetary and cost control	Partners must be prepared to account to each other for their actions and performance on all issues that arise – and must be prepared to account to other stakeholders for the overall performance of the partnership
Equalities and social inclusion	These issues will only be considered in so far as they are included in the contract specification (although some firms may, independently, be committed to improving their record of corporate social responsibility)	Accepted as core values in the working of the partnership – partners are expected actively to seek innovative ways of improving performance against these principles
Ethical and honest behaviour	Staff must act legally and within professional codes of conduct	Accepted as core values in the working of the partnership – partners must actively seek innovative ways of improving performance against these principles
Equity (fair procedures and due process)	Staff must act within organizational procedures, which must ensure consistent treatment of all individuals within any group and must accord priority to different groups as set out in the contract	Accepted as core values in the working of the partnership – partners must continuously seek innovative ways of improving performance against this principle
Willingness and ability to collaborate	Valuable but not essential characteristic of relationships with other organizations	Critical success factor for all partners
Ability to compete	Critical success factor for the provider in the contract (incorporating both cost consciousness and customer focus)	Critical success factor for the partnership as a whole (incorporating both cost consciousness and customer focus)
Leadership	Necessary in each organization to ensure good contract management – timely, accurate and efficient meeting of contract specification	Necessary at all levels of the partnership as a whole, in each of its constituent organizations and in the communities that it serves
Sustainability	The contractor must demonstrate conformity with all sustainability criteria set out in the contract	Partners must continuously seek improved ways of increasing the sustainability of policies and activities

These criteria are demanding – as they are meant to be. It is therefore to be expected that, on occasion, they will bring howls of protest from partnerships which feel that it is too difficult to comply with them. However, the importance of these criteria is already being brought home to many partnerships that have suffered severe damage to their reputations, and lost the confidence of their funders and customers, because these principles have been ignored – most notably in relation to unfair employment practices in development projects sponsored by governments and multilateral aid agencies in parts of Asia. Indeed, international organizations are already monitoring the achievement of these principles by governments and partnerships (and also, in some cases, by large multinational, private corporations) – examples include Transparency International in relation to transparency, corruption and freedom of information; Human Rights Watch and Child Labour News Service in respect of human rights, equalities and fair employment; Greenpeace and Friends of the Earth in relation to environmental sustainability; and Democratic Audit (UK) in respect of 'free and fair elections', the openness, accountability and responsiveness of government, the degree of protection for civil and political rights and freedoms, and the vigour of democratic society (Bovaird and Löffler, 2003).

Just because these 'good governance' principles *could* be implemented in partnerships does not, of course, mean that they *should* be. Indeed, there is an alternative school of thought that believes that there needs to be a careful adaptation of public governance principles to ensure that they are appropriate to the complex and dynamic environments in which they are to be applied. For example, in some countries (such as Scandinavia) more emphasis might be placed on transparency in partnership working, while in other countries issues of social exclusion might be given major emphasis – this would be more likely in a country such as the UK with a high degree of social heterogeneity, compared, for example, with Germany.

Whatever criteria are given highest weight, public sector managers and politicians in every country need to have the assurance that their actions are in accord with good governance principles. However, the extent to which these principles might differ significantly between different contexts in the public sector poses a major challenge for public governance.

This challenge is pointed up well in the suggestion by Perri 6 *et al.* (2002, p. 183) that:

> some of the braver [public managers], or those with more informal and quiet political backing, will find low or lax accountability exactly the environment they need in order to pursue holistic working [i.e. working consistently across all arms and levels of government] in their own way.

They go on to suggest that 'for these more entrepreneurial public managers, accountability arrangements are a nuisance, a brake or at least a very blunt instrument for dealing with an extremely delicate task that requires the sensitivity of the individual public manager' (p. 183). Langford and Harrison (2001) make a similar point when they suggest that many new initiatives in e-government seem to focus upon central control of projects, wrapping them in a web of bureaucratic structures and processes that act against, or, at best, are irrelevant to the creation of strong partnerships and the creation of business value. Clearly these authors are not arguing that accountability does not matter – merely that it is not an absolute good and that it may, in specific contexts, be acceptable to trade off the extent of accountability exercised against the degree of innovation and creativity expected from staff working in public services.

Clearly, such a possibility is rather alarming to some schools of thought. It suggests that 'good governance' is a relative concept, which therefore cannot be assessed without an understanding of the context in which it is applied – an understanding that is likely to be most highly developed by stakeholders embedded within that context, rather than outsiders who might wish to make 'good governance judgements' from afar.

From this, one lesson is immediately clear – partnerships usually mean heterogeneity, not tidiness. Indeed, some authors (e.g. Löffler, 1999) have gone further, suggesting that a major problem with the partnership approach to public issues is that it brings *fragmentation of structures and processes*, which in turn leads to *blurring of responsibilities* and of *accountability* – as each agency has sacrificed some of its sovereignty in joining the partnership, it can also claim that the partnership, rather than itself, is the accountable body – yet there is often no direct mechanism by which these partnerships can be held accountable in a proper fashion. Wettenhall (2001) argues that under NPM in Australia there was a blurring of the sectors, giving rise to governance problems, and that the rise of partnerships has partly been a consequence of this – yet many of these partnerships have, in turn, given rise to similar problems. The issues of accountability and governance are all the more acute when the partnership is reluctant to divulge information to outsiders on grounds of 'commercial confidentiality' (particularly in the case of partnerships that involve private firms) or on grounds of 'data protection' (which can be used as a ground for secretiveness in virtually all partnerships) (Roberts, 2002).

Moreover, ensuring achievement of these principles of good governance is often very difficult in practice, even if they are agreed by all the actors. For example, PPPs are often claimed to have a design that will ensure that the public sector procuring body remains ultimately accountable – usually by ensuring that it has the responsibility for specifying outcomes and standards, monitoring performance, agreeing business plans and controlling payments to the supplier. Of course, the dynamics of organizational behaviour mean that the actual level of 'control' between the procurer and the provider is often difficult to establish – the information supplied by the provider may not well represent the actual state of affairs, whether deliberately or accidentally. We are still far from being able to assess the balance of achievements of partnerships in terms of 'good governance', never mind the overall cost-effectiveness of partnerships, weighing both the governance and service improvement dimensions.

SUMMARY

This chapter has argued that there are major advantages to partnership working in the public domain – but also some important dangers that need to be understood. Just as many case studies demonstrate that partnerships can have very successful outcomes, and that some problems can probably only be tackled by partnerships, often involving private sector partners, there are also some horror stories of where partnership working has gone wrong.

It is important to recognize that most public service partnerships are still young, and their success is not yet clear. For the moment, it is important to experiment with them, as with other approaches to managing the public good – and to watch the results with care. Their evaluation cannot be confined solely to issues of efficiency and cost-effectiveness – it is also essential to subject them to stringent tests of how well they comply with appropriate criteria of public governance.

As the novelty of the 'partnership' fad wears off, it is likely that many partnerships will be seen to have been inefficient, even unnecessary. We can therefore expect to hear more often in the future the advice 'Say "no" to partnerships, where they don't help!'. Similarly, strategic partnerships, such as local strategic partnerships (LSPs), will have to learn that it is not strategic to try to encompass all potential aspects of partnership working that occur within their area.

Moreover, there is a big question mark over the degree of genuine 'partnership' that is the norm in many partnerships. The conceptual frameworks and language of 'relational contracting' and 'partnering' may often be used in such arrangements, but the actual relationships appear often to reflect traditional 'transactional' or even 'confrontational' contracting (Bovaird 2004a).

Perhaps the key concern about partnerships, especially PPPs, is the extent to which their governance is appropriate for bodies that have command over the use of public money. The greatest challenge for partnership working is therefore to demonstrate that it can achieve the potential arising from collaborative efforts across many different types of organization, while still conforming to the basic principles of public governance.

QUESTIONS FOR REVIEW AND DISCUSSION

1   What are the main reasons why partnerships may provide better results in the design and delivery of public services than agencies working alone?
2   What are the main governance issues that tend to make PPPs more controversial than other forms of public sector partnership working?

READER EXERCISES

1   How would you distinguish between the concepts 'partnership working', 'collaboration', 'cooperation' and 'coordination'. Find authors in the literature who agree with your definitions and authors who disagree. Identify what factors seem to lie behind these disagreements.
2   Examine copies of high-quality newspapers in your country and identify stories about services that are being delivered by a public service partnership. Can you identify any ways in which the transparency of these services has been hindered by virtue of their partnership form?

CLASS EXERCISE

The class should break into groups of four to six people. Each group should identify a public service that is now being delivered by a partnership. For that partnership, the group should consider why a partnership might in theory be a better arrangement for the design and delivery of this service and should then collect evidence to see whether this potential has been borne out in practice. The groups should then compare their conclusions in a plenary discussion.

FURTHER READING

Robert Agranoff (2007), *Managing within networks: adding value to public organizations*. Washington, DC: Georgetown University Press.

Tony Bovaird (2004a), 'Public private partnerships: from contested concepts to prevalent practice', *International Review of Administrative Sciences*, 70 (2): 199–215.

Tony Bovaird (2005), 'Public governance: balancing stakeholder power in a network society', *International Review of Administrative Sciences*, 71 (2): 217–28.

Tony Bovaird (2007), 'Developing new relationships with the "market" in the procurement of public services', *Public Administration*, 84 (1): 81–102 (2006).

Tony Bovaird and Elke Löffler (2004), 'Evaluating the quality of local governance: some lessons from European experience', *Local Governance*, 30 (4): 178–87.

Tony Bovaird and Elke Löffler (2007), 'Assessing the quality of local governance: a case study of public services', *Public Money and Management*, 27 (4): 293–300.

Andrew Coulson (ed.) (1998), *Trust and contracts: relationships in local government, health and public services*. Bristol: Policy Press.

Kenneth Kernaghan (1993), 'Partnership and public administration – conceptual and practical considerations', *Canadian Public Administration*, 36 (1): 57–76.

Lester M. Salamon (1995), *Partners in public service: government-nonprofit relations in the modern welfare state*. Baltimore, MD: Johns Hopkins University Press.

Helen Sullivan and Chris Skelcher (2002), *Working across boundaries: collaboration in public services*. Basingstoke: Palgrave Macmillan.

Geerd Teisman and Erik-Hans Klijn (2000), 'Public-private partnerships in the European Union: officially suspect, embraced in daily practice', in Stephen Osborne (ed.), *Public-private partnerships: theory and practice in international perspective*. London: Routledge, pp. 165–86.

Karen West (2005), 'From bilateral to trilateral governance in local government contracting in France', *Public Administration*, 83 (2): 473–92.

REFERENCES

J. Ball (1999), 'Marketing a concept abroad', *Project Finance*, 193: 18–19. Cited in Akintola Akintoye, Matthias Beck and Cliff Hardcastle (eds) (2003), *Public-private partnerships: managing risks and opportunities*. Oxford: Blackwell.

Edward Blakely (1994), *Planning local economic development: theory and practice* (2nd edn). Thousand Oaks, CA: Sage.

Tony Bovaird (2004a), 'Public private partnerships: from contested concepts to prevalent practice', *International Review of Administrative Sciences*, 70 (2): 199–215.

Tony Bovaird (2004b), 'Public-private partnerships in Western Europe and the USA: new growths from old roots', in Abby Ghobadian, Nicholas Regan and David Gallear (eds), *Public private partnerships: policy and experience*. Basingstoke: Palgrave Macmillan, pp. 221–50.

Burnham, J. (2001), 'Local public-private partnerships in France: rarely disputed, scarcely competitive, weakly regulated', *Public Policy and Administration*, 16 (4): 47–60.

246

Susan Fainstain (1994), *The city builders: property, politics and planning in London and New York*. Oxford: Basil Blackwell.

R.S. Fosler and R.A. Berger (eds) (1982), *Public private partnership in American cities: seven case studies*. Lexington, MA: Lexington Press.

Chris Huxham (1993), 'Pursuing collaborative advantage', *Journal of the Operational Research Society*, 44 (6): 599–611.

Robert Jones (1999), 'The European Union as a promoter of public-private partnerships', *International Journal of Public-Private Partnerships*, 1 (3): 289–305.

Rosabeth Moss Kanter (1994), 'Collaborative advantage: the art of alliances', *Harvard Business Review*, July–August: 96–108.

John Langford and Yvonne Harrison (2001), 'Partnering for e-government: challenges for public administrators', *Canadian Public Administration*, 44 (4): 393–415.

Patrick Le Galès and John Mawson (1994), *Management innovations in urban policy: lessons from France*. Luton: Local Government Management Board.

Bing Li and Akintola Akintoye (2003), 'An overview of public-private partnership', in Akintola Akintoye, Matthias Beck and Cliff Hardcastle (eds), *Public-private partnerships: managing risks and opportunities*. Oxford: Blackwell.

Elke Löffler (1999), *Accountability management in intergovernmental partnerships*. Paris: OECD.

John Logan and Harvey Molotch (1987), *Urban fortunes: the political economy of place*. Los Angeles, CA: University of California Press.

Perri 6, Diana Leet, Kimberley Seltzer and Gerry Stoker (2002), *Towards holistic governance: the new reform agenda*. Basingstoke: Palgrave.

Alistair Roberts (2002), 'Closing the window: public service restructuring and the weakening of Freedom of Information Law', *Salem Papers* (www.inpuma.net).

Detlef Sack (2003), 'Gratwanderung zwischen partizpation und Finanzenpässen', *Zeitschrift für öffentliche und gemeinwirtschaftliche Unternehmen,* 26 (4): 353–70.

Geerd Teisman and Erik-Hans Klijn (2000), 'Public-private partnerships in the European Union: officially suspect, embraced in daily practice', in Stephen Osborne (ed.), *Public-private partnerships: theory and practice in international perspective*. London: Routledge, pp. 165–86.

R. Wettenhall (2001), 'Machinery of government in small states: issues, challenges and innovatory capacity', *Public Organization Review: A Global Journal*, 1 (2): 167–92.

Oliver Williamson (1975), *Markets and hierarchies: analysis and antitrust implications*. New York: Free Press.

Chapter 17

Decentralized management
Agencies and 'arm's-length' bodies

Christopher Pollitt, University of Leuven, Belgium

INTRODUCTION

Decentralization is tremendously fashionable. In Western Europe and North America you can hardly hear a word against it (just think – are you really in favour of '*centralization*'?). Yet you should be aware from the start that this is just the current turn of a wheel of fashion that has been going round for many decades. Centralization will probably be back (Hood and Jackson, 1991; Pollitt, 2005a), although not right now – or, at least, only in heavily disguised forms.

So decentralization is 'in'. And the fashion has real and important consequences, which this chapter will seek to interrogate. It expresses itself in a wide variety of forms and discourses – so many that they cannot all be examined in one chapter. So here I will focus on one particular manifestation of decentralized management – the idea that all sorts of benefits will be gained if public sector activities are put 'at arm's length' from the centre of political power, whether that be the ministry or the municipality. This has been a very popular idea indeed. During the past two decades it has, for example, fuelled programmes for creating semi-autonomous agencies in Canada, Jamaica, Japan, the Netherlands, Tanzania, the UK and the USA (Pollitt and Talbot, 2004; Pollitt *et al.*, 2004).

LEARNING OBJECTIVES

The learning objectives for this chapter are that you should:

- understand why the arguments for 'arm's length' public bodies have recently proved so attractive in so many countries;
- assess the evidence underpinning this fashion;
- become able to identify some of the key contextual factors that help or hinder successful decentralization;
- become equipped with a set of useful key questions with which to interrogate proposals for the decentralization of managerial authority to arm's-length bodies.

Definitions

First we need to deal with the question of definition. Let us begin with the general concept of *decentralization*, because it encompasses arm's length bodies (and much else besides). What was written half a century ago remains true today:

> It is impossible to standardize the usage of the word decentralization by seeking to give it meanings that would be acceptable universally. The English language took the word from Latin; it shares it with the Romance languages . . . it is a word that is not confined to public affairs and to formal organization in government or business. It is used in every walk of life. It must be accepted as a word of innumerable applications. Throughout all of them, however, runs a common idea, which is inherent in the word's Latin roots, meaning 'away from the centre'.
>
> (Macmahon, 1961, p. 15)

Those of you who want to explore definitions in greater depth are referred to my work elsewhere (Pollitt, 2005a), but for present purposes I will short circuit further debate by specifying the working definition I will use in this chapter. It is that decentralization occurs when:

> authority is spread out from a smaller to a larger number of actors.

Thus taking part of a ministry and turning it into a semi-autonomous executive agency is an act of decentralization in so far as the staff of the new agency are able to take authoritative decisions (e.g. about money, staff, cases) that previously they would have had to clear 'up the line' within the ministry. Of course, this *could* also mean that, while the chief executive of the new agency gained authority, s/he used it to exert even tighter control over rank-and-file staff. So decentralization *to* an arm's length body certainly does not automatically mean that everything *within* that body is decentralized. Note that this definition also implies that decentralization can take place without any arm's length bodies being created at all. Internal decentralization can occur if a ministry (or any other organizational unit) decides to give increased spending or personnel authority to middle managers, or to give increased discretion in case-handling to desk/street level staff. Decentralization may also take place at local levels when public services are no longer provided by the local authority but by newly founded public agencies, which enjoy managerial discretion but are still accountable to the local council. For example, in the state of North Rhine-Westphalia in Germany, the number of semi-autonomous public agencies at local level has increased from 736 in 1997 to 941 in 2007. It is important to note that the degree of decentralization does not go in hand with the legal autonomy of the new agency. Indeed, legally autonomous agencies at local level in Germany (so-called *Zweckverbände* or *öffentlich-rechtliche Anstalten*) may sometimes have less managerial freedom than local authority agencies without an independent legal status (so-called *Eigen-* or *Regiebetriebe*).

A second definitional question is, what is an 'arm's length body' (or 'agency', or 'QUANGO'). Again, I am afraid I am largely going to dodge this, with good reason. The question has been debated endlessly, both in the academic literature (Pollitt *et al.*, 2004, pp. 7–11) and in official reports at the national and international levels. But no great progress towards an agreed definition has been made. What has been revealed by these debates is a whole zoo full of differing titles, concepts and legal frameworks. In different countries, different species of arm's length bodies are termed agencies and non-departmental public bodies (UK), crown entities (New Zealand), special operating agencies (Canada), administrative corporations (Japan), *mydigheter* (Sweden), *établissements publics* (France), *zelfstandig bestuurs organisaties (ZBOs)* (Netherlands), *autorita amministrative independente* (Italy) and many other things (the OECD has nearly given up and has invented a covering term, 'distributed public governance' (OECD, 2001)). Each of these types has a somewhat different set of powers and a somewhat different relationship to its own political system (themselves differing enormously). Since national systems of law are also different, the researcher cannot find refuge in some universal legalistic definition. For the purposes of this chapter my (imperfect and general) working definition will be that an arm's length body is an organization that:

- has its status defined principally or exclusively in public law (though the nature of that law may vary greatly between different national systems);
- is functionally disaggregated from the core of its ministry or department of state;
- enjoys *some* degree of autonomy that is not enjoyed by the core ministry;
- is nevertheless linked to the ministry/department of state. For semi-autonomous agencies this may still permit ministers/secretaries of state to alter the budgets and main operational goals of the organization. For more fully autonomous bodies (such as Dutch ZBOs), ministers may not be able to do this, because the arm's length body has some kind of statutory independence that means it can only be given general directives by the political level, not case-specific instructions;
- in some way exercises public authority (e.g. by regulating activities, providing a public service or exercising quasi-judicial authority);
- is not a commercial corporation.

ARGUMENTS IN FAVOUR OF THE DECENTRALIZATION OF AUTHORITY TO ARM'S LENGTH BODIES

I will first list some of the key arguments that have been used – both by academics and practitioners – in favour of decentralization. One reason why decentralization is so popular is its property of being able to link up with many other arguments and concepts. It is therefore persuasively useful for several different reform agendas at the same time. It appears to bring both administrative and political benefits (Pollitt, 2005a).

Thus decentralization can be political as well as administrative. Although we are here more interested in management issues, it is necessary to be aware of the political arguments, since in practice these are often thoroughly intermingled with their administrative brothers. Some arm's length bodies include their own political element – for example, a wholly or partly elected board. Others may be purely administrative in form, but nevertheless seek to establish participatory mechanisms with citizens (e.g. through residents' panels, user advisory boards, regular open meetings).

BOX 17.1 ARGUMENTS IN FAVOUR OF ADMINISTRATIVE DECENTRALIZATION

1   Decentralization (both vertical and horizontal) speeds decision making by reducing the overload of information that otherwise clogs the upper reaches of a centralized hierarchy. Faster decision-making is more efficient.

2   Decentralization means that decisions are taken closer to the users/consumers of an organization's products and services, and this, in turn, means that decisions are likely to be more responsive to those users.

3   Decentralization improves the ability of an organization to take account of differences between one local context and another. Services can be better 'tuned' to local conditions.

4   Decentralization may be used as one way to reduce political intervention in matters that are best managed without political interference in details (e.g. case work with individual citizens; regulatory functions, etc.).

5   Decentralization encourages innovation (because new ideas no longer have to find their way all the way up the hierarchy to the centre to be approved and authorized).

6   Decentralization improves staff motivation and identification. They feel they can 'belong' to a smaller, more comprehensible organization, rather than just being a cog in a gigantic bureaucratic machine.

BOX 17.2 ARGUMENTS IN FAVOUR OF POLITICAL DECENTRALIZATION

1   Devolution of political power puts it closer to the citizen.

2   Devolution of political power makes politicians less remote, more visible and more accountable.

3   Devolution of power encourages more citizens to play some active part in the democratic process – by voting, attending meetings or even standing for office.

4   Devolution of political power allows for greater expression of legitimate local and regional differences.

If you look back at the arguments listed above you will realize that decentralization sounds wonderful! It seems to solve a whole host of administrative and political problems. However, you probably won't be surprised to hear that:

■   none of these benefits arrives automatically: 'the devil is in the detail';
■   there are some potential tensions or even contradictions between some of the different claimed benefits;
■   there are also some alleged drawbacks to decentralization – and therefore some good arguments in favour of centralization.

I will take these points one by one.

BARRIERS TO DECENTRALIZATION OF AUTHORITY TO ARM'S LENGTH BODIES

The benefits are not automatic

There is nothing automatic or inevitable about the benefits listed above. Much depends on *context* and on *clear-sighted design and implementation*.

An example of *context* would be the establishment of many agencies in Latvia soon after independence from the Soviet Union at the beginning of the 1990s. As in many other East European countries, in the wake of the immensely centralized, slow-moving bureaucracy of Communist times, decentralization was a hugely appealing idea. The problem, however, was the contextual one that, at that time, the ministries had neither the skills nor the resources to steer these agencies properly, and both financial and staffing irregularities resulted (Horvath, 2000). An autonomous public agency that is not properly accountable and transparent in its operations, and that operates without a clear policy direction from the government can be a very dangerous animal indeed. As for skills, the point is that managing arm's length relationships – from either end of the arm – requires a different set of skills and norms from those for managing within a comfortable, traditional hierarchy. Agency management has to learn not to abuse its (semi) autonomy, and the senior civil servants left in the parent ministry have to learn not to interfere on petty issues in the way that perhaps they used to. Evidence from a number of countries indicates that getting the balance right is very difficult indeed (Pollitt, 2005b). In many cases there seems to be a prolonged tug-of-war in which each party thinks the other is not honouring the bargain they thought they had made – from the point of view of the arm's length body either there is too much interference or, in some cases, too little guidance.

Clear-sighted design and implementation imply that the policymakers will be clear about their intentions, and the implementers will be vigorous leaders over the considerable periods of time usually needed to get new organizational forms up and running. Sometimes these conditions are met, often they are not. For example, Van Thiel records considerable vagueness among politicians about what the aims of QUANGO creation in the Netherlands really were (Van Thiel, 2001, pp. 9–14). And in Eastern Europe, the stability and continuity requirements were often breached during the 1990s and 2000s, because governments and their appointees rose and fell within quite short intervals.

But even if politicians are clear in their objectives, and the political system is largely free of the problems that have hampered Eastern European administrations, there are still considerable design hurdles. The modern idea of an agency is founded on the notion that, while it will enjoy managerial freedoms, it will do so within a contract-like steering framework of policy objectives, associated operational targets and performance indicators that measure how far those targets have been achieved (Pollitt *et al.*, 2004, Chapter 2). This framework should ensure that both strategic steering (by ministries/ministers) and public accountability (to legislatures, citizens) are feasible. But designing a comprehensive set of measurable and meaningful indicators is a major technical challenge, and several important pieces of research have revealed that indicator sets are frequently deficient (see Case Example 1).

CASE EXAMPLE 17.1 **GETTING PERFORMANCE INDICATORS TO FIT THE OBJECTIVES**

Talbot (1996) surveyed the executive agencies 'parented' by the Home Office and the Department of Social Security. All these agencies had sets of key performance indicators. But 47 per cent of their official aims and objectives were not covered by these indicators, and a further 31 per cent were only partially covered. Neither were the indicator sets stable over time. During the first half of the 1990s there was a 70 per cent 'churn rate' (turnover) of indicators, with new indicators being introduced and existing indicators modified or dropped. This made it very difficult to follow performance over time.

In such a situation (some objectives not covered by performance indicators, indicators changing rapidly) it is an open question how well public accountability can work, and even how well the ministry can steer the agency.

There are tensions and contradictions

If you look again at the lists of arguments in favour of decentralization, some tensions leap out. For example, how can moving to arm's length simultaneously promote freedom from political interference *and* more local participation. Local participation is almost bound to be, to some extent, political in nature – particular interest groups pushing for the favoured solutions, local business people trying to exert influence and so on. It may not be party politics on the model of national parties, but it is certainly interest-group politics.

Or again, how can decentralization speed decision-making if it also leads to the participation of more local groups and consumers in policy-making? Wider, deeper processes of consultation usually lead to longer, not shorter, decision-making cycles (see Chapter 19).

ARGUMENTS AGAINST DECENTRALIZATION TO ARM'S-LENGTH BODIES

Now consider the following:

1　Centralization enables organizations to benefit from economies of scale.
2　Centralization enables organizations to retain a critical mass of experts (in central think tanks and the 'technostructure' (Mintzberg, 1979)). Small organizations do not have the resources to do this.
3　Centralization, in the form of standardization, leads to greater equity. All citizens in similar circumstances receive the same service. Autonomous local services are more prone to inequities – both intentional and unintentional.

4   Centralization makes the co-ordination of policies and programmes (especially those that cross sectoral or organizational boundaries) easier to accomplish. 'Joined-up' government can be substituted for 'hollowed-out' government.

5   Centralization makes the line of accountability clearer and more easily understood by citizens. In highly decentralized systems, patterns of accountability are complex, and there are too many opportunities for blame-shifting.

These are not inconsiderable advantages that are attributed to centralization. Better coordination ('joined-up government') and clearer lines of accountability are by no means trivial issues. In fact they are among the central aims of many contemporary governments (see, e.g. Perri 6, 2004; Perri 6 *et al.*, 2002). Perhaps they can be achieved through decentralized networks of many arm's length bodies – that is the hope of many current reformers and of some academics – but the possibility is by no means yet proven and is clearly not always achieved (see Case Example 17.3). Indeed, in 2002, a UK review of the Next Steps agency programme came to the conclusion that one of the effects of the creation of so many executive agencies over the previous fifteen years had been some fragmentation and loss of policy coordination (Office of Public Services Reform, 2002).

CASE EXAMPLE 17.2 **LOSS OF ACCOUNTABILITY IN GERMAN ARM'S-LENGTH AGENCIES AT LOCAL LEVEL**

Recent functional and organizational decentralization in German local authorities has meant that the budget of arm's-length agencies now often exceeds the rest of the budget of the local authority, and there can be similar patterns in employment levels – e.g. in the state of North Rhine-Westphalia, 200,000 staff work in local arm's-length agencies, and 220,000 staff continue to work in local authorities. Clearly, decentralization and privatization of local public services have been popular mechanisms for dealing with budget deficits at local level in Germany. However, there have been some concerns about the consequences of this movement. Local arm's-length agencies are always in danger of becoming an easy income-earner for ex-politicians who are often given top management or board positions, although lacking any professional qualifications. Furthermore, elected councillors are often appointed as board members to local public companies, providing a potential conflict of interest with their council role as a guardian of public interest. Board members legally need to safeguard the interest of the company and therefore may not disclose commercially sensitive information to third parties – which sometimes means that they cannot inform other elected members about important business issues with wider political implications.

Source: Adapted from Hanspeter Knirsch (www.knirsch-consult.com)

EVIDENCE ABOUT THE EFFECTS OF CREATING ARM'S-LENGTH BODIES

Given the number of claims that have been made for the benefits of arm's length bodies, you could be forgiven for believing that there must be – somewhere out there – a body of firm empirical evidence that this type of decentralization does indeed bring these claimed benefits. If so, your belief would be mistaken. In fact the evidence is complicated and patchy, and does not seem to tell one simple story (James, 2003; Pollitt, 2005a). It is hard to weigh up. On the one (positive) hand there are some local success stories such as the IB Groep in the Netherlands, where an organization that had been part of the Ministry of Education was converted into an arm's-length ZBO (self-steering organization) and soon improved the quality (but not necessarily the efficiency) of its services (Van Thiel, 2001, pp. 143–65). Or in the UK one might cite the fact that in 1995/96 agencies met, in aggregate, 79 per cent of the 1,091 key performance targets set for them by ministers (Chancellor of the Duchy of Lancaster, 1997, p. 1). On the other (negative) hand, however, there is also a crop of disaster stories such as those concerning the Child Support Agency in the UK or the Prison Service (Gains, 2004) – see Case Example 17.3. And we should not forget Case Example 17.1, that meeting targets is only part of the story – there are also the questions of (a) whether those targets are meaningful and b) whether they cover all the agency's objectives.

Furthermore – and most worrying – there does not seem to be any systematic before-and-after study to demonstrate that (a) major advantages have accrued and (b) that these may safely be attributed to the process of decentralization. On the contrary, academics have searched for such evidence and not found it (James, 2003, pp. 130–2; Pollitt *et al.*, 1998; Talbot, 2004; Van Thiel, 2001). There is therefore always the suspicion that, even where definite improvements are found, they may be caused by factors other than the decentralization. For example, was the Dutch IB Groep's investment in much better software for its grant-

CASE EXAMPLE 17.3 **THINGS CAN GO WRONG**

HM Prison Service became an agency in 1991, having formerly been a department of the Home Office. Derek Lewis, the first Chief Executive, was appointed from the private sector, and declared himself to be in favour of a more performance-oriented culture. Less than three years later he was dismissed by the Home Secretary, Michael Howard, following two highly publicized escapes of dangerous prisoners. Howard thus brushed off responsibility for this 'operational' failure. Lewis, however, had achieved almost all the performance targets he had been set. He contested Howard's interpretation of events and subsequently sued the Home Office for wrongful dismissal. He was eventually awarded an out-of-court settlement of £280,000 (Lewis, 1997).

Nevertheless, the prison service has remained an agency. Despite further high-profile escapes, and other difficulties, subsequent chief executives have managed to avoid the kind of political clash that occurred between Howard and Lewis.

giving services a result of its becoming a QUANGO, or would it have happened anyway – because there was media exposure and public pressure on the organization stemming from its previous poor levels of service?

It is also the case that governments themselves have acknowledged that decentralization can have negative as well as positive effects. In a review of more than a decade's experience with UK Next Steps executive agencies, the Office of Public Services Reform found much to praise, but also acknowledged that 'in too many cases their work has become disconnected from the increasingly well-defined aims of their ministers'. In fact the review concluded that 'the gulf between policy and delivery is considered by most to have widened' (Office of Public Services Reform, 2002, pp. 3 and 6). In order to remedy this gulf, some English agencies have even been brought back into the relevant ministry (e.g. the Courts Service), even where their operational performance has been considered successful.

Finally, we should note that a number of analysts have suggested that the presence or absence of particular factors help to make the attainment of the promised gains from 'agencification' more or less hard to achieve. Among these suggestions we may pick out the following:

- If an agency exists within a stable network or policy community, it is more likely to survive and do well (Gains, 2004). If it has to play its role within a weak or rapidly changing network, it is more vulnerable.

- It is easier for agencies to prosper if the political sensitivity of their main activity is medium or low (e.g. forestry, weather forecasting). If it is high (e.g. prisons, payment of social security benefits), the temptation for politicians to intervene is great (Pollitt et al., 2004). This does not necessarily spell disaster by itself (Gains, 2004), but it creates a tension that, if combined with other problems, can lead to serious difficulties.

- It is easier for agencies to be steered if their outputs are fairly standardized and easily measured (Pollitt et al., 2004). In those cases (e.g. issuing driving licences, warehousing stock or maintaining vehicles), the supervising ministry can more easily set quantitative targets that encompass the core task and then leave the agency management to get on with finding out the most efficient way of organizing that task (Pollitt, 2003). The more ambiguous or difficult it is to measure the outputs, the more challenging is the role of the supervising ministry. For example, delivering mental health counselling to disturbed teenagers is a highly unstandardized task where, apart from counting the number of 'sessions' delivered (fairly meaningless), it is hard to find good measures of what has been done, still less what has been achieved.

- It is easier for politicians to remain 'hands off' if the total budget size of the agency is small or medium. The reason here is that really big budget agencies inevitably attract the attention of ministries of finance/treasuries whenever the macro-economic cycle means that public expenditure cuts have to be made. This is one reason why researchers found that agencies responsible for paying social security benefits (big budget) tended to be 'interfered with' in greater detail and more often than small budget agencies such as meteorological offices (Pollitt et al., 2004).

257

- Broader cultural factors may also play a part. In Japan, for example, it has been suggested that, despite considerable legal autonomy, the new administrative agencies will not, in practice, have much independence because most of them are headed by senior civil servants who are likely to continue to observe the strongly hierarchical and obedient Japanese civil service traditions (Yamamoto, 2004).

Of course, these various factors do not all pull in the same direction. A small-budget agency can be very politically sensitive. An agency with standardized outputs might be large budget, or might exist within a very weak network. So for any given agency (or proposed agency) one needs to look carefully at a variety of contextual factors.

SUMMARY

The idea of decentralizing public authority to arm's-length bodies of one sort or another has proved to be a very appealing one in many countries. Many arguments – not all of them mutually compatible – have been put forward in its favour. However, the practice of doing this has produced a tremendous variety of results, ranging from policy reversal to on-going crisis, to disappointing sameness, to incremental change, to major improvements in efficiency and/or quality of service. It seems, therefore, that there must be intervening factors that determine the degree of success or failure. Research has pointed towards what some of these might be, but the picture is as yet incomplete, and the complexity of possible interactions is high.

QUESTIONS FOR REVIEW AND DISCUSSION

1   Taking into consideration the factors mentioned above, choose two functions, one of which would be a good candidate for agency status and one which would, because of its characteristics, be high risk.
2   Why have politicians been so keen to set up new agencies when the evidence on results is so patchy?

READER EXERCISES

1   Find an example (e.g. in a newspaper or on the Internet) of a public agency in your country that is in the news for some failure or other. Examine the story for evidence of whether this failure has been caused by the agency's poor internal management or because of its inappropriate relationship with its 'home' ministry or local authority.
2   In relation to the same agency (or another of your choice), examine the managerial qualifications of the top management of the agency and the qualifications of the board members. What do you think this tells you about the relationship of agencies and the 'home' ministry or local authority?

CLASS EXERCISE

List as many reasons for creating decentralized agencies as you can think of. Then discuss how many of these reasons apply to each of the following:

- a unit that gives grants to university students;
- a unit that conducts driving tests and issues licences to successful candidates;
- a civil service recruitment agency;
- an immigration office;
- a rural development agency.

FURTHER READING

George Boyne, Catherine Farrell, Jennifer Law, Martin Powell and Richard Walker (2003), *Evaluating public management reforms*. Buckingham, Open University Press.

Francesca Gains (2004), '"Hardware, software or network connection?" Theorising crisis in the UK next steps agencies', *Public Administration*, 82 (3): 547–56.

Christopher Hood (1991), 'A public management for all seasons', *Public Administration*, 69 (1): 3–19.

Oliver James (2003), *The executive agency revolution in Whitehall: public interest versus bureau-shaping perspectives*. Basingstoke, Palgrave Macmillan.

David Lewis (1997), *Hidden agendas: politics, law and disorder*. London: Hamish Hamilton.

OECD (2001c), *Distributed public governance: agencies, authorities and other autonomous bodies* (preliminary draft). Paris: OECD.

Christopher Pollitt (2005a), 'Decentralization: a central concept in contemporary public management', in E. Ferlie, L. Lynn and C. Pollitt (eds), *The Oxford handbook of public management*. Oxford: Oxford University Press, pp. 371–97.

Christopher Pollitt and Geert Bouckaert (2004), *Public management reform: a comparative analysis* (2nd edn). Oxford: Oxford University Press.

Christopher Pollitt, Colin Talbot, Janice Caulfield and Amanda Smullen (2004), *Agencies: how governments do things through semi-autonomous agencies*. Basingstoke: Palgrave Macmillan.

Colin Talbot (2004), 'Executive agencies: have they improved management in government?', *Public Money and Management*, 24 (1): 104–11.

REFERENCES

Chancellor of the Duchy of Lancaster (1997), *Next steps: agencies in government: review*, Cm 4011. London: Stationery Office.

Francesca Gains (2004), '"Hardware, software or network connection?" Theorising crisis in the UK next steps agencies', *Public Administration*, 82 (3): 547–56.

Christopher Hood and Michael Jackson (1991), *Administrative argument*. Aldershot: Dartmouth.

Tamas Horvath (ed.) (2000), *Decentralization: experiments and reforms. Local governments in central and eastern Europe*. Budapest: Open Society Institute.

Oliver James (2003), *The executive agency revolution in Whitehall: public interest versus bureau-shaping perspectives*. Basingstoke: Palgrave Macmillan.

Arthur Macmahon (1961), *Delegation and autonomy*. London: Asia Publishing House.

Henry Mintzberg (1979), *The structuring of organizations: a synthesis of the research*. London: Prentice Hall.

OECD (2001c), *Distributed public governance: agencies, authorities and other autonomous bodies* (preliminary draft). Paris: OECD.

Office of Public Services Reform (2002), *Better government services: executive agencies in the 21st century* (www.civilservice.gov.uk/agencies, accessed 12 June 2002).

Perri 6 (2004), 'Joined-up government in the western world in comparative perspective: a preliminary literature review and exploration', *Journal of Public Administration Research and Theory* (J-Part) 14 (1): 103–38.

Perri 6, Diana Leat, Kimberly Seltzer and Gerry Stoker (2002), *Towards holistic governance: the new reform agenda*. Basingstoke: Palgrave.

Christopher Pollitt (2003), *The essential public manager*. Buckingham: Open University Press.

Christopher Pollitt (2005a), 'Decentralization: a central concept in contemporary public management', in E. Ferlie, L. Lynn and C. Pollitt (eds), *The Oxford handbook of public management*. Oxford: Oxford University Press, pp. 371–97.

Christopher Pollitt (2005b), 'Ministries and agencies: steering, meddling, neglect and dependency', in M. Painter and J. Pierre (eds), *Challenges to state policy capacity: global trends and comparative perspectives*. Basingstoke: Palgrave Macmillan, pp. 112–36.

Christopher Pollitt and Colin Talbot (eds) (2004), *Unbundled government*. London: Taylor & Francis.

Christopher Pollitt, Johnston Birchall and Keith Putman (1998), *Decentralizing public service management: the British experience*. Basingstoke: Macmillan.

Christopher Pollitt, Colin Talbot, Janice Caulfield and Amanda Smullen (2004), *Agencies: how governments do things through semi-autonomous agencies*. Basingstoke: Palgrave Macmillan.

Colin Talbot (1996), 'Ministers and agencies: responsibilities and performance', in the Public Service Committee, *Second Report Ministerial Accountability and Responsibility*, Vol. II. Minutes of Evidence, HC313, Session 1995–96. London: HMSO, pp. 39–55.

Colin Talbot (2004), 'Executive agencies: have they improved management in government?', *Public Money and Management*, 24 (1): 104–11.

Sandra Van Thiel (2001), *QUANGOs: trends, causes and consequences*. Aldershot: Ashgate.

Kiyoshi Yamamoto (2004), 'Agencification in Japan: renaming, or revolution?', in C. Pollitt and C. Talbot (eds), *Unbundled government*. London: Taylor & Francis, pp. 215–26 (Chapter 11).

Chapter 18

Public leadership

Mike Broussine, University of the West of England, UK

INTRODUCTION

In today's interconnected and interdependent world, public leadership has to be more than just leading public sector organizations. Public organizations are often slow to address new problems, are hampered by all kinds of constraints, and have short time frames – usually election to election. 'Wicked' problems that cross organizational boundaries can only be addressed successfully by networks of public, private and non-profit organizations, community groups and citizens and other inter-organizational arrangements (see Chapter 15).

This means that the engagement of citizens in public issues (see Chapter 19) becomes a key attribute of public and community leadership. In order to solve complex problems, public leaders have to be able to initiate concerted action not only within their own organizations but among a set of stakeholders with different and competing interests. This means that traditional models of organizational leadership have their limitations, as they may help to make public organizations more performance and customer-oriented but they are not adequate to address boundary-spanning problems in a context of fragmented authority. Without any doubt, the 'learning organization' requires a new concept of leadership (see Chapter 22).

The trouble is that there is no one view about what leadership is. There are several ways of looking at it. Those who have reviewed numerous studies, e.g. Yukl (2002) and Horner (1997), have concluded that, well . . . your view of leadership depends on where you are coming from and who you are. Yukl says, 'The definition of leadership is arbitrary . . . there is no single "correct" definition' (pp. 6–7). It is better to see leadership as a complex multifaceted phenomenon. The width of meanings about leadership is represented in this chapter by the boxed quotes from 'real' public service leaders. It may be difficult to define, but you recognize it when you see it, or are in it. Because most people agree that leadership is key to an organization's effectiveness, the lack of agreement about what it is should stimulate us to try to understand it more.

> **LEADERSHIP IS . . .**
>
> Political Leadership to me is about developing a vision, and a direction, that will captivate and inspire those around to transform it into a reality.
>
> *Source*: Mike Whitby, Leader, Birmingham City Council, 13 June 2008

There are three further factors that complicate the study of leadership. The first is that leadership does not just reside with the women and men at the top of organizations, but is exercised throughout – by team leaders, senior practitioners, and by teams of managers and professionals. A second issue is that the language of organization is shifting away from management towards leadership: yet both of these functions are necessary for organizational functioning. Third, the omnipotence that we often project onto our leaders has taken several knocks in recent years – now everyone knows that our leaders are human, make mistakes, take risks, and do not know what is going on all the time. Many leaders of public organizations admit in their candid moments to feeling powerful and in control sometimes, but powerless and out of control at other times. These emotional boundaries – between omnipotence and impotence – are shared by leaders who are working under conditions of unpredictability and flux – a feature of today's public service organizations.

LEARNING OBJECTIVES

- To be aware of the current emphasis on leadership in public governance;
- to be aware of the history of the study of leadership;
- to understand the differences between leadership and management;
- to understand the interrelationships between leadership, power and politics;
- to be aware of the gender dimension in leadership;
- to understand the keys issues in community leadership;
- to recognize the complex relationship between organisational leadership and political leadership;
- to understand what leaders need to learn if they are to become effective.

THE CURRENT EMPHASIS ON LEADERSHIP IN PUBLIC GOVERNANCE

The emphasis on leadership in today's public services is remarkable. One Audit Commission inspection report of a city council's corporate governance mentions leadership twenty-eight times in forty-eight pages. The Bristol Royal Infirmary Inquiry (2001) put the children's heart surgery scandal down in part to 'poor teamwork' and 'a clear lack of effective clinical leadership'.

OECD (2001b, p. 13) suggests that a changing environment requires a new type of leadership because:

- the growing need to address interconnected problems in a public policy context of shared power demands leaders to pay more attention to policy coherence;
- leadership is a key component to make the public sector a competitive employer;
- a knowledge-intensive economy and public sector call for a new type of leadership that inspires others to create and share knowledge;

■ there is a continuing need for public sector organizations to adapt, which requires leadership not just amongst senior managers but amongst all public officials, elected and appointed.

LEADERSHIP IS . . .

. . . about challenging everyone in the organization to raise their game. It is about creating the energy and enthusiasm necessary to take the organization forward. The leader's role is to create, and then manage, the tensions between the short and the long term, current performance and future ambition, restructuring and revitalization. It is about injecting the necessary idealism and foresight to imagine possibilities of a better future for the organization combined with the pragmatism to recognize that whilst some people and systems may be outdated they still have a contribution that they can make.

Source: Hugh Burnard, Regional Head, Regional Business Service South, HM Customs and Excise

---

OECD concluded that the managerial skills that have been emphasized since the 1980s are not sufficient to cope with future challenges.

In similar vein, Hartley and Allison (2000) have looked at the role of leadership in the modernization of public services in the UK. They begin by outlining how important leadership seems to be in current thinking about the improvement of public services. Leadership has been included in the titles of influential government policy papers (e.g. DETR, 1998b, 1999b), and the government has promoted the setting up of new leadership academies – for school leadership, for the NHS, and for local authority councillors. They ask, 'Is [leadership] simply a mantra, or is there some logic to the promotion of leadership in public services?' (Hartley and Allison, 2000, p. 35).

The influential Performance Improvement Unit (PIU) report on leadership (Cabinet Office, 2001) started with the assumption that good leadership is too scarce in the public sector. While the PIU admits that there are many examples of good leadership, there is a scarcity of 'top-level' leaders, and the demands on leaders are growing (e.g. because of rapid technological change, greater organizational complexity, increased consumer expectations, and more demanding stakeholders).

The implicit meanings that are given to leadership in these developments differ significantly. It is interesting to note how often 'strong' is associated with 'leadership' in this discourse, for example in the titles of government reports (e.g. DTLR, 2001). The PIU study refers to 'strengthening' leadership; and 'stronger leadership with a clear sense of purpose' was one of six key themes of the Civil Service Reform Programme after 1999.

It is also important to notice that many pronouncements on leadership are concerned with leaders at the top of their organizations. Leadership is conceived predominantly as, first, the attribute of an individual person or role; and second, as a top-down process. The White Paper on *Modernising Government* (Cabinet Office, 1999d) mentions 'the leadership needed to drive cultural change in the civil service' (p. 20). Such a view would suppose that leadership is not exercised anywhere else in the organization.

Critical analysis of the language used – an essential aspect of studying leadership – can reveal the 'theories-in-use' that policymakers adopt. Given the dominance of powerful voices that influence how public organizations are organized – with direct effects on the working lives of public service employees and users – it could be assumed that the idea of the strong top-level leader is the only legitimate view in town.

However, this suggests a simplified view of organizations that does not accord with reality. As Hartley and Allison (2000) point out, while the role of individual leaders in shaping events is clear, the 'lionization' of the individual leader assumes that she or he has pre-eminent capacity and power (p. 36). Vaill (1999) says: 'Leadership is not the behaviour of a person at all but rather a property of a social system' (p. 121). From a relational perspective, leadership may be seen as arising from the support (or, at minimum, the acquiescence) of followers. That is why a definition of leadership that concentrates only on the qualities of individual leaders tells only half the story. A better definition of leadership is that *it mobilizes the capacities of others inside and outside the organization*.

A BRIEF HISTORY OF THE STUDY OF LEADERSHIP

A succinct and engaging summary of the various approaches to the study of leadership from the 1920s was given by Gareth Jones (1998):

> There have been three major schools of leadership study. The first is called *trait theory*, where behavioural scientists tried to identify effective leaders by looking at what they had in common. Trait theory broke down when an expensive American study stated, with a straight face, 'We have studied 400 effective leaders and we can conclude that they are either above average height or below'.
>
> By then the behavioural scientists had a new toy, the camera. They started to film people and said that effective leaders had a distinctive *style*. This approach was particularly associated with the human relations movement in the 1940s in America. The concept of leadership within this school was open, pseudo-democratic, personal, almost affectionate. Then the 1950s came along and, with the world on the edge of thermonuclear destruction, a whole new leadership style seemed appropriate: the Cold War warrior. Managers were buying rimless glasses whether they needed them or not. That was the end of style theory.
>
> Then it was decided to study not leaders but leadership, i.e. the relationship between leaders and the led. It explains why you have different leaders in a shipyard, a school, a hospital and an advertising agency. You first have to ask who you are trying to lead, then identify the critical parameters of the task. Finally you look for characteristics of the situation that can be turned to your advantage. These three issues form the basis of the latest and best theory, sometimes called *situation leadership theory*.
>
> (Jones, 1998, p. 81–2)

Jones's brief tour gives a useful indication of the historical trends in the study of leadership. Horner (1997) and Yukl (2002) provide extensive and detailed reviews of these theories.

Situation leadership theory represents the most modern ideas about leadership. However, trait theory still has a major place in contemporary discourse about leadership, as does the notion of the *command-and-control* approach – born out of classical management principles in the early twentieth century. Whenever I ask a group of students or managers to give me their first thoughts about leadership, they invariably mention notable individuals from history such as Winston Churchill and Margaret Thatcher.

The advantage of situational theory is that we can see how leadership depends on a relationship between the leader and the situation that the leader is working in, including followers. Such theories are sometimes called contingency theories. This means that leadership can vary according to the situation – so that the British electorate rejected its wartime leader, Winston Churchill, in 1945, preferring new leaders in the immediate post-war era. This gives us a more realistic view of leadership (though admittedly a more complex one), because we now have to deal with several factors in addition to the charisma or strength of the individual leader. But, as we have seen, the notion of the 'strong' leader features to a considerable extent in the language of public service modernization.

THE DIFFERENCES BETWEEN LEADERSHIP AND MANAGEMENT

Any serious attempt to understand organizational leadership needs to distinguish between leadership and management. To put it succinctly: *Leadership shapes the future; management delivers it.*

There is now broad agreement that leadership and management are different (see Table 18.1). Of course, managers lead, and leaders manage, so the distinction can be seen as just playing with words. However, to conflate the two processes would be wrong. Gabriel (1999, Chapter 6) provides a useful analysis of the difference between leadership and management: 'It is possible to manage inanimate objects – a diary, a farm, a stamp collection – but it is only possible to lead people' (p. 139).

LEADERSHIP IS . . .

. . . about having a clear vision based on core values and beiefs. Leaders must have conviction, drive, and commitment to empower others to work towards the achievement of the vision. Leaders must not falter in the face of difficulties. They must have self-reliance to persevere with resilience and tenacity to withstand setbacks, disappointments and failure and to lift and carry their people through disappointments to progress on towards success. These are the true strengths of leadership.

Source: Steve Pilkington, Chief Constable, Avon and Somerset Police

---

Table 18.1 *Management versus leadership*

What managers do	What leaders do
Focus on the present situation	Focus on the future
Organise our current resources so that we can use them effectively	Invent an image of the future that is so persuasive that we are willing to commit our efforts, time and resources to turn image into reality
Have a keen eye for detail	
Think of ways of stretching resources further	

Source: Based on Gabriel (1999, p. 139)

The distinction between management and leadership frees us to ask questions such as whether or not organizations are over-managed and under-led and whether or not the roles of leadership and management are invariably held in the same person.

The distinction between management and leadership represents an important boundary for leaders – how they see the boundary is wrapped up in their self-identity, affecting the style with which they exercise the role . Will they see their role primarily as working with the new, the radical and risky, with uncertainty, encouraging creativity, and looking outside current parameters or constraints – in short requiring leadership? Or, will they see their role as mostly to do with acquiring resources, increasing efficiency, reducing costs, and solving today's rather than tomorrow's problems – requiring management? The answers to such questions can exert considerable influence on the culture and functioning of the organization.

LEADERSHIP, POWER AND POLITICS

I am obsessed with power! Let me rephrase that. We have to understand power and organizational politics if we are to approach an understanding about how leadership works, or doesn't. I am sure you have been asked to do something by your boss, and inwardly have thought to yourself, 'What an idiot!' The authority, power and legitimacy of leaders are potentially contestable, and conflict suffuses organizational functioning. This is especially the case in public services where it is difficult to see the 'bottom line', and where there is much scope for disagreement on aims and means. There is always a political (small 'p') dimension to leadership: organizational members will often seek '. . .to mobilize support for or against policies, rules, goals, or other decisions in which the outcome will have some effect on them. Politics, therefore, is essentially the exercise of power' (Robbins, 1987, p. 194).

LEADERSHIP IS . . .

- providing direction for the organization;
- delivering results;
- building capacity for the organization to address current and future challenges;
- acting with integrity.

Source: Roy Stephenson, Deputy Director, Cabinet Office

The formal authority that goes with a leader's role is an important, usually hierarchically based, source of power (note that formal authority may be an attribute of a team, board or committee, not just a person). However, *formal role authority* is just one power base for organizational leadership. Burnes (2000, pp. 178–9) lists four other kinds:

- *coercive power* – the threat of negative consequences should compliance not be forthcoming;
- *remunerative power* – the promise of material rewards as inducements to cooperate;
- *normative power* – the allocation and manipulation of symbolic rewards, such as status symbols, as inducements to obey;
- *knowledge-based power* – the control of unique information that is needed to make decisions.

You can understand an organization's politics and power structures by seeking to find out who is included in, and who is excluded from, decision-making. Except in the most authoritarian organizations, authority for decision-making will be delegated throughout the organization. Similarly, the four power bases, to greater or lesser extents, may be distributed through all levels of the hierarchy. Knowledge-based power, especially, goes with the professional expertise that is the basis of much of the front-line work of the public services. Indeed, something will have gone wrong if the chief executive and his or her board try to deny the utility of front-line knowledge-based power. However, we may know of instances where 'constructive dissent' among workers wasn't listened to by formal leaders, with the result that the solutions to organizational problems – already known to the workers – took a long time to implement:

> . . . a solution to excessive waiting times and chronic staff shortages is to allow the 'subordinate' nurses the freedom to solve the problems that they could have solved years ago – if only someone had thought to ask them and to implement their suggestions.
>
> (Cabinet Office, 2001, Annex D)

Leadership occurs among groups of people as well as highly placed individuals. Power is more diffuse than we might at first imagine, and does not operate only through orthodox hierarchy. A corollary is that leadership is exercised in a political environment – a seen and unseen network of relations and tactics that people employ to either commit to, or dissent from, decisions that affect them.

THE GENDER DIMENSION OF LEADERSHIP

It is important to study leadership from the gender point of view for several reasons. First, a large number of public service employees are women. Second, public service organizations purport to have advanced equal opportunities policies. Third, the main users of many public services such as health and social care tend to be women, simply because they tend to live longer than men. For these reasons, you might expect that women are at least equally represented in the leadership of UK public services as men – but, if so, you would be wrong.

267

The belief that there are distinguishable 'male' and 'female' styles of leadership is widespread. Many people feel, for example, that women especially hold 'people skills' and those associated with bringing about transformational change. Care is needed in jumping to such conclusions. Women in our research into UK local government (Fox and Broussine, 2001) emphasized that they did not have a monopoly of these skills and attributes. The idea of male and female approaches to leadership could itself be stereotypical, denying both men and women the opportunity to exercise different skills. Furthermore, appreciation of womanly qualities (usually described as caring and relational) could be another way of restricting women to certain kinds of role, for example, careers in the personnel function. Nevertheless, despite such cautions, it was clear that, for many female senior managers, and their male colleagues, the gendered distinction in leadership styles was based in some kind of reality.

Our research also showed that the perpetuation of classical 'command-and-control' and 'macho' assumptions about leadership was strongly associated with stereotypical views among those responsible for appointing women chief executives. The range of blatant and subtle discriminatory behaviours that many women experienced had the effect of marginalizing or belittling their authority as leaders. Even in organizations with good equal opportunity initiatives, the informal organization could continue to transmit cultural messages about the 'proper place' for women. Almost all women chief executives reported that, even after they had been in post for a while, they often felt under scrutiny and judged in different ways to men.

A particular tension centred on the issue of change. Coffey *et al.* (1999) identified an 'organizational schizophrenia' by which an organization can promote a woman to senior management, 'and genuinely welcome that appointment, and can at the same time manifest . . . behaviours that make it very hard for her to succeed' (p. 73).

The growth in recent years of performance targets and other managerialist approaches may create more 'macho' – individualistic and competitive – organizational cultures. In addition, as argued earlier, it is likely that traditional, so-called 'male' command-and-control assumptions about leadership are being perpetuated by the emphasis on 'strong' leadership in the 'modernizing government ' agenda. It is not surprising that this kind of environment has led some women junior managers to question whether promotion is worth going for. Many in our study thought that it was not.

COMMUNITY LEADERSHIP

Public leadership is as much about relationships with external stakeholders and communities as it is about mobilization of internal organizational capacities. Public leaders – at whatever level in the organization – need to be able to operate at the boundaries between the organization and its environment. In the public services, this is not easy because that environment is complex. For one thing, it consists of a range of stakeholders (citizens, service users, customers, community groups, individuals), whose needs and wants cannot be presented in a uniform way. Second, in these days of 'partnership working' between public agencies and communities, the idea of a clear line of demarcation between an organization and its environment is unhelpful.

Case Example 18.1 demonstrates how community leadership may be seen as the mobilization of others' leadership capacities. It also shows that community leadership is about providing an environment that enables different professions, working with those most affected,

CASE EXAMPLE 18.1 **SOLVING LOCAL PROBLEMS THROUGH COMMUNITY LEADERSHIP**

In a major residential area of Falmouth in Cornwall, concerned professionals in the local authority, Carrick District Council, and the health authority, working together with a small number of activists in the community, helped to initiate major improvements to the condition of the housing, especially in respect of heating and insulation. As residents saw the improvements in quality of life that were brought about by this programme, they became more interested in working on a series of further initiatives on the estate, covering estate management, housing repairs, crime watch, youth training schemes, etc. These schemes were largely led and managed by the residents themselves. As the initiatives proved successful, the strength of resident involvement grew and some of the residents decided to become politically active on a formal basis, e.g. getting elected as councillors. One of the strengths of the approach was that residents always had a majority on the project management committee, which was an independent legal entity, but the committee also included all the main public sector organizations with responsibilities for services provided in the housing estate.

Source: Bovaird and Owen (2002, pp. 57–73)

to act together to resolve social problems. We may see public leadership therefore as *working at boundaries*, developing effective relationships between professions, between agencies and organizations, and between all these and the communities they serve. Thus, public leadership can't only be seen as the relationship between leaders and followers (in the case study, just who are the leaders, and who are the followers?). It needs to be seen also as resulting from collaboration and cooperation, resulting possibly in new and unexpected forms of leadership.

THE RELATIONSHIP BETWEEN ORGANIZATIONAL LEADERSHIP AND POLITICAL LEADERSHIP

Another challenge in studying public sector leadership is that it is exercised in a political context, where ministers and elected councillors play important roles. The political dimension is one of the principal distinguishing features of the public services as compared with the private sector. One of the difficult and controversial questions in this political context is about precisely who exercises leadership, over what and whom.

Leadership is . . . about creating a sense of purpose and direction . . . communicating and legitimising belief and passion . . . creating, not consuming, energy . . . fostering creativity . . . and most of all it's about building, winning and retaining . . . trust.

Source: Sir Michael Bichard (formerly permanent secretary at the Department for Education and Employment)

269

Morrell and Hartley (2006, pp. 484–5) have usefully summarized the basis for political leaders' claims to authority. They define political leaders as:

- democratically elected;
- representatives;
- vulnerable to deselection;
- operating within, as well as influencing, a constitutional and legal framework;
- having authority that is based on a mandate, i.e. 'permission to govern according to declared policies, regarded as officially granted by an electorate . . . upon the decisive outcome of an election' (*Chambers Dictionary*, 1993);
- requiring the consent of those whom they govern and serve.

The relationship between organizational and political leadership can be fraught. On the one hand we get occasional insights into the 'power struggles' and tensions between politicians and civil servants or officers. As Richards (2000, p. 21) put it:

> The tensions began almost as soon as Labour got into power. Some permanent secretaries departed at the earliest possible moment. Senior press officers went even more quickly. The clashes seemed to subside, but, in reality, they just faded from public view. If anything, ministerial frustration has increased. 'We've got to kill off the idea that the Civil Service is some kind of Rolls-Royce machine that we've been fortunate to inherit,' confides a minister who has served in two departments. The complaint is that, in Whitehall, everything happens so slowly. 'Most civil servants', said another minister, 'are not interested in delivery. They like to be involved in policy-making, but delivery and measuring the success of the policies are seen to be lower-grade activities.'

Such conflicts and struggles may be seen as an exercise in attempted domination and subordination. They may have a range of causes such as an incoming administration wishing at the outset to exercise control over civil servants or officers; or an anxiety that one side will 'lose out' in a new restructuring proposal or as a result of a renewed call for strong political leadership. For some in local government, the advent of cabinets has created the spectre of charismatic local leaders who are unfettered by the necessity for strategic or policy advice from officers. However, for some observers of the UK local government scene, there exists the equal and opposite possibility of 'weak' elected members who, in their disempowerment, become increasingly dependent on an increasingly important professional officer cadre, the dangers here being that managerialism takes over and authorities lose touch with the needs of communities (Broussine, 2001). The same principles apply to the relationships between civil servants and their political 'masters' (as it is often put) – listen to the following *cri de coeur* from this American commentator:

> Reasonable people can differ on such matters of policy and politics. But these issues obscure a deeper and more fundamental management problem. It's clear now that the chaos in Iraq could have been at least mitigated if the political leaders in the Bush

administration had listened to the civil servants who work for them. Instead, they consistently failed to heed the advice of people who have devoted their careers in government to analyzing situations like the one that unfolded in Iraq and giving leaders the information they need to make informed decisions.

(Shoop, 2004, p. 70)

The power relationships between organizational leadership and political leadership is typically considered to be a 'zero sum game', i.e. the possession of leadership power or authority by one party diminishes that of the other party – a struggle for the exercise of 'strong top leadership' that was explored earlier in this chapter. Yet this picture of a contest to be 'number one' may be misleading. Some research (Broussine, 2000) has suggested that the local authority chief executive's capacity to work with the political dimension is regarded as the most challenging and problematic aspect of his or her role. It demands the most emotional energy and ability, and presents the greatest degree of paradox, ambiguity and risk. Chief executives in our sample sought to manage the relationship with their elected members in a range of ways, including (Broussine, 2000, pp. 502–3):

- knowing where their role ends and that of politicians starts;
- mixing one's own ideas with political reality;
- balancing what is 'rational' and what is 'political';
- turning members' ideas into something realizable;
- facilitating members' understanding of the needs of communities;
- asking members to look ahead and decide what they want to achieve;
- dealing with elected members' changing expectations;
- maintaining an appropriate relationship with the Leader of the Council;
- building relationships and trust;
- spotting potential political trouble by working informally with members.

These chief executives felt that the most complex aspect of their roles was working at the boundary between politics and management. A visit to practically any local authority, or a candid discussion with a senior civil servant, will reveal that this form of boundary working requires a great deal of sensitivity and skill. Greenwood (2000) discusses how both Tony Benn and Margaret Thatcher – coming from completely opposite ends of the political spectrum – used to complain about civil servants imposing their wills on ministers. Tony Benn saw the civil service as part of the 'establishment' (e.g. traditionally from public schools), while Margaret Thatcher regarded civil servants as too wedded to 'the interventionist policies of "big government"' (p. 65). The fact that a recent Home Secretary called his new department in May 2006 'seriously dysfunctional' shows that this tension between administration and politics is alive and well today.

This boundary working, or relationship handling, has its comedic side – the TV series *Yes Minister* is required viewing for the student of public leadership – but the intersection between political and organizational leadership brings both stress and competitiveness to the key players on both sides of the political/managerial divide. Working together to play different but complementary roles is not easy.

271

Nevertheless, when you delve a bit deeper, you can find that the effective and smooth running of public services is often characterized by key organizational and political players playing their respective leadership roles in a situation of mutually understood interdependence, each acknowledging the other's legitimacy. Broadly, elected politicians and their leaders have the capacity to exercise political judgement in developing policy and strategy in their area, while chief executives, and their colleagues, have the capacity to lead, manage and develop the organization's effectiveness in the pursuit of goals.

The idea that there can be a collaborative model of political and organizational leadership may come as a surprise to some who work in the public services, but Case Example 18.2 shows that this is not just a theoretical possibility.

CASE EXAMPLE 18.2 **HOW GOOD OFFICER/MEMBER RELATIONS SUSTAINED CULTURE CHANGE AT ST HELENS METROPOLITAN BOROUGH COUNCIL**

St Helens was one of five case study local authorities that participated in a study of exemplary practice in developing gender equal cultures (Fox and Broussine, 2005). The importance of leadership was emphasized time and again in interviews and focus groups with elected members, the chief executive, managers and front-line staff. One of the factors that was felt to be important was the appointment of a woman chief executive some twelve years before the study. However, what was notable in addition was the sense of collaboration and empathy that pervaded the organization, which respondents attributed to good relations between top managers and councillors. The consistency with which the group of organizational leaders – the Chief Executive and Leader of the Council, Corporate Management Team members (male and female) and elected members – espouse and enact values supporting equality and performance sent powerful explicit and subliminal messages through the organization and in its dealings with groups and organizations in the community:

> Leaders – the Chief Executive and the Leader of the Council – provide strong models. They call people by their first names.
>
> (Female middle manager)

> The Leader, Chief Executive and members – they do speak to you; relationships are fine and friendly.
>
> (Male front-line staff)

> There is lots of communication in the authority including from the Leader and the Chief Executive who get themselves around the place including talking to front-line staff.
>
> (Male senior manager)

> . . . there's a good officer/member relationship here – we need each other to do our jobs. The member training includes equalities. There are some from the 'old school', but you can be challenging of them. Members recognise people; on the whole they're extremely supportive and appreciate staff. The female Leader is very approachable, and praises the team.
>
> (Female middle manager)

KEY LEARNING FOR PUBLIC LEADERS

We arrive finally at the question of what leaders need to learn if they are to be effective. Given the complexities of leadership in public organizations, our contention is that *leadership and learning go together*. This view suggests that leaders get their authority from their ability to learn and their ability to develop the organization's capacity to learn. Thus organizations with good leaders are more likely to respond effectively in providing appropriate services to the public and to work effectively with other stakeholders in the public policy arena.

This view is not often mirrored in practice. Leaders are often set up, or set themselves up, as people with all the answers. Their followers become highly dependent on their omniscience – they wish to hear the 'path to the future' articulated with confidence and eloquence. Such leaders present themselves as leaders who can 'take a grip' and, consequently, they mask all the uncertainty and fallibility inherent in the system.

> ### LEADERSHIP IS . . .
>
> . . . sometimes about stepping out in front of the crowd offering a vision to follow. More often it's about carving out and holding open a space for the ideas and expertise of others to grow and take shape. This is the challenge – leadership is about making a space for the leadership of others to come through.
>
> *Source*: Liz Kidd, Planning and Development Manager, Children and Families Division, Wiltshire County Council

> ### LEADERSHIP IS . . .
>
> . . . to look far ahead without losing sight – not only hearing but listening, not only working but creating.
>
> *Source*: Prof. Dr Marga Pröhl, Director-General, European Institute for Public Administration, Maastricht

In such situations leadership is the antithesis of learning. Leaders 'know', and therefore do not need to learn. Indeed admission of a need to learn will evidence vulnerability, and threaten the image of certainty and security offered by these leaders. However, such an illusion of infallibility is difficult to sustain and, when reality intrudes, such leaders may fall.

An alternative view holds that uncertainty pervades any complex human system. Leadership needs to acknowledge this and to engage with uncertainty in a positive way. It needs people to build resilience to deal with the uncertainties. The ability to learn is a vital tool in the context of change and uncertainty (Vaill, 1999). Furthermore, 'it is not enough for one or two individuals to develop these [leadership] skills. They must be distributed widely throughout the organization' (Senge, 1998, p. 302). Of course, this view of leadership differs a lot from that of the charismatic decision-maker, a view based on trait theory.

So what capacities do today's public service leaders need to learn in practice? I think that they need the capacities to:

- tolerate ambiguity and uncertainty;
- recognize the impossibility of omniscience;

- maintain personal perspective and self-knowledge;
- critically reflect – to ask oneself continuously whether current ways of leading need changing according to changed circumstances;
- develop leaders and leadership throughout the organization, and in the community in which their organization is embedded;
- watch out for 'dependency cultures';
- recognize that leadership and learning go together.

Many public service leaders now recognize the value of finding the space to reflect critically on how they are doing. Action learning sets, personal role supervision and mentoring, each in their ways provides this space. As public services continue to change rapidly, organizational leaders need increasingly to see their roles as requiring self-knowledge, inner confidence, and a 'good enough' sense of identity. They need to be able to think . . . but also act.

SUMMARY

A strong political emphasis on good leadership lies at the heart of the governance agenda. However, we need to look critically at some of the assumptions and language about leadership. Leadership is not just the property of one person. Leadership can be found at all levels of the organization, as well as outside the organization in the community. It is often a function carried out by teams and committees. We also need to distinguish between management and leadership.

Leadership occurs in a complex political environment, in which different bases of power are at play in visible and invisible ways at different levels of the hierarchy. To see leadership only in terms of formal authority and hierarchy leads to a limited view. However, classical, orthodox and 'male' views of leadership – especially 'command-and-control' – prevail in the public services.

More inclusive views of leadership need to be developed in the public services, and there is evidence that this is happening in practice. There is growing recognition that, in a complex and changing system, we need to see leadership and learning as simultaneous if not synonymous activities. Finally, we need to see leadership as the mobilization of stakeholders – in terms of financial and staff resources, their expertise or 'everyday' knowledge and their willingness to cooperate to solve interconnected problems that impact on their lives or organizations.

QUESTIONS FOR REVIEW AND DISCUSSION

1 Explain why the *command-and-control* notion of leadership remains influential in some public agencies at the beginning of the twenty-first century.
2 How can leaders lead when they don't know everything that's going to happen?
3 What strategies would you recommend to develop collaborative relationships between political and organizational leaders in central and local government?

READER EXERCISES

1 Interview two organizational leaders, one in the private, and one in the public sector. You might ask:
   - Do you see yourself as a *leader* or as a *manager*?
   - How would you describe the responsibility of being a leader?
   - What do people expect of you as leader?

   Can you deduce any differences between public and private sector leadership?
2 Pick out two of the boxed *Leadership Is . . .* quotes that seem to contrast with each other in some way. Examine each quote carefully. What are the assumptions and values about leadership that attach to each quote? What are the differences in emphasis?
3 Explore the statistics on female representation in leadership of public sector organizations at www.eoc.org.uk. What are the statistics for your particular public service?

CLASS EXERCISE

Work as a team with three other students in this three-part task:

1 Research sources in the library, and find an article or paper that reports on some recent (i.e. later than 2003) research into organizational leadership.
2 Write a summary of this study.
3 Present your summary to your colleague students. Include in your presentation something about what you have learned about your own leadership approaches and styles as you carried out this exercise.

FURTHER READING

Cabinet Office (2001), *Strengthening leadership in the public sector: a research study by the Performance and Innovation Unit*. London: Cabinet Office.

Eileen Milner and Paul Joyce (2005), *Lessons in leadership: meeting the challenges of public service management*. Abingdon: Routledge

John Storey (ed.) (2004), *Leadership in organizations – current issues and key trends*. Abingdon: Routledge.

Gary A. Yukl (2002), *Leadership in organizations*. Englewood Cliffs, NJ: Prentice Hall.

REFERENCES

Tony Bovaird and Mike Owen (2002), 'Achieving citizen-led area regeneration through multiple stakeholders in the Beacon Housing Estate, Cornwall', in Tony Bovaird, Elke Löffler and Salvador Parrado Díez (eds), *Developing local governance networks in Europe. Local governance in Europe*. Baden-Baden: Nomos Verlag, pp. 57–73.

Bristol Royal Infirmary Inquiry (2001), 'Learning from Bristol: the report of the public inquiry into children's heart surgery at the Bristol Royal Infirmary 1984–1995', Cm 5207, London: Stationery Office.

Mike Broussine (2000), 'The capacities needed by local authority chief executives', *The International Journal of Public Sector Management*, 13 (6): 498–507.

Mike Broussine (2001), 'A stalemate in the power game', *Municipal Journal* (23 Feb – 1 March): 17.

Bernard Burnes (2000), *Managing change – a strategic approach to organisational dynamics*. Harlow: Pearson Education.

Cabinet Office (1999d), *Report to the prime minister from Sir Richard Wilson, Head of home civil service*. London: Cabinet Office.

Cabinet Office (2001), *Strengthening leadership in the public sector: a research study by the Performance and Innovation Unit*. London: Cabinet Office.

Elizabeth Coffey, Clare Huffington and Peninah Thomson (1999), *The changing culture of leadership – women leaders' voices*. London: The Change Partnership.

DETR (1998b), *Modernising local government: local democracy and local leadership*. London: Stationery Office.

DETR (1999b), *Local leadership, local choice*. London: Stationery Office.

DTLR (2001), *Strong local leadership – quality public services*, Cm 5237. London: Stationery Office.

Pam Fox and Mike Broussine (2001), *Room at the top? A study of women chief executives in local government in England and Wales*. Bristol: Bristol Business School.

Pam Fox and Mike Broussine (2005), *Gender isn't an issue! Case studies of exemplary practice in promoting gender equality and diversity in local authorities*. Bristol: Bristol Business School.

Yiannis Gabriel (1999), *Organizations in depth*. London: Sage.

John Greenwood (2000), 'Should the civil service become fully politicised?', in Lynton Robins and Bill Jones (eds), *Debates in British politics today*. Manchester: Manchester University Press, pp. 63–77.

Jean Hartley and Maria Allison (2000), 'The role of leadership in the modernization and improvement of public services', *Public Money and Management*, April–June.

Melissa Horner (1997), 'Leadership theory: past, present and future', *Team Performance Management*, 3 (4): 270–87.

Gareth Jones (1998), 'The leadership of organisations', *RSA Journal*, 3 (4): 81–3.

Kevin Morrell and Jean Hartley (2006), 'A model of political leadership', *Human Relations*, 59: 483–504.

OECD (2001b), *Public sector leadership for the 21st century*. Paris: OECD

Sue Richards (2000), 'Why Labour ministers rage against Whitehall', *New Statesman*, 129 (4489): 21–2.

Stephen Robbins (1987), *Organization theory: concepts, controversies and applications*. Englewood Cliffs, NJ: Prentice Hall.

Peter Senge (1998), *The fifth discipline: the art and practice of the learning organization*. London: Century Business.

Tom Shoop (2004), 'Unheeded advice', *Government Executive*, 36 (9): 70.

Peter Vaill (1999), *Spirited leading and learning: process wisdom for a new age*. Englewood Cliffs, NJ: Prentice Hall.

Gary A. Yukl (2002), *Leadership in organizations*. Englewood Cliffs, NJ: Prentice Hall.

Chapter 19

Engaging with citizens and other stakeholders

Steve Martin, Cardiff University, UK

INTRODUCTION

Public participation is not new. There were attempts to promote local involvement in planning decisions in a number of Western countries as long ago as the 1960s. User involvement has long been a feature of some social services. And 'community involvement' has been a pre-condition of funding for most UK and EU regeneration programmes for the last decade or more (Foley and Martin, 2000). Until relatively recently, though, mainstream services remained firmly under the control of expert professionals who were trusted to act in the best interests of service users and the public at large. Voters could remove unpopular politicians through the ballot-box, but they were not expected to take much of a direct interest in policy debates or the management of public services between elections.

A RECENT OECD REPORT CONCLUDED

... democratic governments are under pressure to adopt a new approach to policy-making ... which places greater emphasis on citizen involvement both upstream and downstream to decision-making ...

Source: Coleman and Gøtze (undated, p. 4)

Current attempts to improve services and modernize governance systems have, however, placed public engagement at centre stage. Rapidly expanding choice in the private consumer goods market has fuelled rising expectations of public services. Meanwhile declining voter turnout, dwindling participation in civic life, and growing cynicism towards politicians, political institutions and politics parties are all seen as pointing to a need to reinvent the relationship between the citizen and institutions of government if a 'crisis of legitimacy' is to be averted. Policymakers in Western democracies appear united in the belief that increased public engagement offers the means of both rebuilding trust in government and ensuring that services are more responsive to changing needs and rising aspirations. A growing number of local politicians see engagement with the public as a means of substantiating their claim to be 'close to the citizen'. Meanwhile, in the age of 'spin', national governments have increasingly turned to assorted panels, opinion polls and focus groups to help inform political priorities, policy development and presentation.

LEARNING OBJECTIVES

This chapter considers four key sets of issues:
- the arguments in favour of engagement with service users and citizens;
- the main forms of public engagement;
- practical approaches to public engagement;
- obstacles to effective engagement and ways of overcoming these.

WHY ENGAGE WITH THE PUBLIC?

OECD (2001a) argues that engaging with citizens is 'a core element of good governance'. It claims that the benefits include:

- improving the quality of policy-making by allowing government to tap wider sources of information, perspectives and potential solutions;
- facilitating greater and faster interaction between citizens and governments;
- increasing accountability and transparency, which in turn increase
- representativeness and public confidence.

The current UK government also sees public engagement as vital. Three main arguments in favour of engagement feature implicitly and sometimes explicitly in the current policy discourse.

First, many public policy issues can only be addressed effectively through prevention as well as cure. Governments therefore need to become better at informing public attitudes and influencing behaviour. Long-term gains in health, for example, depend as much as on changes in lifestyle (diet, smoking habits, exercise and so forth) as they do on advances in the treatment of acute illness in better managed hospital budgets. Levels of educational attainment depend not just on the skills of teaching staff but also on the attitudes of students and their parents. Informing people of the cost of clearing chewing gum from the pavement and providing bins into which it can be discarded are likely to be more cost effective means of addressing the problem than simply scraping the streets clean. And so forth.

Second, those on the receiving end of public services are often able to suggest ways in which services can be tailored to their needs, thus exerting pressure on unresponsive and inefficient public bureaucracies.

Third, it is believed that citizen engagement will increase the perceived legitimacy of government – both by alerting the public to the constraints on governments and by encouraging more effective 'community leadership' at a local level (see Chapter 18).

As noted above, the arguments for more participative forms of engagement have been strengthened by the declining faith in representative forms of democracy, reflected in low, and falling, levels of turnout in elections in many Western Europe countries (see Table 19.1).

The rapid growth in *direct* participation has been reflected in the growth of participatory budgeting and a plethora of local community-based partnerships (see Case Example 19.1).

Table 19.1 *Average turnout in sub-national elections (%)*

	Pre-1995	Post-1995	Change
Austria	82	79	−3
Denmark	80	72	−8
France	68	72	+4
Germany	72	70	−2
Ireland	60	50	−10
Italy	85	80	−5
Netherlands	54	47	−7
Sweden	85	79	−6
UK	40	35	−5

Source: Rallings *et al.* (2000), *Turnout at local government elections: influences on levels of voter registration and electoral participation* (www.dca.gov.uk/elections/elect_odpm_turnout.pdf, accessed 16 May 2008)

CASE EXAMPLE 19.1 **THE *NEW DEAL FOR COMMUNITIES* AND *COMMUNITIES FIRST* PROGRAMMES**

The *New Deal for Communities* programme, run by the UK government's Neighbourhood Renewal Unit, provided £2 billion to thirty-nine of the most deprived areas of England. Local schemes were designed to improve employment prospects, educational attainment, health, housing and the physical environment and to reduce crime. There was a strong emphasis on community ownership of the programmes. Ministers insisted that funding was given direct to community groups that 'have not traditionally led regeneration programmes' and relaxed monitoring requirements placed on previous local authority led programmes for fear that they would inhibit community involvement. A similar scheme, *Communities First*, operated in Wales. Its objective was 'to empower individuals and communities by enabling them to work with local service providers and others to draw up and implement strategies to address those communities' own priorities'.

Further details of the *New Deal for Communities* can be found at www.neighbourhood. gov.uk/page.asp?id=617 (accessed 16 May 2008).

The emphasis on increased public involvement in the planning and delivering of local services in the UK was reflected in Clause 3.1 of the 1999 Local Government Act, which required local councils, police and fire authorities and a range of other statutory agencies to consult not only service users and taxpayers (both individuals and businesses) but also anyone else who they deem to have legitimate interest in the area (which might, for example, include

281

commuters, tourists and representatives of voluntary and community organizations). In addition, councils had to ensure that their staff were 'involved in any plans to change the way in which services are provided' (DETR, 1998c).

These requirements undoubtedly increased both the scale and scope of engagement by local authorities with local people. And since the 1990s, many councils in England have introduced consultation into services where there was previously little direct contact with the public. Many have adopted a range of new, more interactive approaches and also sought to reach communities and groups with which they had traditionally not engaged (Martin et al., 2001).

At national level, there has been a strong emphasis in the UK on 'listening' to the public. The 'People's Panel', consisting of a representative sample of 5000 people, was used as an important 'sounding board', and ministers toured the country attending so-called 'listening events' at which 'ordinary people' could air their views (see Case Example 19.2).

More recently, the UK government has restated its commitment to encouraging public engagement. Ministers have spoken of the need for 'double devolution', whereby power is dispersed from central to local government and local councils, which then hand over increased control to neighbourhoods and local communities. A report entitled *Citizen Engagement and Public Services: Why Neighbourhoods Matter* argued strongly for increased engagement with communities and set out a wide range of examples of mechanisms whereby neighbourhoods have become involved in decision-making and service design (ODPM, 2005). And the Local Government White Paper published in England in 2006 stated that 'People no longer accept the "one size fits all" service models of old. They want choice over the services they receive, influence over those who provide them, and higher service standards'. Local people, it said, need 'to be given more control over their lives; consulted and involved in running services; informed about the quality of services in their area; and enabled to call local agencies to account if services fail to meet their needs' (CLG, 2006). The Local Government and Public Involvement in Health Act 2007, which followed the 2006 White Paper, gave local authorities a new duty to 'inform, consult and involve' local people. It also set up Local Involvement Networks (LINks), based on Primary Care Trust boundaries, which are meant to involve local people in discussions about local health and other public services.

CASE EXAMPLE 19.2 **THE PEOPLE'S PANEL**

The People's Panel was set up in 1998 and ran for five years. It comprised 5,000 members of the public who were representative of the UK population as a whole in terms of age, gender, region and a wide range of other demographic indicators. Data were collected on use of, and attitudes to, public services by the panel members and members of their households.

An independent evaluation of the panel found that it had provided a useful 'high level feel' about public opinion, had stimulated new forms of customer research in the public sector and helped to demonstrate the Government's commitment to public engagement. But it concluded that there were weaknesses in the design of the panel and criticized the newsletter produced by the Cabinet Office for being unduly self-serving.

FORMS OF PUBLIC ENGAGEMENT

The rhetoric of public service 'modernization' and public service improvement, including many of the initiatives outlined above, frequently conflates very different kinds of public participation. Recent government statements in the UK have, for example, referred to the importance of 'consultation', 'listening', 'being in touch with the people', 'involving users', 'devolving power to neighbourhoods', strengthening 'accountability to local people' and 'empowerment', almost as if these often very different types of activity were synonymous or interchangeable. In fact, they represent a wide spectrum of different types of interaction.

One of the most widely quoted typologies is the 'ladder of participation' developed by Sherry Arnstein (1969) (see Figure 19.1).

On the lower rungs of the ladder she placed manipulation of the public. What she saw as 'tokenistic' activities – 'informing' and 'consultation' – came in the middle section. At the upper end were approaches that in her view genuinely empower the public. This typology is

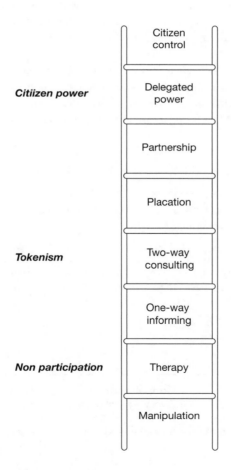

Figure 19.1 _Ladder of participation_
Source: Adapted from Arnstein (1969)

misleading, however, in that it implies that some forms of engagement are inherently superior. In practice, what matters most is that the form of participation used is fit for the purpose. A more useful typology is perhaps that shown in Figure 19.2.

All three of these activities are likely to be important components of an organization's strategy for engaging with its service users and other stakeholders.

Information

Some commentators have echoed Arnstein's scepticism about insincerely motivated forms of participation. Pollitt (1988), for example, dismisses what he dubs the 'charm school and better wallpaper end of the spectrum'. However, honest and effective informing of the public is a legitimate and necessary function, providing people with the means to access services and engage in an informed dialogue with providers. At the very least the public needs clear information about what services are on offer, when and where, in order to be able to access them. Anyone who wants a greater level of involvement in policy decisions is likely first to need information about current service standards, standards achieved by other providers, the reasons for resource allocation decisions made by their provider, and any constraints operating on services in their area.

This is important in the UK where research has shown alarmingly low levels of awareness of which agencies are responsible for the delivery of local public services. One survey found that in some areas almost half the population believed that the local council managed hospitals (Bromley et al., 2000). (Most hospitals are in fact operated by trusts, ultimately accountable

---

The Dutch ICT and Government Committee recently asserted that:

> Government in the Netherlands will face an insidious crisis if it does not quickly take measures to support new democratic processes. Failure to take such action will result in loss of legitimacy.

And the Swedish Government's Democracy Commission advocated:

> Using IT in order to publicise views presented by consultative parties and increase the opportunities for citizens to have insight in and opportunities to influence bases for decisions.

Source: Coleman and Gøtze (undated)

Information	Consultation	Co-production
One-way flow of information from public agencies to the public	Two-way dialogue between public agencies and the public	Active involvement of the public in policy decisions and/or service design/delivery

Figure 19.2 Public participation spectrum

to central government ministers.) Opinion polls have also shown that young people in particular feel they lack information about their local authority, and there is evidence of a link between public satisfaction and the degree to which people feel that they are being kept informed by government.

Consultation

Consultation differs from information in that it involves two-way communication of information and views between governments/service providers and the public. It covers a wide range of activities involving differing levels of engagement. In some cases, the public is presented with a narrow range of options and asked to decide which it prefers. In others, people are consulted at a very early stage and may be given the chance to shape and play a role in conducting the consultation exercise. However, where consultation has become mandatory (as is increasingly the case in the UK), many exercises appear tokenistic: service users or citizens are often consulted on issues at a late stage in the decision-making process, when the key decisions have already been taken. Long-drawn-out consultation processes can be used by policy-makers to defer difficult decisions, as was the case with the health reforms in Canada. And many public agencies fail to provide adequate feedback to consultees, sometimes on the grounds that they cannot afford the cost of doing so. This means that, in practice, 'consultation' can become a one-way flow of information from consultees to public service providers. Worse still, in some cases the results of 'consultations' run by staff low down in the hierarchy or by external consultants do not reach more senior decision-makers for whose benefit they were theoretically designed. And many consultations involve fairly narrowly defined groups of the 'usual suspects'. There is much talk in the UK of 'consultation fatigue'. However, in practice, it is only some groups that are 'over-consulted', while the views of others are still not heard. So-called 'hard to reach' groups often find public service providers difficult to engage with, and public agencies often want to keep control and have the last word. They are therefore naturally cautious about engaging with groups who might pose a serious challenge to existing ways of doing things. As a result consultation can cause particular difficulties in cases where public responses conflict with policymakers' thinking (see for example Case Example 19.3).

Co-production

The efficacy of many public services depends not only on the performance of the providers but also the responses of users and the communities in which they live (Bovaird, 2007). Raising levels of educational attainment, for example, is not just a question of good classroom teaching. It also depends on the capacity and willingness of students to learn and levels of parental support. Similarly, mortality rates depend not only on how good medical treatments provided by health services are but also on the lifestyle choices of the public (including diet, exercise, smoking and so forth). Many services therefore benefit from the active involvement of users in design and production. This can help to increase the chances that services meet users' needs. It can also play an important part in the 'social role valourization' of, for example, people with learning disabilities, increasing their self-esteem and self-confidence and changing the

285

CASE EXAMPLE 19.3 **E-PETITIONS ON ROAD TRAFFIC PRICING**

In November 2006 the British Prime Minister's Office established a facility on its website that enables the public to create and sign online petitions to which the Prime Minister then gives a response. This attracted a great deal of public interest but had the potential to pose future problems for policymakers. For example, a petition in February 2007, which called on ministers to rule out the introduction of a national road pricing policy designed to reduce traffic congestion, attracted more than 1.8 million signatories and widespread media interest. The Government was believed to favour the introduction of a pricing scheme, but such a strong display of public disapproval made it much more difficult to pursue, at least in the short term.

Details can be found at: www.petitions.pm.gov.uk (accessed 16 May 2008).

image others have of them. Co-production therefore seeks to go beyond an attempt to attune public services to the wishes of passive recipients (see Chapter 15). Its aim is to empower users to take greater control over, and responsibility for, their lives.

PARTICIPATION BY WHOM?

Another important issue is with whom governments and service providers need to engage (see also Chapters 6 and 15). There are three key groups:

- *Customers* – In some cases the input of users/clients will be the most valuable form of engagement; for example, in informing service providers about their satisfaction with a service received.
- *Citizens* – In others, the citizenry as a whole has an important stake in the decision-making process. For example, taxpayers who do not use a service themselves (such as prisons) may nevertheless have a legitimate interest in the relative costs of alternative approaches to service delivery, and their preferences may well be at odds with those of service users.
- *Communities* – In the case of initiatives designed to benefit particular neighbourhoods or sections of the population, it may be important to engage with specific communities of place, identity or interest.

Combining the three types of interaction identified in Figure 19.2 with this threefold categorization of the main stakeholder groups provides a useful typology of different modes of engagement (see Figure 19.3 below).

Experience suggests that it is important to be clear from the outset about what the objectives of each exercise in public participation are, because this helps to ensure that the right tools and techniques are used and the right groups are involved. It can also help to clarify what

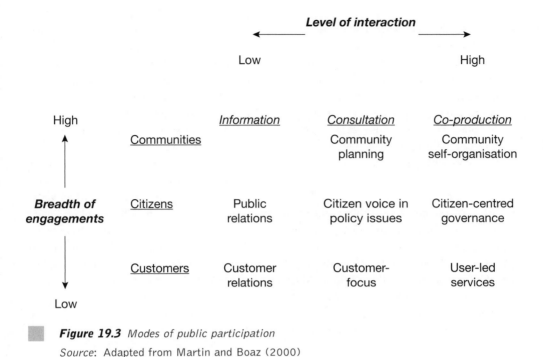

Figure 19.3 *Modes of public participation*
Source: Adapted from Martin and Boaz (2000)

level of influence is being offered to the public, thus reducing the risk of disillusionment among consultees. It also helps to highlight the kind of feedback that consultees can expect. This is important because engagement is only sustainable if stakeholders see that their views have at least been listened to.

PRACTICAL APPROACHES TO PUBLIC ENGAGEMENT

There is a plethora of good toolkits and consultation manuals for practitioners wishing to engage with the public. The aim of this section is not therefore to give a comprehensive guide but to provide a flavour of the range of techniques currently in use.

Information tools

Bristol City Council is one of many local councils to have set up multi-media kiosks around the city, which provide free access to its website and other sources of information.

Governments at local and national levels use a wide variety of media to provide information to the public. Traditional approaches include noticeboards, council newspapers, service directories, videos, roadshows, exhibitions and public awareness campaigns.

287

'Herefordshire in Touch' aims to use government-funded regeneration programmes to provide broadband access to information about council services. It has developed a joint website with the police, health service, chamber of commerce and voluntary sector that will enable residents to access information about all services through a single address.

In recent years electronic information and communications technologies have provided new ways of disseminating information — including websites, community information points (e.g. in libraries) and CD-ROMs. Some public agencies see the Internet as particularly important in serving the needs of sparsely populated areas and citizens who are relatively immobile.

Increasing attention is being given to websites and other sources of information in improving communication by governments to the public. Scott (2006) reports that the principal cities in the US now offer a wide array of information and transaction services via their websites, which he believes have made local governments much more accessible and accountable to local people. Tolbert and Mossberger (2006) found that members of the public who use these websites expressed higher levels of confidence in both federal and local government than those who did not. And Chadwick and May (2003) point to initiatives such as the Minnesota E-Democracy project, the Phoenix-at-your-fingertips and the Santa Monica Public Electronic Network as positive examples of local participatory networks facilitated by the web.

Consultation methods

Lowndes *et al.* (1998) found that the vast majority of British local authorities used traditional consultative mechanisms. Nine out of ten held public meetings ran complaints/suggestions schemes and undertook written consultations. Two-thirds organized service user forums, 62 per cent had area forums, and half had forums focussing on particular issues or services. Many were also developing more 'deliberative methods'. Half reported using focus groups, a quarter had involved the public in 'visioning exercises' or community appraisals, and 5 per cent had held citizens' juries. In the subsequent ten years, these proportions have almost certainly risen.

Some councils have arranged 'listening days' during which senior managers and councillors have gone out into the streets to talk to shoppers and householders. Others have opened up council meetings to local people and scheduled regular public question times. Some broadcast committee meetings on the Web. Free phone lines to enable citizens to record comments and suggestions are now widespread, and at least one UK council has installed video booths in the town so that residents can record video messages.

Although they were relatively rare until the early 1990s, almost all local councils, and many other local service providers, now regularly conduct residents' and users' surveys to gauge public satisfaction with existing services. Central government has also invested heavily in recent years in surveys of the general public (see Box 19.1).

Many local councils, police forces and health authorities in the UK have used citizens' panels (with representative samples, typically of 1,000 to 2,000 local people) as regular sounding boards on key policy issues. Panels of service users and particular communities are also now commonplace.

> **BOX 19.1 MAJOR SURVEYS IN THE UNITED KINGDOM**
>
> The Home Office commissions an annual 'British Crime Survey', of 40,000 to assess attitudes to and experiences of crime, the police and the courts.
>
> The Department of Health's 'Through the Patient's Eyes' survey assesses hospital in-patients' views on the way they were treated in hospital.
>
> The Strategic Rail Authority runs a twice-yearly 'National Passenger Survey', which analyses the views of train passengers about the punctuality and frequency of trains and ticket prices.
>
> Communities and Local Government intends to run a Place Survey every two years (from 2008), interviewing a large sample of the population about their attitudes to the place they live, their quality of life and the service outcomes they experience on a wide range of dimensions.

Citizens' juries bring together a small group of laypeople (selected as a representative sample of the population as a whole) to consider evidence from experts on a specific policy or service issue and to produce recommendations. Juries have been used in the USA and Germany for some years (see Renn *et al.*, 1995) and have recently been used by health authorities and local authorities in the UK (see below).

Some agencies have also developed what are in effect larger citizens' juries, often called 'public scrutiny workshops' or 'consensus conferences', to explore key policy issues.

> Milton Keynes and Bristol City Councils have both held referenda on the level of council tax, offering residents a range of optins and spelling out the implications for service budgets.

Interactive ICT is being used to consult individual local people, for example, through message boards and online discussions with policymakers, and an increasing number of local councils are consulting the public in participatory budgeting exercises (see Chapter 15), e.g. through referenda on the level of council tax or discussions on the allocations between services or projects.

Central governments also increasingly use ICT mechanisms to seek the views of the public, even in law-making, which used to be reserved to debates within government and Parliament, as Case Example 19.4 from Estonia shows.

Co-production

Co-production is less common than consultation but can take a number of different forms – including public involvement in formulating strategies (e.g. 'planning for real', 'visioning exercises' and community appraisals), designing services, co-managing them and monitoring performance (Bovaird, 2007). User groups can have roles in providing services, working in partnership in developing services, and campaigning for more resources and policy change (Barnes *et al.*, 2007).

CASE EXAMPLE 19.4 **NATIONAL ONLINE CONSULTATION ON NEW LAWS IN ESTONIA**

In June 2001 the Estonian Government launched the *Tana Otsustan Mina (Today I Decide)* website. This enables citizens to comment on draft laws and submit their own ideas for new legislation. A proposal for a new law is subject to a two-week period of online discussions, after which the proposer has three days in which to revise his/her idea. It is then put to an online vote. Proposals that receive more than 50 per cent of the vote are forwarded to the appropriate government department, which considers them and posts a response on the website. Several proposals have been carried through into legislation, and the site receives 190,000 hits per month.

Source: Adapted from Coleman and Gøtze (undated)

OBSTACLES TO EFFECTIVE ENGAGEMENT

Power to the people?

Increased public participation does not enjoy unqualified support among public officials and politicians. Not surprisingly, some see it as a threat to their professional judgement or democratic legitimacy, fearing 'governance by referendum' in which their role is reduced to that of 'rubber-stamping' decisions made by the public or brokering the views of different groups in the community. Some authors have even argued that participation (admittedly, mainly in the context of development and poverty alleviation) is tyrannical, in that it allows the illegitimate and/or unjust exercise of power (Cooke and Kothari, 2001).

> Unraveling the interests of different groups in our services will be one of the key roles of councillors; their job will be to act as community leaders and to act as brokers, balancing the different interests of different groups and developing integrated policies which meet local needs best.
>
> *Source*: City of York Council

However, in practice, engagement with users and citizens does not obviate the need for service experts or for political judgement. In most cases, it simply provides more information about the range of, often conflicting, views among the public. Politicians and officials still need to decide how best to reconcile competing interests and to allocate resources accordingly.

Have we got the right approach?

Many public sector organizations focus a great deal of effort on choosing the 'right' approach to public participation. In practice, however, there is rarely one correct method. Some of the approaches described above, for example public meetings, citizens' juries and focus groups, offer high levels of interaction but reach only a small proportion of the population. They are also relatively costly, time-consuming and require skilled facilitation. Other methods, such as panels of citizens and users and surveys of residents, offer breadth of coverage and can be relatively cheap, but provide less in-depth interaction.

Most organizations therefore need to have a balanced portfolio of approaches that fit:

■ the objectives of engaging with users and citizens;
■ the resources available to those managing the process;
■ the timescale for the decision-making process; and
■ the capacity of the respondents.

Let's work together

It is quite common for several local agencies, or even international organizations, to pursue very similar consultation exercises in parallel with each other, unaware that their efforts are being duplicated. In some cases, organizations repeat consultations unnecessarily, not realising

> We usually ask a question ten times and use the information once. We must learn to ask once and use the answer ten times in different settings.

that they already have the information on file. This is problematic for two reasons. First, it is a waste of resources. Second, it increases the risk of 'consultation fatigue' among the public.

In order to avoid duplication and bring together disparate initiatives, some organizations have developed databases of previous consultations. And in some areas joint consultation strategies are being developed by local councils, health authorities, the police and other agencies to ensure that they coordinate their initiatives better or, better still, pool their resources.

Overcoming apathy

Another problem is that many members of the public are unwilling to engage in the ways and to the degree that governments wish. Research suggests, for example, that only one in five citizens in the UK wants to engage more closely with their local authority (Box 19.2).

By definition, the minority who do get involved are therefore unlikely to be representative of the community as a whole, particularly because the most vulnerable groups, those on lower incomes, young people, older people, members of households with a disabled person and members of ethnic minority communities, are usually the least inclined to be involved. Moreover, most people express a strong preference for relatively passive forms of engagement. A survey in the UK showed that the public strongly favoured one-off consultations conducted via postal surveys and face-to-face interviews. Very few were prepared to participate in in-depth consultations – only 13 per cent said they would be willing to go to public meetings, just 6 per cent said they would participate in a citizens' panel, and only 3 per cent would take part in a citizens' jury (Martin and Boaz, 2000).

One way of alleviating this problem is to focus on those policies and issues that citizens say matter most to them – usually issues such as community safety, street cleaning, leisure

BOX 19.2 PUBLIC ATTITUDES TO PARTICIPATION

- ■ I'm not interested in what the Council does, or whether they do their job – 1 per cent.
- ■ I'm not interested in what the Council does as long as they do their job – 16 per cent.
- ■ I like to know what the Council is doing, but I'm happy to let them get on with their job – 57 per cent.
- ■ I would like to have more of a say in what the Council does and the services it provides – 21 per cent.
- ■ I already work for/am involved with the Council – 3 per cent.
- ■ Don't know – 1 per cent.

Source: Martin and Boaz (2000, p. 51)

facilities for young people. Almost all citizens care about at least one issue or service – but sometimes service providers do not take sufficient care to ensure that they are consulting them about the things which they are most interested in.

Another approach is to use the consultation methods that members of the public say they are most comfortable with – and avoid those they dislike. For example, participatory budgeting in the UK has put a strong focus on public meetings, even though this makes it very hard to attract those people who usually do not get engaged.

As noted above, it is also vital to give feedback on how results are used – what decisions were taken and why – so that people can see that their views were taken seriously and made a real difference. This need only involve short flyers with attractive layouts (ideally including photos of consultees and the issues consulted on), with the clear messages 'this is what you said' and 'this is what we are going to do'. There may be a need to reduce the number of consultation exercises in order to do a smaller number properly, but this is a price that is worth paying.

Finally, some public service providers that have made important strides in engaging with the public have been less adept at consulting their own staff. This is a missed opportunity, because front-line staff often live locally, and they and their families therefore use local services and are in a position to provide valuable feedback.

Ensuring it makes a difference

One of the major reasons for citizens' unwillingness to engage is widespread scepticism about whether governments and public service providers are willing to respond to public opinion. In many cases the scope for action will be constrained by the fact that an agency has only limited control over a policy area. Local authorities in the UK, for example, have little or no direct influence over many of the key issues about which local people feel most strongly, including health, community safety and employment, and often have limited room for manoeuvre in terms of the services they do provide directly owing to centrally determined performance targets and 'ring-fenced' budgets.

> If voting changed anything, they'd abolish it.
>
> *Source*: Ken Livingstone, Mayor of London (2000–8)

It is therefore important to make clear at the outset what the parameters of engagement are, what issues are up for negotiation, what changes are possible and what is 'off-limits'. It is also crucial that there is effective communication with users and citizens throughout the process and, where possible, that some early 'wins' are achieved and celebrated – communities often complain that decision-making processes are too slow, and lose interest if improvements do not materialize fairly rapidly.

Evaluating participation

There is now a strong body of knowledge about public participation, its potential and pitfalls both in the UK and in many other Western countries. For example, Coote and Lenaghan (1997) and McIver (1997) evaluate the use of citizens' juries in the health service. Hall and Stewart (1997) provide a detailed account of early experiments with juries in six local authorities in England, covering subjects as diverse as library services, waste management, drugs in the community, community facilities in rural areas and regeneration.

However, public service providers often fail to tap this reservoir of existing knowledge or to reflect properly on their own experiences of public participation (see Chapter 22). The result is that they risk 're-inventing the wheel' and repeating mistakes made elsewhere.

Given the increasing number of consultations being carried out by public agencies, there is growing interest in assessing their cost-effectiveness and benefits. One framework that has gained a lot of interest among civil servants in Europe is the CLEAR model, refined by Lowndes *et al.* (2006) from an original model tested by twenty-three municipalities in five countries in 2006 (see Box 19.3).

BOX 19.3 AN AUDITING TOOL FOR CITIZEN PARTICIPATION AT LOCAL LEVEL

The CLEAR tool builds on a framework for understanding public participation, which argues that participation is most successful where citizens:

Can do – i.e. have the resources and knowledge to participate.
Like to – i.e. have a sense of attachment that reinforces participation.
Enabled to – i.e. are provided with the opportunity for participation.
Asked to – i.e. are mobilized by official bodies or voluntary groups.
Responded to – i.e. see evidence that their views have been considered.

The tool is organized around these five headings and provides a focus for individuals to explore participation in their area.

Source: www.dmu.ac.uk/faculties/business_and_law/business/research/lgru/lgru_local_participation.jsp (accessed 16 May 2008)

SUMMARY

Engaging service users and citizens in policy-making and the design and delivery of services is not new, but it is being seen increasingly as a key to good governance in most Western democracies. As a result there has been a plethora of new programmes and initiatives designed to ensure greater public participation.

Engagement can take many forms. Less interactive approaches involve information – the one-way flow of information from policymakers and managers to the public. More interactive approaches include consultation – a two-way flow of information, views and perspectives between policymakers/managers and users/citizens – and co-production – involving active partnership between providers and the public to develop strategies, design and deliver services and monitor standards.

Participation may include a range of different stakeholder groups. In some circumstances it is appropriate to engage first and foremost with service users. In others it is necessary to involve the public as a whole. In some cases it is important to work with particular communities of place or interest.

There is a vast array of techniques for public engagement. What matters most is that the tools used by an organization are fit for purpose and appropriate to its own capacity and that of the groups with which it is seeking to engage.

Public participation offers a range of potential benefits but also entails formidable challenges. There is a lot of experience that can be tapped from across a range of services and different countries. It is important that policymakers, politicians and public service managers take enough time and are sufficiently open-minded to draw upon this growing body of evidence, when developing their own organization's approach to public engagement – and that they consider carefully the scope for coordinating their actions with those of other local agencies.

QUESTIONS FOR REVIEW AND DISCUSSION

1 In what ways can engagement with users and other stakeholders enhance public services?
2 What are the benefits of representative democracy? How can these be reconciled with increasing direct public participation in policy decisions?
3 How might public engagement undertaken by public organizations need to differ from engagement with stakeholders by private sector organizations?

READER EXERCISES

1 Think of your own experience as a user of public services. What services or issues would you like to have more influence over? How might the organization(s) responsible for these services engage most effectively with you?
2 Interview a local councillor to get his or her views as to how his or her role has changed as a result of more public engagement.

294

CLASS EXERCISES

Work in groups on this exercise.

Access information provided to residents by a local authority (ideally the council where you study, work or live). You may want to look at:

- its website;
- the information it provides with council tax bills;
- the council newspaper (if it has one);
- information about council services provided in libraries or council offices.

Write a short report on the strengths and weaknesses of the council's communications, taking into account questions such as:

- How easy was it to obtain information?
- How user-friendly is it?
- Is it sufficiently comprehensive?
- In your view is it likely to be useful to local people?
- Is there adequate provision for those with particular needs (e.g. are translations and large-print versions available)?
- Does it communicate a clear sense of the organization's values and mission?
- Does it make clear how local people can contact the council with queries and complaints?
- Is there provision for people to feed back their views to the council easily?

Draw up an action plan to address the weaknesses you have identified in the council's communications approach. Explain your proposals to the other groups.

FURTHER READING

Rhys Andrews, Richard Cowell, James Downe, Steve Martin and David Turner (2006), *Promoting effective citizenship and community empowerment*. London: Office of the Deputy Prime Minister (www.communities.gov.uk/documents/communities/pdf/143519.pdf, accessed 16 May 2008).

Future Services Network (2006), *From rhetoric to reality: engaging users in public services*, London: National Consumer Council (www.ncc.org.uk/nccpdf/poldocs/NCC163pd_from_rhetoric_to_reality.pdf, accessed 16 May 2008).

Improvement and Development Agency (2008), *Connecting with communities: communications toolkit*. London: IDeA (www.idea.gov.uk/idk/core/page.do?pageId=7816073, accessed 16 May 2008).

REFERENCES

Sherry Arnstein (1969), 'The ladder of citizen participation', *Journal of the American Institute of Planners*, 35 (4): 216–24.

Marian Barnes, Janet Newman and Helen Sullivan (2007), *Power, participation and political renewal: case studies in public participation*. Bristol: Policy Press.

Tony Bovaird (2007), 'Beyond engagement and participation – user and community co-production of public services', *Public Administration Review*, 67 (5): 846–60.

Catherine Bromley, Nina Stratford and Nirmala Rao (2000), *Revisiting public perceptions of local government: a decade of change?*, London: Department of the Environment, Transport and the Regions.

Andrew Chadwick and Christopher May (2003), 'Interaction between states and citizens in the age of the Internet: "e-government" in the United States, Britain, and the European Union', *Governance*, 16 (2): 271–300.

CLG (2006), *Strong and prosperous communities: the local government White Paper*. London: Communities and Local Government.

Stephen Coleman and John Gøtze (undated), *Bowling together: online public engagement in policy deliberation*. London: Hansard Society.

Bill Cooke and Uma Kothari (2001), *Participation: the new tyranny*. London: Zed Books.

Anna Coote and Jo Lenaghan (1997), *Citizen's juries: theory into practice*. London: IPPR.

DETR (1998c), *Modernising local government: improving services through best value*. London: Stationery Office.

Paul Foley and Steve Martin (2000), 'A new deal for community involvement?', *Policy and Politics*, 29 (4): 479–91.

Vivien Lowndes, Lawrence Pratchett and Gerry Stoker (2006), 'Diagnosing and remedying the failings of official participation schemes: the CLEAR framework', *Social Policy and Society*, 5 (2): 281–91.

Vivien Lowndes, Gerry Stoker, Lawrence Pratchett, David Wilson, Steve Leach and Melvin Wingfield (1998), *Enhancing public participation in local government*. London: DETR.

Shirley McIver (1997), *An evaluation of the King's Fund citizen's juries programme*. Birmingham: Health Services Management Centre.

Steve Martin and Annette Boaz (2000), 'Public participation and citizen-centred local government: lessons from the Best Value and Better Government for Older People pilot programmes', *Public Money and Management*, 20 (2): 47–54.

Steve Martin, Howard Davis, Tony Bovaird, James Downe, Mike Geddes, Jean Hartley, Michael Lewis, Ian Sanderson and Phil Sapwell (2001), *Improving local public services: final evaluation of the Best Value pilot programme*. London: Stationery Office.

ODPM (2005), *Citizen engagement and public services: why neighbourhoods matter*. London: Office of the Deputy Prime Minister.

OECD (2001a), *Citizens as partners: OECD handbook on information, consultation and public participation in policy-making*. Paris: OECD (www.partnershipsforwater.net/psp/tc/TC_Tools/022T_Citizens%20as%20Partners.pdf, accessed 16 May 2008).

Christopher Pollitt (1988), 'Bringing consumers into performance measurement: concepts, consequences and constraints', *Policy and Politics*, 16 (2): 77–87.

Ortwin Renn, Thomas Webler and Peter Wiedemann (1995), *Fairness and competence in citizen participation*. Dordrecht: Kluwer Academic Publishers.

James Scott (2006), '"E" the people: do US municipal government web sites support public involvement?', *Public Administration Review*, 66 (3): 341–53.

Caroline Tolbert and Karen Mossberger (2006), 'The effects of e-government on trust and confidence in government', *Public Administration Review*, 66 (3): 354–69.

Chapter 20

Changing equalities
Politics, policies and practice

Janet Newman, Open University, UK and
Rachel Ashworth, Cardiff Business School

INTRODUCTION

Concepts of equality and inequality are fundamentally *political* concepts that have become institutionalized in the public sector in particular ways. Yet, along with concepts such as 'fairness', social justice' or, more recently, 'social exclusion', they are historically rooted and mutable. In recent years, the meaning of such concepts has shifted, reflecting changing social, economic and political conditions. These include the demise of taken-for-granted assumptions about the welfare state as the guarantor of universal rights and benefits; the increasing importance of social movements around disability, age and sexuality; the changing role of women in both the labour market and in public life; and, in the UK, the fundamental reassessment of institutional cultures and practices following the Macpherson Report of 1999. This reported on the failure of the police to deal effectively with the death of a young black teenager, Stephen Lawrence, in 1993. It introduced the concept of 'institutional racism' into the political lexicon and led to the amendment of UK legislation on race relations. Each of these movements and events is framed in broader patterns of political change, notably the shift in language away from re-distributive meanings of equality and towards the more cultural interpretations implied in the idea of social exclusion; and from the formalized concept of equality to more fluid notions of social diversity.

These transformations have produced major challenges for the public sector. Its capacity to respond is influenced by a number of different issues, not least the ways in which new business and management practices have been adopted; the ways in which notions of consumerism have reshaped relationships between public services and the public; and the effects of the emerging patterns of governance described in Chapters 2, 4 and 15. Where are we at the beginning of the twenty-first century? And what is the capacity of the public sector to deliver equality goals in the midst of these profound social and political trans-formations?

LEARNING OBJECTIVES

- ■ To understand the politics of equality, and the different notions of justice that it draws on;
- ■ to understand how far equality and diversity policies can be viewed as simply a matter of 'good business practice';
- ■ to be able to identify the difficulties inherent in translating policy into practice;
- ■ to understand how to rethink equality and diversity in the context of new forms of governance.

CHANGING POLITICS: ADMINISTRATIVE JUSTICE OR SOCIAL JUSTICE?

Equality is not an essential, unchanging and universal principle of public management. Equality legislation and equality policies are the product of struggles by particular groups to overcome patterns of structural inequality – around social divisions such as class, gender, race, disability and sexuality. Most of what we take for granted as citizens is the product of such struggles. The politics of equality is not settled, but is the continued focus of social action as groups face new forms of disadvantage or attempt to enlarge the opportunities open to them. It is also open to various forms of 'backlash', as those whose power bases are threatened mobilize their resources – ideological, legal and institutional – to resist change. Equality, diversity and social justice are, then, all *political* concepts that are the focus of different interpretations and give rise to different strategies of enactment and resistance.

The form of equality that became enshrined in the UK public sector over recent decades was based on the concept of administrative justice – a concept that tended to strip it of these political inflections (see Box 20.1).

BOX 20.1 THE TWO PRINCIPLES OF ADMINISTRATIVE JUSTICE

The first principle derives from the notion of citizenship in welfare democracies. *All citizens are considered to have equal claims on welfare services,* so that given the same circumstances, they could expect to receive the same benefits, wherever – and to whomever – they made their claims.

The second principle is that of the *impartiality of public service officers* – an impartiality guaranteed by the bureaucratic rules and norms of the organizations in which they work.

Administrative justice is, however, a poor means of redressing inequality. Subjecting everyone to the same rules is not enough to compensate for injustices inherited from the past. Administrative justice gives rise to an individualized and passive conception of equal opportunities that enables dominant cultures to reproduce themselves. That is, to succeed, individuals may take on the characteristics of the dominant groups in whose image organizational cultures have been moulded over successive generations. In this way, little structural change – particularly the shifting of power relations – can take place, and the same groups of staff, users or citizens tend to remain excluded from the centres of power and decision-making. Despite the rules of impartiality and equality, some groups may perceive that their interests are marginalized, their voices unheard, or that they are treated unjustly.

The politics of equality has been through two key shifts in recent years. The first has been an increasing emphasis on diversity – that is, a recognition of the need to respond to difference rather than simply providing equality of opportunity. The second – less embedded – has been an attempt to transcend the passive and formalized notion of equality with a more active and dynamic concept of social justice – see Box 20.2. This shifts attention to the outcomes of policies and practices rather than to the processes through which they are delivered.

BOX 20.2 THE DIFFERENCE BETWEEN ADMINISTRATIVE AND SOCIAL JUSTICE

Administrative justice is about *processes and rules* – for example, the process of staff selection; the rules by which resources are distributed.

Social justice is about the *outcomes* of policies and practices – for example, the overall profile of a labour force; the extent to which resources are redistributed.

CHANGING POLICIES: DIVERSITY AS A BUSINESS ASSET?

The emergence of the diversity agenda

Public service organizations have experienced profound changes over the last twenty years with the introduction of markets and extension of contracting out, a new emphasis on efficiency goals and 'value for money', increasing downwards pressure on public sector pay and a series of attacks on trades union powers (see Chapter 7). Many organizations introduced flexibility strategies that adversely affected their lowest paid workers, among whom women and black and ethnic minorities were disproportionately represented. Despite some notable exceptions, equality goals became subordinated to business and efficiency goals.

However, more recently, there has been a resurgence of interest in the possible benefits of diversity strategies for organizations across the private and public sectors (Fischer, 2007). This interest has been driven by a HRM agenda aimed at 'managing diversity' (see Chapter 9). This agenda has, in turn, been underpinned by a 'business case' that advocates the enlargement of recruitment pools so staff can be more representative of society and therefore more responsive to societal needs (Rees, 2005). In addition, public service organizations have been cast as the 'model employer', leading the way on equalities for their counterparts in the private sector to follow – see Case Example 20.1.

In the public policy literature, the ethos is that equality and diversity are simply a case of being 'responsive' to the different needs of diverse groups of users or citizens (Audit Commission, 2002b). However, the academic literature suggests that responsiveness may not always deliver equality: the results of public consultation exercises may override

CASE EXAMPLE 20.1 **DELIVERING A DIVERSE CIVIL SERVICE IN THE UK**

Sir Gus O'Donnell, Cabinet Secretary and Head of the Home Civil Service has unveiled a Ten-Point Plan to raise the pace towards a representative workforce:

> I want the Civil Service to be a beacon for change and a model of best practice for all organisations. A truly representative workforce, including at the most senior levels, will enable policies and services to be developed in ways which will result in better outcomes for everyone in society. That is why this must happen. Diversity is a key part of the wider Civil Service reform programme. Together with improved leadership and professionalism, improved diversity is essential to build the Service's capacity to deliver.

The Ten-Point Plan sets out commitments on ten key areas that are intended to achieve broad and deep cultural change across the Civil Service. It was developed following a review of equality and diversity in employment in the Civil Service by Waqar Azmi, the Chief Diversity Adviser to the Civil Service. Across the Civil Service, HR Directors, the Council for Civil Service Unions, corporate staff networks and other key stakeholders have also had the opportunity to contribute to the development of the plan.

The aims of the plan are:

1   To improve delivery of services for everyone in society through achieving a truly diverse Civil Service workforce at all levels.
2   To achieve by 2008 the agreed targets of:
    (a) 37 per cent of the Senior Civil Service to be women;
    (b) 30 per cent of top management posts to be filled by women;
    (c) 4 per cent of the Senior Civil Service to be from minority ethnic backgrounds;
    (d) 3.2 per cent of the Senior Civil Service to be disabled people.
3   To use this visible change to lead broader change across the Civil Service in the way we manage and value equality and diversity at all levels, in all aspects of our business.

Source: Adapted from www.cabinetoffice.gov.uk (accessed 16 May 2008)

professional notions of equality, and consumer power tends to be weak as a driver of equality (Harrow, 2002; Clarke *et al.*, 2007). The solution to this dilemma is to develop strong, rather than weak, notions of diversity and forms of consultation, i.e. linked to concepts of social, rather than administrative justice (Young, 1990). A positive notion of diversity acknowledges the wide plurality of interests and complexity of identifications among the public, rather than resting on crude conceptions of 'consulting the whole (i.e. undifferentiated) community' or dividing the public into distinct categories ('the black and ethnic minority community', 'women', 'the elderly' etc. (Barnes *et al.*, 2007). Rather than simply sampling pre-formed 'opinions' through survey techniques, consultation should enable different groups to be informed about the issues and to engage in dialogue – with each other and with public agencies (see Chapter 19).

Diversity policies have been criticized because of their focus on individuals, rather than groups; and because of their focus on assimilation. That is, diverse groups may be absorbed or incorporated into the mainstream and so lose their distinct forms of identity and patterns of allegiance (Prasad *et al.*, 1997). The existence of a diverse workforce will not yield the benefits of enhanced innovation, responsiveness, market sensitivity and so on if the organization is modelled on an image of a holistic, consensual culture in which all sign up to the 'ownership' of the same goals and values, as often demanded by 'total quality management' gurus, and are expected to adopt the dominant ethos. A diverse organization is necessarily a dynamic organization: one in which there is likely to be conflict between different values and norms, in which minority voices are able to raise challenges to conventional practice, and in which power imbalances and discriminatory practices can be recognized and discussed. That is, it is one that recognizes that change involves politics as well as management.

Despite these difficulties, the links being made between diversity and organizational effectiveness potentially place equality agendas at the core of organizational strategies, rather than consigning them to the backwaters of HRM. However, researchers have observed that, in practice, equality policies often lack substance and are little more than 'an empty shell' (Hoque and Noon, 2004). Clearly, politics and business make uneasy partners, and it is important to hold on to the idea that equality and diversity are contested ideas around which a number of conflicts are played out. Only then can we understand why, while equality and diversity are concepts to which everyone may ascribe in principle, few translate into practice in a way that makes a real and sustainable difference.

CHANGING PRACTICE: BARRIERS TO CHANGE

Why, given the centrality of equality in public services over many decades, has so little been achieved? The data here are compelling – see, for example, Audit Commission (2002b) and the recent Equalities Review conducted for the Cabinet Office (2007). Given this lack of progress, current approaches to equality in the UK, reflected in new legislative duties and the work of the recently created Commission for Equality and Human Rights, have placed a heavy emphasis on 'capabilities' – a person's ability to achieve a given state of well-being by combining the different 'functionings' available to them (e.g. meeting their basic physical needs, achieving social integration and self respect, etc.) (Nussbaum and Sen, 1993). The capabilities approach moves beyond 'equal opportunities' by suggesting that some citizens

301

will require additional support in order to take up opportunities such as, for example, extra resources for disabled people or childcare for working lone parents (Widdowson, 2008). However, despite these recent developments, progress on narrowing inequalities remains slow. There are a number of potential explanations for this that are presented in the following section at three different levels of analysis: the institutional, the organizational and the personal.

Institutional explanations explore the ways in which organizations adopt norms and practices in order to enhance their legitimacy in the eyes of external stakeholders. Equality policies are part of a dominant 'logic of appropriate action' within public services. These logics are based on norms and conventions developed through interaction with peers and within particular professional groups (HR managers, equality officers, professional associations, trades unions, etc.). These norms differ subtly between different services (e.g. social service organizations talk about 'anti-oppressive practices', while police services may be oriented towards eradicating 'institutional racism'). They also vary geographically (with a higher legitimacy afforded to equality issues in, say, metropolitan rather than rural areas).

Equality policies and programmes may be partly ceremonial, their function being to secure organizational legitimacy in the institutional environment. There may be a host of signs and symbols (e.g. 'we value diversity' statements on job adverts, photos of black officers in publicity materials, or perhaps a lone woman promoted to an otherwise all male senior management team). However, these signs and symbols may be 'loosely coupled' to the realities of everyday practice (Meyer and Rowan, 1991). Loose coupling allows multiple goals to be pursued in different parts of the system independently of each other. A delicate balance has to be struck between being seen to support equality goals while not allowing them to get in the way of operational efficiency So, for example, there may be a formal job share policy, but an informal set of rules about where this policy can, and cannot, be applied. In order to secure efficiency goals, new working practices may be introduced that adversely affect the pay and conditions of low-paid workers, and so further disadvantage women and ethnic minority staff. The corporate centre may adopt a policy on social exclusion that has little impact on service planning or operational management. Tighter coupling brings a closer alignment between policies and outcomes, with outputs monitored and outcomes evaluated.

Organizational explanations tend to focus on the intractibility of organizational cultures (Itzin and Newman, 1995). This focus stems from a recognition that individuals and groups may be disadvantaged not by overt discrimination (e.g. the old height rule in the police force, or the bar on married women in the civil service) but by norms and practices that influence their experience of the workplace. Expectations about working hours, access to flexible working and job sharing opportunities, norms about an appropriate work/life balance, may all be applied 'fairly' (i.e. even-handedly) but may be profoundly discriminatory in their effects. Issues of language, humour and normative assumptions about lifestyle and relationships can all contribute to the marginalization of particular groups and disable them from making an effective contribution. Assumptions about the characteristics of users and communities – about young black males, Asian women, young single mothers, gays and lesbians, travellers, the homeless – may be enshrined in the culture and passed on from one generation of practitioners to the next. Such assumptions may not be held consciously by any particular individual, but nevertheless may become institutionalized in the culture, influencing a myriad of informal practices that may be experienced as discriminatory by the groups concerned.

However, culture change strategies are rarely successful on their own – the hearts and minds of those whose power and status may be threatened by equality issues cannot necessarily be won by a succession of mission statements and corporate goals. People may learn a new language without changing their behaviour. There may be a backlash against those promoting equality values and actions, coupled with subtle strategies of resistance. Culture change programmes need to be supported by 'harder' organizational change strategies such as equality audits, targets linked to performance indicators, careful use of disciplinary procedures to signal behaviours that are unacceptable, resource allocation strategies that reward positive outcomes, and the monitoring and evaluation of outcomes.

Personal explanations explore the ways in which individuals experience the implementation of equality policies. Enacting the equality agenda through one's own behaviour is threatening, not only to established power bases but also to workers' views of their own competence and professional expertise (Lewis, 2000a). For example, a black hospital worker may experience racial abuse from a white patient, or a white worker may be asked to collude in racist comments about a black colleague, but neither may feel able to respond because of their concern that they may, in so doing, undermine their own professional standards (and status) by showing lack of respect for the patient's vulnerable or dependent status. A care worker's sense of competence may be challenged by the distressing behaviour of a client – or carer – from a different cultural background to their own. A white social work manager may feel that her authority is threatened by the claims of her 'multi-racial' team and may feel tentative about exercising proper performance management in the case of black colleagues. A male police officer may marginalize a gay or lesbian member of the team from the informal bonds of collegiality on which the team's proficiency depends. Such personal fears, emotions and responses tend to be viewed as outside the domain of rational management practice. Yet, they may lead to strategies of avoidance that further marginalize groups that are already disadvantaged. Only in organizational cultures that acknowledge the emotional, as well as the managerial, dynamics of change, and where there is a culture of learning rather than blame, can these fears be confronted and addressed.

CHANGING FORMS OF GOVERNANCE

In the new governance literature, notions of networks, partnerships, participation and involvement all tend to be conceptualized in terms of a predominantly optimistic reading of change in the public policy system, i.e. as a welcome release from the inflexibilities of hierarchy or the fragmenting consequences of markets (see Chapter 15). There is, however, a need for more careful attention to be paid to the patterns of inclusion and exclusion that they may produce or reproduce.

Networks and partnerships are viewed as a response to the increasing complexity and ambiguity of the public realm. As the site of action shifts, so equality agendas must be renegotiated. Newman (2002) suggests two alternative scenarios for what the outcomes of these negotiations might be. The first is a pessimistic reading in which the power dominance of statutory agencies means that radical perspectives from 'outside' are absorbed, deflected or neutralized. For example, organizations may engage in forms of consultation in which the rules of debate are firmly set by the statutory body, thus excluding or marginalizing alternative forms of dialogue. Dissenting or difficult voices may be dismissed as 'unrepresentative', and groups likely to challenge the mainstream consensus may be excluded through a range of informal strategies.

The second scenario is one in which the public sector becomes more open to challenges from groups historically marginalized from decision-making processes. This scenario also emphasizes the possibility of socially oriented action on the part of public service workers committed to equality goals. The opening up of organizations to greater influence by users, citizens and communities – including community activists and politicized user groups – can be a major impetus for innovation. They also potentially provide new forms of legitimacy for those public service professionals seeking to engage with social and political change.

RECENT DEVELOPMENTS

The final section of the chapter examines recent developments on equality and diversity that have occurred at the three levels of analysis: the institutional, the organizational and the personal.

Institutional: New legislative developments

Driven by EU legislation, the UK Labour Government has introduced a series of 'equalities duties', which place a binding duty upon public authorities to promote equality and eliminate discrimination (see Box 20.2 for examples). This set of duties aims to shift the burden of responsibility from the individual to the public organization and, to a degree, takes organizations beyond notions of administrative justice. This is especially so in relation to the Disability Discrimination Act, which requires public organizations to make 'reasonable adjustments' for disabled staff and service users.

Organizational: New approaches to equality

We have also seen developments in terms of new organizational approaches to equality, more specifically, a movement from a focus on equal treatment and positive action to 'mainstreaming' or 'transforming' equality (see Box 20.3).

This has been especially developed in relation to gender mainstreaming – see Case Example 20.4.

Personal: Firmer application of existing legislation

There is evidence to suggest that individuals and groups are using equalities legislation to a greater extent than in the past. For example, there has been concerted action on the part of women workers to enforce sex discrimination legislation in recent years (see Box 20.5). High-profile cases relating to the availability of overtime payments and bonuses are being won by women, with substantial compensation being awarded. These legal judgements are imposing substantial compensation payments on organizations ranging from the US retail giant Wal-Mart to UK local councils.

BOX 20.2 NEW EQUALITY DUTIES FOR UK AGENCIES

The Gender Equality Duty came into force in April 2007 and requires public sector organizations to promote gender equality and eliminate sex discrimination. The duty places the legal responsibility on public authorities to demonstrate that they treat men and women fairly. The duty will affect policy-making, public services such as transport, and employment practices such as recruitment and flexible working.

The Disability Equality Duty came into force on 4 December 2006. This legal duty requires all public bodies to actively look at ways of ensuring that disabled people are treated equally. All of those covered by the specific duties must also have produced a Disability Equality Scheme, which they must now implement. It links to the Disability Discrimination Act 1995, which aimed to end the discrimination faced by many disabled people. Key rights under the Act include: the right to fair employment, the right to access to goods, facilities and services, the right to have 'reasonable' adjustments made to premises or workstations by employers, the right to let or sell land or property and the right to education in any school, and in further education, higher education, adult and community education.

The Race Relations Duty (2001, 2006) requires a listed public authority, 'in carrying out its functions, to have due regard to the need to: eliminate unlawful discrimination, and promote equality of opportunity and good relations between persons of different racial groups.' Authorities are expected to consider the implications for racial equality for everything they do, from allocating council housing, to closing or opening a hospital or a school, or managing prisons. The aim of the duty is to make the promotion of racial equality central to the work of the listed public authorities. The general duty also expects public authorities to take the lead in promoting equality of opportunity and good race relations, and preventing unlawful discrimination. In practice, this means that listed public authorities must take account of racial equality in the day to day work of policy-making, service delivery, employment practice and other functions.

BOX 20.3 MODELS OF EQUALITY

Equal treatment – 'tinkering':
- focuses on individual rights;
- legal remedies.

Positive action – 'tailoring':
- focuses on group disadvantage;
- 'special' projects and measures.

Mainstreaming – 'transforming':
- focuses on systems and structures that give rise to group disadvantage;
- integrates equality into mainstream systems and structures.

Source: Adapted from Rees (2005, p. 557)

CASE EXAMPLE 20.2 **TOTAL E-QUALITY CERTIFICATE FOR THE CITY OF MUNICH**

On 2 June 2005 the City of Munich for the third time won an award from the independent association TOTAL-E-QUALITY in Germany. This award is given for three years to organizations for developing long-term mainstreaming strategies in their HRM system.

Munich has been a pioneer in Germany as far as gender mainstreaming is concerned. In 1984 the local council produced the first report on the situation of female staff in the council. Since 1992 this has been produced regularly and generates a lot of interest in German business and public agencies. In 1985 Munich founded the first Equality Office in Bavaria, which initiated and subsequently developed and refined equality policies for women in order to reform staff recruitment procedures. Today Munich is renowned for good practices in making work and family life compatible, staff training in gender mainstreaming and targets to increase the percentage of women in managerial positions.

The results speak for themselves: 55 per cent of the 26,000 staff are female, 43 per cent of about 2,600 managerial posts are occupied by women, about 25 per cent of staff work part-time (85 per cent of part-time staff are women) and 506 managers and their deputies work part-time, including 324 women.

Source: Adapted from www.muenchen.de and www.total-e-quality.de
(accessed 16 May 2008)

BOX 20.5 COUNCILS FACE HUGE EQUAL PAY BILL

Local authorities face paying billions in compensation to women workers in equal pay cases. Councils in North-East England have already paid about £100m, while in Scotland pay-outs could reach £560m, according to an IDS report.

Other councils had 'larger workforces and therefore larger equal pay liabilities', the research group said. IDS said pay-outs had been made to women denied access to bonuses that could add up to 80 per cent to basic pay.

Sally Brett, of IDS, said: 'Women working as school caterers or home helps are doing jobs of equal value to men, working in refuse collection, gardening or maintenance, and have been on the same pay grade as them for many years, but they have been denied access to the regular bonus payments that the men have received.'

IDS said local authorities were struggling to implement new equality-proofed pay and grading structures without additional government funding similar to that given to other parts of the public sector like the NHS.

The women's campaigns have been backed by the GMB and Unison unions in the past and IDS said no-win, no-fee lawyers were seeking to represent workers with 'such transparent equal pay claims'. 'We could soon see the bill for back pay compensation in local government reaching into the billions,' said Ms Brett.

Source: Summarized from http://news.bbc.co.uk (accessed 5 April 2006)

SUMMARY

Concepts of equality and inequality are fundamentally *political* concepts. In recent years, the language has tended to shift away from redistributive meanings of equality and towards the more cultural interpretations implied in the idea of social exclusion; and from the formalized concept of equality to more fluid notions of social diversity.

Equality is not an unchanging and universal principle of public management. Equality legislation and equality policies are the product of struggles by particular groups to overcome patterns of structural inequality – around social divisions such as class, gender, race, disability and sexuality. In recent years, there has been an increasing emphasis on diversity – that is, a recognition of the need to respond to difference and to pursue a more active and dynamic concept of social justice.

As diversity becomes seen as contributing to business effectiveness, equality agendas are more frequently to be found at the core of organizational strategies. However, it remains the case that equality and diversity are contested ideas. This may be part of the reason why rather less has been achieved than hoped in recent years. Barriers to change can be identified at three different levels of analysis: the institutional, the organizational and the personal. Recent developments at each of those levels of analysis include new legislative duties and a movement to 'mainstreaming' or 'transforming' equalities, but progress so far has been judged to be patchy.

Finally, network forms of governance in the public sector mean that a host of actions, which appear to have little relationship to issues of difference, are likely to be highly significant in terms of their consequences for patterns of equality and inequality – including network governance approaches to consultation; representation on partnership bodies; the selection of staff to develop new projects or initiatives; methods of developing community strategies and local strategic partnerships; the types of contract with voluntary or community sector organizations; and the ways in which 'community', 'diversity' and 'difference' are conceptualized (Newman, 2005).

QUESTIONS FOR REVIEW AND DISCUSSION

1   Why do policies or practices based on the concept of administrative justice fail to deliver change in historical patterns of discrimination or exclusion?
2   How might 'equality' and 'efficiency' goals be in conflict, and how might organizations attempt to reconcile them?
3   Why do new forms of governance mean rethinking the traditional conception of equal opportunities in the public sector?

READER EXERCISES

1   'Bureaucracy' has become unfashionable as an organizational form. What are the implications for ensuring fair treatment for citizens – and staff – in more flexible, devolved organizational forms?

307

2   What strategies or practices might your organization or service adopt to enhance its legitimacy in the eyes of particular groups who may have been subject to institutionalized patterns of discrimination or exclusion in the past?

3   The 'welfare state' is undergoing important shifts as demand on some services exceeds the capacity – or willingness – of the state to supply them. Services are increasingly being targeted to particular groups, rationed through various means, or subjected to the logic of the marketplace. It is also argued that the receipt of services should be conditional on notions of responsibility or deserts – in the familiar phrase of new Labour, that 'rights' come with 'responsibilities'. What ideas of equality or justice do you think underpin such measures? And what might be the implications for our understanding of citizenship in the twenty-first century?

CLASS EXERCISES

1   Look up the definition of 'institutional racism' that was set out in the Macpherson Report (Macpherson, 1999). Consider how the concept of institutional bias might influence practice in relation to other forms of discrimination – for example, in terms of gender, disability, age, sexuality – in your own organization or service *or* a service you use.

2   Obtain a recent report from an organization such as the Commission for Equality and Human Rights on the distribution of top jobs in the public and/or private sector (or find press reports or websites summarizing such data). Explore how far each of the three levels of analysis (institutional, organizational, personal) might be used to explain these data, and identify strategies that might be used to bring about change at each level.

3   Research the way in which a sample of large public and private sector organizations develop and monitor their equality policies. Are there any differences between the public and private sectors? And how might such differences be explained?

FURTHER READING

Marion Barnes, Janet Newman and Helen Sullivan (2007), *Power, participation and political renewal*. Bristol: Policy Press.

Jenny Harrow (2002), 'The new public management and social justice: just efficiency or equity as well?', in Kate McLaughlin, Stephen Osborne and Ewan Ferlie (eds), *New public management: current trends and future prospects*. London: Routledge, pp. 141–60.

Kim Hoque and Mike Noon (2004), 'Equal opportunities policy and practice in Britain: evaluating the "empty shell" hypothesis', *Work, Employment & Society*, 18 (3): 481–506.

Janet Newman and Nicola Yeates (eds) (2008), *Social justice*. Buckingham: Open University Press/ McGraw-Hill.

REFERENCES

Audit Commission (2002c), *Equality and diversity*. London: Audit Commission.

Marion Barnes, Janet Newman and Helen Sullivan (2007), *Power, participation and political renewal*. Bristol: Policy Press.

Cabinet Office (2007), *Fairness and freedom: the final report of the Equalities Review*. London: Cabinet Office.

John Clarke, Janet Newman, Nick Smith, Elizabeth Vidler and Louise Westmarland (2007), *Creating citizen-consumers: changing publics and changing public services*. London: Sage.

Michael Fischer (2007), *Diversity management and the business case*. Research Paper 3–11. Hamburg: HWWI

Jenny Harrow (2002), 'The new public management and social justice: just efficiency or equity as well?', in Kate McLaughlin, Stephen P. Osborne and Ewan Ferlie (eds), *New public management: current trends and future prospects*. London: Routledge, pp. 141–60.

Kim Hoque and Mike Noon (2004), 'Equal opportunities policy and practice in Britain: evaluating the "empty shell" hypothesis', *Work, Employment & Society*, 18 (3): 481–506.

Catherine Itzin and Janet Newman (eds) (1995), *Gender, culture and organizational change*. London: Routledge.

Gail Lewis (2000a), 'Introduction: expanding the social policy imaginary', in Gail Lewis, Sharon Gerwirtz and John Clarke (eds), *Rethinking social policy*. London: Open University Press, pp. 1–21.

Sir William Macpherson (1999), *The Stephen Lawrence enquiry*. London: Stationery Office.

John Meyer and Rowan, B. (1991), 'Institutionalized organizationations formal structure as myth and ceremony', in Walter Powell and Paul Dimaggio (eds), *The new institutionalism in organizational analysis*. Chicago, IL: University of Chicago Press, pp. 41–62.

Janet Newman (2002), 'Changing governance, changing equality? New Labour, modernization and public services', *Public Money and Management*, 22 (1): 7–14.

Janet Newman (2005), 'Re-gendering governance', in Janet Newman (ed.), *Remaking governance: policy, politics and the public sphere*. Bristol, Policy Press.

Martha Nussbaum and Amartya Sen (eds) (1993), *The quality of life*. Oxford: Clarendon Press.

Pushkala Prasad, Albert Mills, Michael Elmes and Anshuman Prasad (1997), *Managing the organizational melting pot: dilemmas of workplace diversity*. Thousand Oaks, CA: Sage.

Teresa Rees (2005), 'Reflections on the uneven development of gender mainstreaming in Europe', *International Feminist Journal of Politics*, 7 (4): 555–74.

Beth Widdowson (2008), 'Well-being, harm and work', in Janet Newman and Nicola Yeates (eds), *Social justice*, Buckingham: Open University Press/McGraw-Hill, Chapter 3.

Iris Young (1990), 'Justice and the politics of difference', in Susan Fainstein and Lisa Servon (eds), *Gender and planning: a reader*. Rutgers, NJ: Rutgers University Press, pp. 86–103.

Chapter 21

Ethics and standards of conduct

Howard Davis, Warwick Business School, UK

INTRODUCTION

Concern to ensure high standards of behaviour is by no means a new phenomenon. Indeed, demands for ethical conduct on the part of politicians and public officials predate the modern concern for the rule of law (*'Rechtsstaat'*) and can be traced back at least to Greek and Roman times. These concerns have risen to prominence again in recent years because of the changing context of public policies (see Chapter 2) and because of changes in both the management and governance arrangements in the public sector (see Chapters 4 and 15).

In spite of evidence of improved efficiency and service practices in public sector organisations, as they implemented the first wave of public sector reforms (see Chapter 4), citizens' trust in government by and large has fallen in most industrialised countries in recent decades – for example, in the USA in the 1990s, roughly three in four citizens didn't trust the government to do the right thing, whereas it had been only one in four in the 1960s (Putnam, 2001, p. 47). However, it would seem premature to say that this is owing to an increase in corruption in the public sector, as critics of managerial reforms often claim. As a matter of fact, there is little empirical evidence as to whether the level of corruption has increased in the public sector in the last ten years or not in most OECD countries. Indeed, one line of argument is that the public sector has become more transparent in recent years, and that therefore more cases of corruption have become more exposed, which does not mean that corruption as a whole has increased. The picture is complicated by the possibility that lower standards of conduct may themselves be the result of new public management practices, particularly the growth of contracting to the private sector, which has always been one of the arenas in which the potential for corruption is particularly high (see Chapter 7).

Whatever the reason for their growth in recent years, 'sleaze', corruption scandals and allegations of dishonesty have clearly affected the confidence and trust that citizens have in public representatives and officials. These attitudes in turn are likely to have played some part in the undermining of democratic activity in many OECD countries, particularly the low voter turnout at elections (with turnout of the voting age population in the US presidential election of 2004 at 55.3 per cent and generally less than 40 per cent – and often considerably less than that – in local elections in the United Kingdom), sinking memberships of political parties and a general disinterest in conventional politics and even disrespect towards politicians.

Moreover, high levels of corruption are also likely to impact upon economic performance, since it means that the costs (in the widest sense of that word) of service production go up, less efficient providers are used, discriminatory behaviour favours certain groups and harms some other groups, and there are significant losses of potential tax income (with the knock-on effect of lower public expenditure). Consequently, international organisations such as the World Bank and the OECD have taken a strong interest in material corruption in recent years. And with the accession of countries such as Romania and Bulgaria, ethics in the public sector have become a key concern to the European Union.

However, increasingly governments are recognising that 'ethics' is not just an issue for others, but that it is necessary for them to clean up their own doorstep, often in the aftermath of revelations about the alleged unethical behaviour of civil servants or politicians. Ethics is now on the agenda of many developed countries, and many public agencies have considered it necessary to increase transparency and to take action to ensure the fair and honest behaviour of individuals and organisations acting in the public domain.

LEARNING OBJECTIVES

This chapter will help readers to identify:

■ the reasons for the current emphasis on ethics and standards of conduct in the public sector;

■ the spectrum of unethical behaviour in the public sector, from corruption to minor infringements of ethical codes;

■ the rationale behind the recent move to strengthened codes of conduct in the United Kingdom and elsewhere;

■ the pros and cons of control-oriented and prevention-oriented approaches to ensure ethical behaviour;

■ the role for transparency as a mechanism for fighting unethical behaviour.

In Brighton she was Brenda
She was Patsy up in Perth,
In Cambridge she was Caina
The sweetest girl on Earth.
In Stafford she was Stella,
The pick of all the bunch,
But down in his expenses,
She was Petrol, Oil and Lunch.

Source: Anon.

ETHICS AS A KEY GOVERNANCE ISSUE IN THE PUBLIC SECTOR

As the definitions in Chapter 15 illustrated, ethics is either explicitly or implicitly considered a part of 'good governance'. How has the renewed emphasis in recent years on fair, just and ethical behaviour come about?

There are no empirical grounds for claiming that managerialism, as an ideology or a codified set of practices, has given explicit incentives that would encourage unethical behaviour. Nevertheless, it seems fair to say that the switch to a focus on results (outputs and outcomes), and away from processes, may have had some unfortunate side-effects. The simple truth that 'processes matter' (and that 'the ends do not necessarily justify the means') seems sometimes to have been forgotten. If processes are not regulated, then some unfair and dishonest processes can occur.

Consequently, the stronger focus on economically driven values and business management methods in the public sector – stronger in countries such as the UK and much weaker in other countries such as France – has generated a new discussion about the values and (written and unwritten) norms of public service. Indeed, one must now ask, rather than take for granted, whether, in any given country, a public service ethos still exists or whether public service culture has become almost identical with business culture (see Box 21.1).

Furthermore, the introduction of contract management (see Chapter 7) and the increasing blurring of boundaries between various sectors (see Chapter 3) mean that decision-makers in the public sector face new, unfamiliar situations and dilemmas, which require new guidelines to clarify how they should be properly tackled from an ethics perspective. Equally, those used to operating in business may find that practices acceptable in the private sector are unacceptable when working with public sector bodies.

In particular, the following changes in public management have raised questions as to what the 'new rules of the game' are:

- New levels and intensity of interactions between the public, private and non-profit sectors have led to all kinds of partnership, with an associated blurring of responsibilities – this brings a need for clarity of roles and transparency in decision-making, not only inside partnerships but between them and external stakeholders.
- Managers – and also to some extent front-line staff – have increased flexibility in the use of financial and staffing resources. For example, in some Continental European countries, many public agencies such as utilities now operate within a private law framework, very different from the previous public sector framework with its rather rigid staff regulations and financial accounting systems.
- With deregulation taking place in many OECD countries, including the UK, many new regulatory agencies have been created, often without clarity as to whom the

BOX 21.1 STANDARDS IN PUBLIC LIFE, UK

Decentralisation and contracting out have varied the format for organisations giving public service. There is greater interchange between sectors. There are more short term contracts. There is scepticism about traditional institutions. Against that background it cannot be assumed that everyone in the public service will assimilate a public service culture unless they are told what is expected of them and the message is systematically reinforced. The principles inherent in the ethic of public service need to be set out afresh.

Source: Committee on Standards in Public Life (1995, p. 17)

regulators are actually accountable. Given the power of these bodies, it is not surprising that some individuals who serve in them occasionally abuse their position. For instance, there are recurring concerns worldwide about potential corruption in police drugs squads and in Customs, both of which have access to high-value goods that are being traded illegally.

■ Increased mobility of staff between different sectors introduces new values into the public sector. While this may have been useful in inculcating a more entrepreneurial spirit in the public sector, it has also meant the dilution of traditional understandings of 'public service'. It also raises the thorny issue of how staff moving between jobs treat confidential information – a particular difficulty when public officials move on to jobs in the private sector.

The increasing use of contracting (particularly, but not only, with the private sector) in the provision of local services has sharpened some of the ethical issues involved in inter-organisational relationships. For example, Seal and Vincent-Jones (1997) summarised one set of concerns about the extension of trust-based, relational contracting to local government services, arguing that:

> [The] positive image of trust that emerges from the literature is based on an implicit assumption that trusting relationships are somehow welfare enhancing. Less obvious are the negative aspects of trust – trust between members of self-serving elites which may flourish within bureaucracies.
>
> (Seal and Vincent-Jones, 1997, p. 7)

Davis and Walker (1997; 1998) have argued that different parties in any contract inevitably have different primary objectives. The first objective for a contractor has to be to survive. A contractor's staff are ultimately not there to provide the best possible public service, but to provide the best possible public service *in accordance with a profitable contract* – however this may be dressed up.

As a result of these changes to the basic value system operating in the public sector, public officials and political representatives often find themselves in hazy areas, where it is no longer clear what constitutes proper behaviour. Of course, there are also cases of deliberate wrong-doing in spite of clear guidance through legal regulations or standards of conduct. However, these are likely only to be the tip of the iceberg, with many other undesirable behaviours occurring more through ignorance or confusion.

CORRUPTION

Media attention tends to focus gleefully on corruption scandals – see Case Example 21.1 – but there are many other forms of unethical behaviour which are usually not reported by the media such as disadvantaging citizens who do not have a strong voice or excluding certain user groups from access to public services. The question therefore arises as to what distinguishes corruption scandals from other forms of unethical behaviour?

CASE EXAMPLE 21.1 A FAMOUS CORRUPTION SCANDAL IN THE UK

'Flagship' Conservative-controlled Westminster City Council in London has been the subject of a long-running alleged 'homes for votes' scandal. In May 1996 auditor John Magill accused former council leader Dame Shirley Porter and five others of 'wilful misconduct' and 'disgraceful and improper gerrymandering' between 1987 and 1989. He also made them jointly and severally liable to repay the £31.6 million that he estimated to have been wrongly spent as they allegedly tried to 'fix' election results in marginal wards by selling council homes cheaply under the right to buy scheme to people thought to be more likely to vote Conservative. The 'surcharge' was later reduced to £26.5 million. After appeal hearings going in different directions the House of Lords, in December 2001, re-imposed the surcharge on Dame Shirley and her former deputy. In April 2002 Dame Shirley lodged a formal complaint against the ruling with the European Court of Human Rights. August 2002 saw Westminster City Council win a High Court summary judgement to help it recover the £26.5 million plus some interest. In November 2003, assets worth millions of pounds and said to be controlled by Dame Shirley were frozen by court orders secured by Westminster Council. Following negotiations and mediation, a settlement of £12.3 million was agreed in mid 2004.

Source: *The Guardian* and BBC News, various dates

The European Union Convention on the fight against corruption, involving officials of the European Communities or officials of Member States of the European Union (Council Act of 26 May 1997) defines active corruption as 'the deliberate action of whosoever promises or gives, directly or through an intermediary, an advantage of any kind whatsoever to an official for himself or for a third party for him to act or refrain from acting in accordance with his duty or in the exercise of his functions in breach of his official duties' (Article 3). Passive corruption is defined along the same lines.

Source: www.conventions.coe.int/Treaty/EN/Reports/HTML/173.htm (accessed 16 May 2008)

Defining corruption, never mind measuring it, is far from straightforward. The legal definition of what constitutes corrupt practices varies from country to country. International regulations only focus on specific forms of corruption, such as the OECD Convention on Combatting Bribery of Foreign Public Officials in International Business Transactions.

Similarly, what public opinion considers as 'corrupt practices' varies from country to country. For example, while many countries have a culture of giving tips for private services, tips are considered as 'unethical' in Finland. Typically, public views as to what is considered 'corrupt behaviour' go beyond what can be prosecuted as an offence under national criminal law. This has implications, for example, for cross-national contracting for major public contracts.

315

Transparency International measures the perception of corruption in different countries (see Box 21.2 below).

It is evident that what is defined as corruption is also culture-bound. For example, while it is totally unacceptable for any public officials in the UK to accept gifts, this is part of many Asian cultures.

BOX 21.2 PERCEPTION OF CORRUPTION WORLDWIDE

Transparency International is an international non-profit organisation that is dedicated to increasing the transparency of decision-making in the public and non-profit sector around the world and to exposing and combating corruption. One of its activities is the compilation and publication of an international Corruption Perceptions Index (CPI).

The CPI is a poll of polls, reflecting the perceptions of business people and country analysts, both resident and non-resident, and ranking countries in terms of the degree to which corruption is perceived to exist among public officials and politicians. First launched in 1995, the CPI in 2007 drew upon 14 surveys and expert assessments. For a country to be included it must feature in at least three of these surveys or assessments.

In 2007, this index ranked 180 countries: close on three-quarters (73 per cent) scored less than five out of a clean score of ten, and over 40 per cent scored less than three, indicating a severe corruption problem. Corruption was perceived to be most rampant in Somalia, Myanmar, Iraq and Haiti.

The countries whose scores indicated the greatest increase in perceived corruption between 2006 and 2007 were Austria, Bahrain, Belize, Bhutan, Jordan, Laos, Macao, Malta, Mauritius, Oman, Papua New Guinea and Thailand. Countries showing 'noteworthy improvements', i.e. a decline in perceptions of corruption, included Costa Rica, Croatia, Cuba, Czech Republic, Dominica, Italy, Macedonia, Namibia, Romania, Seychelles, South Africa, Surinam and Swaziland.

The eight countries with very low levels of perceived corruption were predominantly rich countries, namely Denmark, Finland, New Zealand, Singapore, Sweden, Iceland, the Netherlands and Switzerland. The UK ranked joint twelfth (with a score of 8.4), and the USA ranked twentieth (with a score of 7.2). Transparency International notes that, while it is the 'poorest countries [that] suffer most under the yoke of corruption', it is the case that

> corruption by high-level public officials in poor countries has an international dimension . . . Bribe money often stems from multinationals based in the world's richest countries. It can no longer be acceptable for these companies to regard bribery in export markets as a legitimate business strategy.

Transparency International calls for 'concerted efforts in rich and poor counties to stem the flow of corrupt monies and make justice work for the poorest'.

Source: Adapted from Transparency International, *Corruption Perceptions Index 2007*, www.transparency.org (accessed 16 May 2008)

Nevertheless, a key question must always be, in whose interest does a particular arrangement or relationship operate? In any relationship the full details of it, and what makes it work successfully, may well be opaque to outsiders. In the public service there is a continuing difficulty in ensuring that arrangements and relationships work in the public interest and are clearly seen to do so. The closer that any relationship becomes, the greater the potential for corrupt practice and corruption of purpose. Cosy and exclusive relationships sit uneasily with public probity expectations. The move from cliques to cosiness to collusion to corruption is all too easy without adequate safeguards.

It is also important to note, however, that double standards may sometimes be applied and that this could damage public service. Increasingly the public and media appear to demand that their politicians and public servants are totally without blemish in every regard – in spite of the fact that those criticising any slips from perfection by their public servants are often far from meeting these standards themselves. If anybody putting themselves forward for public office is going to have their whole life history raked over in minute detail, this may discourage many individuals from doing so and result in 'blamelessness' rather than ability to contribute being the main criterion for achieving public office.

This leads to difficult dilemmas about balance. Are there ethically acceptable levels of corruption? Should the standards of conduct applied to those in public life and public service differ from those that the public and media apply to themselves?

THE ROLE OF CODES OF CONDUCT IN THE PUBLIC SECTOR

Because of the lack of a comprehensive legal framework for dealing with unethical behaviour, in recent years there has been an explosion of codes of conduct and/or expectations in 'Westminster-type' countries. These have typically been drawn up either by public organisations or by the professional associations whose members work in public organisations.

CASE EXAMPLE 21.2 **THE 'OLIGARCHS OF RIGA'**

According to a report of the *Frankfurter Allgemeine Zeitung*, Latvia risks becoming a new hub for Russian corruption. Unethical behaviour is said to have been facilitated by:

- opportunities arising from privatisation of the oil industry and the shipping of Russian oil through the harbour of Ventspils;
- the power acquired by the four 'oligarchs', based originally on Moscow contacts, including the Deputy President, and now bolstered by owning their own newspapers and television stations;
- the high number of banks (compared with surrounding neighbouring countries), where clients enjoy a high level of protection in spite of the national money-laundering laws;
- weakening effectiveness of the media and other watchdogs.

Source: Adapted from *Frankfurter Allgemeine Zeitung* (13 September 2004, p. 4)

317

A well-known example of such a code is the 'seven principles of public life' set out by the Committee on Standards in Public Life – see Case Example 21.3 below. This UK Committee, initially chaired by the judge Lord Nolan, was established by the Conservative government in 1994, following a series of allegations about parliamentarians (such as 'cash for questions', sexual liaisons and alleged dishonesty) and concerns at the cumulative effect of these events on public confidence in politicians and the system of government.

The Committee was established on a standing basis and given a wide remit to examine

> current concerns about standards of conduct of all holders of public office, including arrangements relating to financial and commercial activities, and make recommendations as to any changes in present arrangements which might be required to ensure the highest standards of propriety in public life.
>
> (*Hansard*, 25 October 1994, col. 758)

In assessing whether these principles are honoured, none of them can be assumed to be in place – the onus is on demonstrating that they are honoured in practice. Furthermore,

CASE EXAMPLE 21.3 **THE SEVEN PRINCIPLES OF PUBLIC LIFE, UK**

Selflessness Holders of public office should take decisions solely in terms of the public interest. They should not do so in order to gain financial or other material benefits for themselves, their family, or their friends.

Integrity Holders of public office should not place themselves under any financial or other obligation to outside individuals or organisations that might influence them in the performance of their official duties.

Objectivity In carrying out public business, including making public appointments, awarding contracts, or recommending individuals for rewards and benefits, holders of public office should make choices on merit.

Accountability Holders of public office are accountable for their decisions and actions to the public and must submit themselves to whatever scrutiny is appropriate to their office.

Openness Holders of public office should be as open as possible about all decisions and actions that they take. They should give reasons for their decisions and restrict information only when the wider public interest clearly demands.

Honesty Holders of public office have a duty to declare any private interests relating to their public duties and to take steps to resolve any conflicts arising in a way that protects the public interest.

Leadership Holders of public office should promote and support these principles by leadership and example.

Source: Committee on Standards in Public Life (1995, p. 14)

such assessment often throws up systemic issues that need to be considered across the sector, not just in one organisation. For example, the first principle, 'selflessness' is undoubtedly threatened by some of the fragmented ways of working in the mixed economy of provision that now characterises local government in the UK, particularly where contracting is the norm.

It is interesting to note some omissions from these principles, e.g. *competence,* which is arguably central to 'proper' public service. There must be grave doubts about the ethics of an organisation providing a service where it no longer has the competence to deliver it to the desired standard.

The above seven principles have strongly influenced codes of conduct in other countries. They have been adopted in particular in Central and Eastern Europe (even though most of these countries follow the German legalistic tradition), but it is often unclear what their legal standing is.

Some see the standards agenda as a new bureaucracy, or pure political window-dressing, but behind the agenda are concerns both to prevent corruption and improper behaviour and, in so doing, to bolster the regard in which politicians and public servants are held, with its consequent impact on both the credibility of government bodies and their ability to act.

Another problem is 'ownership' of standards. In many cases codes of conduct are drafted by a committee, the members of which may represent different backgrounds and values from those espoused by those who have to conform to the standards. Nor is this the only potential value clash – Eleanor Glor (2001) stresses the differences in values between different generations. To this we might add the different value systems that can be observed between people from different genders, races, religions, regions, beliefs, etc. Clearly, getting owner-ship of a single set of standards is often going to be difficult.

There is currently general acceptance that expectations as to what constitutes ethical behaviour have to be made explicit. Nevertheless, there is a strong argument that these standards still need to be negotiated between the various stakeholder groups of each public sector organisation, rather than being simply imposed by some external body.

CONTROL-ORIENTED AND PREVENTION-ORIENTED MECHANISMS

It is important to note that not only what is defined as unethical behaviour is strongly culture-bound but that 'Western' countries also tend to have different traditions regarding the combat of corruption and other forms of unethical behaviour. In particular, two major traditions can be identified: 'Westminster-type' countries such as the UK, New Zealand and Australia (and also the US) have a long tradition of addressing questions of values and moral behaviour directly on a case-by-case basis. In Continental European countries such as Germany and France, ethical issues are more normally addressed indirectly through general laws. In particular, the French Napoleonic Code of 1810 is a landmark, introducing penalties to combat corruption in public life and even today France is renowned for its emphasis on professional ethics and the study of duties (the so-called *déontologie*) in various sectors (Vigouroux, 1995). In Germany, the rule of law (*Rechtsstaat*) was codified in the Prussian state in the nineteenth century, and the ethos of the civil service that it embodied has been further codified in Article 33 of the German constitution. Although the values of German civil servants have greatly changed from the original ideals of the Prussian state, the legal tradition is still strong today. These differences

319

are interestingly highlighted by the fact that *Public Administration Times* (the monthly magazine of the American Society for Public Administration) always includes a case study dealing with some ethical issue and some model solution from a managerial or political perspective, whereas the corresponding journal for German civil servants always highlights a legal disciplinary case, with a model solution based on some court rulings.

There is a general agreement that ethics management should always involve both control-oriented and prevention-oriented mechanisms – controls include mechanisms for ensuring accountability and limiting and clarifying discretion, while prevention concentrates on increasing transparency and awareness of unethical behaviour.

An OECD survey in 1999 showed that control-oriented mechanisms, such as independent financial and legal scrutiny, were considered to be the most important mechanisms for combating corruption (OECD, 1999, p. 22). Many OECD countries have also taken measures to protect 'whistle-blowers' and to encourage staff to report wrongdoing. Much less common are participatory approaches to counter unethical behaviour by involving citizens in the policing of public activity– see Case Example 21.4 below.

CASE EXAMPLE 21.4 **THE INDEPENDENT COMMISSION AGAINST CORRUPTION (ICAC), HONG KONG**

Hong Kong's Independent Commission Against Corruption (ICAC) was set up originally in 1974. There had been rapid change in Hong Kong in the 1960s and 1970s, providing a fertile environment for the unscrupulous. Corruption was seen to be a very serious problem in the public sector. Vivid examples included firefighters soliciting 'water money' before they would turn on hoses to put out a fire and ambulance attendants demanding 'tea money' before picking up a sick person. From the outset the ICAC adopted a three-pronged approach of investigation, prevention and education to fight corruption. The Commission aims to:

- pursue the corrupt through effective detection, investigation and prosecution;
- eliminate opportunities for corruption by introducing corruption resistant practices;
- educate the public on the evils of corruption and foster their support in fighting corruption.

This approach is embodied in the Commission's three Departments of Operations, Corruption Prevention and Community Relations. In 2006 the ICAC had a strength of 1,314 staff. Its approach to reaching out to the public includes television and radio drama series based on real corruption cases, print advertisements, organising corruption prevention programmes and activities through regional offices across Hong Kong and a 'specific programme plan' aimed at specific target groups such as businessmen, professionals, public servants and young people.

Source: Independent Commission Against Corruption (Hong Kong), www.icac.org.hk (accessed 16 May 2008)

It is clear that controls are always costly and can never be watertight. Consequently most countries have focused their efforts on risk management. That implies that controls are particularly frequent and intensive in areas where the risk of corruption is high, such as in public procurement and public finance. For example, most organisations place ceilings on the amount of expenditure that can be authorised by any individual manager, and contracts invariably have to be awarded by more than one person.

Besides more effective controls, many countries have also taken prevention measures, including such instruments as:

- measures to avoid conflicts of interest (or at least to make them open), such as declarations of financial and business interests of public officials and politicians or regulations for staff moving between sectors.
- affirmative action by supporting disadvantaged groups (minority ethnic groups, women, etc.) to gain access to managerial positions or to bridge the digital divide by making them fit for the information society;
- public education programmes that aim to raise awareness about desirable forms of behaviour and perceptions of unethical behaviour.

This latter group of prevention measures reminds us that ethics always involves values. All control mechanisms will fail if actors do not try to live up to the values that are implicit or explicit in various standards of conduct. But can values be taught? Both in the US and in the UK it appears that academics, at least, think so – ethics typically forms an important part of public management education and training curricula.

TRANSPARENCY

There is common agreement that transparency is important in order to fight corruption and other forms of unethical behaviour. The assumption is that increased transparency brings about a decrease in corruption. Indeed most OECD countries have recently passed freedom of information laws that give third parties access to government information. In many cases freedom of information laws also provide remedies for citizens who believe that their right of access to information has not been respected – in some cases, citizens may complain to an information officer or an ombudsman or ask courts to enforce their access rights.

Clearly, in each case a balance needs to be struck between the public interest and the need to protect personal privacy and to respect confidentiality of information. For example, in Canada, most freedom of information legislation does not apply to public-private partnerships. It is argued that this could impinge on private interests and endanger the confidentiality of commercial information.

Again, the degree to which various stakeholders in different countries wish to be transparent is culture-bound. Scandinavian countries have a comparatively high degree of transparency in the public sector. For example, the Swedish 'principle of public access' means that the general public and the media are, with a few exceptions, 'guaranteed an unimpeded view of activities pursued by the government and local authorities'. The principle of public access manifests itself in various ways:

321

CASE EXAMPLE 21.5 **THE SWEDISH PARLIAMENTARY OMBUDSMEN – JUSTITIEOMBUDSMÄNNEN**

Sweden has had an Ombudsman institution since 1809. An Ombudsman is an individual elected by the Swedish Parliament (*Riksdag*) to ensure that courts of law and other agencies, as well as the public officials they employ (and also anyone else whose work involves the exercise of public authority), comply with laws and statutes and fulfil their obligations in all other respects. An Ombudsman is elected for a four-year period and can be re-elected. Today there are four Ombudsmen, two women and two men. Each Ombudsman has her or his own area of responsibility. Each Ombudsman has a direct individual responsibility to the Riksdag for his or her actions.

An Ombudsman's inquiries are based on complaints from the general public, cases initiated by the Ombudsmen themselves and on observations made during the course of inspections. A complaint can be made by anybody who feels that he or she or someone else has been treated wrongly or unjustly by a public authority or an official employed by the civil service or local government. The most extreme sanction allows an Ombudsman to act as a special prosecutor and bring charges against the relevant official for malfeasance or some other irregularity. Although this very rarely happens the awareness of this possibility is important to the Ombudsman's authority. The most frequent outcome is a critical advisory comment from an Ombudsman or some form of recommendation.

Source: Riksdagens Ombudsmän (Sweden), www.jo.se (accessed 16 May 2008)

- Everyone is allowed to read public documents held by public authorities.
- Civil servants and others who work in the central government sector or for local authorities have freedom of expression – the right to tell outsiders what they know.
- Civil servants also enjoy special freedoms to provide information to the mass media.
- Court proceedings are open to the public, as are meetings of legislative assemblies.

(*Source*: Ministry of Justice, Sweden)

In Finland, transparency even extends to tax information – national newspapers and the website of the Finnish broadcasting company Yle (www.yle.fi/verokone, accessed 16 May 2008) tend to publish tax information of Nokia celebrities and senior politicians. If a Finnish citizen wants to know how much his/her neighbour or colleague earns before tax from income and capital, his/her respective tax rate and total wealth, it is possible to get this information from the tax administration (at a cost of €0.36 per item, but with a €20 minimum charge). Although there has been some discussion in Finland about the privacy issues arising, so far the principle of transparency has protected publication of this information, which would be regarded as an intrusion into privacy in most other countries and be socially and politically unacceptable (for evidence, see Case Example 21.6).

CASE EXAMPLE 21.6 **EVERY ITALIAN'S INCOME POSTED ON INTERNET**

The income of every Italian citizen was published on the web without any prior warning by the government, just days before it was due to leave power.

Claiming it was part of a crackdown on tax evasion, the finance ministry put details of the declared taxable income of every citizen on the country's tax website.

The site proved hugely popular. Surprised Italians, delighted at the chance to find out how much their neighbours, colleagues, and high-profile celebrities were earning, bombarded the site within hours of it going live.

Critics condemned the publication, however, saying it was an outrageous breach of privacy as the government did not have consent to make the information public.

'It's a clear violation of privacy law,' ADOC, the Italian consumer group, told Reuters. 'There is a danger of an increase in crime and violence as the data are an irresistible source for criminals.'

The treasury finally suspended the website last night after the country's privacy watchdog issued a formal complaint.

The tax minister, Vincenzo Visco, was quoted in Italy's *Corriere della Sera* as saying: 'It's all about transparency and democracy. I don't see the problem.'

But the timing of the release of the information has been viewed with scepticism. 'It's a very strange thing to do on the last day before clearing off,' Guido Crosetto, a member of Berlusconi's party, said. 'Taxpayers need to pay less tax, not to know how much all the other Italians are paying.'

Source: Adapted from Rachel Stevenson and agencies, *The Guardian*, 1 May 2008.

Without doubt, the media also play an important role in this context. In particular, particularly in the information age, they are often considered as the 'fourth estate' in the political system. Of course, the media themselves come under attack when they abuse the freedom of the press to violate personal rights to privacy.

E-government may also be used to increase the degree of transparency, as entire documents and accounts can now be disseminated easily and widely – at least to those who have electronic access. However, electronic security is a recurring concern, and cross-border 'scams' can also potentially take place with great ease and speed.

SUMMARY

The standards and conduct of public representatives and officials significantly affect the standing in which they are held. That in turn affects the confidence and respect in which governmental systems are held. High standards of conduct and public confidence go hand in hand. As the Standards Board for English local government says,

> At the heart of good . . . democracy is a bond of trust between the community and the people who represent them – a bond which depends greatly on the conduct of those people. The public have a right to expect the highest standards of behaviour from their representatives and those responsible for the delivery of . . . public services.
>
> (www.standardsboard.co.uk, accessed 16 May 2008)

Many people maintain these standards most of the time. Nevertheless, the need to remain vigilant and alert remains as important today as ever. At the same time, there is a need to balance transparency with the right to privacy of individuals, even those in public office.

QUESTIONS FOR REVIEW AND DISCUSSION

1   Why are high standards of conduct thought to be important for those in public life?
2   What degree of disclosure of private interests is needed from those in public life? How far should such expectations extend to their friends and families?
3   Are ethics and standards of conduct matters for enforcement or education and guidance?

READER EXERCISES

1   Is it right to expect higher standards of conduct from those in public life than we would apply to ourselves?
2   Can you provide a 'watertight' definition of conflicts of interest? Are there any circumstances in which this definition might be relaxed?

CLASS EXERCISE

1   Consider the 'seven principles of public life' (see Case Example 21.3). Are there any principles that you consider inappropriate? Are there any additional principles that you would include? Can these principles be defined in a meaningful way?
2   Do you consider the behaviour of the Italian government (Case Example 19.5) to be ethical? What lessons for government policy or codes of conduct would you draw from this episode?

FURTHER READING

Committee on Standards in Public Life (2001), *The first seven reports: a review of progress*. London: Committee on Standards in Public Life.

OECD (2005d), *Policy brief: OECD guidelines for managing conflict of interest in the public service*. OECD: Paris.

Propriety and Ethics Team (no date), home page of Cabinet Office website (www.cabinetoffice.gov.uk/propriety_and_ethics/index.asp, accessed 16 May 2008).

Standards Board for England website (www.standardsboard.co.uk, accessed 16 May 2008).

United Nations Crime and Justice Information Network website (www.uncjin.org/Documents/corrupt.htm, accessed 16 May 2008).

REFERENCES

Committee on Standards in Public Life (1995), *First report*, Cm 2850–1. London: Stationery Office.

Howard Davis and Bruce Walker (1997), 'Trust based relationships in local government contracting', *Public Money and Management*, 7 (4): 47–54.

Howard Davis and Bruce Walker (1998), 'Trust and competition: blue collar services in local government', in Andrew Coulson (ed.), *Trust and contracts: relationships in local government, health and public services*. Bristol: Policy Press.

Eleanor Glor (2001), 'Codes of conduct and generations of public servants', *International Review of Administrative Sciences*, 67 (3) (September): 524–41.

OECD (1999), *Public sector corruption: an international survey of prevention measures*. Paris: OECD.

Robert Putnam (2001), *Bowling alone: the collapse and revival of American community*. New York: Touchstone.

Willie Seal and Peter Vincent-Jones (1997), 'Accounting and trust in the enabling of long-term relations', *Accounting, Auditing and Accountability Journal*, 10 (3): 406–31.

Christian Vigouroux (1995), *Déontologie des fonctions publiques*. Paris: Dalloz.

Chapter 22

Evidence-based policy and practice

Annette Boaz, University of London, UK and
Sandra Nutley, University of Edinburgh, UK

INTRODUCTION

There is growing interest in the UK and elsewhere in the use of evidence to improve policy-making and public service delivery (Boaz *et al.*, 2008, Shuller *et al.*, 2006). Of course, researchers and analysts have long worked with and in governments. However, in the UK, the election of a Labour government in 1997 revitalized interest in the role of evidence in the policy process. In setting out his modernizing agenda, the then prime minister, Tony Blair, frequently asserted that '*what matters is what works*', a theme developed in subsequent government publications.

The 1990s had seen reduced public confidence in public service professionals, partly because service users were themselves increasingly educated, informed and questioning (see Chapter 19). Moreover, clients were demanding more information about their service choices. The development of evidence-based practice has been one way of addressing these concerns.

This chapter seeks to demonstrate that it is both desirable and practical to ground policy and practice in more reliable knowledge about social problems and what works in tackling them. This does not mean that we have simple faith in the achievement of progress by logical reasoning and evidence. However, it does suggest that effective governance of complex social systems requires opportunities for social and organizational learning, which in turn rely on systems for gathering and using evidence (Sanderson, 2002).

LEARNING OBJECTIVES

- To understand what counts as evidence for what purposes;
- to understand how evidence can be used to improve public services;
- to be aware of the obstacles to the use of evidence in policy-making;
- to understand how evidence-based learning can be encouraged.

WHAT COUNTS AS EVIDENCE FOR WHAT PURPOSES?

There are two main forms of evidence required to improve governmental effectiveness (Sanderson, 2002) – evidence to improve *accountability* (information about the performance of government) and evidence to promote *improvement* (knowledge that enables the design and delivery of more effective policies and programmes). Chapter 14 in this book has discussed the issue of accountability and the role of performance information in facilitating this. Here we consider the use of evidence for improvement purposes – frequently referred to as 'evidence-based policy and practice' (EBPP).

Discussion of EBPP has been focused predominantly on the question of 'what works' – what interventions or strategies should be used to meet specified policy goals and identified client needs (Nutley *et al.*, 2007). However, policy and practice improvement entails a broader range of knowledge than this, including knowledge about the nature of social problems, how potentially effective interventions can be implemented, and who needs to be involved in this process. Furthermore, evidence is also required about the costs of action and the balance between those costs and the likely benefits.

Knowledge about some of these issues is often based more on tacit understandings than on evidence derived from systematic investigations. So, it is no surprise that the UK government works with a broad and eclectic definition of evidence, which includes routine monitoring data, stakeholder consultations and expert opinion.

HOW CAN EVIDENCE BE USED TO IMPROVE PUBLIC POLICY AND PRACTICE?

In this section we consider how research and evaluation evidence can be used. We focus on four main uses of research:

■ to design and develop public policy (also referred to as '*ex ante* evaluation' or 'option appraisal');
■ to assess the impact of policy interventions (also referred to as '*ex post* evaluation');
■ to improve policy implementation (referred to as 'on-going evaluation' or 'monitoring');
■ to identify tomorrow's issues.

Using evidence right from the start: to design and develop public policy

Research has an important role to play at the start of the policy process. It can help to identify the issues to be addressed and whether there are interventions that are likely to be effective in tackling recognized problems.

The choice of a particular policy direction should be informed by existing evidence on what has been tried elsewhere and whether it has been demonstrated to deliver the desired benefits. Typically, this involves commissioning literature reviews, and, in recent years, techniques for undertaking reviews in a more systematic and robust way have been developed.

A distinct feature of systematic reviews is that they are carried out to a set of pre-agreed standards. The main standards are as follows:

- Focus on answering a specific question(s).
- Use protocols to guide the review process.
- Seek to identify as much of the relevant research as possible.
- Appraise the quality of the research included in the review.
- Synthesize the research findings in the studies included.
- Update in order to remain relevant.

Although there are definite benefits of such a process, not least in terms of its coverage and replicability, a recent study of the use of evidence in UK policy-making found that those policymakers who had heard of systematic reviews were concerned about the time involved in conducting reviews, and, hence, their utility (Campbell *et al.*, 2007). There are also concerns that the outputs of such reviews are not always as useful as they need to be (Lavis *et al.*, 2005).

Consultation exercises and market research are often used, alongside more formal research, to explore the views and priorities of key stakeholders and the public (see Chapter 19). Research can also be used to understand more fully the context and challenges facing a proposed policy. At this stage a range of techniques can be used. These may assess the likelihood of alternative future scenarios, e.g. the 'Scenarios for Scotland' project, or they may focus on forecasting more specific impacts of a proposed policy, such as regulatory impact assessments (see Case Example 22.1). As Deelstra *et al.* (2003) point out, such research tools can be beneficial for politically weak stakeholders who cannot undertake such analysis themselves, but much effort is needed to generate convincing and relevant results, involve and build consensus between stakeholders, and identify windows of opportunity in the policy debate when this evidence is likely to be taken seriously.

In recent years pilots have increasingly been used in the design and development of public services. A policy can be trialled with a small group of organizations to identify potential problems and refine the policy before wider implementation – so-called 'prototyping' (Sanderson, 2002). Pilots are usually subject to some form of evaluation, often with the aim of distilling the learning from pilot sites to feed into the subsequent roll-out of the policy. Recent UK examples of policy development through evaluated pilots include Best Value (see Chapter 11) and the New Deal for Communities programme (see Chapter 19). Although the potential benefits of policy pilots are clear, there are concerns that policy decisions often seem to be made prior to their evaluation.

Finally, the design of policy implementation strategies requires consideration of how to bring about practitioner change. Research on alternative implementation strategies and studies of individual and organizational behaviour may be used to determine the available options and what seems to work best in what circumstances. There have also been systematic reviews of the options available. For example, the Cochrane Effective Practice and Organisation of Care Group (EPOC) draws together international evidence on the effectiveness of different strategies for changing the behaviour of health care practitioners, such as issuing practice guidelines or using financial incentives.

329

CASE EXAMPLE 22.1 **IMPROVING THE QUALITY OF REGULATIONS THROUGH REGULATORY IMPACT ANALYSIS**

Regulatory Impact Analysis (RIA) is a multiple stakeholder assessment of the economic, environmental and social impact of regulations. The OECD and European Union have strongly promoted this evidence-based approach towards legislation. The latest OECD survey reveals that, in 2005, all member countries use some form of RIA on new regulations.

While every country has developed its own system of RIA, OECD has assessed the effectiveness of various RIA systems and developed a set of best-practice guidelines for the design and development of RIA systems, which recommends:

1   Maximize political commitment to RIA.
2   Allocate responsibilities for RIA programme elements carefully.
3   Train the regulators.
4   Use a consistent but flexible analytical method.
5   Develop and implement data collection strategies.
6   Target RIA efforts.
7   Integrate RIA with the policy-making process, beginning as early as possible.
8   Communicate the results.
9   Involve the public extensively.
10 Apply RIA to existing as well as new regulation.

However, as OECD admits, there are 'significant challenges' to measuring the benefits of tools such as RIA, since the links between improved outcomes in terms of improved productivity or investments and the quality of regulations tend to be weak.

Source: OECD (2007b; 2008)

Using evidence right to the end: evidence of effectiveness/impact

Existing knowledge about the effectiveness of many policy and practice interventions is partial at best (see also Chapter 11). Hence, while systematic reviews of the knowledge base may suggest promising policy directions, there is still a need to evaluate their impact in specific contexts, which in turn adds to the evidence base.

Evaluating evidence of effectiveness often involves the use of experimental methods, such as randomized controlled trials (RCTs). Although RCTs have been mainly used to measure the effectiveness of clinical interventions, they have also been applied in other areas, including the effectiveness of continuing education programmes, offender rehabilitation programmes and alternative welfare regimes. However, there are ongoing debates about the desirability and practicality of using RCTs to assess the effectiveness of many social interventions (Chalmers, 2005; Hammersley, 2005). Knowledge of what works in social policy tends to be provisional and highly context-dependent. This has led to calls for a realist approach to social policy evaluations (Pawson and Tilley, 1997), which begins with a theory of causal explanation and gives research the task of testing theories of how programme outcomes are generated by specific mechanisms in given contexts. Theory development draws on the knowledge of different stakeholders in the policy process, getting them to articulate their views of what works for whom in what circumstances. Subsequent evaluation involves making inter- and intra-programme comparisons in order to see which configurations of context-mechanism-outcome are efficacious.

Regardless of the evaluation methodology employed, a key challenge facing those tasked with evaluating effectiveness is the difficulty of measuring the outcomes of many social interventions (see Chapter 11), which are only really understood by those experiencing them. Thus knowledge of 'what works' tends to be influenced greatly by the kinds of question asked, who is asked, when they are asked, and depends greatly on the context.

Using evidence throughout: improving policy implementation

Impact studies need to be complemented by research to explore progress towards goals, to assess the costs involved in the intervention, to understand the processes involved and from this to learn the lessons that will improve policy implementation. This calls for rigorous, ongoing monitoring and evaluation throughout the life of a policy or programme.

There is a long tradition of evaluating process and implementation issues, using a wide variety of research methods and approaches. For example, action research models involve practitioners in designing and carrying out research. One of the strengths of this approach is that the practitioner does not have to wait for a final research report, but is in a position to integrate learning into their work as it emerges – see Case Example 22.2.

Using evidence to break the mould: identifying tomorrow's issues

Alongside the increased emphasis on building an evidence base for policy and practice, there has been a plea that researchers continue to explore a wider set of ideas than those defined by the current policy agenda – 'blue skies' thinking, keeping sight of the 'bigger picture', looking more widely for ideas and problems, and challenging current thinking. The way in which pure research can help reframe current thinking is illustrated by the design of the auction of third generation mobile phone licenses in the UK: pioneering research on game theory at the Centre for Economic Learning and Social Evolution, in University College London, was used in 2000 to design a new style of auction for mobile phone licences, which raised £22 billion for the UK Treasury, much more than had originally been expected.

Because of their distance from policy and practice, academic researchers are in a good position to challenge current thinking. Research councils and independent organizations, such as the Joseph Rowntree Foundation in the UK and the Rockefeller Foundation in USA, currently take a lead role in supporting and nurturing curiosity-driven research.

Overall, we can see that research and evaluation can be used for many different purposes, each requiring somewhat different evidence-gathering techniques and methodologies (see Table 22.1).

331

CASE EXAMPLE 22.2 **ACTION RESEARCH INTO TWO-TIER PARTNERSHIP WORKING**

In two-tier local government areas in England, local strategic partnerships (LSPs) have been established at both county and district levels. This has created some uncertainty about the respective roles of county and district based LSPs, their relationships and the arrangements that might be needed to avoid overlap, duplication or competition. As a result, an action learning set (ALS) was set up, facilitated and supported as part of an action research and evaluation programme sponsored by the Department for Communities and Local Government. Its purpose was to learn about existing practice, to understand and clarify the barriers to, and opportunities for, collaborative working, and to consider good practice in relation to two-tier working. Within these broad objectives, the ALS defined its own programme of work, focusing on the issues where members thought their efforts should be concentrated. Thus the agenda was set by LSPs themselves rather than being predetermined by the research team or sponsors.

The conclusions from the ALS helped in the formulation of government advice to LSPs in two-tier areas. However, inevitably, the participants in the ALS were drawn from areas where there was trust between the county and district, and consequently the conclusions presume a willingness to work together. Stronger government guidance may be necessary in areas where collaboration is not taking place.

Source: Adapted from Geddes (2007)

Table 22.1 *Evidence uses and methods*

Purposes	Methods and approaches might include:
Identify key issues	Review existing literature, surveys, group discussions, interviews
Understand the views of stakeholders	Interviews, group discussions, surveys
Explore contextual factors (including opportunities and costs)	Impact assessment, cost benefit analysis, interviews and discussion groups
Prepare guidance for those implementing a policy	Synthesizing the best available evidence, consulting key stakeholders, cost benefit analysis
Evaluate the effectiveness of a policy intervention Understand what works with whom and in what circumstances	Experimental and quasi-experimental studies, economic evaluations, realist evaluations, evaluations of pilots
Evaluate the processes involved Explore the issues involved in implementing the policy	Case studies, observations, documentary analysis, interviews, group discussions and surveys
Monitor progress	Management data, surveys and interviews
Generate new ideas and alternatives, highlight issues for future consideration	'Blue skies' research, syntheses of existing research, interviews, group discussions

WHAT ARE THE OBSTACLES TO THE IMPROVED UTILIZATION OF EVIDENCE?

Many have argued that it is self-evident that policy and practice benefit from being more rather than less informed by evidence (Hammersley, 2001). However, studies of utilization have frequently expressed concern about the apparent under-use of research (Weiss, 1998). How should this problem of *underuse* be tackled, where findings about effectiveness are either not applied, or are not applied successfully? And, conversely, should we also be concerned about *overuse* of research, for example the rapid spread of tentative findings, and about *misuse*, especially where evidence of effectiveness is ambiguous (see Case Example 22.3)?

CASE EXAMPLE 22.3 **THE CURIOUS INCIDENT OF RESEARCH IN THE PAPERS**

On Thursday, 8 July 2004, the London *Evening Standard* ran its lead story on research into children in childcare and the government's cautious response. For nearly three weeks there was a flurry of press interest, largely around the issue of whether very young children are more aggressive if looked after in day nurseries, rather than by their mothers.

What do we observe going on in this curious incident of research in the news? Certainly, many contributions to public debate. But also contributions where everyone – journalists, lobbyists, politicians and researchers – used all the rhetorical tricks in the book: loaded words, selective quotation, reframing the issue, attribution of unseemly motives to opponents, generalizing from personal experience, accusations of misrepresentation, concealment of interests, and false modesty. It should remind those of us who look to research and evaluation to improve the quality of public debate and decisions of a few home truths:

- The development of policy is largely achieved through argumentation, often behind closed doors, with policymakers compelled to act before the evidence is in – researchers must take their chances as they occur.
- How the argument is joined is unlikely to be of our choosing – we either have to go with how others choose to frame the debate or, more boldly, seek to change the terms of engagement by seeking a public platform ourselves.
- Let's not kid ourselves that our contribution will be seen as more objective than that of others – the media care little for academics' much vaunted quality control procedures.
- The scope for misrepresentation is immense by mediators who have other ambitions than ours. We should think twice about intentionally choosing the media as a channel for communication of our research to policymakers, programme managers, lobbyists, consumers. Better to find some direct, unmediated, channel for that purpose.

Source: Adapted from William Solesbury (2004)

Nutley *et al.* (2007) in a review of ways of increasing the impact of research found evidence of a number of barriers and enablers to increased research use (see Box 22.1). The problem of under-utilization is frequently considered to stem from the fact that researchers and research users (policymakers and practitioners) occupy different worlds: they operate on different time-scales, use different languages, have different needs and respond to different incentive systems (Locock and Boaz 2004). This leads to a call for better dissemination strategies to bridge the gap between the two communities and enable research to be communicated effectively to policymakers and practitioners.

BOX 22.1 BARRIERS AND ENABLERS TO THE USE OF RESEARCH

The nature of the research

Research is more likely to be used that:

- is high quality and comes from a credible source;
- provides clear and uncontested findings;
- has been commissioned by, or carries, high-level political support;
- is aligned with local priorities, needs and contexts;
- is timely and relevant to policymakers' and practitioners' requirements;
- is presented in a 'user-friendly' way – concise, jargon-free and visually appealing.

The personal characteristics of both researchers and potential research users

- Policy-makers and practitioners with higher levels of education or some experience of research are more likely to be research users.
- Lack of skills to interpret and appraise research can inhibit research use.
- Some individuals may be hostile towards the use of research, or to research more generally.
- Researchers may lack the knowledge and skills to engage effectively in dissemination and research use activities.

The links between research and its users

- Research use may be inhibited where policymakers and practitioners have limited access to research.
- Knowledge brokers – both individuals and agencies – can play an effective 'bridging' role between research and its potential users.
- Direct links between researchers and policymakers or practitioners also support research use. Face-to-face interactions and two-way exchanges of information are most likely to encourage the use of research.

The context for the use of research

Context plays a key role in shaping the uptake of research.

■ In policy contexts, research is more likely to be used where:
- it is aligned with current ideology and individual and agency interests;
- its findings fit with existing ways of thinking or acting or with other information within the policy environment;
- open political systems exist;
- institutions and structures bring researchers and policymakers into contact;
- at a local level, an organizational culture exists that is broadly supportive of evidence use.

■ In practice contexts, local organizational, structural and cultural issues may limit the use of research, for example:
- lack of time to read research;
- lack of autonomy to implement the findings from research;
- lack of support – financial, administrative and personal – to develop research-based practice change;
- local cultural resistance to research and its use.

■ In research contexts, a number of barriers inhibit the flow of findings to policy-makers and practitioners:
- lack of incentive or reward for engaging in dissemination and research use activities;
- high value placed on traditional academic journal publications at the expense of 'user-friendly' research outputs;
- lack of time and financial resources for research use activities;
- a set of attitudes among some academic researchers that dissemination is not part of their role.

Source: Adapted from Nutley *et al.* (2007: 81–3)

However, this conceptualization of the problem is in danger of overplaying the potential role of research evidence and underplaying the role of other forms of knowledge and experience in the development of policy and practice. The 'two communities' view is also in danger of over-simplifying the political landscape by ignoring others involved in policy development. Delafons (1995) suggests that potential sources for new policy ideas include: political parties, ministers, Parliament, pressure groups, lobbyists, international bodies, academics and the research community. These groups may draw on research evidence to develop their ideas, but other forms of knowledge may play a more prominent role. For example, the Minister is likely to be influenced not only by formal research, but also by the views of constituents, the results of opinion polls, the party manifesto on which he or she was elected, his or her formal learning, and knowledge gained through both work and personal experience. As a consequence, one of the problems facing decision-makers, is the sheer volume of evidence available to them. As John Maynard Keynes famously concluded, *'there is nothing a government hates more than to be well informed; for it makes the process of arriving at decisions much more complicated and difficult'* (Skidelsky, 1992).

In addition to information overload, decision-makers have to wrestle with political and organizational factors, particularly the need to conciliate between all the interests represented in the policy-making process. All stakeholders are likely to use evidence both strategically and politically – we can view this as part of their 'game-playing' (Perri 6, 2002). It should be stressed that, while it is tempting to think of evidence being used directly to make rational and informed decisions, reality is often far more messy and overtly political than this.

There are at least four ways in which evidence might influence policy (see Box 22.2), and the direct use of research in decision making (instrumental use) is in fact quite rare. It is most likely where the research findings are non-controversial, require only limited change and will be implemented within a supportive environment: in other words, when they do not upset the *status quo* (Weiss, 1998).

In general, there is more cause for optimism about the use of evidence if research utilization is more broadly defined than its direct use in making decisions, as the impact of research is often more indirect than this.

BOX 22.2 FOUR MAIN TYPES OF RESEARCH UTILIZATION

1 Instrumental use

Research feeds directly into decision-making for policy and practice.

2 Conceptual use

Even if it seems impossible to use findings directly, research can provide new ways of thinking about a situation and offer insights into the strengths and weaknesses of particular courses of action. New conceptual understandings can then sometimes be used in instrumental ways.

3 Mobilization of support

Here, research becomes an instrument of persuasion. Findings – or simply the act of research – can be used as a political tool, to legitimate particular courses of action or inaction.

4 Wider influence

Research can have an influence beyond the institutions and events being studied. Research adds to the accumulation of knowledge which ultimately contributes to large-scale shifts in thinking, and sometimes action.

Source: Adapted from Weiss (1998)

HOW CAN EVIDENCE-BASED LEARNING BE ENCOURAGED?

In the UK, although there is a prominent debate about the use of evidence in many policy areas (e.g. criminal justice, education, health care and social care), there are important differences both within and between sectors in the concept of EBPP being promoted (Nutley *et al.*, 2007).

Here we limit discussion to just two of the dimensions that characterize EBPP: the *type of evidence* being used (evidence from research *versus* evidence from routine data); and the *focus of attention* (the individual practitioner *versus* the broader organization/system for service delivery) – together, these give four ways of conceptualizing EBPP (see Table 22.2):

- The evidence-based problem solver – here the emphasis is on the ways in which individuals use research evidence to make decisions and solve problems on a day-to-day, case-by-case basis.
- The reflective practitioner is one who uses observational data (including that arising from routine monitoring systems) to inform the way s/he learns from the past and makes adjustments for the future.
- System redesign emphasizes the importance of using evidence to reshape total systems – often a top-down, centrally driven concept of evidence-based practice, using evidence to redesign service systems and frontline practices.
- System adjustment refers to organizational or system level use of monitoring data to make ongoing adjustments to service delivery – sometimes referred to as single loop learning (see Box 22.3).

These are pure types, and practice is likely to spill across these boxes. However, many existing strategies for promoting EBPP either seem to rely on the hope that increased dissemination of research findings will lead to their increased use or they tend towards more wholesale intervention in the form of system redesign. The latter can be seen where the centre has translated research evidence into practice protocols, backed up by audit and inspection regimes to ensure these protocols are used in practice (e.g. the *What Works* initiative in Probation). This imposed approach runs the danger of inhibiting rather than promoting individual and organizational learning. The generation of new knowledge often relies on local invention and experimentation, which may be stifled by centralized control of what counts as evidence or what practices are approved. The concept of organizational learning suggests

Table 22.2 Types of evidence-based practice

Focus	Evidence	
	Research	*Monitoring data*
Individual	Problem solver	Reflective practitioner
Organization/system	System redesign	System adjustment

Source: Nutley *et al.* (2003, Figure 2)

BOX 22.3 SOURCES OF INSIGHT INTO ENCOURAGING EVIDENCE-BASED LEARNING

Knowledge management

Knowledge management is concerned with developing robust systems for storing and communicating knowledge. There are two main approaches: a codification strategy and a personalization approach (Hansen *et al.*, 1999). Codification strategies tend to be computer-centred: knowledge is carefully codified and stored in databases. In a personalization approach it is recognized that knowledge is closely tied to the person who develops it, and, hence, what is needed are enhanced opportunities for sharing knowledge through direct person-to-person contact. The role of information and communication technology within this is to help people communicate knowledge, not to store it.

Individual learning

Social psychology has long been concerned with understanding the process by which individuals learn. Behaviourialists have studied the effects of different stimuli in conditioning learning, while cognitive psychologists have sought to understand the learning processes that occur within the 'black box' between the stimulus and the response. Models of the process of learning include Kolb's learning cycle (Kolb, 1983), with its emphasis on promoting better understanding of different individual learning styles. Organizational psychologists have enhanced our understanding of the factors that help or hinder individual learning within organizations. Recent concerns have focused on how to promote lifelong learning and the benefits of self-directed and problem-based professional education regimes in achieving this.

Organizational learning

Organizational learning is concerned with the way organizations build and organize knowledge and routines and use the broad skills of their workforce to improve organizational performance. Factors that seem to affect ongoing learning include: the importance of appropriate organizational structures, processes and cultures; the characteristics of individuals who bring new information into the organization; and the role of research and development departments. Analyses of the learning routines deployed by organizations have distinguished between adaptive and generative learning. Adaptive (or single-loop) learning routines can be thought of as those mechanisms that help organizations to follow pre-set pathways. Generative (or double-loop) learning, in contrast, involves forging new paths. Both sorts of learning are said to be essential for organizational fitness, but by far the most common are those associated with adaptive learning.

that an approach to EBPP that casts the practitioner as a problem solver (as in evidence-based medicine) may be better suited to the development of learning organizations than the top-down implementation of detailed guidelines and protocols.

Building upon this line of thinking, in the field of education there has been a call to rethink research utilization in terms of 'knowledge transformation', described as a 'knowledge-led, problem-constrained learning process' (DesForges, 2000). It is argued that four conditions are necessary for such learning:

- a knowledge base;
- a problem definition related to that knowledge base;
- transformation/ learning strategies involving various modes of representing 'old' knowledge as well as the acquisition of 'new' knowledge;
- appropriate motivation.

However, it is probably unrealistic to expect all frontline practitioners to become evidence-based problem solvers, given the limited time they have available to keep up to date with research. Some systematization of evidence in research-based guidelines and protocols seems inevitable, especially as there are also demands for consistent service provision. The promoters of EBPP have to learn how to balance the continuing need for individual innovation and experimentation with system-level concerns about compliance and consistency of service. There are no easy solutions to this conundrum. However, a better understanding of how public service organizations can manage knowledge and how they encourage individual and organizational learning is likely to lead to better long term service improvement strategies (see Box 22.3).

SUMMARY

We have argued in this chapter that evidence can be used both to facilitate *accountability* and to promote *improvement* in policy-making, programme development and service delivery. We have focused on the latter and have considered four main uses of research for policy and practice:

- to design and develop public policy;
- to assess the impact of policy interventions;
- to improve policy implementation;
- to identify tomorrow's issues.

Research has important insights to offer in each of these areas. Each requires different forms of evidence, which in turn employ different methods for gathering evidence. We therefore need to work with inclusive definitions of both evidence and research and to emphasize a 'horses for courses' approach, adapting our evidence-gathering approaches to specific policy and practice issues.

Research evidence must, of course, compete with other forms of knowledge and experience, and the passive dissemination of research evidence is unlikely to impact significantly on

339

policy development or service delivery. Existing research on the effectiveness of evidence-based strategies suggests the critical need for better ongoing interaction between researchers and research users, in long-term partnerships that span the entire research process, from the definition of the problem to the application of findings.

Overall, the emerging lesson is that there are many challenges facing the development of evidence-based policy and practice. There are many good reasons why policymakers and practitioners should rise to this challenge, but evidence will and should remain just one of the influences that shape policy development and service delivery.

QUESTIONS FOR REVIEW AND DISCUSSION

1   Why is evidence a useful resource for policymakers?
2   What are the main obstacles to, and enablers of, evidence-based policy and practice?
3   How might the concept of organizational learning be used to inform thinking about how to change service delivery practice so that it is more evidence-based?

READER EXERCISES

1   Identify a policy and practice initiative that has been labelled as being based on good evidence (such as 'Sure Start'). Search for information on this initiative (via websites and journal articles) and write a report that describes and appraises the use of evidence within the initiative.
2   Scan recent newspapers for a high-profile report of a research project. Consider how the research has been presented and how it might be used by different stakeholders (e.g. policymakers, researchers, journalists, professional bodies and other interest groups).

CLASS EXERCISES

1   You are a cross-government group of people brought together to take a fresh look at policy development in relation to smoking. You have been asked to consider how smoking should be framed as a policy problem. For example, it might be viewed as a health problem, a fiscal matter or as an environmental/ regulatory issue.

   ■   If seen as a health problem, then the focus is likely to be on the relationship between smoking and ill-health.
   ■   If viewed as a fiscal issue, then the focus might be on ensuring that tobacco taxes cover the social and health costs of smoking, or interest might lie in addressing issues such as smuggling and duty avoidance.
   ■   If seen as an environmental/ regulatory problem then the focus might be on passive smoking and the regulation of smoking at work and in public places.

Discuss in class what sorts of evidence you would need to help you determine the most appropriate ways of framing smoking as a policy problem.

2   You are a group of staff within a government education department with responsibility for primary school education policy. A recent review of the evidence on how to teach maths at primary school level has concluded strongly that one particular approach is more effective than others. Discuss how you go about trying to change teaching practice so that it is in line with the recommended approach to maths teaching. Reflect upon your initial thoughts by considering how they fit with the ideas of knowledge management, individual learning and organizational learning.

FURTHER READING

Huw Davies, Sandra Nutley and Peter Smith (2000), *What works? Evidence-based policy and practice in public services*. Bristol: Policy Press.

Louise Locock and Annette Boaz (2004), 'Research, policy and practice? Worlds apart?', *Journal of Society and Social Policy*, 3 (4): 375–84.

Sandra Nutley, Isabel Walter and Huw Davies (2007), *Using evidence: how research can inform public services*. Bristol: Policy Press.

OECD (1997b), *Regulatory impact analysis: best practice in OECD countries*. Paris: OECD.

Public Money and Management (2000), 'Theme issue on "Getting Research into Practice"', *Public Money and Management*, 20 (4): 3–50.

Tom Shuller, Wim Jochems, Lejf Moos, Van Agnes Zanten (2006), 'Evidence and policy research', *European Educational Research Journal*, 5 (1): 57–70.

Further information and suggested reading are also available from two key websites:

1   The Centre for Evidence and Policy, based at King's College London is intended to foster the exchange of social science research between policy, research and practitioners. The Centre is also host to the journal Evidence and Policy. For more information visit www.evidencenetwork.org.

2   The Strategy Unit (part of the UK Cabinet Office) was originally given the task of promoting practical strategies for evidence-based policy-making. This programme of work has moved, with the Government Social Research Unit (GSRU), to HM Treasury. GSRU continues to support the policy hub website providing access to knowledge pools, training programmes and government departments' research programmes. For more information visit www. policyhub.gov.uk/ and www.gsr.gov.uk/.

REFERENCES

Annette Boaz, Lesley Grayson, Ruth Levitt,and William Solesbury (2008), 'Does evidence-based policy work? Learning from the UK experience', *Evidence and Policy*, 4 (2): 233–53.

Siobhan Campbell, Siobhan Benita, Elizabeth Coates, Phil Davies and Gemma Penn (2007), *Analysis for policy: evidence based policy in practice*. London: Government Social Research Unit.

Ian Chalmers (2005), 'If evidence-informed policy works in practice, does it matter if it doesn't work in theory?', *Evidence and Policy*, 1 (1): 227–42.

Ytsen Deelstra, Sibout Nooteboom, Ralph Kohlmann, Job Van den Berg and Sally Innanen (2003), 'Using knowledge for decision making purposes in the context of large projects in The Netherlands', *Environmental Impact Assessment Review*, 23: 517–41.

John Delafons (1995), 'Planning research and the policy process', *Town Planning Review*, 66 (1): 41–59.

Charles DesForges (2000), *Putting educational research to use through knowledge transformation.* Keynote lecture to the Further Education Research Network Conference, Coventry: Learning and Skills Development Agency.

Mike Geddes (2007), *An action learning set on two-tier partnership working* (www.oecd.org/data oecd/38/11/39954484.pdf).

Martin Hammersley (2001), 'On "systematic" reviews of research literatures: a narrative response to Evans and Benefield', *British Educational Research Journal*, 27 (5): 543–54.

Martin Hammersley (2005), 'Is the evidence-based practice movement doing more good than harm? Reflections on Iain Chalmers' case for research-based policy-making and practice', *Evidence and Policy*, 1 (1): 85–100.

Morten Hansen, Nitin Nohria and Thomas Tierney (1999), 'What's your strategy for managing knowledge?', *Harvard Business Review*, March–April: 106–16.

David Kolb (1983), *Experiential Learning.* New York: Prentice Hall.

John Lavis, Huw Davies, Andy Oxman, Jean-Louis Denis, Karen Golden-Biddle, Ewan Ferlie (2005), 'Towards systematic reviews that inform health care management and policy making', *Journal of Health Services Research and Policy*, 10: 35–48.

Louise Locock and Annette Boaz (2004), 'Research, policy and practice? Worlds apart?', *Journal of Society and Social Policy*, 3 (4): 375–84.

Sandra Nutley, Isabel Walter and Huw Davies (2003), 'From knowing to doing: a framework for understanding the evidence-into-practice agenda', *Evaluation*, 9 (2): 125–48.

Sandra Nutley, Isabel Walter and Huw Davies (2007), *Using evidence: how research can inform public services.* Bristol: Policy Press.

OECD (2008), 'Measuring regulatory quality', *Policy brief.* Paris: OECD.

Ray Pawson and Nick Tilley (1997), *Realistic evaluation.* London: Sage.

Perri 6 (2002), 'Can policy be evidence based?', *MCC: building knowledge for integrated care*, 10 (1): 3–8.

Ian Sanderson (2002), 'Evaluation, policy learning and evidence-based policy-making', *Public Administration*, 80 (1): 1–22.

Robert Skidelsky (1992), *John Maynard Keynes: a biography. Vol. 2: The economist as saviour, 1920–1937.* London: Macmillan.

William Solesbury (2004), 'The curious incident of the research in the papers', *The Evaluator*, Winter: 15–16.

Carol Weiss (1998), 'Have we learned anything new about the use of evaluation?', *American Journal of Evaluation*, 19 (1): 21–33.

Bibliography

Accenture (2006), *Leadership in customer service: building the trust* (www.accenture.com).

Robert Agranoff (2007), *Managing within networks: adding value to public organizations*. Washington, DC: Georgetown University Press.

Richard Allen and Daniel Tommasi (eds) (2001), *Managing public expenditures: a reference book for transition countries*. Paris: OECD.

Graham Allison (1994), 'Public and private management: are they fundamentally alike in all unimportant respects?', in F.S. Lane (ed.), *Current issues in public administration* (5th edn). New York: St Martin's Press, pp. 14–29.

Alan Andreason and Philip Kotler (2008), *Strategic marketing for nonprofit organizations* (7th edn). Upper Saddle River, NJ: Prentice Hall.

Rhys Andrews, Richard Cowell, James Downe, Steve Martin and David Turner (2006), *Promoting effective citizenship and community empowerment*. London: Office of the Deputy Prime Minister (www.communities.gov.uk/documents/communities/pdf/143519.pdf, accessed 16 May 2008).

Sherry Arnstein (1969), 'The ladder of citizen participation', *Journal of the American Institute of Town Planners*, 35 (4): 216–24.

Audit Commission (2000), *Aiming to improve: the principles of performance measurement*. London: Audit Commission.

Audit Commission (2002a), *Quality of life: using quality of life indicators*. London: Audit Commission.

Audit Commission (2002b), *Equality and diversity*. London: Audit Commission.

Audit Commission (2008), *Positively charged: maximising the benefits of local public service charges*. London: Audit Commission.

Michael Baker (1976), 'Evolution of the marketing concept', in Michael Baker (ed.), *Marketing theory and practice*. London: Macmillan.

J. Ball (1999), 'Marketing a concept abroad', *Project Finance*, 193: 18–19, cited in Akintola Akintoye, Matthias Beck and Cliff Hardcastle (eds) (2003), *Public–private partnerships: managing risks and opportunities*. Oxford: Blackwell.

Gerhard Banner (2002), 'Zehn Jahre kommunale Verwaltungsmodernisierung – was wurde erreicht und was kommt danach?', in Erik Meurer and Günther Stephan (eds), *Rechnungswesen und Controlling*, 4 (June): 7/313–42, Freiburg (Haufe Verlag).

Chester I. Barnard (1968, originally 1938), *The functions of the executive*. Cambridge, MA: Harvard University Press.

Marian Barnes, Janet Newman and Helen Sullivan (2007), *Power, participation and political renewal: case studies in public participation*. Bristol: Policy Press.

Francis M. Bator (1960), *The question of government spending: public needs and private wants*. New York: Harper.

Valerie Beale and Christopher Pollitt (1994), 'Charters at the grass-roots: a first report', *Local Government Studies*, 20 (2): 202–25.

Ian Beardwell and Len Holden (1994), *Human resource management: a contemporary approach*. Harlow: FT Prentice Hall.

Robert D. Behn (2001), *Rethinking democratic accountability*. Washington, DC: The Brookings Institution.

Robert Behn (2007), *What all mayors would like to know about Baltimore's CitiStat performance strategy*. Washington, DC: IBM Center for the Business of Government.

Christine Bellamy and John A. Taylor (1998), *Governing in the information age*. Milton Keynes: Open University Press.

Carolyn Bennett, Donald G. Lenihan, John Williams and William Young (2001), *Measuring quality of life: the use of societal outcome by parliamentarians*. Ottawa: Office of the Auditor General of Canada.

Gwyn Bevan and Christopher Hood (2007), 'What's measured is what matters: targets and gaming in healthcare in England', *Public Administration*, 84 (3): 517–38.

Mark Bevir (2003), 'A decentred theory of governance', in Henrik Paul Bang (ed.), *Governance as social and political communication*. Manchester: Manchester University Press, pp. 200–21.

Mark Bevir and Rod Rhodes (2003), 'Decentring British governance: from bureaucracy to networks', in Henrik Paul Bang (ed.), *Governance as social and political communication*. Manchester: Manchester University Press, pp. 61–78.

Edward Blakely (1994), *Planning local economic development: theory and practice* (2nd edn). Thousand Oaks, CA: Sage.

Annette Boaz, Lesley Grayson, Ruth Levitt and William Solesbury (2008), 'Does evidence-based policy work? Learning from the UK experience', *Evidence and Policy*, 4 (2): 233–53.

R. Bolden (2004), *What is leadership?* Exeter: Leadership South West.

Sandford Borins, Kenneth Kernaghan, David Brown, Nick Bontis, Perri 6 and Fred Thompson (2007), *Digital state at the leading edge*. Toronto: University of Toronto Press.

Jonathan Boston (2000), 'The challenge of evaluating systemic change: the case of public management reform', *International Public Management Journal*, 3 (1): 23–46.

Geert Bouckaert (1992), 'Productivity analysis in the public sector: the case of fire service', *International Review of Administrative Sciences*, 58 (2): 175–200.

Geert Bouckaert (1995a), 'The history of the productivity movement', in Arie Halachmi and Marc Holzer (eds), *Competent government: theory and practice. The best of public productivity review, 1985–1993*. Burke, VA: Chatelaine Press, pp. 361–98.

Geert Bouckaert (1995b), 'Improving performance measurement', in Arie Halachmi and Geert Bouckaert (eds), *The enduring challenges of public administration*. San Francisco, CA: Jossey-Bass, pp. 379–412.

Geert Bouckaert (1995c), 'Measuring quality', in Christopher Pollitt and Geert Bouckaert (eds), *Quality improvement in European public services: concepts, cases and commentary.* London: Sage, pp. 20–8.

Geert Bouckaert and John Halligan (2008), *Managing performance: international comparisons.* Routledge, London.

Geert Bouckaert, Tom Auwers, Wouter Van Reeth and Koen Verhoest (1997), *Handboek Doelmatigheidsanalyse: prestaties begroten.* Brussels: Ministry of the Flemish Community.

Tony Bovaird (2004a), 'Public private partnerships: from contested concepts to prevalent practice', *International Review of Administrative Sciences,* 70 (2): 199–215.

Tony Bovaird (2004b), 'Public-private partnerships in Western Europe and the USA: new growths from old roots', in Abby Ghobadian, Nicholas Regan and David Gallear (eds), *Public private partnerships: policy and experience.* Basingstoke: Palgrave Macmillan, pp. 221–50.

Tony Bovaird (2005), 'Public governance: balancing stakeholder power in a network society', *International Review of Administrative Sciences,* 71 (2): 217–28.

Tony Bovaird (2006), 'Developing new relationships with the "market" in the procurement of public services', *Public Administration,* 84 (1): 81–102.

Tony Bovaird (2007a), 'Beyond engagement and participation – user and community co-production of public services', *Public Administration Review,* 67 (5): 846–60.

Tony Bovaird (2007b), 'Triggering change through culture clash: the UK Civil Service Reform Programme, 1999 – 2005', in Kuno Schedler and Isabella Proeller (eds), *Organisational culture and the outcomes of public management reform.* London: Taylor & Francis, pp. 323–50.

Tony Bovaird and Lucy Gaster (2002), 'Civil service reform: evaluation'. Unpublished case study for Cabinet Office.

Tony Bovaird and Arie Halachmi (1999), 'Community scorecards: the role of stakeholders in performance assessment', in Arie Halachmi (ed.), *Performance and quality measurement in government: issues and experiences.* Burke, VA: Chatelaine Press, pp. 145–55.

Tony Bovaird and Elke Löffler (2002), 'Moving from excellence models of local service delivery to benchmarking of "good local governance" ', *International Review of Administrative Sciences,* 67 (1): 9–24.

Tony Bovaird and Elke Löffler (2003), 'Evaluating the quality of public governance: indicators, models and methodologies', *International Review of Administrative Sciences,* 69 (3): 313–28.

Tony Bovaird and Elke Löffler (2004), 'Evaluating the quality of local governance: some lessons from European experience', *Local Governance,* 30 (4) (2004): 178–87.

Tony Bovaird and Elke Löffler (2007), 'Assessing the quality of local governance: a case study of public services', *Public Money and Management,* 27 (4): 293–300

Tony Bovaird and Mike Owen (2002), 'Achieving citizen-led area regeneration through multiple stakeholders in the Beacon Housing Estate, Cornwall', in Tony Bovaird, Elke Löffler and Salvador Parrado Díez (eds), *Developing local governance networks in Europe.* Baden-Baden: Nomos Verlag, pp. 57–73.

Tony Bovaird and Ken Russell (2007), 'Civil service reform in the UK, 1999–2005: revolutionary failure or evolutionary success?' *Public Administration,* 85 (2): 301–28.

Tony Bovaird, Elke Löffler and Jeremy Martin (2003), 'From corporate governance to local governance: stakeholder-driven community score-cards for UK local agencies?', *International Journal of Public Administration,* 26 (8/9): 1–24.

George Boyne (1997), 'Comparing the performance of local authorities: an evaluation of the Audit Commission indicators', *Local Government Studies*, 23 (4): 17–43.

George Boyne, Catherine Farrell, Jennifer Law, Martin Powell and Richard Walker (2003), *Evaluating public management reforms*. Buckingham, Open University Press.

Bristol Royal Infirmary Inquiry (2001), *Learning from Bristol: the report of the public inquiry into children's heart surgery at the Bristol Royal Infirmary 1984–1995*, Cm 5207. London: Stationery Office.

Catherine Bromley, Nina Stratford and Nirmala Rao (2000), *Revisiting public perceptions of local government*. London: DETR.

Mike Broussine (2000), 'The capacities needed by local authority chief executives', *International Journal of Public Sector Management*, 13 (6): 498–507.

Mike Broussine (2001), 'A stalemate in the power game', *Municipal Journal* (23 Feb – 1 March): 17.

Michael Broussine and Pamela Fox (2002), 'Rethinking leadership in local government – the place of "feminine" styles in the modernised council', *Local Government Studies*, 28 (4): 87–102.

Charles V. Brown and Peter M. Jackson (1990), *Public sector economics* (4th edn). Oxford: Blackwell.

John Bryson (2006), *Strategic planning for public and nonprofit organizations: a guide to strengthening and sustaining organizational achievement* (3rd edn). San Francisco, CA: Jossey Bass.

John Bryson, Fran Ackermann and Colin Eden (2007), 'Putting the resource-based view of strategy and distinctive competencies to work in public organizations', *Public Administration Review*, 67 (4): 702–17.

James M. Buchanan and Richard A. Musgrave (1999), *Public finance and public choice: two contrasting visions of the state*. Cambridge, MA: MIT Press.

Bernard Burnes (2000), *Managing change – a strategic approach to organizational dynamics*. Harlow: Pearson Education.

J. Burnham (2001), 'Local public-private partnerships in France: rarely disputed, scarcely competitive, weakly regulated', *Public Policy and Administration*, vol. 16, no. 4, pp. 47–60.

Cabinet Office (1999a), *Modernising government*, Cm 4310. London: Stationery Office.

Cabinet Office (1999b), *Reform of the civil service*. London: Stationery Office.

Cabinet Office (1999c), *Quality schemes task force*. Report. London: Cabinet Office (http://archive.cabinetoffice.gov.uk/servicefirst/2000/taskforce/report.htm, accessed 25 May 2008).

Cabinet Office (1999d), *Report to the prime minister from Sir Richard Wilson, Head of home civil service*. London: Cabinet Office.

Cabinet Office (2000), *Successful IT: modernising government in action* (McCartney Report). London: Cabinet Office.

Cabinet Office (2001), *Strengthening leadership in the public sector: a research study by the Performance and Innovation Unit*. London: Cabinet Office.

Cabinet Office (2005), *Transformational government: enabled by technology*, Cm 6683. London: HMSO.

Cabinet Office (2007), *Fairness and freedom: the final report of the Equalities Review*. London: Cabinet Office.

Adrian Cadbury (1992), *Report of the Committee on the Financial Aspects of Corporate Governance*. London: Gee & Company.

Nigel Caldwell, Helen Walker, Christine Harland, Louise Knight and Jurong Zheng (2005), 'Promoting competitive markets: the role of public procurement', Special edition on public procurement, *Journal of Purchasing and Supply Management*, 11 (5/6): 242–51.

Siobhan Campbell, Siobhan Benita, Elizabeth Coates, Phil Davies and Gemma Penn (2007), *Analysis for policy: evidence based policy in practice*. Government Social Research Unit: London.

Capgemini (2007), *Benchmarking the Supply of Online Public Services* (http://ec.europa.eu/information_society/newsroom/cf/itemlongdetail.cfm?item_id=3634, accessed 16 May 2008).

CCMD (1998), *Citizen/client surveys: dispelling myths and redrawing maps*. Ottawa: Canadian Centre for Management Development.

Andrew Chadwick (2006), *Internet politics: states, citizens and new communications technologies*. Oxford: Oxford University Press.

Andrew Chadwick and Christopher May (2003), 'Interaction between states and citizens in the age of the Internet: "e-government" in the United States, Britain, and the European Union', *Governance*, 16 (2): 271–300.

Ian Chalmers (2005), 'If evidence-informed policy works in practice, does it matter if it doesn't work in theory?', *Evidence and Policy*, 1 (1): 227–42.

James Champy and Michael Hammer (1993), *Reengineering the corporation*. New York: Harper Business.

Chancellor of the Duchy of Lancaster (1997), *Next steps: agencies in government: review*, Cm 4011. London: Stationery Office.

Chancellor of the Exchequer (1991), *Competing for quality: buying better public services*. London: HMSO.

Alfred Chandler (1962), *Strategy and structure*. Cambridge, MA: MIT Press.

Chartered Institute of Marketing (2007), *Tomorrow's word: reevaluating the role of marketing*. London: CIM (www.cim.co.uk/MediaStore/_Insights/Role%20of%20Marketing%20Agenda%20Paper.pdf, accessed 23 May 2008).

Richard B. Chase, F. Robert Jacobs and Nicholas J. Aquilano (2007), *Operations management for competitive advantage* (11th international edn). Boston, MA: McGraw-Hill, Chapter 5.

Martin Christopher, Adrian Payne and David Ballantyne (1991), *Relationship marketing*. Oxford: Butterworth-Heinemann.

Martin Christopher, Adrian Payne and David Ballantyne (2002), *Relationship marketing: creating stakeholder value*, 2nd edn. Oxford: Butterworth-Heinemann.

CIPD (2001), *Competency frameworks in UK organisations* (Research report). London: CIPD.

Civil Service Department (1975), *Wider issues review*. London: HMSO.

Tom Clark and Andrew Dilnot (2002), *Long-term trends in British taxation and spending*. London: Institute for Fiscal Studies.

John Clarke (2004), *Changing welfare, changing states*. London: Sage.

John Clarke and Janet Newman (1997), *The managerial state: power, politics and ideology in the remaking of social welfare*. London: Sage.

John Clarke, Sharon Gewirtz, Gordon Hughes and Jill Humphrey (2000), 'Guarding the public interest: auditing public services', in John Clarke, Sharon Gewirtz and Eugene McLaughlin (eds), *New managerialism, new welfare?* London: Sage/Open University.

John Clarke, Janet Newman, Nick Smith, Elizabeth Vidler and Louise Westmarland (2007), *Creating citizen-consumers: changing publics and changing public services*. London: Sage.

CLG (2006), *Strong and prosperous communities: the local government White Paper*. London: Communities and Local Government.

CLG (2008), *Communities in control: real power, real people*, Cm 7427. London: Stationery Office.

Elizabeth Coffey, Clare Huffington and Peninah Thomson (1999), *The changing culture of leadership – women leaders' voices*. London: Change Partnership.

Stephen Coleman and John Gøtze (undated), *Bowling together: online public engagement in policy deliberation*. London: Hansard Society.

Committee on Standards in Public Life (1995), *First report*, Cm 2850–1. London: Stationery Office.

Committee on Standards in Public Life (2001), *The first seven reports: a review of progress*. London: Committee on Standards in Public Life.

Comptroller and Auditor-General (2007), *Government on the Internet: progress in delivering information and services online*, HC 529 2006–7. London: Stationery Office (www.nao.org.uk/publications/nao_reports, accessed 16 May 2008).

Bill Cooke and Uma Kothari (2001), *Participation: the new tyranny*. London: Zed Books.

Anna Coote (ed.) (2002), *Claiming the health dividend*. London: King's Fund.

Anna Coote and Jo Lenaghan (1997), *Citizen's juries: theory into practice*. London: IPPR.

Andrew Coulson (ed.) (1998), *Trust and contracts: relationships in local government, health and public services*. Bristol: Policy Press.

Michel Crozier, Samuel P. Huntington and Joji Watanuki (1975), *The crisis of democracy*. New York: New York University Press.

Tony Cutler and Barbara Waine (1997), *Managing the welfare state*. Oxford: Berg.

Thomas H. Davenport (1993), *Process innovation: re-engineering work through information technology*. Boston, MA: Harvard Business School Press.

Thomas H. Davenport and Laurence Prusak (1998), *Working knowledge: how organizations manage what they know*. Boston, MA: Harvard Business School Press.

Huw T.O. Davies, Sandra M. Nutley and Peter C. Smith (2000), *What works? Evidence-based policy and practice in public services*. Bristol: Policy Press.

Howard Davis and Steve Martin (eds) (2008), *Public service inspection in the UK*. London: Jessica Kingsley Publishers.

Howard Davis and Bruce Walker (1997), 'Trust based relationships in local government contracting', *Public Money and Management*, 17 (4): 47–54.

Howard Davis and Bruce Walker (1998), 'Trust and competition: blue collar services in local government', in Andrew Coulson (ed.), *Trust and contracts: relationships in local government, health and public services*. Bristol: Policy Press, pp. 159–82.

Nicholas Deakin and Kieron Walsh (1996), 'The enabling state: the role of markets and contracts', *Public Administration*, 74 (1): 33–48.

Hans de Bruijn (2002), *Managing performance in the public sector*. London: Routledge.

Ytsen Deelstra, Sibout Nooteboom, Ralph Kohlmann, Job Van den Berg and Sally Innanen (2003), 'Using knowledge for decision making purposes in the context of large projects in The Netherlands', *Environmental Impact Assessment Review*, 23: 517–41.

John Delafons (1995), 'Planning research and the policy process', *Town Planning Review*, 66 (1): 41–59.

Christoph Demmke (2004), *European civil services between tradition and reform*. Maastricht/Netherlands: European Institute of Public Administration.

Charles DesForges (2000), *Putting educational research to use through knowledge transformation*. Keynote lecture to the Further Education Research Network Conference, Coventry: Learning and Skills Development Agency.

DETR (1998a), *Modern local government: in touch with the people*. London: Department of Environment, Transport and the Regions.

DETR (1998b), *Modernising local government: local democracy and local leadership*. London: Stationery Office.

DETR (1998c), *Modernising local government: improving services through best value*. London: Stationery Office.

DETR (1998d), *Modernising local government: a new ethical framework*. Consultation paper. London: DETR.

DETR (1999a), *Local Government Act 1999: Part I. Best Value* (Circular 10/99). London: Department of Environment, Transport and the Regions.

DETR (1999b), *Local leadership, local choice*, Cm 4298. London: Stationery Office.

Simon Domberger and Paul Jensen (1997), 'Contracting out by the public sector: theory, evidence and prospects', *Oxford Review of Economic Policy*, 13 (4): 67–79.

John D. Donahue (1989), *The privatisation decision: public ends, private means*. New York: Basic Books.

James Downe and Steve Martin (2007), 'Regulation inside government: processes and impacts of inspection of local public services', *Policy and Politics*, 35 (2): 215–32.

Peter Drucker (1973), *Management: tasks, responsibilities, practices*. New York: Harper Row.

DTLR (2001), *Strong local leadership – quality public services*, Cm. 5237. London: Stationery Office.

Patrick Dunleavy (1991), *Democracy, bureaucracy and public choice*. London: Harvester Wheatsheaf.

Patrick Dunleavy (1994), 'The globalization of public services production: can government be "best in world"?', *Public Policy and Administration*, 9 (2): 36–64.

EC (2006), *Adequate and sustainable pensions: synthesis report 2006*. Brussels: Directorate-General for Employment, Social Affairs and Equal Opportunities.

Efficiency Unit (1988), *Improving management in government: the next steps* (Report to the prime minister). London: HMSO.

Tom Entwistle, Steve Martin and Gareth Enticott (2002), *Making or buying? The value of internal service providers in local government*. Cardiff University: Local and Regional Government Research Unit, for the Public Services Network.

Andrew Erridge (2007), 'Public procurement, public value and the NI Unemployment Pilot Project 2', *Public Administration*, 85 (4): 1023–43.

Andrew Erridge and Jonathan Greer (2002), 'Partnerships and public procurement: building social capital through supply relations', *Public Administration*, 80 (3): 503–22.

European Commission (2001), *White Paper on European Governance*. Brussels: Commission of the European Communities (http://europa.eu.int/comm/governance/white_paper/index_en.htm, from 1 May 2008).

Susan Fainstain (1994), *The city builders: property, politics and planning in London and New York*. Oxford: Basil Blackwell.

David Farnham and Sylvia Horton (1993), *Managing the new public services*. Basingstoke: Macmillan.

David Farnham and Sylvia Horton (1996a), *People management in the public services*. Basingstoke: Macmillan.

David Farnham and Sylvia Horton (1996b), *New public managers in Europe*. London: Macmillan.

David Farnham and Sylvia Horton (2000), *Human resources flexibilities in the public services*. Basingstoke: Macmillan.

David Farnham and Sylvia Horton (2002), 'HRM competency frameworks in the British civil service', in Sylvia Horton, David Farnham and Annie Hondeghern (eds), *Competency management in the public sector: European variations on a theme*. Amsterdam: IOS, pp. 33–47.

David Farnham, Annie Hondeheim and Sylvia Horton (2005), *Staff participation and public management reform: some international comparisons*. Basingstoke: Palgrave Macmillan.

J.M. Fernandez Martin (1996), *The EC public procurement rules: a critical analysis*. Oxford: Clarendon Press.

Michael Fischer (2007), *Diversity management and the business case*, Research paper 3–11. Hamburg: HWWI.

Norman Flynn and Franz Strehl (1996), *Public sector management in Europe*. London: Prentice Hall/Harvester Wheatsheaf.

Paul Foley and Steve Martin (2000), 'A new deal for community involvement?', *Policy and Politics*, 29 (4): 479–91.

R.S. Fosler and R.A. Berger (eds) (1982), *Public private partnership in American cities: seven case studies*. Lexington, MA: Lexington Press.

Pam Fox and Mike Broussine (2001), *Room at the top? A study of women chief executives in local government in England and Wales*. Bristol: Bristol Business School

Pam Fox and Mike Broussine (2005), *Gender isn't an issue! Case studies of exemplary practice in promoting gender equality and diversity in local authorities*. Bristol: Bristol Business School.

Thomas Friedmann (2000), *The Lexus and the olive tree: understanding globalisation*. London: HarperCollins.

Future Services Network (2006), *From rhetoric to reality: engaging users in public services*. London: National Consumer Council (www.ncc.org.uk/nccpdf/poldocs/NCC163pd_from_rhetoric_to_reality.pdf, accessed 16 May 2008).

Yiannis Gabriel (1999), *Organizations in depth*. London: Sage.

Francesca Gains (2004), ' "Hardware, software or network connection?' Theorising crisis in the UK next steps agencies', *Public Administration*, 82 (3): 547–56.

John Kenneth Galbraith (1958), *The affluent society*. Boston, MA: Houghton Mifflin.

Lucy Gaster (1995), *Quality in public services: manager's choices*. Buckingham: Open University Press.

Mike Geddes (2007), *An action learning set on two-tier partnership working* (www.oecd.org/dataoecd/38/11/39954484.pdf).

Eleanor Glor (2001), 'Codes of conduct and generations of public servants', *International Review of Administrative Sciences*, 67 (3): 524–41.

John Greenwood (2000), 'Should the civil service become fully politicised?', in Lynton Robins and Bill Jones (eds), *Debates in British politics today*. Manchester: Manchester University Press, pp. 63–77.

Barry N. Hague and Brian Loader (1999), *Digital democracy*. London: Routledge.

David Hall (1999), *Privatisation, multinationals, and corruption*. London: Public Services International Research Unit, University of Greenwich.

Declan Hall and John Stewart (1997), *Citizen's juries in local government*. London: LGMB.

Gary Hamel and C.K. Prahalad (1994), *Competing for the future*. Boston, MA: Harvard Business School Press.

Martyn Hammersley (2001), 'On "systematic" reviews of research literatures: a "narrative" response to Evans and Benefield', *British Educational Research Journal*, 27 (5): 543–54.

Martin Hammersley (2005), 'Is the evidence-based practice movement doing more good than harm? Reflections on Iain Chalmers' case for research-based policy making and practice', *Evidence and Policy*, 1 (1): 85–100.

Charles Handy (1993), *Understanding organisations* (4th edn). Harmondsworth: Penguin.

Morton T. Hansen, Nitin Nohria and Thomas Tierney (1999), 'What's your strategy for managing knowledge?', *Harvard Business Review*, 77: 106–16.

Jenny Harrow (2002), 'The new public management and social justice: just efficiency or equity as well?', in Kate McLaughlin, Stephen P. Osborne and Ewan Ferlie (eds), *New public management: current trends and future prospects*. London: Routledge, pp. 141–59.

Jean Hartley and Maria Allison (2000), 'The role of leadership in the modernization and improvement of public services', *Public Money and Management*, 20 (2): 35–40.

Harry P. Hatry (1999), *Performance measurement: getting results*. Washington, DC: Urban Institute Press.

Edward Higgs (2004), *The information state in England*. Basingstoke: Palgrave Macmillan.

HM Government (2007), *UK government sustainable procurement action plan*. London: DEFRA.

HMSO (1991), *The citizen's charter*, Cm 1599. London: HMSO.

HM Treasury (1995), *Setting new standards: a strategy for government procurement*, Cm 2840. London: HMSO.

HM Treasury (1998), *Comprehensive spending review on efficiency in civil government procurement expenditure*. London: HMSO.

HM Treasury (2000a), *Government accounting 2000: a guide on accounting and financial procedures for use of government departments*. London: HM Treasury.

HM Treasury (2000b), *Improving police performance: a new approach to measuring police efficiency*. Public Services Productivity Panel Report No. 4. London: HM Treasury.

HM Treasury (2006), *PFI: strengthening long-term partnerships*. London: Stationery Office.

HM Treasury (2007), *Transforming government procurement*. London: HMSO.

Jens Hoff and Jacob Rosenkrands (2000), 'When democratic strategies clash: the citizen card debate in Denmark', in Jens Hoff, Ivan Horrocks and Pieter Tops (eds), *Democratic governance and new technology*. London: Routledge, pp. 101–8.

Home Office (2002), *Entitlement cards and identity fraud*. A consultation paper. London: Home Office.

351

Christopher Hood (1991), 'A public management for all seasons?', *Public Administration*, 69 (1): 3–19.

Christopher Hood (2005), 'Public management: the word, the movement, the science', in Ewan Ferlie, Laurence Lynn Jr. and Christopher Pollitt (eds), *Oxford handbook of public management*. Oxford: Oxford University Press, pp. 7–26.

Christopher Hood and Michael Jackson (1991), *Administrative argument*. Aldershot: Dartmouth.

Christopher Hood, Martin Lodge and Christopher Clifford (2002), *Civil service policy-making competencies in the German BMWi and the British DTI*. London: Industry Forum.

Christopher Hood, Colin Scott, George Jones, Oliver James, and Tony Travers (1998), *Regulation inside government: waste-watchers, quality police and sleaze busters*. Oxford: Oxford University Press.

Kim Hoque and Mike Noon (2004), 'Equal ppportunities policy and practice in Britain: evaluating the "empty shell" hypothesis', *Work, Employment & Society*, 18 (3): 481–506.

Melissa Horner (1997), 'Leadership theory: past, present and future', *Team Performance Management*, 3 (4): 270–87.

Sylvia Horton (2006), 'Competencies in people resourcing', in Stephen Pilbeam and Marjorie Corbridge (eds), *People resourcing: contemporary HRM in practice*. London: FT Prentice Hall.

Sylvia Horton and David Farnham (2007), 'Turning leadership into performance management', in Rainer Koch and Pat Weller (eds), *Public governance and leadership*. Wiesbaden: Gabler Edition, Wissenschaft Deutscher Universitäts-Verlag, pp. 429–55.

Sylvia Horton, David Farnham and Annie Hondeghem (eds) (2002), *Competency management in the public sector: European variations on a theme*. Amsterdam: IOS.

Tamas Horvath (ed.) (2000), *Decentralization: experiments and reforms. Local governments in central and eastern Europe*. Budapest: Open Society Institute.

Gordon Hughes, Robert Mears and Christopher Winch (1996), 'An inspector calls? Regulation and accountability in three public services', *Policy and Politics*, 25 (3): 299–313.

Chris Huxham (1993), 'Pursuing collaborative advantage', *Journal of the Operational Research Society*, 44 (6): 599–611.

Improvement and Development Agency (2008), *Connecting with communities: communications toolkit*, London: IDeA (www.idea.gov.uk/idk/core/page.do?pageId=7816073, accessed 16 May 2008).

Catherine Itzin and Janet Newman (eds) (1995), *Gender and organisational culture: linking theory and practice*. London: Routledge.

Peter Jackson (2001), 'Public sector added value: can bureaucracy deliver?', *Public Administration*, 79 (1): 5–28.

Peter M. Jackson and L. Stainsby (2000), 'Managing public sector networked organisations', *Public Money and Management*, 20 (1): 11–16.

Oliver James (2003), *The executive agency revolution in Whitehall*. Basingstoke: Palgrave.

Peter John (1998), *Analysing public policy*. London: Cassell.

Gerry Johnson and Kevan Scholes (2001), *Exploring public sector strategy*. Harlow: FT Prentice Hall.

Gerry Johnson, Kevan Scholes and Richard Whittington (2008), *Exploring corporate strategy: text and cases* (8th edition). Harlow: FT Prentice Hall.

Gareth Jones (1998), 'The leadership of organizations', *RSA Journal*, 3 (4): 81–3.

Robert Jones (1999), 'The European Union as a promoter of public-private partnerships', *International Journal of Public-Private Partnerships*, 1 (3): 289–305.

Paul Joyce (1999), *Strategic management for the public services*. Buckingham: Open University Press.

Edward J. Kane (1986), 'IBM's quality focus on the business process', *Quality Progress*. Milwaukee, WI: American Society for Quality, pp. 24–33.

Rosabeth Moss Kanter (1994), 'Collaborative advantage: the art of alliances', *Harvard Business Review* (July–August): 96–108.

Robert S. Kaplan and David P. Norton (1996), *The balanced scorecard: translating strategy into action*. Boston, MA: Harvard Business School Press.

Robert S. Kaplan and David P. Norton (2004), *Strategy maps*. Boston, MA: Harvard Business School Press.

Kenneth Kernaghan (1993), 'Partnership and public administration – conceptual and practical considerations', *Canadian Public Administration*, 36 (1): 57–76.

Anne Ketelaar, Nick Manning and Edouard Turkisch (2007), *Performance based arrangements for senior civil servants – OECD experiences*. OECD Governance Working Paper. Paris.

Walter J.M. Kickert and Joop F.M. Koopenjan (1997), 'Public management and network management: an overview', in Walter J. M. Kickert, Erick-Hans Klijn and Joop F. M. Koopenjan (eds), *Managing complex networks: strategies for the public sector*. London: Sage, pp. 35–61.

Ian Kirkpatrick and Miguel Martinez-Lucio, M. (eds) (1995), *The politics of quality in the public sector*. London: Routledge.

Klaus Klaus and Roland Traunmüller (2002), 'Preface to the focus theme on e-government', *EM – Electronic Markets*, 12 (3): 147–8.

Erik-Hans Klijn and G.R. Teisman (1997), 'Strategies and games in networks', in Walter J.M. Kickert, Erick-Hans Klijn and Joop F.M. Koopenjan (eds), *Managing complex networks: strategies for the public sector*. London: Sage, pp. 98–118.

David A. Kolb (1983), *Experiential learning*. New York: Prentice Hall.

Jan Kooiman (ed.) (1993), *Modern governance: new government–society interactions*. London: Sage.

Jan Kooiman (2003), *Governing as governance*. London: Sage.

Philip Kotler and Nancy Lee (2006), *Marketing in the public sector: a roadmap for improved performance*. Upper Saddle River, NJ: Wharton School Publishing.

John P. Kotter and James L. Heskett (1992), *Corporate culture and performance*. New York: Free Press.

John Langford and Yvonne Harrison (2001), 'Partnering for e-government: challenges for public administrators', *Canadian Public Administration*, 44 (4): 393–415.

John Lavis, Huw Davies, Andy Oxman, Jean-Louis Denis, Karen Golden-Biddle and Ewan Ferlie (2005), 'Towards systematic reviews that inform health care management and policy making', *Journal of Health Services Research and Policy*, 10: 35–48.

Patrick Le Galès and John Mawson (1994), *Management innovations in urban policy: lessons from France*. Luton: Local Government Management Board.

Julian Le Grand (1982), *The strategy of equality: redistribution and the social services*. London: Allen & Unwin.

Gabriella Legrenzi and Costas Milas (2002). *Asymmetric and non-linear adjustment in the revenue-expenditure models*. Uxbridge: Brunel University.

Klaus Lenk (2007), 'Reconstruction public administration theory from below', *Information Polity*, 12 (4): 207–12.

David Lewis (1997), *Hidden agendas: politics, law and disorder*. London, Hamish Hamilton.

Gail Lewis (2000a), Introduction: expanding the social policy imaginary', in Gail Lewis, Sharon Gerwirtz and John Clarke (eds), *Rethinking social policy*. London: Open University Press, pp. 1–21.

Gail Lewis (2000b), *Race, gender, social welfare: encounters in a postcolonial society*. Cambridge: Polity Press.

Bing Li and Akintola Akintoye (2003), 'An overview of public-private partnership', in Akintola Akintoye, Matthias Beck and Cliff Hardcastle (eds), *Public-private partnerships: managing risks and opportunities*. Oxford: Blackwell.

Paul C. Light (2006), 'The tides of reform revisited: patterns in making government work, 1945–2002', *Public Administration Review*, 66 (1): 6–19.

Michael Lipsky (1980), *Street-level bureaucracy: dilemmas of the individual in public services*. New York: Russell Sage Foundation.

Louise Locock and Annette Boaz (2004), 'Research, policy and practice? Worlds apart?', *Journal of Society and Social Policy*, 3 (4): 375–84.

Elke Löffler (1999), *Accountability management in intergovernmental partnerships*. Paris: OECD.

Elke Löffler (2001), 'Quality awards as a public sector benchmarking concept in OECD countries: some guidelines for quality award organisers', *Public Administration and Development*, 21 (1): 25–47.

Elke Löffler (2006), 'Lessons from Europe: innovations in public sector quality', in Ministry of Public Administration (ed.), *Good practices in Slovenian public administration*. Ljubljana, Slovenia: Ministry of Public Administration, pp. 25–36.

Elke Löffler, Salvador Parrado and Tomás Zmeskal (2007), *Improving customer orientation through service charters: a handbook for improving quality of public services*. Paris: OECD, Ministry of the Interior of the Czech Republic and Governance International.

John Logan and Harvey Molotch (1987), *Urban fortunes: the political economy of place*. Los Angeles, CA: University of California Press.

Vivien Lowndes, Lawrence Pratchett, and Gerry Stoker (2006), 'Diagnosing and remedying the failings of official participation schemes: the CLEAR framework', *Social Policy and Society*, 5 (2): 281–91.

Vivien Lowndes, Gerry Stoker, Lawrence Pratchett, David Wilson, Steve Leach and M. Wingfield (1998), *Enhancing public participation in local government*. London: DETR.

J.J. Lynch (1992), *The psychology of customer care*. London: Macmillan.

David Lyon (1994), *The electronic eye: the rise of the surveillance society*. Cambridge: Polity Press.

David Lyon (ed.) (2003), *Surveillance as social sorting. Privacy, risk and digital discrimination*. London: Routledge.

Robert MacIntosh (2003), 'BPR: alive and well in the public sector', *International Journal of Operations & Production Management*, 23 (3): 327–44.

Shirley McIver (1997), *An evaluation of the King's Fund citizen's juries programme*. Birmingham: Health Services Management Centre.

Leo McKinstrey (2006), 'Sign here – you know this is good for you: private contractors everywhere must now prove their devotion to the new creed of political correctness', *The Times*, 27 April.

Arthur Macmahon (1961), *Delegation and autonomy*. London: Asia Publishing House.

Sir William Macpherson (1999), *The Stephen Lawrence enquiry*. London: Stationery Office.

Nick Manning and Neil Parison (2003), *International public administration reform: implications for the Russian Federation* (series: Directions in development). Washington, DC: World Bank.

Michael Margolis and David Resnick (2000), *Politics as usual: the cyberspace 'revolution'*. Thousand Oaks, CA: Sage.

Steve Martin and Annette Boaz (2000), 'Public participation and citizen-centred local government', *Public Money and Management*, 20 (2): 47–54.

Steve Martin, Howard Davis, Tony Bovaird, James Downe, Mike Geddes, Jean Hartley, Mike Lewis, Ian Sanderson and Phil Sapwell (2001), *Improving local public services: final evaluation of the Best Value pilot programme*. London: Stationery Office.

Alex Matheson, Boris Weber, Nick Manning and Emmanuelle Arnould (2006), 'Managing the political/administrative boundary: study on the political involvement in senior staffing decisions and on the delineation of responsibilities between ministers and senior civil servants', unpublished. Paris: OECD.

A. Mendelow (1991), Proceedings of the second international conference on information systems. New York, 16–18 December.

John Meyer and B. Rowan (1991), 'Institutional organizations: formal structure as myth and ceremony', in Walter Powell and Paul J. DiMaggio (eds), *The new institutionalism in organizational analysis*. Chicago, IL: University of Chicago Press, pp. 41–62.

John L. Mikesell (1995), *Fiscal administration*. Belmont, CA: Wadsworth.

Eileen Milner and Paul Joyce (2005), *Lessons in leadership: meeting the challenges of public service management*. Oxford: Routledge.

Ministry of Justice (2007), *The governance of Britain*, Cm 7170. London: HMSO.

Henry Mintzberg (1979), *The structuring of organizations: a synthesis of the research*. London: Prentice Hall.

Henry Mintzberg (1987), 'The strategy concept 1: five Ps for strategy', *California Management Review*, 30 (1): 11–24.

Henry Mintzberg (1992), 'Mintzberg on the rise and fall of strategic planning', *Long Range Planning*, 25 (4): 99–104.

Mark H. Moore (1995), *Creating public value: strategic management in government*. Cambridge, MA: Harvard University Press.

Elaine Morley, Scott P. Bryant and Harry P. Hatry (2001), *Comparative performance measurement*. Washington, DC: Urban Institute Press.

Kevin Morrell and Jean Hartley (2006), 'A model of political leadership', *Human Relations*, 59: 483–504.

Laurie Mullins (2005), *Management and organisational behaviour*. London: Prentice Hall.

Richard A. Musgrave (1959), *The theory of public finance*. New York: McGraw-Hill.

Richard A. Musgrave (1998), 'The role of the state in fiscal theory', in Peter Birch Sorensen (ed.), *Public finance in a changing world*. London: Macmillan, pp. 35–50.

Ralph Nader (1965), *Unsafe at any speed: the designed-in dangers of the American automobile*. New York: Grossman.

Andy Neely, Mike Kennerly and Angela Walters (2006), *Performance measurement and management: public and private*. Cranfield: Cranfield School of Management.

Janet Newman (2001a), *Modernising governance: New Labour, policy and society*. London: Sage.

Janet Newman (2001b), '"What counts is what works"? Constructing evaluations of market mechanisms', *Public Administration*, 79 (1): 89–103.

Janet Newman (2002), 'Changing governance, changing equality? New Labour, modernization and public services', *Public Money and Management*, 22 (1): 7–14.

Janet Newman (2005), 'Re-gendering governance', in Janet Newman (ed.), *Remaking governance: policy, politics and the public sphere*. Bristol: Policy Press.

Janet Newman and John Clarke (2009), *Publics, politics and power: remaking the public in public services*. London: Sage.

Janet Newman and Nicola Yeates (eds) (2008), *Social justice*. Buckingham: Open University Press/ McGraw-Hill.

Kohn Nomden (2000), 'Flexible working patterns in European public administration', in David Farnham *et al.* (eds), *Human resources flexibilities in the public services*. London: Macmillan, pp. 280–97.

Fritz Nordsieck (1932), *Die schaubildliche Erfassung und Untersuchung der Betriebsorganisation*. Stuttgart: C.E. Poeschel.

Dan Norris (2007), 'Hain, not Reid'. Letter in *New Statesman*, 2 April, p. 6.

Sandra Nutley, Isabel Walter and Huw Davies (2003), 'From knowing to doing: a framework for understanding the evidence-into-practice agenda', *Evaluation*, 9 (2): 125–48.

Sandra Nutley, Isabel Walter and Huw Davies (2007), *Using evidence: how research can inform public services*. Bristol: Policy Press.

Martha Nussbaum and Amartya Sen (eds) (1993), *The quality of life*. Oxford: Clarendon Press.

ODPM (2002), *Connecting with communities: improving communications in local government*. London: Office of the Deputy Prime Minister.

ODPM (2005), *Citizen engagement and public services: why neighbourhoods matter*. London: Office of the Deputy Prime Minister.

OECD (1993), *Public management developments: survey*. Paris: OECD.

OECD (1997a), *In search of results: performance management practices*. Paris: OECD.

OECD (1997b), *Regulatory impact analysis: best practice in OECD countries*. OECD: Paris.

OECD (1999), *Public sector corruption: an international survey of prevention measures*. Paris: OECD.

OECD (2001a), *Citizens as partners: OECD handbook on information, consultation and public participation in policy-making*. Paris: OECD (www.partnershipsforwater.net/psp/tc/TC_Tools/ 022T_Citizens%20as%20Partners.pdf, accessed 16 May 2008).

OECD (2001b), *Public sector leadership for the 21st century*. Paris: OECD.

OECD (2001c), *Distributed public governance: agencies, authorities and other autonomous bodies* (preliminary draft). Paris, OECD.

OECD (2003), *Policies for an ageing society: recent measures and areas for further reform* (Working Paper No. 369). Paris: OECD.

OECD (2005a), *Modernising government: the way forward*. Paris: OECD.

OECD (2005b), *Policy brief – public sector modernisation: open government* (www.oecd.org/dataoecd/1/35/34455306.pdf). Paris: OECD.

OECD (2005c), *Performance-related pay policies for government employees*. Paris: OECD.

OECD (2005d), *Policy brief: OECD guidelines for managing conflict of interest in the public service*. Paris: OECD.

OECD (2006), *The challenges of managing government employees in the context of an ageing population in OECD member countries*. Paris: OECD.

OECD (2007a), *Ageing and the public service: human resource challenges*. Paris: OECD.

OECD (2007b), *Measuring government activity*. Paris: OECD.

OECD (2008), 'Measuring regulatory quality', *Policy brief*. Paris: OECD.

Office of the e-Envoy (2000), *UK online action plan*. London: Cabinet Office.

Office of Public Services Reform (2002), *Better government services: executive agencies in the 21st century* (www.civilservice.gov.uk/agencies, accessed 12 June 2002).

Office of the Vice President (1993), *From red tape to results. Creating a government that works better and costs less*. Report of the National Performance review. Washington, DC: US Government Printing Office.

OGC/Office of the e-Envoy (2002), *In the service of democracy. A consultation paper on a policy for electronic democracy*. London: Office of Government Commerce/Office of the e-Envoy.

Olov Olson, James Guthrie and Christopher Humphrey (1998), *Global warning: debating international developments in new public financial management*. Oslo: Cappelen Akademisk Forlag.

Edoardo Ongaro (2004), 'Process management in the public sector. The experience of one-stop shops in Italy', *The International Journal of Public Sector Management*, 17 (1): 81–107.

David Osborne and Ted Gaebler (1992), *Reinventing government. How the entrepreneurial spirit is transforming the public sector*. Reading, MA: Addison-Wesley.

Vance Packard (1957), *The hidden persuaders*. New York: D. McKay.

Gabriel A. Pall (1987), *Quality process management*. Englewood Cliffs, NJ: Prentice Hall.

Ray Pawson and Nick Tilley (1997), *Realistic evaluation*. London: Sage.

Janie Percy-Smith (ed.) (2000), *Policy responses to social exclusion: towards inclusion?* Maidenhead: Open University Press.

Perri 6 (2002), 'Can policy be evidence based?', *MCC: building knowledge for integrated care*, 10 (1): pp. 3–8.

Perri 6 (2004), 'Joined-up government in the western world in comparative perspective: a preliminary literature review and exploration', *Journal of Public Administration Research and Theory* (J-Part) 14 (1): 103–38.

Perri 6, Diana Leet, Kimberley Seltzer and Gerry Stoker (2002), *Towards holistic governance: the new reform agenda*. Basingstoke: Palgrave.

Jon Pierre and B. Guy Peters (2000), *Governance, politics and the state*. New York: St Martin's Press.

PIU (2002), *Data sharing and privacy: the way forward for public services*. London: Cabinet Office, Performance and Innovation Unit.

Christopher Pollitt (1988), 'Bringing consumers into performance measurement: concepts, consequences and constraints', *Policy and Politics*, 16 (2): 77–87.

Christopher Pollitt (1995), 'Justification by works or by faith? Evaluating the new public management', *Evaluation*, 1 (2): 133–54.

Christopher Pollitt (2002), 'Clarifying convergence: striking similarities and durable differences in public management reform', *Public Management Review*, 4 (1): 471–92.

Christopher Pollitt (2003), *The essential public manager*. Buckingham: Open University Press.

Christopher Pollitt (2005a), 'Decentralization: a central concept in contemporary public management', in E. Ferlie, L. Lynn and C. Pollitt (eds), *The Oxford handbook of public management*. Oxford: Oxford University Press, pp. 371–97.

Christopher Pollitt (2005b), 'Ministries and agencies: steering, meddling, neglect and dependency', in M. Painter and J. Pierre (eds), *Challenges to state policy capacity: global trends and comparative perspectives*. Basingstoke: Palgrave Macmillan, pp. 112–36.

Christopher Pollitt and Geert Bouckaert (eds) (1995), *Quality improvement in European public services: concepts, cases and commentary*. London: Sage.

Christopher Pollitt and Geert Bouckaert (2003), 'Evaluating public management reforms: an international perspective', in Hellmut Wollman (ed.), *Evaluation in public sector reform*. Cheltenham: Edward Elgar, pp. 12–35.

Christopher Pollitt and Geert Bouckaert (2004), *Public management reform: a comparative analysis* (2nd edn). Oxford: Oxford University Press.

Christopher Pollitt and Colin Talbot (eds) (2004), *Unbundled government*. London: Taylor & Francis.

Christopher Pollitt, Johnston Birchall and Keith Putman (1998), *Decentralizing public service management: the British experience*. Basingstoke: Macmillan.

Christopher Pollitt, Geert Bouckaert and Elke Löffler (2007), *Making quality sustainable: co-design, co-decide, co-produce, co-evaluate*. Finland: Ministry of Finance.

Christopher Pollitt, Colin Talbot, Janice Caulfield and Amanda Smullen (2004), *Agencies: how governments do things through semi-autonomous agencies*. Basingstoke: Palgrave Macmillan.

Christopher Pollitt, Xavier Girre, Jeremy Lonsdale, Robert Mul, Hilkka Summa and Marit Waerness (1999), *Performance or compliance? Performance audit and public management in five countries*. Oxford: Oxford University Press.

Michael Porter (1985), *Competitive advantage*. New York: Macmillan.

Michael Power (1993), *The audit explosion*. London: Demos.

Michael Power (1997), *The audit society*. Oxford: Oxford University Press.

Pushkala Prasad, Albert J. Mills, Michael Elmes and Anshuman Prasad (eds) (1997), *Managing the organizational melting pot: dilemmas of workplace diversity*. London: Sage.

Lawrence Pratchett (2002), *The implementation of electronic voting in the UK*. London: Local Government Association.

Robert Putnam (2001), *Bowling alone: the collapse and revival of American community*. New York: Touchstone.

Colin Rallings, Michael Thrasher and James Downe (2000), *Turnout at local government elections: influences on levels of voter registration and electoral participation* (www.dca.gov.uk/elections/elect_odpm_turnout.pdf, accessed 16 May 2008).

Stuart Ranson and John Stewart (1994), *Management for the public domain: enabling the learning society*. Basingstoke: Macmillan.

Teresa Rees (2005), 'Reflections on the uneven development of gender mainstreaming in Europe', *International Feminist Journal of Politics*, 7 (4): 555–74.

Ortwin Renn, Thomas Webler and Peter Wiedemann (1995), *Fairness and competence in citizen participation*. Dordrecht: Kluwer Academic.

Rod Rhodes (1997), *Understanding governance: policy networks, governance, reflexivity and accountability*. Buckingham: Open University Press.

Sue Richards (2000), 'Why Labour ministers rage against Whitehall', *New Statesman*, 129 (4489): 21–2.

Stephen P. Robbins (1987), *Organization theory: concepts, controversies and applications*. Englewood Cliffs, NJ: Prentice Hall.

Alistair Roberts (2002), 'Closing the window: public service restructuring and the weakening of Freedom of Information Law', *Salem Papers* (www.inpuma.net).

Detlef Sack (2003), 'Gratwanderung zwischen partizpation und Finanzenpässen', *Zeitschrift für öffentliche und gemeinwirtschaftliche Unternehmen*, 26 (4): 353–70.

Lester M. Salamon (1995), *Partners in public service: government-nonprofit relations in the modern welfare state*. Baltimore, MD: Johns Hopkins University Press.

Lester M. Salamon (2002), *The tools of government*. Oxford: Oxford University Press.

Ian Sanderson (2002), 'Evaluation, policy learning and evidence-based policy making', *Public Administration*, 80 (1): 1–22.

Adrian Sargeant (2004), *Marketing management for nonprofit organizations* (2nd edn). Oxford: Oxford University Press.

Wallace Sayre (1958), 'Premises of public administration: past and emerging', *Public Administration Review*, 18 (2): 102–5.

Fritz W. Scharpf (1978), 'Interorganizational policy studies: issues, concepts and perspectives', in K.I. Hanf and Fritz W. Scharpf (eds), *Interorganizational policy making: limits to coordination and central control*. London: Sage, pp. 345–70.

Allen Schick (2005), 'The performing state: reflection on an idea whose time has come but whose implementation has not'. Paper prepared for the OECD Senior Budget Officials Meeting in Bangkok, Thailand (www.oecd.org/dataoecd/42/43/35651133.pdf). OECD. Paris

James Scott (2006), '"E" the people: do US municipal government web sites support public involvement?', *Public Administration Review*, 66 (3): 341–53.

Michael Scott Morton (ed.) (1991), *The corporation of the 90s: information technology and organizational transformation*. Oxford: Oxford University Press.

Willie Seal and Peter Vincent-Jones (1997), 'Accounting and trust in the enabling of long-term relations', *Accounting, Auditing and Accountability Journal*, 10 (3): 406–31.

Peter Self (1993), *Government by the market?* London: Macmillan.

Peter M. Senge (1998), *The fifth discipline: the art and practice of the learning organization*. London: Century Business.

Jean Shaoul (2005), 'A critical financial analysis of the private finance initiative', *Critical Perspectives on Accounting*, 16: 441–71.

Rod Sheaff (1991), *Marketing for health services*. Buckingham: Open University Press.

359

Rod Sheaff (2002), *Responsive healthcare: marketing for a public service*. Buckingham: Open University Press.

Tom Shoop (2004), 'Unheeded advice', *Government Executive*, 36 (9): 70.

Tom Shuller, Wim Jochems, Lejf Moos and Van Agnes Zanten (2006), 'Evidence and policy research', *European Educational Research Journal*, 5 (1): 57–70.

Sir Neville Simms (2006), *Procuring the future: Sustainable Procurement National Action Plan: recommendations from the Sustainable Procurement Task Force*. London: DEFRA.

Herbert A. Simon (1945), *Administrative behavior*. New York: Free Press.

Robert Skidelsky (1992), *John Maynard Keynes: a biography. Vol 2: The economist as saviour, 1920–1937*. London: Macmillan.

Arthur Smith (2003), 'Public-private partnership projects in the US: risks and opportunities', in Akintola Akintoye, Matthias Beck and Cliff Hardcastle (eds), *Public-private partnerships: managing risks and opportunities*. Oxford: Blackwell.

Social and Cultural Planning Office (2004), *Public sector performance: an international comparison of education, health care, law and order, and public administration*. Netherlands: The Hague (www.scp.nl/english/publications/books/9037701841.shtml).

William Solesbury (2004), 'The curious incident of the research in the papers', *The Evaluator*, Winter: 15–16.

David Stasavage (2006), 'Does transparency make a difference? The example of European Council of Ministers', in Christopher Hood and David Heald (eds), *Transparency: the key to better governance?* Oxford: Oxford University Press, pp. 165–79.

Miekatrien Sterck, Wouter Van Dooren and Geert Bouckaert (2006), *Performance measurement for sub-national service delivery*. Report for OECD. Leuven: Public Management Institute, Katholieke Universiteit.

Gerry Stoker (2004), *Transforming local governance: from Thatcherism to New Labour*. Basingstoke: Palgrave Macmillan.

John Storey (1995), *Human resource management: a critical text*. London: Routledge.

John Storey (ed.) (2004), *Leadership in organizations – current issues and key trends*. Abingdon: Routledge.

Helen Sullivan and Chris Skelcher (2002), *Working across boundaries: collaboration in public services*. Basingstoke: Palgrave Macmillan.

Surveillance Studies Network (2006), *A report on the surveillance society*. Wilmslow: Information Commissioner's Office.

Gillian Symon (2005), 'Exploring resistance from a rhetorical perspective', *Organization Studies*, 26 (11): 1641–63.

Colin Talbot (1996), 'Ministers and agencies: responsibilities and performance', in the Public Service Committee, *Second Report Ministerial Accountability and Responsibility*, Vol. II. Minutes of Evidence, HC313, Session 1995–96. London: HMSO, pp. 39–55.

Colin Talbot (2004), 'Executive agencies: have they improved management in government?', *Public Money and Management*, 24 (1): 104–11.

Vito Tanzi and Ludger Schuknecht (2000), *Public spending in the 20th century*. Cambridge: Cambridge University Press.

Geerd Teisman and Erik-Hans Klijn (2000), 'Public-private partnerships in the European Union: officially suspect, embraced in daily practice', in Stephen Osborne (ed.), *Public-private partnerships: theory and practice in international perspective*. London: Routledge, pp. 165–86.

Melissa A. Thomas (2001), 'Getting debt relief right', *Foreign Affairs*, 80 (5): 36–45.

Robyn Thomas and Annette Davies (2005), 'Theorizing the micro-politics of resistance: new public management and managerial identities in the UK public services', *Organization Studies* 26 (5): 683–706.

Caroline Tolbert and Karen Mossberger (2006), 'The effects of e-government on trust and confidence in government', *Public Administration Review*, 66 (3): 354–69.

Derek Torrington and Laura Hall (1987), *Personnel management*. Hemel Hempsted: Prentice Hall.

Max Travers (2007), *The new bureaucracy: quality assurance and its critics*. Bristol: Policy Press.

Gordon Tullock (1967), 'The welfare costs of tariffs, monopolies and theft', *Western Economic Journal* (June): 224–32.

UK Public Administration Select Committee (2003), *On target? Government by measurement*. Fifth Report of Session 2002–3, Vol. I (www.publications.parliament.uk/pa/cm200203/cmselect/cmpubadm/62/62.pdf, accessed 16 May 2008). London: House of Commons.

UNCTAD (2007), *World investment report*. New York: United Nations.

Peter B. Vaill (1999), *Spirited leading and learning: process wisdom for a new age*. Englewood Cliffs, NJ: Prentice Hall.

Wouter Van Dooren, Miekatrien Sterck, Zsuzsanna Lonti and Dirk-Jan Kraan (2007), 'The institutional drivers of efficiency in the public sector', unpublished OECD paper. Paris: OECD.

Sandra Van Thiel (2001), *QUANGOs: trends, causes and consequences*. Aldershot: Ashgate.

Thorstein Veblen (1994), *The theory of the leisure class* (1st edn, 1899). New York: Dover Publications.

Christian Vigouroux (1995), *Déontologie des fonctions publiques*. Paris: Dalloz.

John A. Wagner III (1994), 'Participation's effects on performance and satisfaction: a reconsideration of research evidence', *The Academy of Management Review*, 19 (2): 312–30.

Kieron Walsh (1991a), *Competitive tendering of local authority services: initial experience*. London: Department of the Environment.

Kieron Walsh (1991b), 'Quality and public services', *Public Administration*, 69 (4): 503–14.

Kieron Walsh (1993), *Marketing in local government*. London: FT Prentice Hall.

Max Weber (1956), *Wirtschaft und Gesellschaft* (4th edn). Tübingen: Johannes Winckelmann.

Karl Weick (1979), *The social psychology of organizing*. Reading, MA: Addison-Wesley.

Karl E. Weick and Robert. E. Quinn (1999), 'Organizational change and development', *Annual Review of Psychology*, 50: 361–86.

Carol H. Weiss (1998), 'Have we learned anything new about the use of evaluation?', *American Journal of Evaluation*, 19 (1): 21–33.

Darrel M. West (2007), *Global e-government 2007*. Providence, RI: Brown University (www.inside politics.org, accessed 16 May 2008).

Karen West (2005), 'From bilateral to trilateral governance in local government contracting in France', *Public Administration*, 83 (2): 473–92.

R. Wettenhall (2001), 'Machinery of government in small states: issues, challenges and innovatory capacity', *Public Organization Review: A Global Journal*, 1 (2): 167–92.

Geoff White (2000), 'Pay flexibility in European public services: a comparative analysis', in David Farnham *et al.* (eds), *Human resources flexibilities in the public services*. London: Macmillan, pp. 255–79.

Beth Widdowson (2008), 'Well-being, harm and work', in Janet Newman and Nicola Yeates (eds), *Social justice*. Buckingham: Open University Press/McGraw-Hill, Chapter 3.

Oliver Williamson (1975), *Markets and hierarchies: analysis and antitrust implications*. New York: Free Press.

Michael Woolcock (1998), 'Social capital and economic development: toward a theoretical synthesis and policy framework', *Theory and Society*, 27 (2): 151–208.

World Bank (1989), *Sub-Sahara Africa: from crisis to sustainable growth. A long-term perspective study*. Washington, DC: World Bank.

Kiyoshi Yamamoto (2004), 'Agencification in Japan: renaming, or revolution?', in C.Pollitt and C.Talbot (eds), *Unbundled government*. London: Taylor & Francis, pp. 215–26 (Chapter 11).

Iris Young (1990), 'Justice and the politics of difference', in Susan Fainstein and Lisa Servon (eds), *Gender and planning: a reader*. Rutgers, NJ: Rutgers University Press, pp. 86–103.

Gary A. Yukl (2002), *Leadership in organizations*. Englewood Cliffs, NJ: Prentice Hall.

Valarie A. Zeithaml, A. Parasuraman and Leonard L. Berry (1990), *Delivering service quality: balancing customer perceptions and expectations*. New York: Free Press.

Index

Page references in *italics* indicate illustrations.

eBooks

eBooks – at www.eBookstore.tandf.co.uk

A library at your fingertips!

eBooks are electronic versions of printed books. You can store them on your PC/laptop or browse them online.

They have advantages for anyone needing rapid access to a wide variety of published, copyright information.

eBooks can help your research by enabling you to bookmark chapters, annotate text and use instant searches to find specific words or phrases. Several eBook files would fit on even a small laptop or PDA.

NEW: Save money by eSubscribing: cheap, online access to any eBook for as long as you need it.

Annual subscription packages

We now offer special low-cost bulk subscriptions to packages of eBooks in certain subject areas. These are available to libraries or to individuals.

For more information please contact webmaster.ebooks@tandf.co.uk

We're continually developing the eBook concept, so keep up to date by visiting the website.

www.eBookstore.tandf.co.uk